Why Do You Need this New Edition?

The past decade has seen major advances in our understanding of interpersonal and organizational conflict and communication. These advances in theory and practice have been incorporated into this Sixth Edition to provide you with the most cutting-edge and strategy-rich resource for using communication to deal with conflict. All of the revisions in the Sixth Edition are designed to significantly improve student learning and to make learning and teaching from the book a rewarding and enjoyable experience for both students and instructors. What follows are just some of the changes that are new to the Sixth Edition.

- We have reorganized Chapter 2, The Inner Experience of Conflict, around two major themes: (1) emotion and conflict interaction; and (2) social cognition in conflicts. These two topics integrate many of the theories covered in the Fifth Edition and incorporate fresh insights from recent research on the two processes. A final section discusses the relationship between emotion and social cognition in conflict interaction. We have included several new case studies throughout the text that deal with leadership, family, and neighborhood conflict, making the material even more engaging and relevant.
- We have reorganized Chapter 3, Conflict Interaction, to pull all of the theories of conflict interaction into an organized framework that shows how they relate to one another. We have updated references extensively throughout the text to highlight the most current research in the area of conflict studies.
- We have moved up our discussion of conflict styles to Chapter 4, so the styles are more directly connected to conflict interaction. The tactics discussed in Chapter 7 of the Fifth Edition are now covered throughout the book.
- We have expanded Chapter 7, which previously focused solely on climate, to cover the Context of Conflict, which includes personal history, climate, and organizational characteristics.
- We have reworked Chapter 8 to present an integrated model of conflict management as well as techniques for managing conflict.

PEARSON

Working Through Conflict

Working Through Conflict

Strategies for Relationships, Groups, and Organizations

SIXTH EDITION

Joseph P. Folger

Temple University

Marshall Scott Poole

University of Illinois Urbana-Champaign

Randall K. Stutman

CRA, Inc.

PEARSON

Boston New York San Francisco
Mexico City Montreal Toronto London Madrid Munich Paris
Hong Kong Singapore Tokyo Cape Town Sydney

Acquisitions Editor: *Jeanne Zalesky*
Project Manager: *Lisa Sussman*
Series Editorial Assistant: *Susan Brilling*
Marketing Manager: *Suzan Czajkowski*
Production Supervisor: *Liz Napolitano*
Editorial Production Service: *Pre-Press PMG*
Manufacturing Buyer: *JoAnne Sweeney*
Electronic Composition: *Pre-Press PMG*
Cover Designer: *Kristina Mose-Libon*

For related titles and support materials, visit our online catalog at
www.pearsonhighered.com.

Between the time website information is gathered and then published, it is not unusual for some sites
to have closed. Also, the transcription of URLs can result in typographical errors. The publisher would
appreciate notification where these errors occur so that they may be corrected in subsequent editions.

ISBN-10: 0-205-56989-7

Library of Congress Cataloging-in-Publication Data

Folger, Joseph P.
  Working through conflict: strategies for relationships, groups, and organizations / Joseph P.
Folger, Marshall Scott Poole, Randall K. Stutman. — 6th ed.
     p. cm.
  ISBN 978-0-205-56989-2
  1. Social conflict.   2. Conflict (Psychology)   3. Conflict management.   4. Social interaction.
5. Interpersonal conflict.   I. Poole, Marshall Scott, 1951.   II. Stutman, Randall K., 1957.
III. Title.
  HM1121.F65 2009
  303.6—dc22

                                                        2008020447

Printed in the United States of America

10 9 8 7 6 5 4 3 2   HAM 12 11 10 09

Credits: p. 56, Excerpt from *Negotiating in Organizations* by Bazerman. Copyright 1983 by Sage
Publications Inc Books. Reproduced with permission of Sage Publications Inc Books in the format
Textbook via Copyright Clearance Center; p. 67, Excerpt from Wallace Shawn and André Gregory,
My Dinner with André. Copyright 1981. Reprinted by permission of Grove/Atlantic.

To our parents:

Ed and Virginia
Ed and Helen
Bernie and Marge

Contents

List of Cases

Preface

The Study of Conflict

The main objective of the sixth edition of *Working Through Conflict* is to provide a summary and synthesis of social science research and theory on conflict. It offers students of conflict a review of the core concepts and theoretical frameworks that enhance an understanding of human behavior in a wide range of conflict situations. The research and theory covered in this book reflect the many social science disciplines that have contributed to the study of conflict.

Although it takes an interdisciplinary view of conflict, this book emphasizes understanding conflict as a communication phenomenon. It assumes that conflict is something that people create and shape as they interact with each other. Sometimes conflict interaction is immediate and face-to-face. In other instances, it is played out in a series of moves, actions, and responses that occur over time and in different places. This book highlights the interactive nature of conflict, no matter what form it takes. This focus on communication means that readers gain an appreciation for how mutual influence occurs, how language and message choices shape conflict, and how patterns of behavior and the structure of human discourse create important dimensions of any unfolding conflict.

In addition, *Working Through Conflict* offers a road map for how theory and research can be used to understand and influence conflict dynamics in everyday life. The field of conflict management is supported by a long history of useful research and theory that form a basis for a wide variety of conflict management work. This book demonstrates how conflicts across settings can be understood by seeing them through a range of theoretical lenses. It illustrates how students of conflict can begin thinking and acting in ways that can have profound effects on the dynamics of difficult conflicts.

Developing Theory-Based Intuition

It is often said that people who are good at their work have excellent intuition. Usually this means that they instinctively make good decisions and employ effective strategies to create change or accomplish productive objectives. Intuition is often assumed to be innate—it is seen as a gift that some people have. But in most cases effective professional intuition comes from a broad background of knowledge, study, and experience gained over time. *Working Through Conflict* is written for those who want to develop good intuition about how to react, interact, and intervene in conflict situations. Conflict is usually complex—it is often multilayered, steeped in a history of events, and shaped by diverse perspectives and understandings.

As a result, having good intuition about conflict starts by mastering a broad repertoire of ideas—ideas that create different possible explanations for why conflict interaction moves in destructive or constructive directions.

Working Through Conflict covers a wide range of essential concepts and theories that clarify the practical implications for managing conflicts in relationships, groups, teams, and organizations. It is a primer for those who might want to pursue professional work in the conflict management field as mediators, ombudspersons, facilitators, or conciliators. It can also help build a strong intuition in those who deal with conflict daily in work and professional settings and in those who want to have an impact on conflicts in their personal lives within families, romantic relationships, marriages, and friendships.

Key Features of Sixth Edition

Several changes have been made to help strengthen the sixth edition of *Working Through Conflict* and to incorporate helpful suggestions from those who have read prior editions.

The current edition has been thoroughly revised to reflect the newest theory and research. Specifically:

- We have rewritten Chapter 2 with a focus on emotion and social cognition in conflicts.
- We have revised Chapter 3 to focus on interaction processes.
- We have reworked Chapters 2 and 3 to provide greater continuity of narrative.
- We have moved Chapter 4, on conflict styles, up from its previous position as Chapter 7. The relationship between conflict styles and conflict interaction is now more immediately evident.
- We have revised Chapter 7 to cover context in general, addressing three elements of the context of conflict: history, climate, and organizational dispute resolution systems.
- We have reworked Chapter 8 to discuss more specific procedures for managing conflict.

We have moved some sections from previous editions into the Instructor's Manual, which has been thoroughly revised for this edition.

We have updated references to research and theory throughout the book to capture the most current thinking about the topics covered. In many instances, we retain older references because they point to core work in the field that has served as 4 foundation for more recent studies. Current developments are important, but we believe that students should also be aware of the field's conceptual roots as represented in classic conflict literature.

We have added several new case studies to this edition of *Working Through Conflict*. Not only do the cases help to illustrate the various theories covered in the book, but they also demonstrate the complexity and nuances of real-life conflict. We have found that case studies stimulate thoughtful discussion of strategies and ethics, as well as intervention possibilities. They also serve as excellent models for students who want or need to write their own case analyses. Inevitably, readers will notice how almost all theories covered here have specific case illustrations. This allows students to see how they might analyze conflicts they have observed or experienced themselves and to see the utility of providing contrasting theoretical understandings of the same conflict events.

We consider conflicts occurring in a wide range of arenas, from intimate relationships and friendships to group, inter-group, organizational, and negotiation settings. This added breadth makes the book suitable as a primary text for courses in conflict and conflict management, as well as a useful supplement to courses that devote substantial attention to conflict or third-party work.

The title of this book is an intentional double entendre. Because its major emphasis is on communication patterns people use when attempting to manage conflict, we hope that the book will help people successfully *work through* difficult conflicts. The book is also built on the assumption that effective work is often promoted *by the emergence and productive use of conflict*. It is our hope that this book will encourage and assist people to confront their conflicts and to work through them creatively rather than suppressing or superficially "resolving" conflicts.

Acknowledgments

Thanks are still due to those who helped make the first edition possible. We owe our greatest debt to our colleagues at the Center for Conflict Resolution in Madison, Wisconsin. We are very grateful to Lonnie Weiss for her insight and help with our analyses. We also thank Syd Bernard, Jim Carrilon, Jay Herman, Jan Shubert, Rick Sloan, Dennis Smith, and Kathy Zoppi for reacting to parts or all of the manuscript. In addition, we turned to Betsy Densmore, Robert Everett, and Tommy Vines for an evaluation of the manuscript from a managerial perspective. We also thank Linda Klug, Jean Kebis, and Wayne Beach for supplying the transcript of interaction in Chapter 6.

We thank Melissa Dobosh for her help with research for the current revision and Leanne Knoblach for reading and commenting on the revised Chapter 2. We also thank Bethany Sills and Phoebe Kruger, Portland State University, who found in reviewer in Table 4.1. Once again, this sixth edition is the product of many valuable comments and contributions from students and instructors. We are grateful to the students in our classes who became enthusiastic about documenting and analyzing real-life conflicts. Over the years, they have contributed several detailed cases to the book.

We appreciate the feedback reviewers provided for this revision: Cheryl Brattlie, St. Edward's University; Lori A. Byers, University of North Texas; Rachel L. DiCioccio, University of Rhode Island; Jessica Katz Jameson, North Carolina State University; and Chris Kennedy, Western Wyoming Community College. Our continued gratitude goes to reviewers of earlier editions: Wayne Beach, Tom Biesecker, Lori Carrell, Steven Colmbs, Charles R. Conrad, Alice Crume, Robert J. Doolittle, David A. Frank, Dennis Gouran, Bruce Gronbeck, Dale Hample, Thomas Harris, Gary Hartzell, Tricia Jones, Keven E. McCleary, Laura L. Jansma, Sara E. Newell, Linda Putnam, Mistee and Kevin Real, Susan Rice, Gale Richards, Tracy Routsong, Dale L. Shannon, Cynthia Stohl, Michael Sunnafrank, Stella Ting-Toomey, Shirley Van Hoeven, Hal R. Witteman, and Paul Yelsma.

The excellent editorial and production staff at Allyn & Bacon including Lisa Sussman, Jeanne Zalesky, Karon Bowers, and Liz Napolitano have assisted greatly with the production of this volume.

Joseph P. Folger

Introduction

Conflict offers a mixture of the good, the bad, and the uncertain. On the positive side, conflicts allow us to air important issues; they produce new and creative ideas; they release built-up tensions. Handled properly, conflicts can strengthen relationships; they can help groups and organizations to re-evaluate and clarify goals and missions; and they can also initiate social change to eliminate inequities and injustice. These advantages suggest that conflict is normal and healthy, and they underscore the importance of understanding and handling conflict properly.

But perhaps more familiar is the negative side of conflict. Heated exchanges spiral out of control, resulting in frustration, tension, hard feelings, and, ultimately, more conflict. Low-grade family conflicts, perpetuated through criticism, arguments, nagging, and verbal abuse, not only distance parents from children and spouses from one another, but also lower self-esteem and create problems that can follow people throughout their entire lives. Additionally, conflicts are sometimes violent, not only between strangers, but also in the workplace and within the family. Sometimes *not being able* to start a conflict is the source of frustration. If one friend persistently denies that a problem exists or changes the subject when it comes up, the other cannot discuss the things that are bothering her or him, and the friendship suffers. The various negative experiences we all have with conflict are reinforced in the media, where it often seems that the only effective way to solve problems is to shoot somebody.

Conflicts also bring uncertainty. As we will see, the great "unpredictables" in life often arise in interactions we have with others. Conversations, meetings, conflicts all have in common the fact that they may suddenly turn in unexpected directions. Indeed, the uncertainties that arise during conflicts often cause them to turn in negative directions.

The twists and turns of the following case—in this instance a conflict in a small office—offer a good illustration of the positive, negative, and uncertain sides of conflict.

The conflict at the women's hotline initially exhibits several negative features and might easily turn in a destructive direction.

First, the situation was tense and threatening. This was a difficult time for the workers. Even for "old hands" at negotiation, conflicts are often unpleasant and frightening. Second, the parties experienced a great deal of uncertainty. They were unable to understand what is going on and how their behavior affected the conflict. Conflicts are confusing;

CASE I.1A • *The Women's Hotline Case*

*Imagine yourself as a staff member in this organiza-
tion: How would you react as this conflict unfolded?
What is it about this particular conflict that makes it
seem difficult to face—let alone solve?*

Women's Hotline is a rape and domestic
crisis center in a medium-sized city. The center
employed seven full- and part-time workers. The
workers, all women, formed a cohesive unit and
made all important decisions as a group. There were
no formal supervisors. The hotline started as a
voluntary organization and had grown by capturing
local and federal funds. The group remained proud
of its roots in a democratic, feminist tradition.

The atmosphere at the hotline was rather
informal. The staff members saw each other as
friends, but there was an implicit understanding
that people should not have to take responsibility
for each other's cases. Because the hotline's work
was draining, having to handle each other's wor-
ries could create an unbearable strain. This norm
encouraged workers to work on their own and
keep problems to themselves.

The conflict arose when Diane, a new counselor who had only six months of experience, was
involved in a very disturbing incident. One of her
clients was killed by a man who had previously
raped her. Diane had trouble dealing with this
incident. She felt guilty about it; she questioned
her own ability and asked herself whether she
might have been able to prevent this tragedy. In the
months following, Diane had increasing difficulty
in coping with her feelings and began to feel that
her co-workers were not giving her the support she
needed. Diane had no supervisor to turn to, and,
although her friends outside the hotline were helpful, she did not believe they could understand the
pressure as well as her co-workers could.

Since the murder, Diane had not been able to
work to full capacity, and she began to notice some
resentment from the other counselors. She felt the

other staff members were more concerned about
whether she was adding to their work loads than
whether she was recovering from the traumatic
incident. Although Diane did not realize it at the
time, most of the staff members felt she had been
slow to take on responsibilities even before her
client was killed. They thought Diane had generally
asked for more help than other staff members and
that these requests were adding to their own
responsibilities. No one was willing to tell Diane
about these feelings after the incident, because they
realized she was very disturbed. After six months,
Diane believed she could no longer continue to
work effectively. She felt pressure from the others at
the center, and she was still shaken by the tragedy.
She requested two weeks off with pay to get away
from the work situation for a while, to reduce the
stress she felt, and to come back with renewed energy. The staff, feeling that Diane was slacking off,
denied this request. They responded by outlining, in
writing, what they saw as the responsibilities of a
full-time staff worker. Diane was angry when she
realized her request had been denied, and she
decided to file a formal work grievance.

Diane and the staff felt bad about having to
resort to such a formal, adversarial procedure. No
staff member had ever filed a work grievance, and
the group was embarrassed by its inability to deal
with the problem on a more informal basis. These
feelings created additional tension between Diane
and the staff.

Discussion Questions

- Can you foresee any benefits to this conflict?
- Is it possible to foresee whether a conflict
  will move in a constructive or destructive
  direction?
- What clues would lead you to believe that
  this conflict is going to be productive?

actions can have consequences quite different from what is intended because the situation
is more complicated than we had assumed. Diane did not know her co-workers thought she
was slacking even before the tragedy. When she asked for time off, she was surprised at
their refusal, and her angry reaction nearly started a major battle.

Third, the situation was fragile. A conflict may evolve in very different ways depending on the behavior of just a single worker. If, for example, the staff chose to fire Diane, the conflict may have been squelched, or it may fester and undermine relationships among the remaining staff. If, on the other hand, Diane won allies, the others might split over the issue and ultimately dissolve the hotline. As the case continues, observe staff members' behavior and their method of dealing with this tense and unfamiliar situation.

CASE I.1B   *The Women's Hotline Case (Continued)*

Imagine yourself in the midst of this conflict: What would you recommend this group do to promote a constructive outcome to this conflict?

The committee who received Diane's grievance suggested that they could handle the problem in a less formal way if both Diane and the staff agreed to accept a neutral third-party mediator. Everyone agreed that this suggestion had promise, and a third party was invited to a meeting where the entire staff would addresses the issue.

At this meeting, the group faced a difficult task. Each member offered reactions they had been unwilling to express previously. The staff made several pointed criticisms of Diane's overall performance. Diane expressed doubts about the staff's willingness to help new workers or to give support when it was requested. Although this discussion was often tense, it was well-directed. At the outset of the meeting, Diane withdrew her formal complaint. This action changed the definition of the problem from the immediate work grievance to the question of what levels of support were required for various people to work effectively in this difficult and emotionally draining setting.

Staff members shared doubts and fears about their own inadequacies as counselors and agreed that something less than perfection was acceptable. The group recognized that a collective inertia had developed and that they had consistently avoided giving others the support needed to deal with difficult rape cases. They acknowledged, however, the constraints on each woman's time; each worker could handle only a limited amount of stress. The group recognized that some level of mutual support was essential and felt they had fallen below that level over the past year and a half. One member suggested that any staff person should be able to ask for a "debriefing contract" whenever he or she felt in need of help or support. These contracts would allow someone to ask for ten minutes of another person's time to hear about a particularly disturbing issue or case.

The group adopted this suggestion because they saw that it could allow members to seek help without overburdening each other. The person who was asked to listen could assist and give needed support without feeling that she had to "fix" another worker's problem. Diane continued to work at the center and found that her abilities and confidence increased as the group provided the support she needed.

Discussion Questions

- In what ways did the parties in this conflict show "good faith"?
- Is "good faith" participation a necessary prerequisite to constructive conflict resolution?

This is a "textbook" case in effective conflict management because it resulted in a solution that all parties accepted. The members of this group walked a tightrope throughout the conflict, yet they managed to avoid a fall. The tension, unpleasantness, uncertainty, and fragility of conflict situations make them hard to face. Because these problems make it difficult to deal with issues constructively and creatively, conflicts are often terminated by force, by uncomfortable suppression of issues, or simply by exhaustion after a prolonged fight—all outcomes that leave at least one party dissatisfied. Entering a conflict is often like making a bet against the odds: You can win big if it turns out well, but so many things can go wrong that many people are unwilling to chance it.

The key to working through conflict is not to minimize its disadvantages, or even to emphasize its positive functions, but to accept both and to try to understand how conflicts move in destructive or productive directions. This calls for a careful analysis of both the specific behaviors and the interaction patterns involved in conflict and the forces that influence these patterns.

This chapter introduces you to conflict as an interaction system. We first define conflict and then introduce the four arenas for interpersonal conflict that this book explores. Following this, we discuss an important reference point—the distinction between productive and destructive conflict interaction—and the behavioral cycles that move conflict in positive and negative directions. Finally, we lay out the plan of this book, which is written to examine the key dynamics of conflict interaction and the forces that influence them.

I.1 Conflict Defined

Conflict is the interaction of interdependent people who perceive incompatibility and the possibility of interference from others as a result of this incompatibility. Several features of this definition warrant further discussion.

The most important feature of conflict is that it is a type of human *interaction*. Conflicts are constituted and sustained by the behaviors of the parties involved and their reactions to one another, particularly verbal and nonverbal communication. Conflict interaction takes many forms, and each form presents special problems and requires special handling. The most familiar type of conflict interaction is marked by shouting matches or open competition in which each party tries to defeat the other. But conflicts also can be more subtle. People may react to conflict by suppressing it. A husband and wife may communicate in ways that allow them to avoid confrontation, either because they are afraid the conflict may damage a fragile relationship or because they convince themselves that the issue "isn't worth fighting over." This response is as much a part of the conflict process as fights and shouting matches. This book deals with the whole range of responses to conflict and how those responses affect the development of conflicts.

People in conflict perceive that there is some existing *incompatibility* with others and that this incompatibility may prompt others to interfere with their own desires, goals, personal comforts, or communication preferences. The key word here is *perceived*. Regardless of whether incompatibility actually exists, if the parties believe incompatibility exists, then conditions are ripe for conflict. Whether one employee really stands in the way of a co-worker's promotion, if the co-worker interprets the employee's behavior as interfering with his promotion, then a conflict is likely to ensue. Communication is important because it is the key to shaping and maintaining the perceptions that guide conflict behavior.

Communication problems can be an important source of incompatibility. You may have experienced times when you got into a disagreement with someone else, only to realize it was due to a misunderstanding, rather than a real conflict of interest. However, although communication problems may contribute to conflicts, most conflicts cannot be reduced to communication. Rather, real conflicts of interest underlie most serious conflicts.

Conflict interaction is influenced by the *interdependence* of the parties. Interdependence determines parties' incentives in the conflict. There is an incentive to cooperate when parties perceive that gains by one will promote gains by the other or losses for one party will result in corresponding losses for the other. There is an incentive to compete when parties believe that one's gain will be the other's loss. Resentment to Diane built up among the other workers at the hotline because they felt that if she got what she needed—time off—it would result in more work and pressure for them. This set up a competitive situation that resulted in conflict escalation. However, purely competitive (or cooperative) situations rarely occur. In most real situations there is a mixture of incentives to cooperate and to compete. The other staff members at the hotline wanted to maintain a cordial atmosphere, and several liked Diane. This compensated to some degree for their resentment of Diane and set the stage for a successful third-party intervention.

The greater the interdependence among people, the more significant the consequences of their behaviors are for each other. The conflict at the hotline would not have occurred if Diane's behavior had not irritated the other workers and if their response had not threatened Diane's position. Furthermore, any action taken in response to a conflict affects both sides. The decision to institute a "debriefing contract" required considerable change by everyone. If Diane had been fired, that, too, would have affected the other workers; they would have had to "cover" Diane's cases and come to terms with themselves as co-workers who could be accused of being unresponsive or insensitive.

There is one final wrinkle to interdependence: When parties are interdependent, they can potentially aid or interfere with each other. Parties know about their respective abilities to cooperate or to compete, and their interpretations of each other's communication and actions shape how the conflict develops. In some instances, one party may believe that having his or her point accepted is more important, at least for the moment, than proposing a mutually beneficial outcome. When Diane asked for two weeks off, she was probably thinking not of the group's best interest, but of her own needs. In other cases, someone may advance a proposal designed to benefit everyone, as when the staff member suggested the debriefing contract. In still other instances, a comment may be offered with cooperative intent, but others may interpret it as one that advances an individual interest. Regardless of whether the competitive motive is intended by the speaker or assigned by others, the interaction unfolds from that point under the assumption that the speaker is competitive. As we will see, subsequent interaction is colored by this negative interpretation, and people's experiences may further undermine their willingness to cooperate in a self-reinforcing cycle. The same cyclical process also can occur with cooperation, creating a positive momentum.

I.2 Arenas for Conflict

This book examines a broad range of conflicts in four general settings. One important conflict arena is the *interpersonal relationship.* Interpersonal conflicts include those between spouses, siblings, friends, and roommates. But interpersonal relationships are broader than this, encompassing those among co-workers, supervisors and employees, landlords and tenants, and neighbors. Interpersonal conflicts tell us a great deal about styles of conflict interaction, emotional and irrational impulses, and the diversity of resources people exchange in close or long-term relationships.

A second important genre of conflicts are those that occur in groups or teams. This arena includes families, work teams, small businesses, classes, clubs, juries, and even therapy or consciousness-raising groups. Because much work is done in groups, this arena has been studied extensively and offers a wide range of conflict situations for analysis. Conflicts in this arena offer insights about group cohesion; the influence of climates, coalitions, and working habits; and the distribution of power.

A third important arena for conflict is the *organization*. Many relationships and groups are embedded in organizations. Organizations often engender conflict when they create issues for parties, such as struggles over promotion, battles over which projects should be funded, debates over strategic directions. Sometimes conflicts in organizations are displaced: parties angry due to perceived personal slights may express their frustration in ways that are more legitimate to the organization, such as attacking a plan the transgressor is presenting in a meeting. By cloaking their personal grievance in formal terms, they are able to exercise their anger. Organizations also constrain conflict behavior. In an organization that is comfortable with disagreement, expressing conflict is acceptable. In one that is uncomfortable, conflicts may be suppressed.

Finally, the book examines conflicts that occur in *intergroup* settings. In this case, the focus is on individuals as representatives of social groups rather than as unique and special individuals. This arena includes conflicts among people who represent different gender, ethnic, or cultural groups. Intergroup conflicts also can arise among parties who are viewed as representatives of different teams, organizations, or political action groups. In these conflicts, the individual's identity is supplanted by issues of group identity. Prejudice, stereotyping, and ideologies often come into play (Putnam & Poole, 1987).

The four arenas differ in several respects. One obvious difference is in the number of people typically involved in a conflict. Interpersonal conflicts are characterized by face-to-face exchanges among a small number of people. The parties may belong to a larger group or organization (for example, siblings are part of the same family), but the divisive issues are those that the parties view as centrally their own. The conflict is played out between them and not in the group as a whole. Group conflicts involve a number of people who are members of some larger unit. The parties know each other, have interacted with each other in meetings or work settings, and attempt to reach decisions as a group. The divisive issues in these conflicts are central to the entire group. Intergroup conflicts involve parties representing two or more large groups such as organizations, cultural groups, or genders. Issues in intergroup disputes are often carried over from long-standing grievances and conflicts between the "parent" units.

As the number of people involved in a conflict increases, important features of the interaction change as well. For example, in interpersonal conflicts, people usually speak for themselves. In group, organizational, or intergroup conflicts, spokespersons, representatives, or various counselors, such as attorneys, union representatives, or presidents of organizations, are more likely to speak for the collective. In addition, the group, team, or organizational climate becomes important as the number of people in a conflict increases.

These arenas of conflict also differ in the type of interdependence that typically exists among the parties. The resources available to parties shift across these contexts. In interpersonal relationships, parties depend on each other for a wide range of emotional, psychological, and material resources (Levinger, 1976; Roloff, 1981; Cahn, 1990a). Among the resources exchanged in interpersonal relationships are: emotional support; images one holds of oneself as a talented, generous, loving, sensuous, or loyal person; financial security; and the ability to meet physical needs. These resources are at stake when conflicts emerge in interpersonal relationships. In group and intergroup conflicts, the range of interdependence is generally narrower. In task-oriented units, people are dependent on each other for achieving the goals the group has set for itself, for financial security (if the group provides income for members), and for a person's professional or public identity (for example, images parties hold of themselves as competent, fair-minded, or cooperative). In intergroup relationships, individuals are dependent on each other for the advancement and continuation of the group vis-à-vis other groups (for example, some Shiites in Iraq worked to achieve control by attacking other groups such as the Sunnis), and also for their identities as members of a well-defined social unit (for example, the sense of self one has as a human being, a Christian, a Hispanic American, a Republican). The different types of interdependence in each arena make the use of power different in each of them.

Although these arenas differ in important ways, they are similar in one important sense: in all of them interaction is central to conflict (Roloff, 1987a). Regardless of the number of parties involved or the type of interdependence among them, conflict unfolds as a series of moves and countermoves premised on people's perceptions, expectations, and strategies. Because of this fundamental similarity, many of the principles of conflict examined apply across the arenas. As Putnam and Folger (1988, p. 350) put it:

> Theoretical principles apply across (conflict) contexts because interaction processes form the foundation of conflict management. Fundamental to all conflicts are the series of actions and reactions, moves and countermoves, planning of communication strategies, perceptions, and interpretations of messages that directly affect substantive outcomes.

Because interaction is the key feature of conflict across all four arenas, they share a number of common characteristics as well. For example, violent exchanges can occur in interpersonal, intragroup, organization or intergroup conflicts. So too, can parties engage in negotiation in any of these settings. Because labor–management or political negotiations are the most commonly reported examples in the media, people often think of negotiation or bargaining as a separate arena. However, husbands and wives can negotiate divorce agreements, a professor and student can negotiate a grade, environmental groups can negotiate a land-use policy, or neighborhood groups can negotiate historical preservation standards. Another aspect of conflict common to all four arenas is power, because power is integral to all forms of interdependence. These and other commonalities are explored throughout this book.

I.3   Productive and Destructive Conflict Interaction

As previously noted, people often associate conflict with negative outcomes. However, there are times when conflicts must be addressed regardless of the apprehension they create. When differences exist and the issues are important, suppressing conflict is often more dangerous than facing it. The psychologist Irving Janis points to a number of famous political disasters, such as the failure to anticipate the Japanese attack on Pearl Harbor, where poor decisions can be traced to the repression of conflict by key decision-making groups (Janis, 1972). The critical question is: What forms of conflict interaction will yield obvious benefits without tearing a relationship, a group, a team, or an organization apart?

The sociologist Lewis Coser (1956) distinguished realistic from nonrealistic conflicts. *Realistic* conflicts are based on disagreements over the means to an end or over the ends themselves. In realistic conflicts, the interaction focuses on the substantive issues the participants must address to resolve their underlying incompatibilities. *Nonrealistic* conflicts are expressions of aggression in which the sole end is to defeat or hurt the other. Participants in nonrealistic conflicts serve their own interests by undercutting those of the other party involved. Coser argues that because nonrealistic conflicts are oriented toward the expression of aggression, force and coercion are the means for resolving these disputes. Realistic conflicts, on the other hand, foster a wide range of resolution techniques—force, negotiation, persuasion, even voting—because they are oriented toward the resolution of some substantive problem. Although Coser's analysis is somewhat oversimplified, it is insightful and suggests important contrasts between productive and destructive conflict interaction (Deutsch, 1973).

What criteria could be used to evaluate whether a conflict is productive? In large part, productive conflict interaction depends on *flexibility*. In constructive conflicts, members engage in a wide variety of behaviors ranging from coercion and threat to negotiation, joking, and relaxation to reach an acceptable solution. In contrast, parties in destructive conflicts are likely to be much less flexible because their goal is more narrowly defined: They are trying to defeat each other. Destructive conflict interaction is likely to result in uncontrolled escalation or prolonged attempts to avoid issues. In productive conflict, on the other hand, the interaction changes direction often. Short cycles of escalation, de-escalation, avoidance, and constructive work on an issue are likely to occur as participants attempt to manage conflict.

Consider the Women's Hotline Case. The workers exhibited a wide range of interaction styles, from the threat of a grievance to the cooperative attempt to reach a mutually satisfactory solution. Even though Diane and others engaged in hostile or threatening interactions, they did not persist in this mode, and when the conflict threatened to escalate, they called in a third party. The conflict showed all of the hallmarks of productive interaction. In a destructive conflict, the members might have responded to Diane's grievance by suspending her, and Diane might have retaliated by suing or by attempting to discredit the center in the local newspaper. Her retaliation would have hardened others' positions, and they might have fired her, leading to further retaliation.

In an alternative scenario, the Hotline conflict might have ended in destructive avoidance. Diane might have hidden her problem, and the other workers might have consciously or unconsciously abetted her by changing the subject when the murder came up or by avoiding talking to her at all. Diane's problem would probably have grown worse, and she might have had to quit. The center then would have reverted back to "normal" until the same problem surfaced again. Although the damage caused by destructive avoidance is much less serious in this case than that caused by destructive escalation, it is still considerable: the Hotline loses a good worker, and the seeds for future losses remain. In both cases, it is not the behaviors themselves that are destructive—neither avoidance nor hostile arguments are harmful in themselves—but rather the inflexibility of the parties that locks them into escalation or avoidance cycles.

In productive conflicts, all parties believe they can attain important goals (Deutsch, 1973). Productive conflict interaction exhibits a sustained effort to bridge the apparent incompatibility of positions. This is in marked contrast to destructive conflicts, where the interaction is premised on participants' belief that one side must win and the other must lose. Productive conflict interaction results in a solution satisfactory to all and produces a general feeling that the parties have gained something (for example, a new idea, greater clarity of others' positions, or a stronger sense of solidarity). In some cases, the win–lose orientation of destructive conflict stems from the fear of losing. People attempt to defeat alternative proposals because they believe that if their positions are not accepted they will lose resources, self-esteem, or the respect of others. In other cases, win–lose interaction is sparked, not by competitive motives, but by the parties' fear of working through a difficult conflict. Groups that rely on voting to reach decisions often call for a vote when discussion becomes heated and the members do not see any other immediate way out of a hostile and threatening situation. Any further attempt to discuss the alternatives or to pursue the reasons behind people's positions seems risky. A vote can put a quick end to threatening interaction, but it also induces a win–lose orientation that can easily trigger destructive cycles. Group members whose proposals are rejected must resist a natural tendency to be less committed to the chosen solutions and avoid trying to "even the score" in future conflicts.

Productive conflict interaction is sometimes competitive. Both parties must stand up for their own positions and strive for perceived understanding if a representative outcome is to be attained (Cahn, 1990b). This may result in tension and hostility, but they should be regarded as paths to a higher goal. Although parties in productive conflicts hold strongly to their positions, they are also open to movement when convinced that such movement will result in the best decision. The need to preserve power, save face, or make the opponent look bad does not stand in the way of change. In contrast, during destructive conflicts parties may become polarized, and the defense of a "noble," nonnegotiable position often becomes more important than working out a viable solution.

Of course, this description of productive and destructive conflict interaction is an idealization. It is rare that a conflict exhibits all the constructive or destructive qualities just mentioned. Most conflicts exhibit both productive and destructive interactions. However, better conflict management will result if parties can sustain productive conflict interaction patterns, and it is to this end that this book is dedicated.

I.4 Judgments About Conflict Outcomes

To this point we have focused on assessing conflict interaction. This is because we believe it is important to know where a conflict is heading while we are in the midst of it. But the outcomes of conflicts are also important. Parties must live with the outcomes, and whether they accept and are satisfied with them determines whether the conflict is resolved or continues to smolder, waiting for some future spark to set it off again.

The most obvious and most desirable outcome measure would give an objective account of the *gains and losses* that result for each party. If these can be assessed in an objective manner for each party, they can then be compared to determine things such as who won, how fair the outcome of the conflict was, and whether a better outcome was possible. We can determine relative gains and losses in more or less objective terms if the outcome can be stated in numerical terms. Some numerical measures use values that correspond to real things (for example, money or the number of hours in a day someone agrees to work), whereas others simply measure value on an arbitrary scale such as the "utility" of an outcome to a party.

As desirable as it is, determining gains and losses is more difficult for outcomes that cannot be reduced to numerical terms. For example, the outcome of a conflict between a brother and sister over who gets the corner bedroom is difficult to quantify, though a winner and loser can be identified immediately afterward—who got the bedroom? However, over the longer term, the "winner" may discover that he or she finds the room too hot because of the sun beating through the windows and too noisy because it is right over the game room. Outcomes, such as bedrooms, are complicated to measure, and although there might be gains on some dimensions, there may be losses on other dimensions. Whether there is an overall gain or loss may depend as much on what aspects parties choose to emphasize as on "real" values of the items. If the winner chooses to regard the sun as cheerful (but hot!) and instead focuses on the nice furniture in the room, outcomes are more favorable than if heat is the main focus. Moreover, as our example illustrates, outcomes can change over time. What appears to be a fine outcome right after the conflict is settled may turn out to be negative over the long run, and vice versa.

A second way to evaluate conflicts is in terms of the level of *satisfaction* people feel about the resolution. One definition of an integrative resolution is the solution that all parties are most satisfied with. This criterion gets around some of the limitations of objective outcome measures because we can always determine parties' perceptions and evaluations, even when there is no direct measure of outcomes. The satisfaction criterion also enables us to compare outcomes—at least in relative terms—because parties may be more or less satisfied.

Two other judgments that can be made about conflict outcomes concerns their fairness. Two types of *fairness,* or *social justice,* have a bearing on evaluation of conflict outcomes. *Distributive justice* refers to the fair allocation of resources among two or more recipients. *Procedural justice* is concerned with the fairness of the process by which decisions are made to resolve the conflict.

The answer to the key question regarding distributive justice—have outcomes been allocated fairly?—depends on the value system we apply. Thompson (1998, p. 194) distinguished three value systems: (a) "The *equality rule,* or blind justice, prescribes equal shares for all." The U.S. legal system is an example of this value system. (b) "The *equity rule,* or *proportionality of contributions principle,* prescribes that distribution should be proportional to a person's contribution." A case in which it was decided that workers who put in more hours on a project should get a greater share of the bonus earned than should those who put in relatively little effort would be following the equity rule. (c) "The *needs-based rule,* or *welfare-based allocation,* states that benefits should be proportional to need." Universities give out much of their financial aid based on this principle. Exactly what is regarded as a just outcome will differ depending on which of these three systems applies.

Judgments about procedural justice focus on the process by which outcomes are determined and concern whether this process is legitimate and fair. Consider the example of grade appeals. Most colleges have specific procedures in place to handle student grade appeals. In one college, there is a three-step process. The student must first talk to the instructor. If this does not result in a satisfactory resolution, the student can then appeal to the department chair. The next step is to take the appeal to a committee consisting of three professors and four students. There are detailed rules specifying what types of evidence are required and how the committee hearing will be held. The procedure allows each appeal to be thoroughly considered. The final step involves judgment by the student's peers, who are in the majority on the committee that makes the final determination. The process is set up the way it is so that both students and faculty will agree that there has been a fair hearing. Regardless of the outcome, if students and faculty believe they have participated in a legitimate process, they are more likely to accept the outcome and they are also likely to have their faith in the "system" renewed. So procedural justice can be just as important as the actual outcome.

In evaluating the outcomes of conflict, it is important not to emphasize one of these four criteria—gains and losses, satisfaction, distributive justice, or procedural justice—so much that we forget about the others. Each of the outcomes may cloud the others. For example, an objectively good outcome for both parties may also be perceived as unfair because the proper procedures were not followed. And an outcome that satisfies both parties may be grossly unfair from the viewpoint of distributive justice. Ideally all four criteria will be considered in evaluating the outcomes of a conflict.

I.5 Plan of the Book

The key question this book addresses is: How does conflict interaction develop destructive patterns—radical escalation, prolonged or inappropriate avoidance of conflict issues, inflexibility—rather than constructive patterns leading to productive conflict management? A good way to understand conflict interaction is to think of parties in a conflict as poised on a precipice. The crest represents productive conflict management, and the chasm below the downward spiral into destructive conflict. Maintaining a productive approach to a conflict requires diligence and the ability to strike a careful balance among all of the forces that influence interpersonal conflict interaction. Managed properly, these forces can be used to maintain a proper balance and to keep the conflict on a constructive path. However, lack of attention to powerful dynamics surrounding conflicts can propel them into developing a momentum that pushes the parties over the edge in an accelerating plunge.

This book considers several major forces that direct conflicts and examines the problems people encounter in trying to control these forces to regulate their own conflict interactions. To sort out the most influential forces in moving conflicts in destructive or constructive directions, we examine the major theoretical perspectives on communication and conflict. Chapter 1 offers an introduction to communication in conflict centered on four properties of conflict interaction, each of which highlights key influences on conflict. Chapter 2 focuses on the inner experience of conflict—psychological dynamics that influence conflict interaction, specifically emotion and social cognitive processes that affect conflict. Chapter 3 then considers conflict interaction and reviews a number of processes that affect conflict.

Building on this theoretical foundation, we devote the next four chapters to understanding important forces that influence conflict interaction—styles, power, face-saving, and context—and how to work with each of them to encourage productive conflict management. Chapter 8 discusses conflict management. Chapter 9 turns to third-party intervention in conflicts, and examines how third parties can facilitate constructive conflict interaction.

I.6 Summary and Review

What is conflict?

Conflict is interaction among parties who are interdependent and perceive incompatibility with one another. It is important to recognize that conflicts can be driven by perceptions, not merely by the objective situation. Interdependence plays a critical role in conflict because it sets up tendencies to compete or cooperate that drive conflict interaction.

What are important arenas for interpersonal conflict?

Interpersonal conflicts occur in interpersonal relationships, small groups, organizations, and intergroup settings. Each of these arenas differs in terms of the number of people potentially involved in the conflict and in the type of interdependence among parties. They have in common the fact that conflict in all four arenas is first and foremost a type of interaction.

What is the role of interaction in conflict?

Conflicts are constituted by interaction among parties in that conflicts only exist in the moves and countermoves of parties. Conflicts unfold as parties act them out. This means that conflict is never wholly under the control of any single party; all parties involved have at least some degree of control over how the conflict is to be pursued over time. One particularly strong force in conflict interaction is the tendency of behavioral cycles to be self-reinforcing such that competitive behavior begets competition in response, and cooperative behavior prompts cooperative responses, and so on, in a repeating spiral.

Can different types of conflict be distinguished?

Scholars have distinguished productive from destructive modes of conflict. In productive conflicts, parties take flexible approaches and believe a mutually acceptable solution can be developed. Destructive conflicts are characterized by inflexible behavior and attempts to defeat the other party. In destructive conflicts, parties' goals often shift from achieving an acceptable outcome to defeating the other party, regardless of other considerations. It is worth noting, however, that destructiveness and competitiveness are not synonyms. Competition can occur in constructive conflicts; it just never leads parties to excesses.

What are the standards by which conflict outcomes can be evaluated?

We can distinguish four different criteria that can be used to evaluate conflict outcomes—objective gains/losses, participant satisfaction, distributive justice, and procedural justice. Because most conflicts are complex, it is desirable to use more than one of these criteria to judge the quality of outcomes for participants.

What are the major factors influencing conflict interaction?

As we will see in the remainder of this book, particularly important factors are power, face-saving, context, and the strategies employed by parties. Several other psychological and social dynamics also play a role in conflicts, and we will consider them as well. One moral of this book is that *conflict is a complex phenomenon,* and that no single factor is the key to effective conflict management. Like all communication skills, conflict management requires us to be aware of the forces that influence conflict and to be capable of working with those forces to channel conflicts in productive directions.

1

Communication and Conflict

We have argued that conflicts are best understood if we view them as a form of interaction. But interaction is an extraordinarily complicated phenomenon. How can we get a grasp on what happens in conflicts? How can we use that knowledge to turn conflict interaction in productive directions?

This chapter provides an introduction to conflict interaction. First, we describe a model of conflict interaction as a "balancing act." The model proposes that in order to manage a conflict effectively, parties must first articulate and understand the differences in their positions and interests. Only after this has been done can they move toward a mutually acceptable, integrative solution. However, this is a precarious process, fraught with difficulties. If parties make the wrong moves, their differentiation may spiral into uncontrollable escalation or, alternatively, to rigid suppression and avoidance of a conflict that they should be able to face and manage. Walking the tightrope to productive conflict management requires insight into the forces that push conflict in negative directions and the appropriate actions required to control them.

The second part of this chapter presents four basic properties of conflict interaction, which suggest a number of factors that are important in conflicts. These factors, discussed in subsequent chapters, can move conflict in productive and destructive directions and suggest various levers parties can use to manage conflict effectively.

1.1 A Model of Effective Conflict Management

At the outset it is a good idea to consider effective conflict management, the type of interaction that will lead to productive conflict. In his book, *Interpersonal Peacemaking,* Richard Walton (1969) describes a simple yet powerful model of conflict management that reflects insights on conflict management echoed by a number of other influential writers (Deutsch, 1973; Fisher & Ury, 1981; Pruitt & Carnevale, 1993; Thomas, 1975). The model views conflict in terms of two broad phases: a differentiation phase followed by an integration phase. In *differentiation,* parties raise the conflict issues and spend sufficient time and energy clarifying positions, pursuing the reasons behind those positions, and acknowledging their differences. At the point where further escalation seems fruitless, an *integration* phase begins. Parties begin to acknowledge common ground, explore possible options, and move toward some solution—sometimes one that meets everyone's needs, but sometimes simply one that they can live with. If integration is not completely success-ful, the conflict may cycle back through a new differentiation phase.

This two-phase model of conflict may seem elementary, but it is highly suggestive because it indicates what parties must do to move through a conflict successfully. How and whether conflict interaction moves from differentiation through integration is complicated. We will consider in further detail some of the dynamics of this two-stage model of conflict.

1.1.1 Moving Through Differentiation and Integration

The differentiation stage of conflicts is often difficult because of the seemingly unbridge-able differences that emerge and the intense negative emotions these differences often spark. The combination of hostility and irreconcilable positions may encourage behavior that spurs uncontrolled escalation into a destructive conflict. In a different overreaction, parties fearful of escalation and loss of control, may "sit on" and suppress the conflict, which then festers and undermines their relationship. But it is important to navigate differentiation successfully to get to integration, during which "parties appreciate their similarities, acknowledge their common goals, own up to positive aspects of their ambiva-lence, express warmth and respect, and/or engage in other positive actions to manage their conflict" (Walton 1969, p. 105). The simultaneous need for and fear of differentiation poses a difficult dilemma for parties who want to work through important conflicts.

Adequate differentiation is necessary for constructive conflict resolution. Without a clear statement of each party's position, finding a problem-solving solution—one in which "the participants all are satisfied with their outcomes and feel they have gained as a result of the conflict"—is a hit-or-miss venture (Deutsch, 1973, p. 17). Unless parties honestly ac-knowledge their differences and realize that they must tackle the conflict and work it out, they may not be sufficiently motivated to deal with the problem. And unless they understand their points of difference, they do not have the knowledge required to find a workable solution.

Here, however, is the rub. Differentiation may also lead to open confrontation and competition. Discovering that others disagree or want something that threatens our best interests is frustrating. Others may be combative, demanding, and angry, or whiny and insistent, when they express their demands or grievances. Differentiation may initially in-volve personalizing the conflict, as parties clarify their stands and identify with posi-tions. Due to these and other potential problems, parties may be reluctant to openly explore and understand their differences.

Paradoxically, though, it is not until opposing positions are articulated that the conflict can finally be managed. Once individual positions have been clarified, it is just a short step to the realization that the heart of the conflict lies in the *incompatibility* of positions and is not the fault of the other party. If parties can clarify the issues and air diverse positions without losing control (a difficult problem in its own right), they can recast the conflict as an external obstacle that they can work together to surmount.

Once achieved, this depersonalized and accurate view of the issues serves as a basis for commonality. It often marks the beginning of an integrative phase, but by no means does it signify the end of the conflict process. The parties must still generate ideas and choose a solution that, as Simmel (1955, p. 14) puts it, "resolves the tension between contrasts" in the group or social relationship. From this point of view, people can build on the accomplishments of differentiation.

Differentiation and Escalation.   Although differentiation is necessary for constructive conflict resolution, it can also nourish destructive tendencies. Differentiation surfaces disagreements and makes them the center of attention. This makes the stakes seem high, because an unsuccessful attempt to resolve an issue means that members must live with a keener awareness of differences and a more vivid understanding of the negative consequences of leaving the issue unresolved.

In some cases, the process of differentiation can spiral out of control into "malevolent cycling"—highly personalized or hostile conflict that is not directed toward issues (Walton 1969). Baxter, Wilmot, Simmons, and Swartz (1993) conducted open-ended interviews with students that suggested that spiraling escalation is common in interpersonal conflicts. One commonly occurring type of conflict in their interviews they labeled "Escalatory Conflict" because it involved increasing emotional intensity and multiple stages in which the scope and intensity of the conflict increased over time. One female respondent provided this example from a romantic relationship: "I might bring up a topic. Then he will get mad that I brought up this particular topic. Then I will lose my patience and get frustrated. He, in turn, will get more mad" (Baxter et al., 1993, p. 98). Roloff and Soule (2002) summarize considerable evidence that "serial arguing" is a common feature of many interpersonal relationships.

This type of escalation also occurs in workplace conflicts, conflicts between groups, and international conflicts (Poole & Garner, 2005; North, Brody, & Holsti, 1963; Walton, 1969). As we discuss in Chapters 2 and 3, it is fueled by negative emotions such as anger and hurt, by social cognitive processes such as attributing fault for the conflict to the other, and by interaction processes such as reciprocity.

Differentiation and Avoidance.   A second, equally damaging pattern in conflict interaction is overly rigid avoidance. Parties may sometimes fear the consequences of open conflict so much that they refuse to acknowledge the conflict and avoid anything that might spark a confrontation. They may respond to potential conflicts with ambiguous statements ("I'm not sure how I feel about that") and skirt troublesome issues. They may openly suppress discussion of the conflict ("Let's not talk about that") and refuse to acknowledge it ("There's really no problem here"). Even when both parties know there is a conflict, they may simply avoid discussing it, even if there is palpable discomfort with that "elephant in the corner," the potential conflict.

The problem with this approach is that parties may never realize their own potential for finding creative solutions to important problems (Poole & Garner, 2005; Tjosvold, 1995; Pruitt & Lewis, 1977). Trying to avoid conflict at all costs, parties may quickly accept a solution that leaves them feeling lukewarm and dissatisfied after the fact. Several studies of conflict interaction illustrate this.

A classic study by Guetzkow and Gyr (1954) provides a vivid picture of the consequences of rigid avoidance. In a sample of 72 decision-making groups they compared interaction in groups with high levels of *substantive* conflict (conflict focused on the issues and on disagreements about possible solutions) to interaction in groups with high levels of *affective* conflict (interpersonal conflict characterized by extreme frustration, according to an outsider's observations). They were interested in the difference between substantive and affective conflicts because affective conflicts are more likely to exhibit spiraling escalation. Affective conflict was highly correlated with how critical and punishing members are to each other and how unpleasant the emotional atmosphere is. In essence, affective conflict is a sign of differentiation gone awry. The objective of Guetzkow and Gyr was to determine what conditions allowed groups with substantive and affective conflict, respectively, to reach consensus.

Guetzkow and Gyr found that different behaviors contributed to each group's ability to reach consensus. Groups that were high in substantive conflict and were able to reach consensus sought three times as much factual information and relied on that information more heavily in reaching a decision than did groups that were not able to reach consensus. In other words, substantive conflict was resolved by determined pursuit of the issue.

In contrast, groups high in affective conflict engaged mostly in flight or avoidance to reach consensus. Members withdrew from the problem by addressing simpler and less controversial agenda items, showed less interest in the discussion overall, and talked to only a few others in the group. When consensus was achieved in the affective conflict groups, it was most often the result of ignoring the critical problem at hand and finding an issue on which members could comfortably reach agreement. If the primary goal is to reduce tension and discomfort at any cost, then flight behaviors will serve well.

When people cannot easily ignore an issue, however, destructive tension can result from their inability to pursue the conflict. Baxter et al. (1993) also found this type of avoidance in their study of interpersonal conflict. One of the interviewees in their study called this type of conflict "don't talk about it" conflict. When confronting particularly serious issues, friends reported that they would change the subject and avoid the conflict because they did not want to threaten their relationship. Results similar to those in the two studies just summarized have been found in numerous other studies (Nicotera & Dorsey, 2005; Poole & Garner, 2005).

Differentiation and Rigidity.   In the Greek epic poem *The Odyssey,* Ulysses and his men must sail through a narrow strait guarded by two monsters. On one side is Scylla, a ravenous six-headed snake who would seize six men from each passing ship to satisfy her ravenous hunger. On the other is Charybdis, a whirlpool that would suck unsuspecting ships into the deeps. Ships had to navigate the strait very carefully to escape the two monsters. To drift too far one way or the other was to court death and disaster. Avoidance and spiraling, hostile escalation are the Scylla and Charybdis of differentiation, and carefully navigating a course that escapes both is key to effective conflict management.

Differentiation is often threatening or anxiety-ridden and this makes sticking to the straight and narrow course toward integration difficult. Threat and anxiety tends to produce rigidity that causes people to cling inflexibly to patterns of interaction that emerge during differentiation.

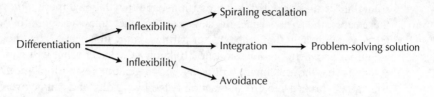

FIGURE 1.1 *Possible Responses to the Demands of Differentiation in Conflict Situations.*

We will consider the relationships among threat, anxiety, and rigidity in more detail in Chapter 2, but we will undertake some preliminary discussion here to explain the normative model. Figure 1.1 expresses the relationship among differentiation, inflexibility, and the course of conflict interaction. Psychodynamics, discussed in Chapter 2, are one source of inflexibility. Psychodynamic theory traces maladaptive, repetitive behavior—behavior that persists despite its destructive outcomes—to a threatening or anxiety-inducing environment (Volkan, 1994).

The psychoanalyst Alfred Adler, for example, maintains that running through a normal person's life is a consistent pattern of responses, a way of reacting to the world. This orientation gives rise to the person's character and a set of guiding principles used to make decisions; to deal with people; and, in general, to give meaning to the events of one's life. Sometimes, however, a person's orientations clash with events in the world, and one or more guiding principles appear false. Adler offers an explanation for why, in some cases, individuals fasten onto their orientations despite severe clashes with reality (cited in Luchins & Luchins, 1959, p. 19):

> The relatively normal person, when he [*sic*] realizes that his scheme is seriously in conflict with reality, is adaptable and modifies his orientation, abandoning what is patently false. But there are certain situations which work against flexibility and adaptability and favor rigid adherence to the guiding fictions. These are conditions in which the individual experiences exaggerated feelings of inferiority and psychological uncertainty, conditions that spell anxiety to him since anxiety is the sensation accompanying a strong uncompensated inferiority feeling. Under such conditions even a normal person may cling to his guiding fictions despite their conflict with reality. There are some individuals who live quite constantly under such anxiety-inducing conditions; and so rigidly do they adhere to their guiding fictions that these become accentuated and create a rigid, hardened lifestyle or character, an orientation out of tune with reality but nonetheless dogmatically maintained.

In much the same way, parties in conflict are faced with anxiety-inducing conditions that work against flexibility and adaptability. These conditions are the result of the inherent demands of differentiation. The conditions that produce anxiety for people are those pressures that work toward radical escalation: (1) an initial personalization of the conflict, (2) the stress of acknowledging opposing stands, (3) hostile and emotional statements, (4) uncertainty about the outcomes of the conflict, and (5) heightened awareness of the consequences of not reaching a resolution (Holsti, 1971; Smart & Vertinsky, 1977).

Failure to differentiate and search for an acceptable resolution can rigidify relationships as well. The Baxter et al. (1993) interviews indicated that relational conflicts sometimes exhibit predictable repetitions, and they labeled these *déjà vu conflicts*. In these cases, the parties enact the same conflict over and over again. In one case, an interviewee indicated that "she and her partner 'know in advance' that they will (a) enact a conflict on a certain topic or issue, (b) know how the conflict will play itself out, and (c) know that the enactment will never end in genuine resolution" (p. 97). This sort of frustrating "broken-record" interaction is fed by rigidity and can be overcome if parties engage and explore their differences directly.

Differentiation is a necessary but anxiety-provoking process that people face during any conflict. If parties pursue issues and work through the demands of differentiation without rigidly adhering to counterproductive interaction patterns, there is a clear promise of innovation and of finding an integrative solution to the conflict (Alberts, 1990). The pressures toward escalation are formidable, however, and the anxiety of differentiation can promote rigidity of behavior, resulting in either spiraling conflict or flight from the issue.

1.1.2   Taking the Middle Path: Moving Toward Integration

The key to effective conflict management is to achieve the benefits of differentiation—clear understanding of differences, acceptance of others' positions as legitimate (but not necessarily agreement with them), and motivation to work on the conflict—and to make a clean transition to integration, which sets the conflict on an entirely different course. Making the transition from differentiation to integration is not always easy. It requires parties to make a fundamental change in the direction of the conflict, turning it from a focus on differences—often accompanied by intense emotions and a desire to defeat each other—to negotiation and cooperative work. Several measures can facilitate this transition.

First, it is important to ensure that differences have surfaced as completely as possible. If parties do not feel that they have articulated their issues completely, they are likely to return to them later on, moving what had been constructive work back into differentiation. There is less temptation to do this if parties attain a thorough understanding of each others' positions, even if they do not agree with each other.

A second condition that promotes a transition to integration is when parties realize that others will not give into them or be pushed into an inferior settlement. It is an old adage that armies go to the negotiating table when they reach a "standoff." Chapter 5 discusses how the balance of power affects conflicts and how parties can attain a workable balance.

Pruitt, Rubin, and Kim (1994) recommend that parties be encouraged to set ambitious goals for themselves in negotiation. If parties "aim high" and strive for outcomes that are truly meaningful to them, rather than settling for sub-par results, they are more likely to stand their ground and act decisively. This, in turn, is likely to convince others that they will not be intimidated or easily moved, and those others are likely to recognize the need to deal with the party on terms other than competition.

Experiencing the negative consequences of differentiation can also motivate parties to work on the conflict. Sometimes parties must inflict serious practical or emotional damage on each other before they realize that it is not appropriate or workable to compete, but that some other route must be taken to resolve the situation. For example, many married couples seek counseling only after repeated, damaging fights. This is unfortunate, but a case can be made that these couples seek counseling only because they finally realize the dire consequences of continuing in their present, miserable patterns. This last point reemphasizes the paradox of the positive results that can emerge from enduring the often negative and unpleasant experience of differentiation.

It is important for parties to synchronize their transition to the integration stage (Walton, 1969). If one party is ready to work on the problem, but the other still wants to fight, the first might give up on cooperation and restart escalating conflict. The burden of synchronizing often falls to the one who first develops cooperative intentions. This party must endure the other's "slings and arrows" and attempt to promote cooperation and a shift to problem solving. The transition to integration will be easier if the other feels that his or her position has been heard. Active listening—in which the party draws out the other's issues and grievances and responds in a respectful manner—encourages concilia- tion. This enables both parties to build "positive face," as explained in Chapter 6.

Chapter 4 discusses strategies and tactics that promote integration. One such strat- egy is the "reformed sinner"—after an initial period of competition, the party offers coop- eration and signs of goodwill in response to the other's behavior; if the other continues to compete, the party responds with competition and then returns to cooperation. This indi- cates that the party could compete if he or she wanted to, but instead prefers cooperation. A final condition that promotes integration is a cooperative climate—the general situation surrounding the conflict is not threatening or defensive. The ways in which climates are created and sustained are discussed in Chapter 7.

In many cases, a third party can be a great help in making the transition from dif- ferentiation to integration. People sometimes become so involved in the conflict that they have neither the motivation nor the insight to take the necessary actions. A third party has a more objective stance and can often determine what must be done to move the con- flict into integration. In addition, individuals often trust the third party and will follow advice that they would not accept from each other. A discussion of third parties and their role in sharpening conflicts and inducing integration can be found in Chapter 9.

One key to moving through differentiation and integration is the ability to recognize destructive and productive patterns, which we will now address.

1.1.3 Recognizing Destructive Cycles

It is often difficult to determine when conflict interaction has turned in a destructive direction. Conflict can develop tendencies in gradual and subtle steps, and sometimes it is difficult to assess the consequences of gradual changes. Conflicts can also be difficult to understand due to conscious efforts by some parties to keep the conflict "hidden"—out of the more public forums in a group or organization (Kolb & Bartunek, 1992). Unsuspecting parties may suddenly find themselves caught in an escalating spiral or persistent avoidance. Once in these destructive cycles, the rigidity that sets in may prevent parties from pulling out. It is important to be constantly on the alert for signs of destructive patterns and to act quickly to alter them. Developing the ability to recognize protracted, destructive spirals is a key conflict management skill because such insight is the first step in taking some control over the conflict. People in conflict must be aware of concrete symptoms that signal the possible onset of escalation or avoidance.

Table 1.1 on page 20 summarizes several symptoms of when a conflict is heading toward destructive escalation or avoidance. The mere appearance of any symptom should not be an automatic cause for concern. Productive conflict interaction can pass through periods

TABLE 1.1 *Interaction Symptoms of Escalation or Avoidance Cycles*

Symptoms of Avoidance	*Symptoms of Escalation*
• Marked decrease in the parties' commitment to solving the problem ("Why would we care?") • Quick acceptance of a suggested solution • Parties stop themselves from raising controversial aspects of an issue • People "tune out" of the interaction • Unresolved issues keep emerging in the same or different form • Discussion centers on a safe aspect of a broader and more explosive issue • Little sharing of information • Outspoken people are notably quiet • No plans are made to implement a chosen solution • No evaluation is made of evidence that is offered in support of claims	• An issue takes much longer to deal with than was anticipated • Parties repeatedly offer the same argument in support of a position • Parties overinflate the consequences of not reaching agreement • Threats are used to win arguments • Mounting tension is felt • The parties get nowhere but seem to be working feverishly • Name-calling and personal arguments are used • Immediate polarization on issues or the emergence of coalitions • Hostile eye gaze or less-direct eye contact occurs between parties • Sarcastic laughter or humor is used as a form of tension release • Heated disagreements seem pointless or are about trivial issues

of escalation, avoidance, constructive work, and relaxation. Cycles only become threatening when they are repetitive and preempt other responses.

Once a destructive cycle has been recognized, parties (or third parties) can intervene to break it. The previous section mentioned some measures, and we will explore these and other interventions throughout the remainder of this book. Countermeasures against destructive cycles need not be formal or particularly systematic. Simply making a surprising comment can jolt a conflict out of a destructive cycle. We recall a group member who recognized a fight developing and suddenly said, "Are we having fun yet?" This cliché got others to laugh at themselves, defusing the situation.

1.1.4 Tacking Against the Wind

Effective conflict management is much like tacking a sailboat to move upstream against an unfavorable wind (and steering it so as to avoid Scylla and Charybdis!). A sailor wishing to move her boat against the wind can do so by directing the boat at an angle, back and forth across the water, taking advantage of the sails' ability to capture some force from the opposing wind if they are set at an angle to it, as illustrated in Figure 1.2. In the same way, the tensions introduced by the danger points of escalation and avoidance may provide useful

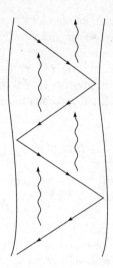

FIGURE 1.2   *Tacking Against the Wind.*

forces to move the conflict in productive directions, because they "jar loose" parties' assumptions that things are going well and encourage them to realize that others may have opinions/needs that differ from their own. Even though tacking a sailboat takes time and does not seem as direct as moving straight to one's destination, it is in fact the only choice we have when we want to steer our ship in a productive direction. There is no way to get a sailboat to go against the wind without tacking, and there is no way to work through a conflict without braving the balance between rampant escalation and stubborn avoidance.

In performing this balancing act, it is important to manage conflict interaction effectively. This is no easy task because, as noted in the introduction, interaction often seems to have a "mind of its own." It seems to be driven by forces beyond our control, and sometimes may even seem incoherent and uncontrollable. This encourages people to ignore the give-and-take of interaction and rely instead on generalizations or rules of thumb.

For instance, there is a temptation to say "she is just a difficult person to get along with" as a way of explaining why discussions with Joelle always seem to end in conflicts. Of course, this ignores the fact that Joelle might be reacting to our rather aggressive presentation of our position. Alternatively, we might assume that "the best way to win our position is to never disclose it, but rather to find out the others' position and try to exploit any weaknesses." This rule of thumb eliminates the need to make sense of an evolving situation because we have decided to do the same thing no matter what the other party does. However, this inflexible approach may discourage a cooperative party and lead her to adopt a competitive stance in the face of manipulation. It is important to avoid these easy paths and to recognize that the key to conflict management is understanding conflict interaction and taking appropriate measures to redirect it in positive directions.

It is easy to say this, but now how do we go about doing it? There is no simple answer to this challenge. However, about fifty years ago scholars in sociology, social psychology, communication, conflict studies, labor relations, and other fields began to untangle the puzzle that is human interaction. Our knowledge has grown rapidly over the past thirty years, to the point where we can understand some of the general contours and also specific dynamics of human interaction. We are not yet at a point where we can predict it with any certainty, and it may be impossible to get to such a point. Additionally, many aspects of interaction remain uncharted territory—unknown, unmapped, unstudied. But some general principles have emerged, and we center this book on them.

1.2 Properties of Conflict Interaction

Four properties of conflict interaction offer keys to understanding the development and consequences of conflicts:

1. Conflict is constituted and sustained by moves and countermoves during interaction.
2. Patterns of behavior in conflict tend to perpetuate themselves.
3. Conflict interaction is influenced by and in turn affects relationships.
4. Conflict interaction is influenced by the context in which it occurs.

By "unpacking" these simple statements, we can discover a number of important points about conflict.

We introduced the idea of conflict as interaction at the beginning of this book, and Property 1 expands this idea by distinguishing moves and countermoves as the basic features of interaction. This suggests that it will be useful to explore various strategies and tactics that can be used to enact conflicts. Property 1 also highlights the importance of power in conflict, because moves and countermoves depend on power. As we will see, power is often regarded as a possession or personal characteristic; for example, it is common to use phrases like "he or she is powerful." In Chapter 5, however, we explain that power is created and sustained during interaction. So moves and countermoves play an important role in determining a person's power in a given situation.

Property 2 expands on the previous section to focus on the momentum that conflicts develop. Sometimes momentum contributes to destructive cycles of avoidance or escalation, but in other cases momentum for productive conflict management develops. Momentum depends on psychological and behavioral dynamics that parties are often unaware of. We will explore these in Chapters 2 and 3. With so many factors, no wonder conflicts sometimes escape our control!

Property 3 directs our attention to relationships. The prior history of the relationships among parties has a powerful influence on conflict. Face, which refers to the side of themselves that people try to present in public, is particularly important in conflict. Interactions go differently for those perceived to be honorable, competent, or intelligent than it does for those perceived to be untrustworthy, incompetent, or simple-minded. During conflicts people often challenge face and the drive to maintain or restore it can dominate all other concerns. In Chapter 6, we explore how face and other relational concerns influence conflicts. Other relational aspects of conflict will be discussed in Chapters 2, 3, and 4, which focus on the psychology of conflict, conflict interaction, and conflict styles, respectively.

Property 4 addresses how context shapes conflict interaction. Several aspects of context are relevant. Previous history strongly shapes conflict interaction. Parties bring a history of personal experiences that affect how they act during conflicts. The parties may also have a previous relationship with each other that contextualizes the conflict. The unfolding situation also has a character—generally known as climate—that represents the immediate context for interaction. Climate refers to the general interpretations that parties attach to a situation, such as whether it is competitive or threatening. Finally, organizations and communities often develop normative systems of norms and procedures for the management of conflict. These, too, form part of the context and shape how the conflict unfolds.

The four properties of conflict interaction suggest points at which conflicts can be influenced by judicious interventions. Many of these interventions can be undertaken by the parties themselves. In some cases, it may be more effective for third parties—facilitators, mediators, arbitrators, even therapists and lawyers—to intervene. We will discuss interventions throughout this book. Chapters 4 through 7 have special sections on intervention, and Chapter 8 focuses on methods for managing conflict. Chapter 9 considers how third parties can help manage conflicts.

Now let us turn to each of the four properties, with special emphasis on the role of communication.

1.2.1 Property 1: Conflict Is Constituted and Sustained by Moves and Countermoves During Interaction

Conflicts emerge as a series of actions and reactions. The "He did X and then she said Y and then he said Z and then . . ." formula is often used to explain a quarrel. When parties try to deal with incompatibilities the way in which their actions mesh plays an important role in the direction the conflict takes.

Suppose Robert criticizes Susan, an employee under his supervision, for her decreasing productivity. Susan may accept the criticism and explain why her production is down, thus reducing the conflict and moving toward a solution. Susan may also shout back and sulk, inviting escalation, or she may choose to say nothing and avoid the conflict, resulting in no improvement in the situation. Once Robert has spoken to Susan and she has responded, the situation is no longer totally under Robert's control: His next behavior will be a response to Susan's reaction. Robert's behavior, and its subsequent meaning to Susan, is dependent on the interchange between them.

The behavioral sequence of initiation–response–counterresponse is the basic building block of conflicts. This sequence cannot be understood by breaking it into its parts, into the individual behaviors of Robert and Susan. It is more complex than the individual behaviors and, in a real sense, has a "life" of its own.

Taylor and Donald (2003) conducted a study of interaction during nine hostage negotiations and 27 divorce mediations that sheds some light on the interconnections between acts during conflict sequences. They found significant amounts of conflict in both and that disputant behaviors could be classified into "avoidant (withdrawal), distributive (antagonistic), and integrative (cooperative) behavior" (Taylor & Donald, 2003, p. 218). This classification reflects the three different trajectories of conflicts described earlier in this chapter, and we will revisit them often in the remainder of this book. However, Taylor and Donald studied individual behaviors or acts that occur during negotiations and conflicts, the "building blocks" of the more general directions that we have discussed. Taylor and Donald found that a four-act sequence served as the basic structure of the interaction in these negotiations.

For example, one sequence might run as follows:

1. Robert: I didn't mean to hurt your feelings (Integrative Act)
2. Susan: But you did hurt me, and I'm mad! (Distributive Act)
3. Robert: I just meant my remark to be constructive criticism (Integrative Act)
4. Susan: OK, I understand . . . but it still hurt (Integrative Act)

In this sequence, Robert makes an integrative move by apologizing. Susan responds with a distributive act that is probably meant more to emphasize her hurt feelings than to actually compete with Robert. Robert then explains more, by way of apologizing. Finally Susan accepts his apologies, but again underscores that she was hurt.

This sequence is also called a "triple–interact" because it strings together three pairs of acts, each of which is called an "interact": act 1–act 2; act 2–act 3; and act 3–act 4. Note that each act serves as the response to the previous act and as an initiator of the next act. For instance, act 2 by Susan is both a response to act 1 by Robert and a stimulus for Robert's act 3.

Taylor and Donald's research indicated that we must consider four-act sequences to adequately understand what is occurring during these negotiations. If we consider just the first two acts, we might conclude that Robert has made an overture for reconciliation and that it was rejected by Susan. However, if we go on to consider all four acts, we see that Susan accepts Robert's apology, but just wants him to know how hurt she was. No single act, or pair of acts, is sufficient to understand or to enact a conflict. Taylor and Donald's (2003) study suggests that the minimal structure in conflict interaction is four acts long. Longer structures may also help us to understand the conflict, but structures shorter than three are not sufficient. This underscores the fact that conflicts cannot be reduced to the acts of individuals. Rather they are composed of interaction among the parties: moves, responses, and countermoves.

Moves and countermoves depend on participants' ability and willingness to exert power. *Power* can be defined as the capacity to act effectively. Power sometimes takes the form of outward strength, status, money, or allies, but these are only the most obvious sources of power. There are many other sources, such as time, attractiveness, and persuasive ability that operate in a much more subtle fashion.

In the Women's Hotline Case (Case I.1) on page 2, for example, Diane might have used the other workers' guilt to try to get her way, and the workers did use their seniority and familiarity with their jobs to pass judgment on her by drafting a list of worker responsibilities. In both cases, power operates much more subtly and indirectly than is commonly assumed. More generally, a person is powerful when he or she has the resources to act and to influence others and the skills to do this effectively. The third party in the hotline case provides a good example of the effective use of power: The third party had certain resources to influence the group—experience with other conflicts and knowledge about how to work with groups—and made skillful use of them to move both sides toward a solution.

Participants' attempts to mobilize and apply power can drastically shift the direction conflict takes. As possible solutions to the conflict are considered, the parties learn how much power each is willing to use to encourage or to prevent the adoption of various alternatives. This is critical in the definition of conflict issues and solutions because it signals how important the issue is.

The balance of power often tips the scale in a productive or destructive direction. If a party perceives that he or she can dominate others, there is little incentive to compromise.

A dominant party can get whatever he or she wants, at least in the short run, and negotiation only invites others to cut into the party's solution. In the same vein, feeling powerless can sap parties' resolve and cause them to appease more powerful individuals. Of course, this method often encourages powerful people to be more demanding. Only when all participants have at least some power is the conflict likely to move in a productive direction.

At the Women's Hotline, the third party was called in only after both Diane and the workers had played their first "trumps"—the workers by informing Diane of her responsibilities, and Diane by filing a grievance. The use of power could have prompted additional moves and countermoves: Rather than calling in a third party, both sides could have continued to try to force each other to yield, and the conflict could have continued escalating. In this case, however, the two sides perceived each other's power and, because they wanted the hotline to survive, backed off. As risky as this process of balancing power is, many social scientists have come to the conclusion that it is a necessary condition for constructive conflict resolution (Deutsch, 1973; Folberg & Taylor, 1984; Pruitt, Rubin, & Kim, 1996).

Power often begets power. Those who have resources and the skills to use them wisely can use them in such a way that their power increases and reinforces itself. Those with little power find it difficult to assert themselves and to build a stronger base for the future. Yet, for conflicts to maintain a constructive direction, there should be a balance of power. This requires members to reverse the usual flow: The weaker parties must build their power; the stronger ones must share theirs, or at least not use it to force or dominate the weaker ones. As shown in Chapter 5, managing this reversal is both tricky and risky. It is tricky because power is difficult to identify, and sharing power may run up against members' natural inclinations. It is risky because the process of increasing some parties' power and decreasing or suspending others' is a sensitive operation and can precipitate even sharper conflicts.

Power is a fact of life in conflicts (Berger, 1994). Trying to ignore power or to pretend power differences do not exist is pointless, because power is operating notwithstanding and will influence the moves and countermoves in the conflict. Chapter 5 discusses the role of power in conflict interaction.

1.2.2 Property 2: Patterns of Behavior in Conflicts Tend to Perpetuate Themselves

As we just noted, conflict often seems to take on a "life of its own." To continue our example, suppose that Susan shouts back at Robert, Robert tries to discipline her, Susan becomes more recalcitrant, and so on, in an escalating spiral. The cycle could also limit itself if Robert responds to Susan's shouting with an attempt to calm her and listen to her side of the story. Conflict interaction acquires a momentum of its own through these self-reinforcing cycles. Such cycles tend to take a definite direction—toward escalation, toward avoidance and suppression, or toward productive work on resolving the conflict.

The depth of the momentum in conflict interaction becomes even more apparent when we remember that Robert formulated his original criticism on the basis of his previous experience with Susan. That is, Robert's move is based on his perception of Susan's likely response. In the same way, Susan's response is based not only on Robert's criticism, but on her estimate of Robert's likely reaction to her response. Usually such estimations are "intuitive"—that is, they are not conscious—but sometimes parties do plot them out ("If I shout at Robert, he'll back down, and maybe I won't have to deal with this"). Parties' actions in conflict are based on their perceptions of each other and on whatever theories or beliefs each holds about the other's reactions. Because these estimates are only intuitive predictions, they may be wrong to some extent. The estimates will be revised as the conflict unfolds, and this revision will largely determine what direction the conflict takes.

The most striking thing about this predictive process is the extraordinary difficulties it poses when we attempt to understand the parties' thinking. When Susan responds to Robert on the basis of her prediction of Robert's answer, from the outside we see Susan making an estimate of Robert's estimate of what she means by her response. If Robert reflects on Susan's intention before answering, we observe Robert's estimate of Susan's estimate of his estimate of what Susan meant. This string of estimates can increase without bounds if one tries to pin down the originating point, and after a while the prospect is just as dizzying as a hall of mirrors.

Several studies of different conflicts in contexts such as arms races (North, Brody, & Holsti, 1963), marital relations (Watzlawick, Beavin, & Jackson, 1967; Rubin, 1983; Scarf, 1987), and employee–supervisor interactions (Brown, 1983), have shown how this *spiral of predictions* poses a critical problem in conflicts. If the parties do not take this spiral into account, they run the risk of miscalculation. However, it is impossible to calculate all of the possibilities. At best, people have extremely limited knowledge of the implications their actions may hold for others, and their ability to manage conflicts is therefore severely curtailed. Not only are parties' behaviors inherently interwoven in conflicts, but their thinking and anticipations are as well.

The tendency of conflicts to develop through repetitive cycles is present in all types of human interaction. Any message is based on some, perhaps only barely conscious, assumption about how it will be received. Each assumption or prediction about the reaction is based on an estimate, a best guess, about the other person or social unit as a whole. The choice of message anticipates and reflects the response it seeks, and thus promotes the reaction included in its construction. A predictable sequence of act–response is often established in conflict interaction because each message in the sequence helps to elicit the response it receives. In the previous section we discussed the tendencies of escalation and avoidance to perpetuate themselves.

Perversely, this tendency toward self-perpetuation is also useful, because it helps parties know what to expect. Even if they are over-simplified, any grounds for predicting how the conflict will go is more assuring than not knowing what will happen next. For this reason, parties are often willing to make assumptions about the way others will act before any move is made.

By acting on the basis of their assumptions about the other, parties run the risk of eliciting the response they assume will occur. As discussed earlier, anticipating that the other will be competitive can encourage the party to make a competitive move. This then is likely to make the other competitive, in a sort of self-fulfilling prophecy. The cycle feeds on itself. In some cases, this may be helpful: Self-reinforcing cycles can be productive if they include a periodic check for possible inflexibility or if they lead to success on "easy" issues, which then carries over to more difficult disputes (Tjosvold, 1995). In other cases, however, the cycles lead to uncontrolled destructive interaction.

The self-perpetuating nature of conflict suggests that when conflict interaction is examined closely, on a turn-by-turn basis, it is often not resolved in any real sense (Vuchinich, 1984). Conflict often unfolds in waves of somewhat repetitive interaction sequences and moves that start and stop in a variety of ways. Repetitive sequences can end, for example, with topic switches, withdrawals, or standoffs, and may resurface later and end differently the next time the repetitive sequence occurs (Vuchinich, 1990). Roloff and Soule (2002) discuss serial arguments, in which the same issues repeat themselves and participants know how the argument will turn out even before the next one starts.

In Chapters 2 and 3 we will discuss psychological and social factors that generate and influence the structure of interaction in conflicts. We will explore the sources of inter-dependencies in conflict interactions, of self-reinforcing cycles, and of the expectations and beliefs about others that are the basis for spirals of predictions. We will also consider the patterns in coherent episodes of conflict, as reflected in stage models of conflict.

Exhibit 1.1 (see page 28) on Confrontation Episodes Theory illustrates one view of the way in which conflicts are enacted. It shows that the conflict consists in the interaction among parties, and also that no individual's actions can account for confrontation episodes. It provides a truly "interactional" view of conflict that is also systematic.

1.2.3 Property 3: Conflict Interaction Is Influenced by and in Turn Affects Relationships

It is easy to focus mainly on the substantive issues in a conflict, on the problem and its proposed solutions. In fact, centering only on issues and ignoring "emotional" aspects of a conflict has sometimes been recommended as the best way to deal with conflicts. However, focusing on the "bare facts" of the case can cause one to overlook the important effects. Conflicts are often emotionally laden and tense. This is in part because participants are concerned about getting (or not getting) what they want, but it also stems from the implications the conflict has for one party's present and future relationship to the other party. The conflict between Robert and Susan, for example, cannot be fully appreciated without considering the emotional side of the issues and the impact of the conflict on the relationships between them.

The interaction in the Women's Hotline situation (Case I.1A, page 2) had the potential to drastically alter the relationships in the group. Until the staff openly challenged Diane for not living up to her responsibilities, she believed she was doing adequate work and was regarded as an equal by the other workers. The reprimand called Diane's competence and responsibility into question, and she realized that the others did not consider her an equal. Her attitudes and assumptions about her relationship with the other workers were challenged, causing her a great deal of self-doubt and soul-searching, as well as stimulating her angry retaliation against the center. The workers' judgment of Diane also affected their attitudes and assumptions about her. Coming to the conclusion that Diane was slacking off generated distrust for her in the minds of the other staff members. It also made them angry at her, and some admitted a tendency to want to "gunnysack"; that is, pile up a long list of problems with Diane and then dump them on her. Luckily, this never happened, and the third party was able to restore some trust and encourage a more open and understanding approach among the parties.

EXHIBIT 1.1 • *Confrontation Episodes Theory*

Newell and Stutman (1988, 1991) developed a theory of social confrontation episodes that is based on a view of communication as an activity in which two parties co-create the episode.

Social *confrontation episodes* involve conflict over conduct and rules of conduct. The confrontation episode is initiated when one party signals the other that his or her behavior has violated a rule or expectation for appropriate conduct within the relationship or situation. The violation could be something as minor as bad manners or a major relational transgression, such as cheating on one's spouse. The social confrontation involves working through disagreement over behaviors and thus negotiating expectations for future conduct.

Social confrontation episodes follow typical issues and sequences of interaction. The first issue, which must be resolved before the problem issue can be explored, is the legitimacy of the rule in question. How the episode unfolds turns on whether the rule is accepted, interpreted, or rejected. Once this is settled, the behavior in question can be assessed with respect to the rule. For example, Jill may confront Jack (the confrontee) over spending money for clothing beyond a budget limit. Once the confrontee acknowledges the legitimacy of this relational rule (budget), questions concerning the act of spending too much for clothing in relation to this rule can be explored. That is, did Jack perform the behavior in question? Does the behavior constitute a violation of this rule? Is there a superseding rule that takes precedence? Is Jack responsible for his or her behavior?

The final resolution of a social confrontation episode is made up of one or more of the following: A *remedy* occurs when the confronter apologizes or makes up for the violation or when the confronter exacts some penalty or punishment. For example, Jack may apologize for overspending. Alternatively, Jill may insist that he not buy any new clothes for the next six months. *Legislation* occurs when parties rework or reinterpret the rule. Jack and Jill may, for instance, agree that they should no longer have a clothing budget. *Remediation* involves one or both parties changing expectations about the rule. Jill might tell Jack that she will no longer expect him to strictly abide by

the rule, that "a little bit over budget" is just fine. *Reaffirmation* occurs when both parties reaffirm the importance of the rule. Finally, *no resolution* occurs when the parties cannot agree. More than one of these results can occur in any episode. For instance Jack may admit he is wrong, which remedies the situation, but also reaffirms the rule that Jill applied.

Newell and Stutman's (1988) model of the social confrontation episode displays the various ways an episode can develop depending on the issues between the parties (Figure 1.3). The purpose of this model is to define the confrontation episode and to illustrate how confrontation episodes differ from one another. While action moves from initiation through development toward some sort of closure or resolution to the problem, the pattern of interaction can vary greatly. Although the confronter may perceive that the confrontee has broken a rule, how the problem ultimately is defined and resolved depends on the interaction. The model illustrates the major variations in how the problem is defined and resolved.

The model in the figure displays the various issues likely to occur within the confrontation as a series of choices (designated A–F). Based on these choices, a particular episode might take any of six paths (designated 1–6) depending on the points of disagreement between the participants. At the end of each path are the outcomes that are likely to occur.

The major split between tracks occurs over whether the confronter's expectations are explicitly or implicitly granted legitimacy by the confrontee, or whether the confrontee challenges the legitimacy of the expectations. The conversation moves along track 1, *nonlegitimacy,* if the confrontee challenges the legitimacy of the confronter's expectations, in essence arguing that the implied rule is not mutually acceptable or agreed on. For instance, Jack might turn the conflict along this path if he responds, "You hold me to standards that are just too high!"

If the confrontee does not challenge the legitimacy of the rule, several other paths remain. On track 2, *justification,* the episode revolves around whether or not this is a special situation for which

(continued)

EXHIBIT 1.1   Continued

A. Is the implied rule mutually accepted as legitimate?
B. Is this a special situation?
C. If invoked, is the superseding rule mutually accepted as legitimate?
D. Did the confrontee actually perform the behavior in question?
E. Does the behavior constitute a violation of the rule?
F. Does the confrontee accept responsibility for the behavior?

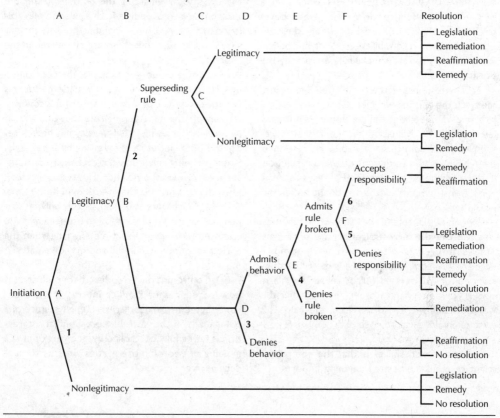

FIGURE 1.3   *An Elaborate Model of Social Confrontation.*

Source: Adapted from Newell and Stutman (1988). Reprinted by permission of Taylor & Francis Ltd. (www.tandf.co.uk/journals).

the confrontee invokes a superseding rule for the extenuating circumstances. Jack might say, "But it's nearly my birthday," for example. This rule is also open to challenges of legitimacy, but this time by the confronter rather than the confrontee. Jill might respond, "But I get to buy you clothes on your birthday, not you," which indicates that Jack's excuse does

not apply and tries to move the episode to a different track.

On track 3, *denies behavior,* the question concerns whether the confrontee actually performed the behavior in question. The response "I did not buy any clothes, John gave me those" starts the episode on track 3. On track 4, *denies rule broken,*

(continued)

EXHIBIT 1.1   Continued

the issue is one of interpretation as to what constitutes a violation of the rule. A bid for track 4 might start "But these are casual clothes. Our budget rule only applies to work clothes." On track 5, *denies responsibility,* the issue revolves around the excuse offered by the confrontee to deny responsibility for the behavior. "I just can't help myself when I see a bargain!" is an effort to move the episode down track 5. On track 6, *accepts responsibility,* the confrontee accepts responsibility for his or her behavior and moves to reaffirm the rule or remedy the situation.

The response of the confrontee determines the track the episode will take. Once on a particular line of development, the confronter is primarily left the job of evaluating the confrontee's response. If the confronter accepts the response, then they move down the track toward resolution. If the confronter challenges the response, the episode may jump to another track and a different resolution.

For an example of the range of possibilities, let's consider the fairly straightforward statement, "You're late." A confrontee might directly acknowledge this as a complaint, remedying the problem by responding: "I'm sorry. I forgot to set my alarm clock. I won't let it happen again." In responding this way the confrontee also reaffirms the rule. This episode unfolded according to path number 6, leading to these two resolutions.

Another possibility is that the confrontee might respond "Did I miss anything important?", which implies that the statement is simply a factual statement that he or she is late without a necessarily negative connotation. This implicit claim that the rule has no legitimacy in this situation has the potential to lead the episode down path 1 to no resolution. However, if the confronter to continue the episode by enlarging the complaint and the confrontee acknowledges it, the episode may follow paths 2 through 6, depending on how the answers to the other questions are negotiated in the interaction.

To give one other example, the confrontee may claim that this is a special situation: "But this has just been the worst day for me." If the confronter accepts the superceding rule that one should be forgiven for being late if the day has been a really bad one, the result of following path 2 is legislation of a new rule, remediation of expectations, and a remedy for the violation. This route also reaffirms the original rule that one should be on time, because it highlights that the rule can only be suspended for special cases. If, on the other hand, the confronter denies the superceding rule, then the episode continues to unfold and may take paths 3, 4, 5, or 6.

Confrontation episodes theory illustrates how sequences of conflict interaction are co-constructed by parties. It gives a fuller picture of a point made in the Introduction: Conflict interaction is never fully controlled by one party, but is a melding of two or more parties' actions to produce a larger episode.

This case illustrates two levels operating in all communication: every message conveys not only substantive content but also information about the relationship of the speaker to the hearer (Watzlawick et al., 1967). If Diane angrily says, "I don't deserve this reprimand. I'm filing a grievance!" to her co-workers, her statements convey two levels of meaning. First, and most obvious, is the information that she is angry and is filing a grievance to challenge the reprimand, a countermove in the conflict. But second, Diane's message also carries the information that she believes her relationship with the workers has deteriorated to the point that she must file a formal grievance: It redefines the relationship between Diane and her co-workers. Even in formal negotiation contexts, verbal and nonverbal cues carry relational information that has significant impact on the relationship between negotiating parties (Burgoon & Hoobler, 2002; Donohue, Diez, & Stahle, 1983).

This relational aspect of communication is critical because it affects both present and future interaction. It affects present interaction because people often respond to relational messages immediately and emotionally. If someone insults us, we may become angry and want to retaliate. If someone implies that our friendship is in jeopardy because of an argument, we may back down and become conciliatory. However, relational communication has its most profound effects through influencing future interaction. How people interact in conflicts is colored by their assessments of others—judgments about things such as others' trustworthiness, intentions (good or bad), and determination to win. These assessments bear directly on the relational aspects of communication and hence people often try to project a certain image in order to shape others' assumptions about their relationship (Canary & Spitzberg, 1989; 1990).

For example, one person may act defiant and angry to project an image of cold determination that tells the other, "Our relationship is not that important to me, as long as I get what I want." If this projection is successful, the second person may back down, believing the first person has no regard for him or her and will go to any lengths to win. Of course, this tactic could also backfire and make the second person resentful and defiant because the first seems cold and ruthless. Attempts at managing image and relationships prompt many moves and countermoves in conflict.

As important as relational management is in conflicts, it is not surprising that it plays a critical role in generating the direction conflicts take. *Face-saving,* parties' attempts to protect or repair their image to others, has great potential to send conflicts into destructive spirals. One particularly dangerous form of face-saving stems from people's fear of losing ground in an exchange (Brown, 1977). People in conflict often believe that if they move from a stated position or back away from a set of demands, they will appear weak or vulnerable in the eyes of the group. This concern for face—a concern for how one appears to others during the conflict interaction and the effects this will have on future relationships—can encourage people to keep arguing for a position even though they no longer believe in it or to back down because they recognize it is not contributing to a workable resolution to the conflict.

A second form of face-saving can prompt parties to continually ignore or avoid an important conflict issue. In relationships with a history of resolving conflicts in a friendly and cooperative manner, a concern for face may prevent parties from raising an issue that is far more threatening than any conflict the parties have previously addressed. People may believe that if they raise the issue, others will perceive it as an attempt to destroy the friendly relationships that have been cautiously protected and valued. This concern for face can prevent parties from calling in a third party when intervention is needed because they are reluctant to admit that they cannot resolve an issue on their own.

A party's ability to define and maintain positive working relationships during conflict interaction depends heavily on how much concern he or she has for saving face. For this reason, it is important to understand how people create pressures or incentives that heighten or lessen concern for saving face during conflict interaction (Cupach & Metts, 1994). Face as a force in conflict interaction is examined in Chapter 6.

1.2.4 Property 4: Conflict Interaction Is Influenced by the Context in Which it Occurs

One of the most robust characteristics of human interaction is that it is strongly influenced by the context in which it occurs. The simple statement "Good morning" means very different things when expressed to a casual acquaintance in the hall at school at 10 A.M. and to one's boss when reporting to work at 5 A.M. The former is something we just toss off as a politeness, while the second is something carefully performed for our manager to let her know that we are ready for work.

So it is with conflict. Important elements of the context include the personal histories of the parties and their relationship, the climate of the situation, and the environment in which the conflict occurs.

History is a complex and important force in conflict. Each of us brings to a conflict a personal history of previous experiences with relationships in general and with conflict in particular. How we have been treated by former managers, for example, creates expectations (justified or unjustified) concerning how our present manager will treat us if a conflict arises. Over the course of our lives we develop a sense of our priorities and what is important for us which affects how we respond to conflicts, what we are willing to fight for, and what is not so important. We also develop "hot buttons," sensitivities that can trigger conflicts when "pressed" by others. Our history is the source of our hopes and dreams, our aspirations about what we want from life, where we are going, and how we should be treated. These and other aspects of our history affect how we respond to conflict.

Research also suggests that our prior experience fosters conflict styles, general tendencies to respond to conflicts in particular ways. For instance, some people tend to respond to conflicts competitively, while others withdraw, and still others see opportunity in conflicts. Styles are influenced by personality traits such as aggressiveness or passivity, but they are much more strongly influenced by our experiences with past conflicts, with what worked and what did not work for us in these situations.

Another important part of personal history is our experience with the other party. If the other betrayed us in the past, for example, we are likely to interpret a friendly overture very differently than if the other has been a steadfast and loyal friend for years. Here is where history and the cyclic nature of conflict come together. Negative cycles of conflict with another party predispose us to approach the other with a negative mindset, while positive cycles have the opposite effect.

The second component of context that we will consider, *climate,* refers to the general atmosphere surrounding a particular situation. For example, most of us have felt the "tension in the air" during a charged confrontation between two people. This generalized sense of the situation is what the concept of climate attempts to capture. Climates may be threatening or safe, warm or cold. They are, as we will see, generated and sustained by the parties to the conflict, as well as by the broader environment surrounding the conflict. Though it may seem intangible, climate provides important information about how conflict is likely to be handled and may "steer" conflict interaction in particular directions. For example, if the climate of an organization seems cold and unsupportive, subordinates may be reluctant to raise issues with their superiors, on the assumption that they will be rejected outright. When a conflict does break out in such an organization, it is likely to be

CASE 1.1 • *The Columnist's Brown Bag*

Imagine yourself as a student attending this seminar: How would you have recognized what was going on?

An editorial columnist from the *New York Times* was asked to participate in one of a series of brown-bag discussions hosted by a Department of Journalism at a large university. Faculty, students, and journalists from the community attended these noon-hour seminars. Although some speakers in this series of talks gave formal presentations and then left a few minutes for questions afterward, this columnist said, at the outset of his talk, that although he had prepared comments on a number of different topics he would rather spend the entire hour responding to questions.

Within a few minutes after the session began, a climate of open communication prevailed. The speaker responded to a wide range of questions. People asked about national economic policy, press coverage of news events, politically-based indictments of the press, and the use and misuse of the term "the media." Despite the potentially controversial nature of many of these issues, there was an expectation set in the group that the questions would seek information or opinions from the columnist, who had more than thirty years of experience at the prestigious newspaper. In his initial answers, the speaker told amusing anecdotes, gave background information about recent news events, and offered unmuted commentary on key issues. The atmosphere was relaxed, almost reverent, and the speaker himself continued to eat his brown-bag lunch as he spoke.

During the last ten minutes of the question-and-answer discussion, a student sitting in the back of the room sat up and leaned forward in his chair. Speaking more loudly than anyone else during the previous forty-five minutes, he said he had a question about editorial responsibility. He said that the *Times* ran a story about atrocities in an African nation, but the paper made no editorial comment on the killings until three years after they had occurred. He wanted to know if the paper had an editorial responsibility to comment on this event at the time it happened. It soon became clear that both the student asking the question and the columnist knew, as the question was asked, that American arms had been used in the killings. The student did not, however, explicitly mention this when he asked the question.

Almost immediately, a journalism professor, who had introduced the speaker and was instrumental in getting him to visit the campus, defended the paper's policy before the guest speaker had a chance to respond. Neither this professor nor anyone else in the group had previously interrupted the question–answer–question format that the group had adopted; no one had previously made a comment in response to any other question. The professor was visibly upset by the student's question, said he had worked on the paper himself at the time the story broke, and contended that the editorial decision was justified because insufficient information was available about the incident for quite some time. The student responded with a pointed declaration of mistrust in the paper. The columnist then took the floor and commented that, although the paper had made several editorial blunders during the years he worked at the paper, he could not accept the accusation that editorial comments were withheld because U.S. arms were involved. There were, he said, too many editorials to the contrary in the paper.

As this exchange occurred, others in the room seemed uncomfortable and tense. Some turned to look back at the challenger, some engaged in side conversations, and a few smiled uncomfortably at each other. A second professor interrupted the columnist and said, in a somewhat self-conscious tone of voice, "We had better leave the seminar room because another class has to meet in it soon."

Discussion Questions

- There was a noticeable shift in climate in this discussion. How did the shift come about?
- How did the shift in climate affect the interaction in this seminar?
- Suppose the seminar had begun with a confrontational climate. What kind of event might cause the climate to shift toward a more relaxed direction?

handled in ways that are not positive or supportive for those involved. For instance, a manager may reprimand an employee for bringing up a complaint, implicitly sending a message to other employees that it is not safe to differ with management.

Climates are not fixed, but may vary, even within a single conflict. Case 1.1 on page 33 illustrates the impact of a change in climate.

The student's question and the professor's initial response changed the established climate in midstream, with significant effects on subsequent interaction. Prior to the question, this was a normal seminar, with a climate of objective interest and scholarly respect. The expectation that the purpose of questions was to seek information or advice from the speaker was redefined by the student's question. The student challenged the politics behind the story and assumed that the speaker would defend himself. The professor's defense of the *Times* reinforced the climate of confrontation and shifted the tone of the interaction to challenge and response. The rest of the group may have resented the change in tone, yet in some ways they facilitated the change by disrupting the seminar's format themselves. The shift in climate resulted in new ways of interacting for everyone in attendance. You can judge for yourself whether it was an improvement.

The third element of context we will consider is the outside *environment* related to the conflict. Environment is a very broad term that refers to characteristics of the society and social unit that may affect the conflict. Where the conflict occurs determines what features of the environment affect it. A conflict between siblings is affected strongly by the nature of their family, including family norms about how conflict should be handled and family history. How the sibling conflict plays out also depends on whether it occurs in the home or outside it, because the family influence is likely to be stronger in the former case, and the familiarity of the home setting may affect the conflict in subtle ways. A conflict on the job is affected by the character of the organization in which it occurs. The prevailing management style, attitudes toward airing differences and grievances, formal and informal systems for resolving conflict in the organization, and other factors affect the conflict.

Chapter 7 discusses the context of conflict in greater detail. There we will explore the role of history, climate, and environment in conflicts.

1.3   *Summary and Review*

What is effective conflict management?

There are a number of excellent models for conflict management, and a particularly useful one distinguishes two stages in a well-managed conflict: a differentiation stage and an integration stage. When differentiation is handled effectively, parties are able to express their positions and emotions. At the end of effective differentiation, parties have come to understand others' positions (though they might not agree with them), to recognize the legitimacy of others, and to have the motivation to resolve the conflict. During effective integration, parties explore a range of solutions, develop a solution that meets the needs of all, and work out a means of implementing the resolution. In order to work through these two stages, parties have to prevent the uncontrolled avoidance and escalation cycles mentioned in the introduction. This requires them to perform a tricky balancing act in which they have to air disagreements, but cannot let their interactions get too far out of control.

What are the dangers in differentiation?

Differentiation initially personalizes the conflict and often involves expression of intense and negative emotions. There is a danger that this can either infuriate parties, resulting in escalation, or terrify them, resulting in rigid avoidance. As long as parties can avoid rigid, in-flexible, knee-jerk responses to differentiation, they have a good chance of navigating to an effective integration phase. As unpleasant as it may be, differentiation is important because it provides the basis for real solutions later on; if parties understand and respect their differ-ences, they have the best chance of working toward a mutually beneficial solution.

What causes rigidity?

Anxieties about differences and emotions in conflicts, as well as the uncertainties about the outcome of the conflict, tend to produce rigid and inflexible behavior in conflicts.

How do parties manage the transition between differentiation and integration?

The transition is easier to make: (a) if parties feel that they have been able to express their positions fully, (b) if they believe that they cannot get what they want by forcing the other or by avoiding conflict altogether, and (c) if they synchronize their cooperative initiatives. A third party is sometimes useful to help move the conflict from differentia-tion to integration.

How do we recognize when destructive cycles have set in?

Table 1.1 summarizes several symptoms or indicators of destructive conflict interaction. Signs of avoidance cycles include quick acceptance of proposals, low levels of involve-ment, and discussion of safe issues. Signs of escalation cycles include threats, difficulty in defining the issues, and sarcasm.

Are there some basic principles of interaction that can help in understanding conflict?

In this chapter, we have defined four basic properties of conflict interaction that highlight the role of communication in conflict: Together, these properties indicate a web of vari-ables and processes that influence conflict.

What does it mean to say that conflict is constituted by moves and countermoves in interaction?

This property builds on the argument from the introduction. Conflicts exist not because of differences between parties, but because of the actions parties take in responding to their differences. These moves and countermoves create and define the conflict, and they sus-tain it insofar as parties continue to make more moves and countermoves. This underscores the importance of power in interpersonal conflicts because the types and effectiveness of moves depends on how skillfully parties use their power.

Why do patterns of behavior in conflicts perpetuate themselves?

Conflicts tend to be perpetuated by self-reinforcing cycles of behavior. They are linked to the human tendency to reciprocate behavior, and also to predictions about others' responses that lead to behavior that elicits the expected response (creating self-fulfilling prophecies). These self-perpetuating patterns give conflicts a momentum of their own and may make it difficult to change the direction of conflicts.

What role do relationships play in conflict interaction?

Conflict obviously can have profound effects on relationships. How conflicts unfold also depends on prior relationships among the parties. A particularly important dimension of relationships in conflict is face—the image a person wants to present to others. Efforts to create and sustain positive face and to save face in response to perceived attacks can exert profound influence on conflicts.

How does the context influence conflict interaction?

Three elements of the context affect conflict. Personal and relational history shape parties' expectations about and reactions to one another. They also influence their general attitudes toward conflict and how they tend to respond to conflicts. Shared interpretations of the conflict situation have been termed the climate of conflict interaction. Climates are composed of generalized beliefs about the situation, including whether it calls for competition or cooperation and how safe it is on a psychological or emotional level. Climates are produced and sustained by interaction among the parties to the conflict and by other important actors in the situation. Finally, those elements of the environment that are relevant to the conflict affect conflict interaction. Different sets of environmental features are relevant to each particular conflict.

How does confrontation episodes theory model conflict?

This theory proposes a set of decision points, organized around key issues, that are likely to occur during a confrontation. Episodes can follow several tracks, including nonlegitimacy, justification, denial of behavior, denial of broken rules, denial of responsibility, and acceptance of responsibility. This theory models conflict at the move–countermove level and provides a framework to help us understand the logic behind moves and countermoves. It represents a common way in which parties' rule systems mesh during conflicts.

1.4 Conclusion

Although shouting matches or heated discussions are often the first images that come to mind when we think of conflict, our conception argues for a more broadly-based understanding of conflict interaction. Active suppression of issues, an exchange over who is an authority on a particular issue, a round of comments explaining positions to a third party, a discussion of the decision-making procedures, or a series of comments that back away from a stand so that one member is allowed to "win" a point are all forms of conflict interaction as well. Conflict interaction is *any* exchange of messages that represents an attempt by participants to address some incompatibility.

We have presented a normative model for conflict management that will continue to be a common theme throughout this book. This model argues that conflicts must develop through two stages, differentiation and integration, to be properly managed or resolved. In both stages the parties do some important work necessary to deal with a conflict adequately, and the functions of the differentiation stage must be accomplished before effective integration occurs. Differentiation must be conscientiously and carefully managed, because it may instead lead to spiraling escalation or rigid avoidance, both of which keep the conflict from moving into the integration stage.

The two-stage model may look neat and straightforward. However, you should not be misled into thinking that conflicts are always divided into two easily recognizable stages. As we will see throughout this book, conflicts are often messy. We may start with spiraling escalation and only after a time get true differentiation, which then leads to an attempt at integration, which then breaks down as escalation occurs again, and then finally moves into true integration. There are many permutations on this theme. Conflicts are neither simple nor straightforward. We advance the normative two-stage model as a guide to tell you what you *must* do to work with conflict effectively, not as an accurate description of conflict.

This chapter also focused on four properties of conflict interaction. These properties draw a complex net of ideas, which we will explore in the remainder of this book. We will constantly return to the point that conflict interaction, deceptively simple on the surface, is actually quite complex and can only be understood by analyzing its flows and the forces that shape them. Conflict, like any other form of behavior, can only be understood at the level of concrete interaction where moves and countermoves take many forms and unfold in diverse episodes (yet maintain some level of coherence), where interaction patterns tend to perpetuate themselves in destructive and constructive cycles, and where messages define and alter relationships among people.

The chapters of this book concern conflict, of course, but they also concern change. Because conflicts are rooted in differences and incompatible interests, conflict always confronts participants with the possibility of change. Indeed, that differences arise at all is a flag indicating a need for adjustment in response to conflicts between members, or a need to resolve an external problem. Once a conflict emerges, resolution of differences may require redefinition of policies or goals, reassignment of responsibilities, shifts in expectations for or of individuals, or even changes in the unit's power and status structures. Members' recognition of these possible changes guides the forms that conflict interaction takes.

The active suppression of issues, the positive or negative evaluation of possible solutions, and the clarification of differences are all forms of conflict interaction, which can be motivated and shaped by the participants' awareness of imminent change. In a very real sense, as a group manages its conflicts, so too does it deal with the need to change in response to its environment or people's needs. Some wise sage in the 1960s said that "not to change is to die." The same can almost be said for failure to work through conflict.

2

The Inner Experience of Conflict

Recall the Women's Hotline Case (Case I.1), page 2. The conflict and how it was resolved were strongly influenced by parties' interpretations of each others' behavior and by assumptions that each side held about the other. For instance, several staff members believed that Diane was not willing to bear her share of the work, while Diane drew the conclusion that the staff was not sympathetic with her problems. The staff made incorrect inferences about Diane's motivations in asking for a leave of absence. Diane's anger at their rejection led her to file a grievance. Sharing their doubts and fears encouraged members to reinterpret Diane's behavior in more generous terms. It is clear that the conflict was strongly influenced by what was going on inside the parties' heads, by emotion and cognition. While conflict is constituted in interaction, the behavior that constitutes that interaction has its origins in the human mind. So it is to the inner experience of conflict that we now turn.

In this chapter we explore the psychological processes that influence conflict interaction. We consider psychological dynamics that affect our perception and interpretation of conflicts, how we process conflict-related information, and how we behave during conflicts. Some of these dynamics are rooted in deep-seated motivations and emotional reactions, and others in our beliefs and thought processes. Thinking and feeling are often regarded as quite different processes, but as we will see, they affect each other in important ways.

This chapter is divided into four sections. The first reviews psychodynamic theory, a psychological theory that influenced classic theories of conflict. Section two explores the role of emotions in conflict. Cognitive processes that influence our interpretations of and reactions to conflicts are the subject of the third section. The final section considers how psychodynamics, emotions, and cognitive processes interact to affect conflict interaction.

To illustrate how the different factors discussed in this chapter figure in conflict, they will be used to illuminate the same conflict case, the Parking Lot Scuffle. Before diving into the next section, refer to Case 2.1, which reviews a conflict between two relative strangers as it was captured by an observer. This is the actual dialogue recorded between the parties; only phrases some readers might find offensive have been changed.

CASE 2.1 • *The Parking Lot Scuffle*

Imagine yourself as Jay: What assumptions are you making about Tim as the conflict unfolds?

Jay drove to work alone every weekday. On this particular Monday morning, he arrived in his office parking lot a few minutes before nine o'clock. He had several thoughts on his mind and was not prepared to see a small moped parked in his reserved spot. In fact, because the moped was set back deep in the spot and between cars, he could not see it until he made the turn into the space. Jay slammed on the brakes but failed to stop before hitting the scooter. The moped wobbled and then fell to the ground. Jay backed up his car and then placed the car in park. He got out and moved quickly to examine the results. He was surveying the damage done to his own bumper when Tim, whom he recognized but could not name, approached him on the run. The following conversation ensued:

1T: What's your problem? What the hell did you do to my Honda? I said, 'What did you do?'

2J: I drove into my spot and didn't see your bike. What was it doing parked there?

3T: Look, my tire's flat. I can't move the wheel. Crushed in and doesn't move.

4J: I didn't see it until I was on top of it.

5T: You are going to have to pay for this. I can't afford this.

6J: What was it doing in a parking space?

7T: What's your problem? It was parked. Look at the wheel. You came around pretty good.

8J: Listen, this is my spot. I didn't see it, and it shouldn't have been there. You're lucky I stopped when I did. Look at my bumper. What was it doing there?

9T: You ass. Who cares whose spot it is? Some jerk like you drives over my Honda and says, 'This is my spot.' I don't care who you are. You will fix my Honda!

10J: You are the one with a problem. Do you work here?

11T: What does that have to do with anything? Stop looking at your bumper; it looks fine. I want your driver's license and insurance.

12J: Who in the hell do you think you are? *(Starts walking away.)*

13T: You are not going anywhere. *(Grabs J's arm.)*

14J: Let go of me. You are screwed. I'm calling the police. *(Turns to move toward the office.)*

15 *Tim slugs Jay from behind. The two scuffle for a few moments until others arrive to break them apart.*

Discussion Questions

- Why did this conflict escalate to physical violence?
- What assumptions does your answer reveal?
- Consider the explanations that have been offered for well-known conflicts: the war in Iraq, the ordination of gay clergy in various religious denominations, the Columbine shootings, or others. What assumptions underlie these explanations?

2.1 The Psychodynamic Perspective

Landmark advances in art and science often elicit as much criticism as praise. At the turn of the century, Freud's psychoanalytic theory altered people's vision of themselves as much as French impressionist art had altered people's view of the world. Yet both Freud and the Impressionists at different times became the target of significant criticism, and even ridicule. Freud and his followers studied the dynamics of the human mind (Freud, 1900/1953, 1925, 1923/1947, 1949; Rapaport, 1951). They tried to explain how intrapersonal states and mental activity give rise to behavior in social contexts. Psychodynamic theory has been overshadowed by experimental and cognitive approaches to psychology in recent years, but it is beginning to receive increased attention in psychological research (Bower, 2007).

One value of the psychodynamic perspective is that it "thinks big," It is concerned with issues like the meaning of life, how we face death, and the origins of love and hate. It deals with fundamental human issues and has generated important insights that have become part of our day-to-day thinking—concepts like the ego, the unconscious, repression, and wish fulfillment. Several ideas from psychodynamics are fundamental to an understanding of conflict (Coser, 1956).

Freud and his followers portray the human mind as a reservoir of psychic energy that is channeled into various activities. This energy is the impulse behind all human activity and can be channeled into any number of different behaviors, ranging from positive pursuits such as work or raising family to destructive impulses such as vandalism or verbal attacks. However it is channeled, this energy must be released. If it is not released through one channel, psychic energy builds up pressure to be released through another. Sometimes the psyche is likened to a system of hydraulic pipes in which turning off one outlet puts pressure on others.

The frustrations and uncertainties involved in conflict generate two powerful impulses—the *aggressive impulse* and *anxiety*—which we must manage. The various ways in which these two forms of energy are channeled play a critical role in conflict interaction because they determine how people react to conflict. The psychodynamic perspective suggests that aggressive energy frequently arises from feelings of guilt, a lack of self-worth, or frustrations resulting from unfulfilled needs or thwarted desires. Aggression may be directed at the actual source of the guilt or frustration, either back at oneself in the form of self-hate or in attacks on another person. However, self-hatred is destructive and aggression toward others is discouraged by moral codes and also by their negative consequences. When this occurs, individuals find various conscious or unconscious ways to redirect their aggressive impulses.

One strategy is to attempt to suppress aggressive drives. *Suppression* can take the form of simply not acknowledging the drives and channeling this energy into an alternative activity. For example, an employee who is angry at his boss for denying him a promotion may simply suppress his anger and re-channel it into working even harder. The psychodynamic perspective stresses the benefits of suppression because it leads to less anxiety, guilt, or pain than attempting to act on a destructive impulse or satisfy a need that is impossible to fulfill. If people recognize their drives explicitly, they must make some conscious response to them, and this can increase anxiety or frustration if the drives go unsatisfied. On the other hand, if a need is never acknowledged, it can be treated as if it were nonexistent, and the energy associated with the need can be diverted into other channels.

Despite its benefits, suppression can be a double-edged sword. Suppressing a need is frustrating, and if no acceptable substitute is found, frustration can fester and erupt more violently later on. Also, when goals are suppressed, people may still be driven by the need without realizing it. Actions may be guided by unconscious drives or needs, and these may direct behavior in destructive ways. Thus, the employee who was not given his promotion might take out his anger unconsciously by organizing his work so that he has too much to do and inadvertently misses the deadline for an important report his boss must give to her superiors. The employee may take some satisfaction in his boss's failure; he is assuaging his anger without openly recognizing it. However, this action may have bad consequences for the employee too—he might lose his job if his boss believes him to be incompetent or vindictive. Facing up to anger directly may be unpleasant for both the employee and his boss, but in this case it would have been less unpleasant than the consequences of suppression.

A second strategy for dealing with aggression is to direct it toward more vulnerable or acceptable targets than the actual source of frustration. This process, *displacement,* is more likely when the actual source of frustration is powerful or valued by the individual. Rather than suffering the consequences of an attack on the actual source, people attribute their frustrations to other parties so that their impulses can be legitimized. They look for distinctions between themselves and others so that "enemy lines" can be drawn and targets for their aggressive urges can be made available.

In his insightful book, *The Functions of Social Conflict,* Coser (1956) notes that the *scapegoating* of a few group members may be the result of displaced aggression. When members of a group face failure or a crisis, they are often reluctant to direct their anger toward the whole group because they fear rejection. To avoid losing the benefits of belonging to the group, they attack a weak member or an outsider. This process is often quite harmful to the scapegoat, but it serves to keep the group together because it allows members to vent aggressive energy. Kenwyn Smith (1989) argues that organizational conflicts are often redirected to issues and people other than those who provoke the initial reaction.

Several conflict scholars suggest that patterns of *cultural displacement* are at the heart of some long-standing ethnic and international conflicts that have produced deep-seated hatred and violence. Volkan (1994) and Gaylin (2003) argue that long-standing ethnic conflicts that have spawned wars and genocide are sometimes the products of large groups of people dealing with the difficulties of their own demeaning existence. When perceived inadequacies and deficiencies weigh on the minds of large groups of individuals, cultures often find a means to displace the feelings of inadequacy by singling out others as enemies. Deep-seated ethnic hatred becomes a form of needed attachment to the defined enemies. Enemies need to be identified and opposed so that members of the deprived culture can externalize the source of the despair or misery they are experiencing. Leaders may prey on this psychological tendency and create the possibility for an ethnic group to act on these forms of rationalized hatred. In this view of the emergence of ethnic conflict, the more "tangible" issues, such as territory, property, or others' resources, that emerge exacerbate conflicts and become a part of them, but the core cause of conflict is seen as psychological. Deep feelings of psychological insecurity produce and propel the need for constant definition of enemies—enemies that become targets of hatred and violence.

In addition to aggressive impulses, *anxiety* is also a by-product of conflict. Anxiety is an internal state of tension that arises when we perceive impending danger. It arises when we believe our drives or needs will be thwarted. Because conflicts involve perceived interference of others, anxiety is likely to persist until there is some hope that an agreement will be reached that meets each person's needs. If there is little reason for hope, or if the party suspects that others do not see their needs as legitimate, then anxiety is likely to increase throughout the conflict.

EXHIBIT 2.1 • *Collusion and Intractable Conflict*

Psychodynamic theories suggest that there are influences on human behavior that lie below people's full consciousness. Often these sub-conscious influences are ones that help people deal with difficult or anxiety-producing situations without having to fully acknowledge that these situations actually exist. The concept of "collusion" is one interpersonal phenomena that illustrates a classic way in which people can be influenced by factors that are kept some distance from their full awareness. Collusion occurs when two or more people "agree" subconsciously to ignore or deny some existing state of affairs or situation. As they interact with each other, they do not acknowledge to themselves or to each other that they are not recognizing a reality that is readily apparent to others. For example, two members of a family may collude that another family member does not have a substance abuse problem, even though the family member does. The collusion enables the family to maintain the status quo and to avoid acknowledging a state of affairs that may be stressful to address and difficult to change.

Sometimes people in engage in a particular form of collusion that contributes to the intractability of an ongoing conflict (Northrup, 1989). This happens when a conflict starts over a particular issue but as it unfolds and develops over time, the conflict comes to have a life of its own—it begins to sustain itself and propels its own escalation. This happens when the parties come to see themselves as less and less like each other and the exaggeration of differences eventually buttresses each person's own identity. The parties become more and more dependent on the conflict to support their own sense of who they are and what they stand for. Each person knows who they are because they are not like the other person. When this happens, the parties often collude to continue the conflict because it serves to support their own sense of identity (Zartman, 2005). Although not admitting (or even seeing) that the conflict is serving this function for themselves or each other, each party becomes invested in the continuation of a conflict, which then becomes highly intractable.

The psychodynamic perspective also points to two other sources of anxiety. First, it suggests that anxiety may result from fear of impulses. As noted, many drives are self-destructive or counterproductive. When people suspect that they may be acting on one of these deep-rooted impulses, they may become anxious. They may be unsure about how far they will go and try to establish limits and prove themselves by engaging in risky or self-endangering behavior. For example, a receptionist in a law office inadvertently overheard an insulting remark one of the lawyers made about her. She was very angry and began to berate the lawyer with insulting jokes in retaliation. Despite the possibility that the lawyer might fire her, she continued joking for several days. When a friend in the office asked her why she took the chance, she commented that she *was* really afraid the lawyer would fire her, but that she had to prove to herself that she was not a "mouse." Persisting in and strengthening counterproductive responses is one way of reassuring oneself that they are permissible.

Anxiety also may result from the judgments people make about themselves. Psychodynamic theory posits that the superego gives people a capacity to make judgments about their behavior. Anxiety ensues when people are uncomfortable with their actions and realize that they would not ordinarily act this way. Even if they disapprove of their own behavior, people may continue with it because at the time there seems to be some legitimate or important reason. They may, for instance, be trying to save face or see themselves using a questionable means to achieve a worthwhile end. The anxiety people experience from engaging in disapproved behaviors may decrease the chances that they will stop these behaviors: Anxiety can cloud thinking and prevent people from understanding their own ambivalence.

Anxiety influences conflict interaction by causing members to be excessively rigid and inflexible. Hilgard and Bower (1966) draw on psychodynamic principles to help explain compulsive or repetitive tendencies that can take hold of people's actions, despite the fact that they carry destructive consequences. The mere repetition of unpleasant behaviors is often rewarding because it allows people to achieve a sense of mastery over some activity. Mastery in itself is rewarding, and, hence, behaviors continue even if they eventually prove to be destructive. Hilgard and Bower note that sense of mastery, and the compulsive behaviors it promotes, may reduce anxiety. It allows people to cope with a trying situation and it leads to overlearned behaviors that are highly resistant to change. Although this account aims to explain neurotic forms of individual behavior, it can also explain the nature of interaction cycles. Counterproductive interaction patterns can persist because they provide a way to deal with the anxiety that conflict produces. As Chapter 1 showed, these cycles, fed by members' rigidity, can be threatening.

The psychodynamic perspective has generated several important insights into conflict interaction (See Table 2.1). The most important achievement is its explanation of the role of impulses, particularly aggression and anxiety, in conflicts. The idea that impulses build up and can be redirected into other activities, including attacks on a third person, is crucial to most conflict theories. The psychodynamic perspective recognizes the importance of substitute activities, displacement, scapegoating, and inflexibility in conflicts, and it allows many subtle processes to be taken into account. The idea of unconscious or subconscious

---

TABLE 2.1 *Psychodynamic Insights into Conflict*

Psychodynamic Theories encourage us to consider the following range of questions about a conflict to help understand its dynamics:

- In what ways are aggressive impulses evident in the communication among the parties? What is prompting or inhibiting the aggression? Does the aggression enhance or detract from the expression of the parties' feelings, views, and perspectives to each other?
- Are any of the parties' suppressing obvious needs? Does the suppression contribute to constructive or destructive influences on the conflict interaction?
- Are negative feelings and frustrations being displaced towards people who are not the source of the frustrations? In what ways does this displacement escalate the conflict? Does the person or group who is the target of the displacement recognize the negative behaviors directed toward them stem from a different source? If they do, how do they respond to the displaced behaviors?
- In what ways are parties' past experiences with similar issues or situations influencing their behavior in the current conflict? Are the parties aware that their behaviors in the current conflict are being influenced by prior and perhaps unrelated events?
- What are the specific sources of anxiety that contribute to the parties' behavior in the conflict? How are the parties managing these sources of anxiety? What could the parties say to each other that might alleviate any of the existing anxiety?
- Are there repetitive behaviors or repetitive cycles of interaction that are particularly revealing about the parties' inability to address their anxieties? What purpose does the repetition serve in managing aggression or addressing anxiety?
- In what ways does the continuation of the conflict help the parties manage their anxieties? Are there ways in which the parties "need" the conflict to continue to serve their own needs, even if the conflict interaction is destructive and counter-productive in other ways?

---

motivation is also important. People do not always understand what is driving their conflict behavior. Unconscious motivation underscores the importance of helping members gain insight into their behavior. Once members understand what is driving conflicts, they can begin to control them. Case 2.2 explores the role psychodynamic processes may have played in the Parking Lot Scuffle.

2.2 Emotion and Conflict

Common sense tells us that emotion is an important part of conflict, and research during the past fifteen years has greatly clarified how emotion influences conflicts (Planalp, 1999; Jones, 2001; Long & Brecke, 2003; Guerrero & LaValley, 2006). Guerrero and LaValley (2006) discuss five points that are important in understanding how emotion shapes conflict:

- "Emotions occur in reaction to stimuli that threaten to interrupt, impede, or enhance one's goals" (p. 70)
- The central constituent of emotional experience is positive or negative affect

---

CASE 2.2 • *Psychodynamic Theory and the Parking Lot Scuffle*

The accident immediately created physiological arousal in Jay and Tim. Both were frustrated and angry—Jay because of the damage to his car and Tim because his scooter was crushed. The energy from this frustration had to be channeled, and it was directed against each other, the source of the frustration. At first, Jay attempted to keep the conflict in check by giving explanations ("I didn't see it") and invoking social norms ("What was it doing in a parking space?"). This represents the action of the superego, which tries to keep the expression of psychic energy within socially approved bounds. However, Tim's attacks made Jay angry, and he dropped his efforts to resolve the conflict through "normal" channels. Escalation developed as the two exchanged insults and aggressive energy fed on itself, further escalating the conflict.

The conflict might have taken a different turn if the two had displaced the conflict by blaming the parking company for mislabeling the parking slots. This would have united them as they redirected their anger at a different target. Another way to manage the psychic energy in this conflict would have been to suppress it. For example, Jay might have toned down his anger and conversed calmly with Tim to help Tim temper his anger. Then the two might have worked out a mutually acceptable resolution. Another way to suppress the conflict would have been for Jay to walk off and find an attendant or police officer who could have taken down the details of the accident. The case would then have been referred to their insurance companies. The two methods of suppressing the conflict would have had very different outcomes. The first approach dissipates the psychic energy associated with the dispute. The second, however, leaves this energy intact, and Tim would need to deal with it, either by displacing it or by finding some way to take it out on Jay, perhaps at a different time or place.

Discussion Questions

- How might anxiety have played a role in this conflict?
- What is a possible source of anxiety, according to psychodynamic theory?

- Physiological changes usually accompany emotional experiences
- "Cognition frames and helps people interpret emotional reactions" (p. 70)
- Specific behavioral tendencies or reactions are associated with emotions

Jones (2001) argues that the same factors that trigger conflict—incompatibilities and interference from another—set off emotional responses. In many cases, a surge of emotion is what makes us aware that we are in a conflict. Typically, the affect associated with the emotional response to conflict is negative, since the conflict is associated with blockage or frustration of goals. One study found that arguments accounted for 80 percent of the variance in subjects' negative mood (Bolger, DeLongis, Kessler & Schilling, 1989). Along with negative affect come physiological changes, particularly in terms of how activated or aroused we are. For example, anger is associated with increased heartbeat and tensed muscles. Physiological responses associated with emotion may impede our ability to listen and understand others, because they are so powerful and immediate. They are associated with the fight/flight response and so predispose us to visceral responses.

The experience of emotion is shaped by our interpretations of the situation. Current models of emotion posit that cognitive processes play a role in how we label emotions (e.g., Lazarus & Lazarus, 1994; Planalp, 1999). Primary and secondary appraisal processes, both of which occur rapidly in response to an event, are involved in the generation of emotional states. *Primary appraisal* determines whether affect is positive or negative and consists of an assessment of whether the event is relevant to us, and if it is deemed relevant, whether it advances or threatens to disrupt attainment of our goals in a situation. In *secondary appraisal* we identify what the emotion is, a process also called labeling. Secondary appraisals involve determining who is responsible for the event that stimulated our affect, the other's intent toward us, the degree of control we have over the event, and whether the situation will get better or worse in the near future. So the same negative affect in response to a tactless joke could be labeled anger, if we interpret the situation as one in which the joker purposely insulted us and we have enough control over the situation to take some action against him, or sadness, if we believe the joke reflected contempt for us and that we are powerless to do anything about it.

Cognitive processes thus play an important role in shaping emotions in conflict. The reverse is also true: emotional states influence cognitive processing. Negative emotions such as anger, hurt, and sadness can predispose us to focus on the negative aspects of the situation and to see the other's behavior in more negative terms than if we were in a positive emotional state.

Emotions tend to elicit certain types of behavioral responses. These biologically-based responses help us to deal with the events that stimulated the emotion. According to Guerrero and LaValley (2006), "Different emotions are associated with various *action tendencies*. For example, the action tendency for anger is to attack, the action tendency for fear is to move away from harm, and the action tendency for guilt is to make amends."

A number of emotions are associated with conflict. Here we will discuss several of the most important and common, both negative and positive. The most common negative emotion associated with conflict is *anger*. Other emotions associated with anger include rage, disgust, contempt, irritation, and exasperation. Angry people typically have accelerated heart rates, feel hot or flushed, and may have tense muscles. Anger is most often triggered, as noted above, when an individual perceives his or her goals to be frustrated or threatened by another. In addition, some individuals have predispositions toward anger due to personality or substance abuse. Infante and Wigley (1986) have proposed that verbal aggressiveness is a personality trait closely connected with anger, and have described verbally aggressive behavior (see the accompanying Exhibit 2.2). Canary, Spitsberg and Semic (1998) found that common specific causes of anger include perceptions of threats to identity or face, aggression by another on oneself or valued others, unfairness or inequity, another's egocentric behavior, and threats to valued relationships.

EXHIBIT 2.2 • *Verbal Aggressiveness*

Infante and colleagues (Infante & Wigley, 1986) proposed a theory of verbal aggressiveness to explain why verbal attacks occur in interpersonal communication. The theory views aggression as a personality trait that represents a learned predisposition to act in response to certain cues that are reminiscent of the context in which the learning occurred. For example, the theory posits that a person who has seen family members aggressively confront, insult, and taunt each other during disagreements would learn this behavior as a response to disagreement. The person would be likely to engage in similar types of aggressive behavior when someone disagrees with him or her. The likelihood of this response depends on (a) how similar the disagreement in question is to those the person experienced in his or her family, (b) how often the person was exposed to the aggressive response in his or her family, and (c) the degree to which rewarding or positive consequences were seen as a result of the aggressive behavior in the person's family.

The theory distinguishes between verbal attacks made against ideas or positions and verbal attacks made against self-concept. *Argument* involves presenting and defending positions on issues while attacking positions held by others. *Verbal aggression,* on the other hand, also includes attacks on another's self-concept. The aggressiveness trait is a predisposition to use personalized attacks in interpersonal communication.

For Infante, verbal aggressiveness is yoked to a trait he labels *argumentativeness.* The theory maintains that to understand aggression, the concept of argumentativeness must be understood. A person's level of argumentativeness is created by two competing motivational tendencies: the motivation to approach argumentative situations and the motivation to avoid such situations. Highly argumentative people perceive arguing as exciting and intellectually challenging, and they experience feelings of invigoration and satisfaction after engaging in arguments. People who are low in argumentativeness find arguments uncomfortable and unpleasant; they generally associate argument with personal suffering. Not surprisingly, these individuals attempt to avoid arguments or keep them from occurring. In the aftermath of arguments, they often feel anxious and unsettled.

As a result of approaching or avoiding argumentative situations, people develop or fail to develop the social skills needed to succeed, so an argument is unavoidable. Highly argumentative people tend to be more skilled at stating controversies in propositional forms, determining the major issues of contention, discovering ways to support a position, and delivering arguments effectively. Among the many factors promoting aggressive behavior, it is skill proficiency that weds the traits of argumentativeness and verbal aggressiveness.

In a series of studies, Infante and colleagues demonstrated that people low in argumentativeness are more likely to resort to attacks against the self-concept of the other party. In other words, low argumentatives are high in verbal aggressiveness. In a manner of speaking, the two

(continued)

EXHIBIT 2.2 Continued

traits represent the opposite poles of a single-skill continuum. Because individuals who avoid argumentative confrontations are often frustrated and lack the skills to succeed in such situations, they turn to verbal aggression.

Argumentative behavior is a positive trait that is distinct from verbally aggressive behavior. The advantages of argumentativeness are numerous. Research has shown that argumentative behavior is positively related to career satisfaction, career achievement, superior–subordinate relationship satisfaction, and other organizational outcomes (Infante & Gorden, 1985).

Verbal aggressiveness is a negative trait that can produce a variety of effects in interpersonal communication, including conflict escalation, long-lasting damage to self-concepts, and deterioration of relationships. Infante believes that teaching people to value argument and providing them with the skills to succeed in argumentative situations will increase productivity in society and reduce the amount of verbally aggressive acts during interpersonal conflicts.

What do we do about verbal aggressiveness? Infante and colleagues propose using workshops and therapy sessions that would focus on making the person aware of his or her tendencies and on developing alternative behavior patterns through rehearsal and feedback. Such measures are time-consuming and require the consent of the verbally aggressive person, so they may not be of much help when confronting such a person during a conflict. When in a conflict with a verbally aggressive person, it is important to maintain distance from the exchange and not be drawn into mudslinging and name-calling. This is difficult to do in the heat of the moment, but it is critical not to buy into the verbal aggressive's assumptions about what is appropriate behavior. Steadfast resistance to the attacks of the verbal aggression is also important, as it signals to him or her that the approach will not work in this case. It is also useful to bear in mind that, in a small proportion of cases, a frustrated aggressive person may resort to physical violence or other means of reprisal; we need to protect ourselves from this possibility.

How do we work with verbal aggressiveness? One step is to become aware of our own tendency to be verbally aggressive. If we recognize that we are low in argumentative skills, we can engage in specific strategies to help prevent ourselves from turning to verbal aggression, including:

- Monitoring our comfort and skill in verbal arguments
- Recognizing that discussion of "hot" topics may trigger verbal aggression due to our frustration with the argument and difficulty in expressing ourselves
- Making conscious commitments about specific words, expressions or sentences that we will not use in a verbal argument
- Talking slowly and deliberately; pausing before giving a response
- Preparing substantive arguments before a discussion
- Disengaging from the interaction if frustration rises beyond a manageable level

When others are low on argumentative skills, it may be useful to approach them thoughtfully to avoid triggering their verbal aggression. Some possible strategies include:

- Giving them advance notice about the need or desire to talk about a controversial topic
- Providing a summary of your point of view in writing before engaging in a face-to-face conversation with them
- Letting them speak first in the interaction about the topic
- Asking them questions before presenting your own arguments
- Paraphrasing their arguments before responding to their substantive points
- Avoiding discussion of differences with them in front of other people

Common responses to anger include physical attacks, verbal attacks, and nonverbal expressions of disapproval (Fehr, Baldwin, Collins, Patterson, & Benditt, 1999). These responses obviously invite reciprocation and can contribute to spiraling escalation of a conflict. Another common response to anger is to avoid the other. There are also more constructive responses to anger, such as expressing hurt feelings and channeling the emotion into a respectful yet assertive response to the other. However, this type of response is more indirect and because it "short-circuits" the general attack response to anger, it may take some effort and self-control to make it.

Another negative emotion that occurs in conflicts is *fear*. Physiological responses to fear include perspiration, muscle tension, pupil dilation, and the hair on arms and legs standing up. In some cases an individual may have a higher heart rate, a "startle" reaction, and involuntarily movement to protect parts of his or her body that seem likely to be harmed. Fear is stimulated by perceived likelihood of harm. Causes of fear in conflict include perception of physical aggression, verbal aggression, threats to face or identity, and possible loss of a person or thing of value. The behavioral tendency associated with fear is flight, and common responses to fear in conflict include withdrawing, accommodating the other, and avoidance of the conflict altogether.

Hurt is the third negative emotion that often occurs during conflict. Hurt results when one feels psychologically injured by someone else. Hurt is associated with other negative emotions such as anger, anguish, sadness, and suffering, and can easily transform into them. Physiological hurt is similar to both anger and sadness, depending on which of these other emotions is associated with the hurt. We have already discussed the physiological correlates of anger. If the hurt is tinged with sadness, then physiological responses may include tears, a lump in the throat, tensed muscles, and quietude. Causes of hurt include accusations, negative evaluations, lies, and betrayal. Another cause are relational transgressions (Metts, 1994), violations of implicit or explicit relational rules that are perceived as betrayal. Relational transgressions include infidelity in interpersonal relationships, disconfirming a friend, going back on a promise, or manipulating a colleague at work.

Behavioral responses to hurt may be similar to those for anger, but also include acquiescence to the other's behavior and expressions of invulnerability (e.g., "sticks and stones may break my bones, but words can never harm me." Other responses affirm the relationship, such as expressions of loyalty (e.g., "I know X didn't mean that" and "I'll work through this because our relationship is more important than this little incident") and integrative communication whereby the hurt party attempts to engage the other to talk things out and repair the relationship with the offender.

Guilt is a negative emotion that results from hurting another. Guerrero and LaValley (2006) note that "people experience guilt when they perceive that they have injured, unjustly hurt, or failed to help someone" (p. 79). It is a self-conscious emotion that involves judging ourselves to have come up short or to have violated our own or generally accepted codes of conduct toward another. Physiological reactions to guilt include a lump in the throat, accelerated heartbeat, irregular breathing and a tension associated with wanting to do something to compensate for our transgression. Guilt may be stimulated by our reflections on our own behavior, but others' communication may also trigger guilt. Vangelisti, Daly and Rudnick (1991) identified several conversational tactics that stimulate guilt, including statements about unfulfilled relational or role obligations (e.g., "but you promised . . ."), bringing up sacrifices (e.g., "I worked overtime this weekend for you, and now you do this!"), and making comparisons that reflect badly (e.g., "You've spent two weekends in a row with Jake. When do I get some time with you?").

In response to guilt, parties may simply refuse to take responsibility (e.g., "I never asked you to work overtime") or they may justify their behavior (e.g., "I was with Jake because his wife is leaving him and he needed me"). Responses that affirm the relationship include offering compensation (e.g., "What can I do to make up for this?"), appeasement (e.g., "All right, let's spend this weekend together") and apologies.

There has been less attention paid to positive emotions in conflict. Since conflict is founded on differences and interference with goals, negative emotional states are primary. However, positive emotions, though secondary, are also relevant to conflict. One response to conflict is *hope* (Lazarus & Lazarus, 1994). Hope is a positive feeling based on anticipation of positive outcomes that is associated with an optimistic outlook. Physiological correlates of hope include moderate levels of activation, a light feeling (as opposed to the heaviness sometimes associated with depression), and some increase in pulse rate. Hope can sometimes be intense, but generally is a more moderate emotional state. Factors that contribute to hopefulness include personality and prior experience with conflict situations that turned out well. An experienced manager, for example, commented that when she was involved in a conflict, she regarded it as an opportunity to improve the situation, rather than something to be dreaded. An optimistic response to a conflict depends on a secondary appraisal that redefines the negative affect as something that can be channeled in positive directions.

Another positive emotion, *energy,* "is the feeling that one is eager to act and capable of acting" (Quinn & Dutton, 2005, p. 36). Also described as vitality and zest, energy is a self-reinforcing experience that is quite pleasant and focusing, one which people try to prolong and enhance. People try to recreate or repeat circumstances that create energy and to avoid those that deplete or dampen it. Physiological correlates of energy include enhanced awareness, focused attention, and sometimes tensed muscles and increased heartbeat. Factors that contribute to energy include positive expectations about a situation, a sense that one is capable of meeting the challenges of the situation, and positive affect and encouragement from others (Quinn & Dutton, 2005). Energy fosters a tendency to view events positively and to invest effort in activities. Hence, it is a valuable emotion that may help move conflicts in positive directions.

There is a tendency to regard emotions primarily as undesirable during conflict. This stems from a long-standing tradition in Western thought that privileges thinking over feeling. Thinking—rationally analyzing the situation and working out alternatives that might resolve a conflict—seems to be preferable to allowing our emotional responses to take over and drive the conflict in nonrational—or even irrational—directions. However, this viewpoint is overly simplistic and based on an oversimplified notion of the role of emotions in conflict.

Emotions are a natural part of all human experience, and they are a natural part of conflict. We would be poorer if we could somehow turn off our emotional reactions to conflict and approach it solely on the basis of reason. Emotions energize our responses to conflict and are just as important to positive integrative movement toward a solution as they are to destructive escalation. So, the issue should not be deciding whether emotion is bad for conflict or not, but *when and under what conditions* it has positive versus negative effects.

Emotions can be so powerful that they overwhelm us, limiting our ability to accurately understand others or to appreciate their positions and reducing our ability to analyze the conflict and think through issues and options. Gottman (1994) discusses *emotional flooding,* when one party is surprised and overwhelmed by the other's negative emotional response. This arouses such strong counter-emotions in the party that the party is unable to process the other's statements and issues properly. This degrades the party's ability to respond to the conflict, and makes an aggressive, attacking response more likely.

Emotional contagion is a more general term that refers to the tendency for emotions to spread among parties in a conflict. Emotional contagion is defined as a tendency to automatically mirror or mimic the emotional response to another, leading to a synchronization of emotional experience and reciprocation of behavioral responses to emotion (Hatfield, Cacioppo, & Rapson, 1994). So, Jack may respond to Jill's angry outburst by becoming angry in return and shouting back at her, which intensifies Jill's anger and encourages her to shout even louder, which infuriates Jack, and so on. As we will see in Chapter 3, reciprocation is a natural and powerful tendency in human interaction. Emotional contagion is one contributing factor to reciprocation.

Jones (2001) cautions us to recognize that emotional contagion—like emotion itself—is not a simple phenomenon. She points out that, "Not only do people differ in their focus on affective communication as information . . . but also they differ in their propensity to be affected by the emotional communication of others" (p. 92). The communication of emotions by others may not affect us if we discount the emotional display (e.g., "He's just tired and grumpy; don't pay attention to that outburst") or when we are aware of potentially harmful impact of emotions and so keep our own responses under control. Booth-Butterfield and Booth-Butterfield (1990) also suggest other reasons that affect might have little effect, including the party's personality. There is also evidence that the nature of the relationship may influence response to emotional communication. Hatfield, Cacioppo and Rapson (1994), for example, report that in situations of intense competition, people are likely to dampen their responses to others' emotional displays. Participants in sports are familiar with this, as they often try to "keep their cool" as the other "experiences a meltdown."

As this discussion illustrates, emotions may have powerful impacts on conflicts, but the impacts are complex. Case 2.3 considers the role emotion played in the Parking Lot Scuffle. Emotional communication can have both positive and negative effects on conflict management. These effects are tightly bound with cognitive processes associated with conflict, to which we now turn. Table 2.2 gives some basic suggestions for working with emotion in conflicts.

CASE 2.3 • *Emotion in the Parking Lot Scuffle*

The predominant emotion at the beginning of this conflict was anger. Jay hit the moped, and his natural reaction was to become upset at the accident. His pulse rate was elevated, and he may have been trembling a bit, a common reaction to an accident that is a "near miss" in which nothing really harmful happened to him. Tim saw his Honda and was angry because his cherished moped had been damaged. Tim launched a verbal attack, a reflexive action triggered by anger.

Tim's attack prompted Jay to reassess his feelings in a secondary appraisal. His physiological reactions were already similar to those of anger, and the anger expressed by Tim elicited a matching anger response from Jay. This emotional contagion put both in similar emotional states, which had the potential to escalate the conflict. As the interchange unfolds, Tim experienced emotional flooding. His anger was so extreme that it seems to block his ability to comprehend Jay. Tim was concerned only with getting reparations from Jay or, if these weren't forthcoming, with taking revenge on Jay.

Another common reaction to anger is to avoid the other party, and this seems to be what Jay was doing near the end of the episode. He turned away from Tim, trying to end the confrontation and calm down. Tim, flooded with anger, hit him.

Discussion Questions

- Was the emotional contagion inevitable?
- Could anything have been done to avoid the escalation of anger and to inject some positive emotion into the situation?

TABLE 2.2 *Working with Emotions: Questions to Ask and Measures to Take Regarding Emotions in Conflict*

- Accept emotion as a natural part of conflict and acknowledge your emotions.
- Identify your emotional states. You may not always be aware of exactly what emotions you are feeling.
- Ask yourself whether the emotion you have labeled your current state with is appropriate for this situation.
- Be aware of the behavioral tendencies associated with various emotions and consider whether these tendencies are constructive or destructive in the current situation.
- Realize the possibility of emotional flooding. If your emotions overwhelm you, find a way to get some distance and perspective on them.
- Be vigilant for emotional contagion. Are you and the other party feeding on each others' emotions? Is there some way to short-circuit this?
- Foster hope and positive energy.
- Own up to your emotions and discuss them with the other party.
- Help the other party discuss his or her emotions. Recognize the other's emotions as legitimate and respect his or her feelings. You will not be able to get someone else to dismiss emotions, but you can help him or her gain insight into them.
- Chapters 7 and 8 provide suggestions for building a climate safe for emotional expression and for communicating in ways that counteract some of the negative impacts of emotional flooding and contagion.

2.3 Social Cognition and Conflict

Social cognition refers to "the organized thoughts people have about human interaction" (Roloff & Berger, 1982, p. 21). Thoughts are organized by various cognitive structures and processes. For our purposes, the structures and processes of interest are those pertaining to conflict and conflict interaction. Roloff and Miller (2005) summarize these in terms of (a) forms of social knowledge that we may have about interpersonal conflict, and (b) cognitive processes that shape our behavior in conflicts. We will discuss each of these in turn.

2.3.1 Social Knowledge About Conflict and Conflict Interaction

Several types of knowledge influence our expectations about conflict and our behavior in conflict interaction. We will consider beliefs about conflict, conflict frames, and conflict scripts.

Beliefs About Conflict.   Roloff and Miller (2006) classify beliefs about conflict into as-sumptions and standards. *Assumptions* are beliefs such as whether conflict is desirable or not, how others will behave in conflict, and how a conflict will turn out. Studies have found that common beliefs related to conflict include (Crohan, 1992; Roloff & Miller, 2006):

- Conflict is destructive.
- The other party cannot change.
- Men and women respond differently to conflict.
- Problems can be overcome.
- Disagreements can be settled if you just talk about them.
- Disagreements in a marriage are healthy.

While these are just a few of the possible beliefs about conflict, generally studies have shown that these beliefs exert the types of influence we might expect over how partners in relationships respond to each other.

Standards are beliefs about how a conflict should be handled. Maxims and sayings reflect various standards about conflict:

- Let sleeping dogs lie.
- Never go to bed mad at each other.
- Arguments only confirm people in their own opinions.
- You can make up after a quarrel, but it will always show where it was patched.
- For souls in growth, great quarrels are great emancipations.

These sayings reflect several aspects of standards. Standards incorporate value judgments about conflict. Standards also include implicit beliefs about how conflicts typically unfold or about their likely outcomes. Finally, standards may guide our behavior in conflict.

Culture is an important influence on beliefs and standards about conflict. We are not born knowing how to think. Patterns of thinking and reasoning are learned as we mature, and the culture we are born into, which favors certain ways of thinking over others, is the primary source of these patterns (Hofstede & Bond, 1984). Glen (1981) distinguished dif-ferent cultures based on their typical thought patterns, and these cultural differences have been linked to different ways of responding to conflicts. Table 2.3 briefly describes the main types of cultures Glen identified.

TABLE 2.3 *Types of Cultures*

Associative Culture

- Reliance on a particular way of thinking—requires close reading of immediate and past contexts
- People are keenly aware of obligations to others
- People value the group over the individual (collectivism)
- People are highly dependent on others in the immediate situation
- Communication is not always open and explicit
- Meanings have to be inferred from contextual cues

Abstractive Culture

- Reliance on a universal way of thinking—knowledge can be shared across large groups
- People value assertion of self over group commitment (individualism)
- Communication is precise and explicit
- Meanings are assumed to be stated openly and interpretations rely less on contextual cues

---

Kozan (1997) has identified three different conflict models that stem from the different ways of thinking in diverse cultures. His framework suggests that people with different cultural backgrounds will have different standards about conflict: They will have different attitudes toward conflict, different expectations about appropriate conflict behavior, as well as different approaches to managing conflict. Kozan's three cultural models—the harmony model, the confrontational model, and the regulative model—are summarized in Table 2.4 on page 54 and represent three general standards people can hold about conflict. The harmony model tends to emerge in associative cultures, while the confrontational and regulative models tend to emerge in abstractive cultures. The confrontational model is more likely to hold in abstractive cultures that assume power should be distributed equally among people (low-power distance cultures). On the other hand, the regulative model is more likely to hold in cultures that accept the existence of differences in power (high-power distance cultures). These culturally-based models of conflict have a significant impact on how conflict interaction unfolds. Differences in conflict styles across cultures have been found in a variety of cross-cultural settings (Zupnik, 2000; Tingley, 2001; Ellis & Maoz, 2002; Nicotera & Dorsey, 2006). These will be discussed further in Chapter 4, which deals with conflict styles.

Conflict Scripts. A *script* is a cognitive structure that describes appropriate sequences of events in an episode. It has been documented that people have scripts for eating in restaurants, for conversations, and for dating. There is also evidence that people have scripts for conflict. Fehr, Baldwin, Collins, Patterson and Benditt (1999) found evidence that men and women had expectations about how they would react to anger and how their partner would respond to their reaction, (though this study did not actually elicit scripts from subjects). The most common expected response to expression of anger for both men and women were that the other would talk it over, be conciliatory, and express hurt feelings.

Miller (1991) elicited scripts from undergraduates about five different conflicts precipitated by, respectively, a broken promise, the cumulative effects of an annoying

TABLE 2.4   *Cultural Models of Conflict and Their Characteristics*

Harmony Model
- Emphasizes maintaining smooth relationships
- Tendency to prevent or avoid open expression of conflict
- Reliance on cooperativeness and connection
- Lack of self-assertion
- Restriction on negative emotional displays
- Emphasis on use of third parties who are from the community
- Preservation of honor, pride, and face
- Strives for long-term, stable outcomes to a conflict

Confrontational Model
- Emphasizes the aggressive pursuit of individual goals
- Conflicts are valued because they can address the needs of individuals
- Less emphasis on relationship or group preservation
- Tendency to open up conflict and to engage in negotiations
- Emotions are experienced intensely and expressed openly
- Use of third parties to help facilitate the negotiation between parties
- Interventions strive for short-term gains

Regulative Model
- Emphasizes settling conflict through application of principles
- Reliance on codes, rules, and laws to address differences or issues
- Personal aspects of the conflicts tend to be underplayed or ignored
- Emotions are underplayed and are seen as less relevant to the conflict resolution process
- Third parties are usually people in ascribed roles who have the power to apply rules to specific conflict situations
- Procedural justice is an important element of conflict resolution process
- Short-term resolutions are valued over long-term concerns

habit, criticism, a rebuff, and an illegitimate demand. She found differences in the scripts across the different types of conflicts. For example, in response to a broken promise the most common script was that the party would ask a question about the promise, the other would make an excuse, the party would accept the apology, and the conflict would be somewhat resolved. In response to the rebuff, in which the other did not invite the party to a social gathering of old friends, in the most common script the party accuses the other, the other makes an excuse, the party grudgingly accepts the excuse, and the conflict is resolved.

Burrell and Buzzanell conducted studies on the mental schemas people held concerning what would typically occur during conflicts (Burrell, Buzzanell, & McMillan, 1992; Buzzanell & Burrell, 1997). To identify these schemas, they analyzed the metaphors workers and students used to describe conflicts in their families and at workplaces. Three distinct metaphorical schemas were found.

The *conflict is war* schema identifies conflict as a battle that involves great cost to the participants. Examples of metaphors reflecting this schema include "clash of the Titans," "fighting like cats and dogs," and "guerilla warfare." The war schema assumes that conflict is a win–lose proposition and that competing and forcing would determine the outcome. The ultimate conclusion of a conflict involving this metaphor is victory for one side and defeat for the other.

The *conflict is impotence* schema depicts conflict as a "victimizing process in which participants were powerless to influence or alter unpredictable events" (Buzzanell & Burrell, 1997, p. 125). The parties see themselves as trapped in a conflict not of their making, often trying vainly to protect themselves or to change a situation that is beyond their control. All this effort is felt to be wasted because they have little control. Metaphors reflecting this theme include "a bear preying on a defenseless infant," "running up a steep hill with lead weights in my pockets," "whatever I say isn't heard," and "I am a ghost."

The third schema, *conflict is a rational process,* portrays conflict in collaborative terms and emphasizes its potentially positive outcomes. This view of conflict emphasizes discussion, debate, and exploring issues. Examples of metaphors in this schema include "a discussion handled responsibly," "the comedy cabaret; we end up laughing most of the time," and "Mother Theresa (my boss never shows anger or reacts in a hostile way; everything is handled in a very cool and collected manner)." This schema implies that conflicts can be constructive.

These studies suggest that many people may have implicit scripts that shape their expectations about how a conflict will unfold. These may be based in part on social norms of acceptable behavior and also, no doubt, on prior experience.

Conflict Frames. A *frame* is a cognitive structure based on previous experience, which guides our interpretation of an interaction or event. There has been a substantial amount of research on conflict frames (Roloff & Miller, 2006). Rogan (2006) attempted to integrate and synthesize this research into a common set of dimensions. He identified six dimensions of conflict frames that guided interpretations of interpersonal conflict:

- ***Instrumentality:*** The degree to which the party focuses on factual or substantive issues and outcomes
- ***Other Assessment:*** The degree to which the party focuses on the other's conduct and judging whether it was good/bad, right/wrong, or fair/unfair
- ***Affect:*** The degree to which the party has negative emotions toward the other or the conflict in general
- ***Face:*** The degree to which the party focuses on issues related to self-image
- ***Affiliation:*** The degree to which the party is concerned with finding a mutually-acceptable solution and maintaining a good relationship with the other
- ***Distributiveness:*** The degree to which the party interpreted the conflict in win-lose or competitive terms

These six dimensions map the various ways in which parties might interpret conflicts, and not all will figure in every interpretation. In terms of our discussion of types of conflicts in the Introduction, realistic conflict would be framed as instrumental and affiliative. In contrast, nonrealistic conflicts would be framed as distributive, emotional, and there would be much concern with assessing the other (primarily negatively) and with self-image.

Again returning to our types in the Introduction, task conflict would be framed as instrumental and affiliative, while relationship conflict would be framed as emotional, distributive, and concerned with assessing the other. Process conflict would be instrumental (since it pertains to how the group members will work together), and it could be framed in positive terms as affiliative or in negative terms as distributive, concerned with other assessment, and concerned with losing one's own face.

Pinkley and Northcraft (1994) studied framing in a simulated conflict. They found that instrumental and affiliative frames resulted in better outcomes than did distributive frames. They also found that subjects who adopted an instrumental frame were more satisfied with the outcome than those who adopted an affective frame.

Research on negotiation has studied how differential framing of bargaining proposals can influence the evaluations and choices made about those proposals (Bazerman, 1983; Bazerman & Neale, 1983). Bargaining proposals can be worded to suggest what might be gained by adopting or accepting the proposal. Or the same proposal can be worded to suggest what will be lost by adopting or accepting the proposal. Both of these frames represent different ways of wording proposals within the instrumental, affiliative, and distributive dimensions of framing.

As an illustration of these gain or loss frames, consider the following example that has been used as a basis for research on negotiations (Bazerman & Neale, 1983, pp. 54–55):

A large manufacturer has recently been hit with a number of economic difficulties, and it appears as if three plants need to be closed and 6,000 employees laid off. The vice president of production has been exploring alternative ways to avoid this crisis. She has adopted two plans:

Plan A: This plan will save one of the three plants and 2,000 jobs.

Plan B: This plan has a 1/3 probability of saving three plants and all 6,000 jobs, but has a 2/3 probability of saving no plants and no jobs.

Which plan would you select?

Note that both of the proposed plans (A and B) are cast in terms of gain (saving plants).

Now reconsider the same problem but with the following alternative choices:

Plan C: This plan will result in the loss of two of the three plants and 4,000 jobs.

Plan D: This plan has a 2/3 probability of resulting in the loss of all three plants and all 6,000 jobs but has a 1/3 probability of losing no plants and no jobs.

Which plan would you select?

Plans C and D are cast in terms of what people can possibly lose if they are adopted. However, these two options are objectively identical to those worded in terms of gains. That is, Plan A is the same as Plan C and Plan B is the same as Plan D. The difference is in the way in which the proposals are framed—as potential gains or losses.

The way options are framed has an important effect on people's preferences. Given the choice between Plans A and B, about 80 percent of people choose Plan A. But given the choice between Plans C and D, the choice is overwhelmingly for Plan D. The difference in framing as potential for gain versus potential for loss is enough to shift the choices that people make. When people choose among options cast in terms of gains, they are more likely to choose the sure thing. In this instance, Plan A is chosen over Plan B because the choice is among plans that offer gain and Plan A is a sure thing, while Plan B is the riskier choice. In contrast, when people choose among options that are cast in terms of losses, they are more likely to choose the riskier option. In this instance, Plan D is chosen over Plan C because the choice is among plans that offer losses, and Plan D is the riskier choice. Research shows that negotiators who view possible outcomes in terms of gains rather than losses are, in some cases, more likely to attain better overall outcomes, because they do not take as much risk (Bazerman, Magliozzi, & Neale, 1985; Neale & Northcraft, 1986). However, this may not be the case in conflicts, since sometimes willingness to take a risk may be associated with trying to find a solution acceptable to everyone (that is, with adopting a collaborating conflict style, as we will see in Chapter 4).

What guides our framing of conflicts? As noted in the definition of frame, past experience plays an important role. Prior experience with the other party encourages us to select certain frames over others. If Jill has been competitive in previous conflicts, we are likely to apply the distributive frame in the future. Gayle and Preiss (1998) found that memory of a negative experience in a previous conflict clouded the subsequent relationships between parties. Our experience in particular contexts or situations also influences the frames we select. If we are working in an organization that values constructive, supportive communication, we are more likely to apply an instrumental and affiliative frame. Past experience with significant others such as our families, friends, and mentors may also shape how we frame conflicts (Roloff & Miller, 2006). There is evidence that experiences we have had in conflicts in important relationships influence how we frame conflicts through transference of the negative or positive feelings from past experience to the present situation (Bower, 2007). For this transference to occur, the other party must have characteristics or mannerisms similar to those of the significant other.

Rogan (2006) reported that men and women differed in the frames they applied in describing previous conflicts. Women applied the affiliative frame more than men, while men had a tendency to use the distributive frame more than women. Culture also seems likely to influence the framing of conflicts. Gelfand et al. (2001) compared the frames used by U.S. and Japanese citizens and found some commonalities, but also some unique frames. Both cultures used frames similar to affiliation and distributive frames, but only the U.S. citizens used an "Infringement of rights" frame similar to the other assessment frame, while the Japanese citizens employed a "Duty to repay obligations" frame. This is consistent with the general tendency for U.S. citizens to emphasize individualism and Japanese collectivism.

Beliefs and scripts are forms of social knowledge that exist prior to and independent of a particular conflict. They tend to be abstract. Parties recall beliefs and scripts when confronted with a potential or actual conflict to help them interpret the situation and for guidance. Frames, on the other hand, emerge in response to the conflict and are tied to the specific context. Of course, the cognitive structures that give rise to frames are pre-existing, and people do seem to have habitual tendencies to frame conflicts in particular ways. However, the particular frame applied is specific to the immediate situation. Case 2.4 shows how social knowledge may have played a role in the Parking Lot Scuffle. Beliefs, scripts, and frames enter into and are shaped by several cognitive processes, to which we now turn.

CASE 2.4 • *Social Knowledge About Conflict and the Parking Lot Scuffle*

Several beliefs about conflicts seem to have affected the development of the Parking Lot Scuffle. Standards about how problems like the accident should be handled are implicit in Jay's reaction, which implies that Tim was responsible for where his moped was parked, and therefore Jay was not to blame. The standard of personal responsibility implied that Tim should back down and take responsibility, thus reducing the conflict. Tim, on the other hand, assumed that damages are the responsibility of the person doing the damage and that Jay was responsible. As the conflict progressed, Jay's behavior reflected the belief that when conflicts get out of hand, one should turn to a third party (the police) to mediate or manage the conflict.

Tim framed the conflict in distributive terms based on an assessment of Jay's behavior as wrong and unfair. Jay also bought into this frame, adding a judgment of Tim as presumptuous, rude, and engaged in inappropriate behavior (physical contact). When both parties frame a conflict in this way, escalation is bound to occur.

Discussion Questions

- Which cultural models of conflict does Tim's behavior most resemble? What standards concerning how conflict should be handled does this imply? What about Jay's behavior?
- How might Jay have framed the conflict so that his frame did not match Tim's so closely? What barriers stand in the way of adopting a different frame?

2.3.2 Social Cognitive Processes and Conflict

The thought processes by which we make sense of and interpret others' behavior during a conflict obviously have an influence on our own conflict behavior. Three processes in particular are likely to influence conflict interaction: expectancy violations, attributions about others, and thinking about the conflict.

Expectancy Violations.   Expectancy violations theory asserts that people have both predictive and prescriptive *expectancies* about others' behavior (Burgoon, Stern, & Dillman, 1995). Predictive expectancies pertain to expectations about how another will act in a particular situation. Prescriptive expectancies pertain to expectations about how another should act in a particular situation. Burgoon and colleagues argue that when the other's behavior falls outside expectancies it creates emotional reactions and attempts to make sense of the situation. If the other's behavior negatively violates the party's expectancies, it is likely to spark negative emotional responses and a behavioral response. In some cases, this response attempts to compensate for the violation and in other cases the response is to reciprocate the negative violation.

The party's assessment of the *potential reward value* of the other party is what determines whether the party compensates or reciprocates. If the party judges that the other has low potential for future reward, the party is more likely to reciprocate negative behavior. For example, if a stranger Jill has never met says something rude, Jill is likely to snub the stranger or perhaps say something rude in return, because she does not expect further contacts in the future. If, however, the party assesses that the other has high potential for reward, compensation is the most likely response. If Jill's boss says something rude, Jill is likely to either ignore the remark or perhaps turn it into a joke, because she knows that her raise depends on her boss's good will.

Conflicts are situations in which expectancy violations are likely to occur, and the associated cognitive dynamics are thus likely to influence conflict. Bachman and Guerrero (2007) studied reactions to hurtful events in interpersonal relationships from an expectancy violation perspective. They argued that when people experience hurtful events such as infidelity, deception, unfair accusations, and rebuffs, they base their responses on their assessment of the potential reward and the intentions of the other. When the other person was highly rewarding, parties tended to respond more constructively, by expressing satisfaction with and commitment to the relationship, by trying to repair the relationship, and by communicating more cooperatively. On the other hand, when the other person was not rewarding and when the hurt was seen as intentional, parties tended to respond by deescalating the relationship and with distributive and vengeful behavior.

Scripts and expectancies are likely to be linked, because we may have expectancies about scripts. Scripts describe sequences of expected behavior, while the expectancies that have been studied are for the most part single responses. It is a straightforward extension to posit that we are likely to have expectancies about the other's part in a script, and that violations of the script elicit similar responses to violations of expectancies.

Expectancy violations theory also points to a connection between emotion and cognition in conflict. Expectancy violations trigger emotional responses, and these emotional responses tend to fuel responses to the violation (Burgoon et al., 1995; Guerrero & LaValley, 2006). Assessments and reactions such as reciprocation, in turn, are likely to produce further emotional responses in both self and other, further shaping cognition, and so on.

Not all expectancy violations are negative. In some cases, another may exceed our expectations. When this occurs, positive emotions and reciprocation of positive behavior follow. This suggests a way in which we can use expectancies to move toward productive conflict management and to dampen escalation tendencies. In Case 2.5 on page 60 we show how expectancy violations likely influenced the Parking Lot Scuffle.

Attribution Processes. In a number of pathbreaking studies and theoretical analyses, Sillars and colleagues applied attribution theory to the study of interpersonal conflict processes (1980a, 1980b, 1980c; Sillars & Parry, 1982; Sillars & Weisberg, 1987; Sillars, Canary, & Tofoya, 2004). Before describing how this theory has been applied in the conflict arena, we will briefly discuss the nature of attribution processes.

At the heart of attribution processes are two premises. First, people interpret behavior in terms of its causes. People naturally attribute characteristics, intentions, and attitudes to the people they encounter. Through this linking process, people attempt to organize and understand the world around them. Second, these causal explanations affect reactions to the judged behavior. Attributions enable actors to behave appropriately toward others in varying contexts.

When trying to make sense of others' behavior, we scrutinize the environments, settings and people's actions in search of reasons behind their actions. After discovering a plausible reason or cause, the other's behavior is attributed to one of two categories: (1) *dispositional factors* or (2) *situational factors*. For example, ability, mood, effort, and

CASE 2.5 • *Expectancy Violations and the Parking Lot Scuffle*

The beliefs and standards the two parties brought to the conflict set up expectations about how the other should behave. Jay expected Tim to accept responsibility for parking his moped in the wrong place. He expected Tim to graciously apologize and not fly off the handle. When Tim's behavior and his accusation of Jay violated these expectations, Jay was taken aback and he experienced a rush of negative emotion. Jay did not expect to work with Tim in the future—after Tim's behavior, he probably never wanted to see him again—so Tim had low potential reward value, and thus Jay was not willing to make excuses for Tim or accept his behavior.

Tim expected Jay to accept responsibility for the accident and offer to repair his moped. When Jay instead asserted his right to the parking spot and refused to accept responsibility, this violated Tim's script for the conflict, and Tim's anger about the accident itself was redirected to Jay. Tim also did not see Jay as potentially rewarding—in fact, he saw Jay more as a barrier to his goal of getting his moped fixed. So he, too, was unlikely to make excuses for Jay or forgive his violation of the script.

This mirroring of expectancy violations between Jay and Tim created a self-reinforcing cycle of negativity that ended in physical violence.

Discussion Questions

- What, if anything, could Jay have done to forestall the impact of expectancy violations on the conflict?

knowledge are dispositional causes arising from the individual, whereas task difficulty, interference, and luck are causes considered to be situational in nature stemming from external sources. In other words, all factors internal to the individual are considered dispositional, and all factors external to the individual are deemed situational. Two critical biases influence the attributions that actors make.

First, individuals commonly attribute others' behavior to dispositional factors and their own behavior to situational factors (Jones & Nisbett, 1971; Ross, 1977). This has been called the *fundamental attribution error,* and it is especially likely to occur when people believe others' behavior is intentional and goal-directed (Heider, 1958). For example, when searching for reasons for our own behavior, such as nervousness in speaking situations, we commonly attribute our unease to the situation, but when confronted with a nervous speaker, we are more apt to attribute his or her unease as a permanent feature of his or her character. The tendency for attributors to underestimate the influence of situational factors and overestimate dispositional factors in attributing others' behavior is remarkably strong. Research confirms that attributors infer attitudes from behaviors even when they know the behavior has been severely constrained (Snyder & Jones, 1974; Miller, 1976). This tendency even occurs when observers are told of this bias.

Second, to maintain and enhance self-esteem individuals often defensively attribute actions resulting in negative consequences to external forces and attribute positive consequences of the action to themselves (Bradley, 1978; Zuckerman, 1979; Snead & Ndede-Amadi, 2002). This *self-serving bias* is especially likely to occur in situations involving success and failure. One educational study nicely illustrates this tendency: Based on test scores, math teachers either believed that a student improved or regressed in math skills (Beckman, 1970). When asked to explain this difference, the teachers consistently attributed student improvement to their teaching prowess, but they attributed lower performance to factors related to the students. Predictably, students reached the opposite conclusion, attributing their success to internal factors and their failure to their teachers.

Attribution processes have important impacts on conflict interaction. In several studies, Sillars and his associates investigated three types of conflict management strategies that we have introduced and will continue to discuss throughout this book: integrative, avoidance, and distributive strategies. Sillars and colleagues defined integrative strategies as messages designed to manage conflict openly through discussion while refraining from negative evaluations of the partner. These benevolent strategies place a premium on collaboration and joint problem solving. Avoidance strategies were defined as attempts to avoid direct discussion and management of the conflict. These strategies include statements that deny the presence of conflicts, shift the focus of conversations, and sidestep discussions about conflict through indirect or ambiguous talk. In moderation, avoidance can be a useful strategy (see Chapter 4); but taken to the extreme it can be destructive, as noted in Chapter 1. Distributive strategies include attempts to resolve the conflict in a zero-sum manner in which one party wins at the others' expense. Distributive messages often include negative evaluations of the partner, such as insults and direct criticism. Again, moderate use of distributive strategies can be productive, but excessive and rigid employment moves conflicts in negative directions, as we have seen in Chapter 1 and will develop further in Chapter 4.

Sillars' research has made a strong case that a party's attributions influence conflict interaction in at least three ways. First, due to the self-serving bias, people are more likely to attribute the negative effects of conflict to partners rather than to themselves. This tends to heighten resentment of others as the negative effects of conflict are felt, which in turn increases people's likelihood of responding distributively. Second, also due to the self-serving bias, people more often think that they use integrative strategies (which are perceived as socially desirable and positive) and that others use distributive or avoidance tactics (Thomas & Pondy, 1977). This can lead parties to mistakenly assume that they are doing more to resolve the conflict than others are.

Third, the fundamental attribution error heightens conflict by encouraging people to see others' behavior as planned and intentional and their own as driven by the situation. So when others act distributively, parties tend to view their actions as intentional aggression. On the other hand, if the party acts distributively toward others, there is a tendency for him or her to view this behavior as a natural response that is called for by the situation (such as the other's distributive behavior). The result is that parties see their own behavior as caused by others and others' behavior toward them as due to others' intentional plans. So they grow angry with others who are acting distributively or avoiding, but they rationalize their own aggression as a sensible response to others'. Clearly this sets up a vicious cycle whereby the party believes his or her distributive or avoidant behavior is justified by another's bad intentions. Roloff and Miller (2006) substantiate this further in their summary of a number of studies that indicate that "making maladaptive attributions promotes negative conflict behavior" (p. 108).

One assumption underlying most attribution research is that the parties have common background knowledge. The fundamental attribution error and self-serving bias occur even in cases in which parties know each other quite well. However, in situations where parties come from very different backgrounds or social groups, errors of attribution are much more likely to occur. Parties from different cultures, genders, or economic classes are particularly prone to misattributions and misinterpretations of one another. Because they have little common experience and no common set of beliefs and values, parties from different groups are prone to major misunderstandings that include, but go well beyond, the two errors we have discussed.

A study by Weisinger and Salipante (1995) highlights serious misattributions between American and Japanese engineers who were asked to discuss the creation of joint business ventures. Parties on both sides tended to judge those of other cultures as less technically competent than they were due to different cultural norms about what competence was. Japanese engineers concluded that American engineers were not very good because they would not teach the Japanese engineers how they did certain types of analyses they employed. Such actions are valued in Japanese engineering culture because it emphasizes sharing responsibility and a team approach to design. However, in American engineering culture such actions signal disrespect for the professionalism of the other because fellow engineers are presumed to be competent due to their certification.

Weisinger and Salipante also found misunderstandings based on incorrect assumptions of shared "traits" of other cultures. For example, in a situation where Americans found out that the Japanese members of their joint venture had been solving joint venture problems among themselves parallel to work that the team was doing, the Americans attributed this to the "sneakiness" of the Japanese. Although cultures do share typical ways of thinking and doing things, there is little worth in such value-laden judgments. The Japanese were proceeding in a way common to their culture, thinking things through in a group, but the Americans, who valued open discussion and individual thinking, found this unacceptable and explained it in prejudicial terms. Note also that the Americans were engaging in the fundamental attribution error (attributing Japanese actions to bad intentions rather than to how things are done in Japanese culture), which compounded the misinterpretation.

Such misunderstandings are commonplace when people from different cultures and backgrounds come together. Attributions are made almost automatically, and generally people are not aware that their conclusions about others are based on faulty reasoning. When mistaken assumptions such as these drive behavior, they keep parties at a distance and feed negative conflict cycles.

Just as conflict is not static, the attributions made by individuals do not remain constant. As a conflict unfolds, attributions may change, thereby promoting use of different strategies. In this sense, the strategies a person uses are part of an emergent process mediated by ongoing reevaluation and attribution. Sillars and Parry (1982) found that as stress levels during conflict situations increase, other-directed blame due to the fundamental attribution error also rises. Spontaneous verbal statements that provide integrative understandings decrease as stress increases.

On the whole, research and theory in this area can be summarized by three propositions. First, people choose conflict resolution strategies based on the attributions they make regarding the cause of the conflict. Second, biases in the attribution process tend to encourage noncooperative modes of conflict. Third, the choice of conflict strategies

CASE 2.6 • *The Role of Attributions in the Parking Lot Scuffle*

At the outset of the conflict Jay engaged in somewhat tentative behavior and attempted to understand the situation and find answers to the dilemma. (Whether Jay's line 2 stands as a question or an accusation is open to debate, but given the context of Jay's justification in line 4, he deserves the benefit of the doubt.) When Jay saw Tim's accusations, negative evaluations, insults, and insistence that Jay pay for repairs, he was likely to make a dispositional attribution that Tim was simply an unreasonable and irrational person. Along with this came a presumption of negative intent. This was likely to make Jay angry toward Tim, partly due to a need to defend himself and partly in response to Tim's "unreasonable" reaction.

From the beginning, Tim attributed both the accident and the escalating conflict that follows to Jay. This dispositional attribution cast Jay as generally uncaring of others' property and unwilling to accept responsibility. From this vantage, it is likely that Tim perceived Jay as the aggressor, and this led him to respond with more negative tactics and, eventually, violence. It is easy for us to see "from the outside" that Tim's anger sparked Jay's. In the heat of the moment, however, attributional "reflexes" told Tim that his behavior was caused by Jay's unreasonable reaction (the situation), while Jay was intentionally trying to weasel out of his responsibility (due to his disposition), and redefine the situation for Tim so that *he* felt perfectly justified in his behavior toward Jay.

Also caught up in the same attributional biases, Jay is likely to have concluded that Tim is generally an aggressive person and deserves the hostility Jay expressed toward Tim in line 14.

Discussion Questions

- What might Jay and/or Tim have done to sort out their mistaken attributions from actual competitive intentions?
- Could the damage done by attribution processes in this conflict have been limited or counteracted?

influences the likelihood of conflict resolution and the degree of satisfaction with the relationship. Case 2.6 considers the role of attributions in the Parking Lot Scuffle.

What can we do about the negative impacts of attribution processes? Measures to enhance understanding and cut through mistaken assumptions are discussed throughout the remainder of the book. Chapter 8 discusses several structured problem-solving and communication methods that are particularly valuable in uncovering and correcting misunderstandings.

One important step in limiting the impact of attributions on conflict is to remember that attribution errors occur constantly and to be watchful for them. We have a tendency to make similar attributions in our conflict experiences across time, partners, and situations (Bono, Boles, Judge, & Lauver, 2002). Research has shown that attributions, once made, are difficult to dismiss. In part this seems to be due to a lack of awareness of typical patterns. One useful corrective is to take attribution errors into account when we try to understand conflicts or disagreements. We can do this by remembering that we are very likely to misinterpret the behavior of people from different cultures, genders, and socioeconomic backgrounds and that it is important to understand their point of view.

Attribution research suggests that we are also more likely to find excuses for our own behavior and to blame others for their behavior. When this blaming occurs—when we assume others' behavior stems from their bad intentions toward us—we should remind ourselves that they may feel driven by the situation as well and look for ways to change the situation to encourage cooperation. Remember too that we tend to credit ourselves for good outcomes and blame others for bad ones. Hence, we should take a good hard look at our behavior to ensure that it is not causing the problem, and we should be more charitable toward others, not presume that they are creating the problems we face.

There is a catch, however. Despite the problems introduced by attribution biases, others may *really* have competitive intentions. If this is indeed true, then our strategy in a conflict could be very different than if we are merely misunderstanding their behavior and assuming bad intentions when none exist. The challenge is sorting things out and deciding how to respond.

Thinking About Conflicts.   Have you ever thought about a conflict that you expected to occur or mulled over one that you previously had? What thoughts ran through your head, and how did you feel? Did thinking about the conflict make you angrier at the other party, or did you feel regretful and wish you'd done something differently? Have you ever rehearsed what you were going to say to someone you were angry at?

Thinking is characteristically human, and so it is not surprising that there is a good deal of evidence that people do think about conflicts before and after, and that thinking influences their emotional reactions and behavior. In summarizing this research, Roloff and Miller (2006, p. 115) note that

> individuals report thinking about (a) their partners' provocative behavior, before they initially confront him or her (Roloff, Soule, & Carey, 2001), (b) the dynamics of the initial confrontation (Roloff et al., 2001), and (c) actions performed in subsequent argumentative episodes (Johnson & Roloff, 1998). In some cases, these thoughts take the form of replaying a prior conflict as an imagined interaction in preparation for another confrontational episode (Edwards, Honeycutt, & Zagacki, 1988).

If these thoughts center on an unpleasant or negative conflict experience, then parties become more negative toward the other, are less likely to be forgiving, and may focus on vengeance in future episodes.

This does not mean that thinking about conflicts or problems is necessarily dysfunctional. There seems to be a distinction between contemplating a problem as a problem and brooding over it. The first approach is likely to help people gain some perspective on the situation and can lead to useful insights that help manage the conflict more effectively. Brooding, however, or ruminating constantly about a conflict has more negative associations. Cloven and Roloff (1991) found that mulling over a conflict with a roommate led to negative emotional states. However, when the subject had a positive interaction with his or her roommate prior to mulling over the conflict, the negative effects of thinking were less pronounced. The positive interaction may have given the parties perspective on the conflict that led to fewer extreme negative thoughts.

So, should we try to limit the amount of thinking we do about conflicts? This seems unlikely to work, as Wenzlaff and Luxton (2003) found that suppressing thinking takes effort and that trying to dampen negative feelings may ultimately lead to more pressure to brood and ruminate. A more constructive alternative is to try to avoid painting an oversimplified, negative picture of the other, and to recognize the other's

TABLE 2.5 *Working with Social Cognition*

- Identify your beliefs about conflict and your scripts for the conflict. Are they realistic in the current conflict? What unwarranted assumptions might you be making?
- How are you framing the conflict? Is your frame constructive? Is there another way to look at the conflict? You may be able to find one by identifying your current frame and reversing some of the assumptions in it.
- What are your expectancies for the other? Are they realistic? Have they been violated? How is this contributing to your view of the other party and the conflict? Can you revise any of your expectancies?
- Remember that attribution errors are very common, especially the tendency to blame the other for the conflict and to deny your own responsibility for it. What part do you play in the conflict?
- If you are thinking about the conflict a lot, do you have an oversimplified, negative view of the other party?
- Communicate with the other party and try to understand his or her point of view. More realistic information is one of the best cures for problems caused by social cognition.

---

legitimate points and how we may be contributing to the conflict. Engaging the other, when possible, is also helpful in short-circuiting the thinking process which is, after all, in anticipation of the interaction. Table 2.5 summarizes some recommendations for counteracting negative impacts of social cognition on conflict interaction.

2.4 The Interaction of Psychodynamics, Emotion, and Social Cognition in Conflict

While each of the psychological processes discussed in this chapter has its own particular effects, the three can interact in ways that increase the potential for destructive responses. Staw, Sandelands, and Dutton's (1981) model of the *threat-rigidity cycle* provides a framework that can integrate the impacts of psychodynamics, emotion, and social cognition. The threat-rigidity cycle, which was briefly previewed in Chapter 1, operates as follows:

1. When individuals feel threatened, they experience an increase in psychological stress and anxiety.
2. This in turn fosters emotional reactions such as fear or anger, and physiological arousal.
3. These reactions in turn result in (a) restricted information processing and (b) constriction of behavior.
   a. Restricted information processing occurs because anxiety, physiological arousal, and emotional responses narrow the range of cues individuals can attend to and increase their tendency to react with habitual or automatic responses. Individuals are "flooded" with emotion and anxiety, and the accompanying physiological arousal so occupies them that it impedes their ability to diagnose, to plan, or to respond to the situation in a discriminating manner. Instead, individuals tend to fall back on previous expectations and habitual ways of thinking, such as the attributional tendencies discussed above. Individuals also tend to pay attention to only a few dominant cues and ignore peripheral information that might qualify or contradict the first cues they fasten on.

  b. Anxiety, emotion, and physiological arousal also constrict the range of behavior by creating increased drive to "just do something" about the situation. The result is a "knee-jerk" resort to typical or habitual responses, without consideration of alternative possibilities.
 4. There are two possible routes the cycle can take, once the individual has responded:
  a. If the habitual responses happen to be appropriate for the situation, then results will be positive. This in turn reinforces the tendency to stick with the habit and continue along the same course of action.
  b. If the habitual responses are inappropriate and make the situation worse, then the perception of threat, stress, and anxiety increase, and the cycle starts over again.

The threat-rigidity model, shown in Figure 2.1, portrays the cycling, self-reinforcing nature of behavior driven by threat, and suggests some points at which the psychological factors and processes discussed in this chapter influence and reinforce one another. It also underscores the tendency we have to fall back on habitual responses when confronted with threatening situations. These habits serve as what the important literary and social critic Kenneth Burke has called "trained incapacities," as discussed in Exhibit 2.3.

Here is one way in which the processes and structures discussed in this chapter might figure in the threat-rigidity cycle. The aggressive impulse from psychodynamics, as well as perceived interference with goal attainment, can lead one party to engage in behavior that constitutes a threat. This threat may be exacerbated if the other shows his or her anger. The threat triggers anxiety and emotions such as anger, fear, or hurt and concomitant physiological arousal, which impede the party's processing of information about the situation and tend to generate reflex-like responses. Expectancy violations add to the

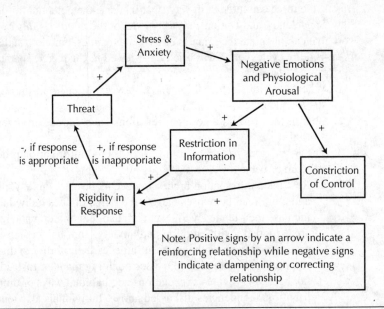

FIGURE 2.1 *The Threat-Rigidity Cycle.*

EXHIBIT 2.3 • *Trained Incapacities and Conflict Interaction*

But, Wally, don't you see that comfort can be dangerous? I mean, you like to be comfortable, and I like to be comfortable, too, but don't you see that comfort can lull you into a dangerous tranquillity? I mean, my mother knew a woman, Lady Hatfield, who was one of the richest women in the world, but she died of starvation because all she would eat was chicken. I mean, she just liked chicken, Wally, and that was all she would eat, and actually her body was starving, but she didn't know it, because she was quite happy eating her chicken, and so she finally died. . . .

Roc used to practice certain exercises, like, for instance, if he were right-handed, all today he would do everything with his left hand. All day—writing, eating, everything—opening doors—in order to break the habits of living, because the great danger for him, he felt, was to fall into a trance, out of habit.

—Wallace Shawn and André Gregory,
My Dinner with André

We often develop habitual interaction strategies to accomplish tasks or solve problems. For example, decision procedures such as voting, leadership styles normally employed in a group, or the practice of frequently joking during meetings to vent the frustrations of work are all examples of working habits. Sometimes habits are formally and consciously adopted, but more often we are not conscious of our habits or their effects.

As noted in the discussion of the threat-rigidity cycle, when confronted with a threatening situation such as conflict, parties often fall back on habits that proved effective in other contexts. However, behaviors effective in some circumstances may actually worsen conflicts. For example, the common practice of openly evaluating ideas or proposals in an attempt to reach a decision can deepen parties' feelings of anger or competition in conflicts, resulting in escalating hostilities. These behaviors hold a

"catch"—because they seem ordinary and have proved useful so often, people may be blinded to the problems they create. The social critic Kenneth Burke (1935) termed this catch a *trained incapacity*. He argued that individuals become so well-trained in their strategies that they begin to serve as blinders. People think they know what to expect, so they ignore signs that something is wrong. The incapacities are particularly pernicious because people may assume they are doing the right thing when actually they are worsening the situation.

Burke offers two simple and somewhat outlandish examples as illustrations of this concept: A chicken can be taught to repeatedly come to a specific place to receive food when it hears a certain pitch of a bell. On one occasion, however, the chicken responds to the bell as it always has by coming to the same place in search of food. This time the chicken finds not food, but the threatening axe of its owner. In Burke's second example, a trout that has had a near miss with a fishhook on its way upstream avoids all food sources that even remotely resemble the color of the bait that nearly caught it. In both cases the animals' past training causes them to misjudge their present situation; their training has incapacitated them.

Certain working habits are adaptive and beneficial in the contexts in which they are learned; however, as conditions change and as conflicts deepen, they become maladaptive, harmful, and irrational. The behaviors are injurious because they shape thinking and perception and, therefore, can prevent recognition of changed circumstances. When this happens, people continue to do "what has always worked," resulting either in no change or in an actual deterioration of the situation.

While some habitual patterns facilitate conflict management; others may immediately seem to improve the situation, but actually cause it to deteriorate over the long run. Patterns can blind people to the negative consequences of their behaviors and prevent them from altering the direction of the conflict when harmful escalation or avoidance cycles begin. Because people cannot recognize that behaviors

(continued)

EXHIBIT 2.3 Continued

that were once beneficial are now counterproductive, they become locked in destructive cycles.

One habit that may become a trained incapacity is our emphasis on achieving goals and planning accordingly. Obviously, having plans or goals serves people well in various ways. Most important, a plan allows for the completion of critical activities and makes it possible to direct and evaluate our actions, because each action can be assessed by determining whether it contributes to successful plan completion.

In conflict situations, one set of goals is the solutions or outcomes parties would like to see adopted. They are the parties' estimates of the best decision or course of action. Entering a discussion with a solution to a problem or conflict in mind is natural and in some respects useful. It is natural because parties often have explicit needs, which they believe can only be met by the adoption of a particular solution. Having a solution in mind can also be useful because it provides clear guidance about the type of communicative behavior parties should engage in during conflict interaction. Each party can argue for the solution he or she wants adopted. If parties start the discussion of an issue by arguing for alternative solutions, the information and arguments in favor of each solution will be aired and points of difference can be clarified. Parties need to hear the pros and cons of suggested solutions to evaluate and choose among them.

Goal-emphasis becomes harmful when it prevents parties from seeing a problem clearly. The experience of a twelve-person food distribution cooperative illustrates this. The members were in conflict over whether to continue publishing the cooperative's newsletter. The conflict was rapidly defined in terms of solutions: either publish the newsletter or discontinue it. The group quickly reached an impasse between these two opposing solutions, and a third-party facilitator was called in. The facilitator turned their attention to the issues behind the conflict; two in particular surfaced. First, a newcomer to the organization was going to succeed to the editorship of the newsletter, and several members doubted that this person could adequately

represent the Coop. A second issue was the need for the Coop to keep in touch with other cooperatives. In the ensuing discussion, members realized that the cooperative could substitute e-mail for the newsletter to keep up with the other cooperatives, and that they could also send out newsbriefs, which any member could submit via an online listserv. So the printed newsletter was discontinued, but its functions were maintained, and all Coop members became "writers" of its news, with the new editor coordinating the stories.

Goal-emphasis becomes an incapacity when (1) it prevents parties from conducting an adequate assessment of the problem underlying the conflict (in other words, when it undercuts the group's attempt to orient itself to the problem), or (2) it becomes a way to quickly make a decision without a complete analysis of the chosen solution (in other words, when it prevents the group from establishing criteria for solutions or examining a solution in light of established criteria). In the case of the newsletter, solutions were debated before the group adequately assessed what functions the newsletter served, what needs prompted its publication, or what the possible consequences of not publishing it were. An examination of these issues gave the members a clearer understanding of the problem they were trying to solve. Once the issues were clarified, criteria for what a good solution might look like emerged.

One way to diagnose the effect of trained incapacities is, therefore, to examine "standard operating procedures" for traps that can provide a set of starting points for a search. Parties can monitor discussions for problems due to goal centeredness, such as insufficient analysis of problems underlying the conflict, or reliance on procedural rules. This monitoring process must go on continuously because people can slip into harmful patterns without recognizing it. Because trained incapacities are "second nature," they are subtle and hard to detect: Parties know something is wrong, but they cannot put their finger on the source. In Chapter 8 we will consider some additional measures that can be taken to counteract trained incapacities and break threat-rigidity cycles.

emotional charge the party feels, which further degrades information processing and encourages unthinking, habitual responses. The party will tend to fall back on the beliefs, scripts, frames, and attributions he or she habitually calls up during conflicts. If these "work," then the party will continue to apply them, rigidifying his or her response. If they do not work and the conflict moves toward spiraling escalation, the cycle starts again with the party feeling threatened, further degradation of information processing, and so on. Even more pressure develops to respond in a rigid, unthinking manner.

If the conflict moves toward avoidance, anxiety and negative emotions tend to decrease, temporarily. This reinforces habitual responses in the future because they seem to have worked. The party may, however, have residual anxiety due to uncertainty as to why the other chose to avoid and whether the conflict will reignite at some point in the future. If the party continues to think about the unpleasant aspects of the conflict, it will add "fuel to the fire" the next time a threat response is triggered.

This negative cycle includes elements of many of the processes and structures that tend to worsen conflicts. What do we do about this? Is this type of cycle inevitable and unstoppable once started? Actually, the different steps in the threat-rigidity cycle are points at which we can break it, if we are aware of their negative effects. For example, we could break the grip of anxiety and negative emotions by reminding ourselves that these are natural feelings under the circumstances, but that the threat might not be as real or substantial as we think it is. We can avoid falling back on habits, if we remind ourselves that we are likely to do so unless we search for additional options or act creatively. Like all human behavioral tendencies, knowing them gives us the power to alter the likely course of events.

2.5 Summary and Review

What is the psychodynamic perspective, and how does it explain conflict?

This perspective began with the work of Freud and has developed in the vibrant field of psychoanalysis. Fundamental is the premise that energy must be managed somehow, either by channeling it directly to the concerns at hand, by redirecting it to a different issue, or by expending energy to suppress the impulse. Two impulses, the aggressive impulse and anxiety, are particularly important in conflicts. Aggression can be handled through directly expressing it, but it may also be suppressed or displaced. Anxiety influences conflict by causing parties to be rigid and inflexible. The psychodynamic perspective is limited by its inability to explain which targets are chosen and how psychic energy is used.

How do emotions influence conflict?

Emotions occur in reaction to events such as conflict that threaten to interrupt, impede, or alternatively enhance our goals. The central constituent of emotional experience is positive or negative affect, and with this come physiological changes and reactions. Cognition plays a role in interpreting and framing our emotions. Specific behavioral tendencies or reactions are associated with emotions. Negative emotions associated with conflict include anger, fear, hurt, and guilt. Positive emotions associated with conflict include hope and energy. Emotion influences conflict through its impact on cognitive processes and through the behavioral tendencies it triggers. For example, anger may encourage us to make negative attributions about others and to engage in verbal attacks or other competitive behavior. Emotional contagion can lead to the spread of similar emotions—negative or positive—among parties.

What role does verbal aggressiveness play in conflict?

Verbal aggressiveness is a predisposition to engage in personalized attacks in response to conflict. It can be contrasted to argumentativeness, the tendency to enjoy the give and take of verbal argument. For obvious reasons, verbal aggressiveness has negative impacts on conflict management and interpersonal relationships. This theory explains conflict behavior in terms of more or less permanent traits, and thus differs from the other explanations, which focus on internal processes or interaction itself.

How does our social knowledge affect conflict interaction?

Several types of social knowledge may influence our interpretations and behavior, including beliefs about conflict, conflict scripts and conflict frames. Beliefs about conflict include assumptions about conflict (e.g., conflict is destructive) and standards about how conflict should be handled (e.g., people should always be civil to one another). These beliefs tend to guide our behavior and also our interpretations of others. Culture has a major influence on beliefs about conflict, because they are commonly learned through interacting with others.

Conflict scripts are expectations about how a conflict will typically unfold (e.g., first Jack will confront Jill, then Jill will apologize, and then Jack will accept the apology). They guide our behavior, because we tend to behave according to the scripts we hold, and they also shape our interpretations of others' behavior and our expectations of what they will do in the conflict.

Conflict frames are cognitive structures that channel our interpretation of conflicts. Six dimensions comprising conflict frames have been identified: instrumentality, other assessment, affect, face, affiliation, and distributiveness. Some of these frames—instrumentality and affiliation—tend to create positive views of a conflict, while others—distributiveness, other assessment, affect, and face—represent negative interpretations of the conflict. Our interpretation of conflicts is reflected by the particular combination of frames we bring to bear on the conflict, and this interpretation, in turn, affects our behavior and shapes our emotional reaction to the conflict.

How do expectancy violations affect our reactions to others?

When someone else's behavior violates our expectations of how others will or should act in a situation, this sparks emotional reactions, and we attempt to understand what the violation means. If the other negatively violates expectancies, then we are likely to experience negative affect and view the violation in negative terms (e.g., as a rebuff or unwarranted aggression toward us). Our particular behavioral response depends on the potential reward value of the other. If the other has the potential to be rewarding to us in the future, the tendency is to compensate for the violation, perhaps by making an excuse or deciding to ignore it. If the other is not likely to be rewarding in the future, the tendency is to reciprocate the negative behavior. So expectancy violations have the potential to trigger conflict.

What is attribution? What tendencies does it encourage?

Attribution is the psychological process in which parties interpret and draw conclusions about others' behavior. It is a fundamental part of all interaction. Through lengthy study of the attribution process, researchers have identified several tendencies. Two that affect conflict are the fundamental attribution error and the self-serving bias.

The fundamental attribution error is a tendency to interpret others' behavior as intentional, but our own behavior as a result of the situation. Hence, parties are likely to interpret others' competitive behavior in conflicts as purposeful, selfish attempts to force others to comply; however, they interpret their own competitive behavior as simply a product of the situation in which they must contend with unreasonable others. This error sets up a situation in which parties are likely to respond to unreasonable and selfish competition with their own competitive moves that simply "respond" to what the other is doing—a dynamic that feeds into escalation cycles. The same process can also lead to cycles of avoidance.

The self-serving bias is a tendency to attribute negative consequences to external situational forces and positive consequences to our own behavior. Hence, parties are likely to conclude that negative experiences during conflicts are the fault of others, whereas the positive outcomes result from what they do. This error sets up a situation where others are faulted for negative feelings and outcomes a party may have, and the party has an incentive to punish others for creating this negative situation.

What impacts does thinking about conflicts have?

People often think about conflicts they expect will occur or ruminate on previous conflicts. The particular way in which people think about conflicts influences whether thinking has positive or negative impacts. Contemplating a conflict and trying to understand it does not seem to have negative effects and may even be beneficial. However, brooding about a conflict, running it over and over in our heads, and focusing on negative aspects of the conflict are likely to have negative effects on future interaction with the other party.

How do psychodynamic processes, emotion, and social cognition interact in conflicts?

Each of these affects the others in numerous ways that may reinforce both negative and positive tendencies. We discussed the threat-rigidity model as one nexus of psychodynamics, emotion, and social cognition.

What are trained incapacities?

People often develop habitual approaches to decision making and problem solving based on what has worked for them in the past. The better these habits work, the more likely people are to stick to them. During conflicts, however, habits that work well in nonconflictive situations can have destructive consequences. The habits become trained incapacities—abilities that blind people to negative consequences—because they assume that their behavior will be beneficial. It is important to be aware of the possibility of trained incapacities and to guard against them.

2.6 Conclusion

The behaviors that constitute conflict interaction originate in psychological processes. Psychodynamic, emotional and social cognitive processes set the stage for conflict, they influence how we understand and interpret conflict, and they motivate and channel how we behave in conflict. An understanding of the psychology of conflict helps us to understand how others see a conflict and how they are likely to react to us.

It is always tempting to assume that if we were just able to be more rational, productive conflict management would be much easier. However, as this chapter shows, emotions and deep-seated drives are part and parcel of all experience. It is simply not possible to separate ourselves from them, to somehow purify ourselves so that we can take a rational approach to conflict. Indeed, it would be harmful to try to do so, because emotion and psychodynamics provide the energy and activation that livens our behavior, and because emotions like sympathy and hope are at the roots of the moral responses that help us to curb our worse tendencies. While they may move conflicts in destructive directions, emotions may also move them down productive paths. A more productive approach is to accept that psychodynamics, emotion, and cognition interact and influence each other, to try to anticipate negative and positive impacts they may have, and to use this knowledge to move conflicts in more productive directions.

While it is important, the inner experience of conflict is not sufficient. It is useful to grasp how individual psychology shapes conflict, but it is even more important to think through how the psychological processes of pairs or groups of parties influence one another. When one party makes a negative attribution toward another, for example, it creates tendencies for the party to act in negative ways toward the other, which encourages the other to make negative attributions, behave negatively toward us, and elicit similar reactions, and so on, in a reinforcing cycle. How others interact with us shapes our emotions and cognitions, and ultimately it is impossible to fully disentangle thinking, feeling, acting, and interacting. The next chapter builds on this one by exploring interaction dynamics that shape conflict.

3

Conflict Interaction

Knowledge of what goes on in parties' heads is useful for understanding conflicts like the Women's Hotline Case (I.1), page 2. It is not the whole story, however. As we argued in Chapter 1, conflicts are constituted in interaction and cannot be reduced solely to psychological terms. From an interactional perspective, conflicts like the Women's Hotline Case emerge from the complex interplay of the parties' behaviors, moves and countermoves.

The interactional perspective assumes that situations are more fluid than fixed, that they evolve as an episode of interaction unfolds. For instance, imagine a common sales encounter in a retail outlet. The service provider approaches the shopper and offers the standard opening: "Hello, may I help you?" As language is a creatively ambiguous code, the customer looks up and says in a highly suggestive tone: "You sure can help me. What are you doing Friday night?" What situation are these people sharing? Are they involved in what is typically called a customer-service encounter? Or is the situation more one of prospective dating? The interactional view suggests that it depends on how the conversation continues to develop. The behavior, not the mental category, will define the situation and, just as important, that definition will change due to subsequent acts.

Consistent with this position, the interactional perspective also embraces the idea of mutual influence. Communication is not so much a product as it is a process that is enacted. As an ongoing process, any given behavior is influenced as much by preceding behaviors as by psychological processes. Concepts of importance to conflict scholars—relationships, power, climate, dominance, and the like—are defined not by a single move or by a single actor but through interaction. In this sense, realities and meanings between people emerge and are negotiated through moves and countermoves during interactions. To be sure, how a particular interaction is accomplished will have an effect on the patterning of future interactions, but the general rule is that what an interaction is about—its purpose and outcomes—are open to continuous negotiation by the participants.

The interactional perspective on conflict emphasizes several questions: What patterns exist in conflict interaction? How do these patterns move the conflict in productive or destructive directions? How do people use messages to accomplish their goals in conflicts? What factors influence how sequences of moves unfold in conflict interaction?

The answers to these questions are not always simple or straightforward. Conflict interaction is quite complex and we do not fully understand how it works. Scholars are making progress, however, and have identified several regularities—common patterns and factors—that can help us understand conflict interaction and guide our actions accordingly. The five sections of this chapter discuss some important regularities in conflict interaction.

The first regularity is represented by stage models of conflict, which give us "the big picture" of how conflicts typically unfold over time. Stage models describe conflicts in terms of key events, specific types of episodes that occur during conflicts, and how one episode leads to another. Stage models are useful because they tell us what to expect during conflicts and suggest things to look for as we move through a conflict.

The next three regularities concern patterns in moves and countermoves in conflict. Section two focuses on interdependence as the fundamental relationship of parties in conflict and on the attitudes and behaviors it fosters. In this section we discuss various types of interdependence, their impact on conflict, and how they are shaped by conflict interaction. Section three explores two critical types of interchanges between interdependent parties, reciprocity and compensation. Reciprocity and compensation are the building blocks of conflicts. They are the source of momentum—for good or ill—in conflicts and the means through which productive changes in the direction of conflicts are enacted. The fourth section shifts our focus to the content of conflicts and explores the framing of issues in conflict interaction. We explore how issues may multiply or narrow as a conflict ensues.

The fifth section of this chapter steps back to consider social identity and intergroup conflict. These bring features of the encompassing social structure such as gender, ethnic, or class differences into the conflict, often to its detriment. We discuss factors that promote the introduction of group differences into a conflict and some ways of responding to them.

Altogether, the five regularities help us understand some important influences on conflict interaction. They do not represent a complete and comprehensive picture, however, because in the end it is simply not possible to fully predict how a conflict will unfold. But they do give us ideas about the dynamics of conflict interaction and suggest some ways in which we might tack in productive directions.

3.1 Stages of Conflict

In Chapter 1 we introduced a normative two-stage model as our reference point for understanding conflict interaction. Other, more elaborate descriptions of the stages of conflicts have also been advanced. These models have been developed based on studies of a wide range of conflicts, including broad societal and international conflicts, conflicts in organizations and small groups, and conflicts in relationships. They describe the emergence and progression of conflicts over the long term and give us important insights into the origins and management of conflict.

3.1.1 Rummel's Five-Stage Model

Based on a study of international conflicts, Rummel (1976) suggested that conflicts pass through five sequential stages:

1. Initially conflict is *latent:* the parties (usually the leaders of the nations involved) hold different dispositions or attitudes that carry the potential for conflict. Differences in values, objectives, and outlooks lay the groundwork for future conflict.
2. During the *initiation stage,* some *triggering event* causes the parties to act. At this point, the potential differences become the basis for conflict.
3. After the conflict has been initiated, the conflict moves into a stage of *open conflict.* In this third stage, parties assess each other's capabilities and willingness to use force, threats, rewards, and sometimes they engage in attack and defense. During this stage the parties confront the issues before them as they try to reach some settlement.
4. The settlement leads to a *balance of power* stage in which the participants come to understand the consequences of the resolution and learn to live with the outcomes. This stage is characterized by the set expectations of individuals and may last for some time until significant changes in circumstances, attitudes, or goals arise.
5. Such evolving changes lead to a *disruption stage* during which parties realize that circumstances are ripe once again for the emergence of potential conflict and eventual confrontation if a new triggering event occurs.

Rummel's model implies a continual cycle—from latency to initiation to balancing power to a balance of power to a disruption, back to a new latency, and so on—until the issue is ultimately resolved, if it ever is.

The first Iraq War in the Middle East can be seen as an example of Rummel's sequence. Saddam Hussein's and U.S. interests in Kuwait had the potential to be in conflict. Saddam wanted the oil resources of Kuwait in order to build a greater Iraq and Iraq had long made territorial claims on Kuwait. The U.S. needed Kuwaiti oil resources as well and had an interest in preserving the pro-Western government of Kuwait. Hence there was a latent conflict. Saddam's invasion was a triggering event that led President Bush to mobilize a multinational effort to pressure Saddam to withdraw. Various types of diplomatic and economic power were used in an effort to get Saddam to pull out of Kuwait. When this failed, a coalition invaded Kuwait and routed Saddam's forces. This led eventually to a new balance of power in which the coalition forces drove Iraq from Kuwait and imposed sanctions on Iraq when it tried to stamp out rebellions by Shiites in southern Iraq and the Kurds in the North. Things settled back into an uneasy peace, full of latent conflict from 1991 to 2001, when another disruption occurred, the attacks on the World Trade Center in New York City on September 11th, 2001.

While this model focuses on international conflict, it can be extended by analogy to other contexts. Conflicts in intimate relationships often follow a similar course. A latent conflict might stir for some time until a triggering event sets it off and the partners confront each other. This confrontation might play out in an open fight that ends in a stalemate, with neither willing to give any ground. The conflict then settles back into latency, but because it really has not been addressed, simmers until the next triggering event occurs.

3.1.2 Pondy's Model

Pondy (1967) articulated a similar five-stage model of the emergence and development of conflict in organizational contexts:

1. Conflict is *latent* when conflicting issues, such as insufficient resources or divergent goals, arise in the organization, but has not yet been recognized by parties.
2. When latent issues reach the awareness of one or more parties, parties are in the *perceived conflict* stage. Pondy also notes that a conflict can be also perceived when no latent conflict exists. This occurs when parties misunderstand each other's positions.
3. Parties then enter a stage of *felt conflict* in which the conflict changes one party's feelings for the other. In this stage the conflict becomes emotionally charged as parties feel anxiety, mistrust, or hostility toward others.
4. *Manifest conflict* occurs when parties act on the perceived and felt differences.
5. Finally, conflict enters an *aftermath stage* in which new relationships and arrangements are formed as a result of how the manifest conflict is handled. During this stage parties assess their outcomes, positive and negative.

3.1.3 Stage Models of Negotiation

Studies of formal negotiations suggest that the negotiation process unfolds in identifiable stages as well (Douglas, 1962; Morley & Stephenson, 1977; Putnam & Jones, 1982b; Putnam, Wilson, Waltman, & Turner, 1986; Holmes, 1992). One ground-breaking study of the interaction in union–management negotiations found that a three-stage framework described conflict development in this context (Morley & Stephenson, 1977):

1. In the first stage, *distributive bargaining,* the parties test the feasibility of possible demands, establish criteria for appropriate settlements, assess the power of each side, and evaluate the strength of each side's case. Here the parties see themselves fulfilling their roles as representatives of a "side" in the negotiations, building planned cases for constituents.
2. In the second stage, *problem-solving,* the parties explore a range of solutions that might satisfy the criteria established at the outset. There is some tactical maneuvering but, by and large, the focus is on establishing a working relationship by proposing and evaluating solutions to identified problems.
3. In the final *decision-making* stage, the parties come to agreement on some terms and explore the implications of their decision. The focus is on reality checking—assessing the feasibility and implementation of terms that both sides support.

As you can see, there is a good deal of similarity among these three models. What do they tell us about conflict?

3.1.4 Insights of Stage Models of Conflict

Stage models are built on an episodic conception of how conflict interaction unfolds. Stages (also called phases by some scholars) are, by definition, periods in which the character of the conflict and conflict interaction is fairly uniform and identifiable. Although somewhat different sequences of episodes are posited for different conflict contexts, the basic premise that conflicts travel through meaningful segments of interaction is common to all of the models. Stage theories offer several important insights about the nature of conflict interaction.

First, stage models suggest that conflicts have a definite pattern or rhythm. The pattern often seems to depend on participants' expectations about likely directions conflicts will take. These expectations are governed by an underlying logic of progressions that conflicts go through and serve to make even apparently confusing interaction understandable over the long run. Looking back and forward simultaneously, parties can see an ambiguous situation of latent conflict growing into a test of power and can anticipate the need to de-escalate the conflict by compromise or at least by backing off. This closely resembles the scripts for conflict discussed in the previous chapter. Conflict scripts are built around stages or steps that conflicts are expected to take, and thus both influence our behavior and help us make sense of how the conflict unfolds.

Stage models imply that an understanding of a conflict comes from taking a broad view of the history of the conflict in terms of the sequence of episodes that the parties have engaged in. Stage models lead to a conception of conflict that includes not only confrontation and discussion of differences between parties, but also intermittent periods of equilibrium and calm when the parties settle into new arrangements resulting from the conflict (Christensen & Pasch, 1993; Putnam, 2005).

A second important implication of stage models is that the same messages, behavior and interaction patterns can serve different functions in different conflict stages. Each stage provides the broader, meaningful context that makes behavior understandable in light of what is going on at any particular conflict stage. Ellis and Fisher (1975) argue, for example, that ambiguous comments occur in both the beginning and ending stages of decision-making conflict in small groups. At the beginning, these comments reflect the ambiguity of indecision; people are unsure about their attitudes and are trying to orient themselves to the issue before the group. In the final stage, however, the ambiguous comments reflect members' moves from one position to another. Members are changing their minds so that agreement can be reached and a group decision can be made. They make ambiguous comments to soften their adherence to previously stated positions without admitting they are wrong. Parties' interpretation of specific acts or interchanges are likely to differ, depending on the stage a conflict is in.

Stage models also suggest that triggering events are particularly important in conflicts. This is not because these events are particularly important in themselves, but because they occur at a critical point in the conflict interaction (Donohue & Kolt, 1992). As a conflict ripens and people feel pressure to face up to the issues, seemingly common and inconsequential events can trigger rapid escalation. A misplaced criticism, teasing, or even a casual reference to a touchy subject can be tinder in a dry forest that soon ignites. While latent differences may influence interaction in subtle and destructive ways, the issues themselves are often hazy or ill-defined until the triggering event brings them out in the open. And how these issues are framed initially influences the subsequent course of the conflict.

Fourth, stage models posit that conflict often includes a testing period before any direct confrontation occurs. This testing period allows parties to reduce their uncertainty about what others will do if they make certain moves. For example, in the face of an impending conflict, one party may want to cooperate but fears being taken advantage of. By making certain subtle cooperative overtures, the party can assess likely responses without taking big risks. By testing the waters, parties gain knowledge of the likely consequences of moves they might make. This knowledge enables parties to develop broad strategies and to choose specific tactics as the conflict unfolds. Stage models suggest that these testing periods can play a critical role in determining the direction conflicts will take.

3.1.5 Multiple Sequences in Conflict

The main weakness in stage models of conflict is that they are often overly simplistic. Critics suggest that research on stages of individual and group processes sometimes overemphasizes the role of a logical step-by-step sequence in the development of conflicts. Poole (1981; Leveque & Poole, 1998), for example, found that the assumption of a set sequence of stages was often not correct for decision-making groups. Instead of a single set of stages applicable to all decisions, studies have found numerous different sequences, depending on how the group chose to attack its problem (Poole & Roth, 1985a; Sambamurthy & Poole, 1992). In a study of forty groups, Sambamurthy and Poole (1992) found four general patterns of response to differences:

1. The first pattern was characterized by low confrontation on conflict issues. Instead of confronting, the group spent most of its time in stages of cooperative, *focused work* broken by *integration* periods consisting of tangential discussions or joking. Conflicts simply never surfaced in this first pattern.
2. A second pattern was characterized by periods of focused work alternating with stages of *critical work* in which members raised alternative points of view but did not openly acknowledge opposition. In critical work periods, differences were aired in a low-key manner. This often proved to be an effective method of working out differences between members. In some instances, groups passed through three or four cycles of focused work stages, alternating with stages of critical work.
3. Neither of the first two patterns confronted conflict directly. A third pattern consisted of stages of focused work and critical work followed by a stage of *open opposition,* in which the conflict surfaced. Once opposition was expressed, members resolved the conflict either by dropping the subject and reentering a period of focused work or by one party giving in to the other. The first method of resolving the opposition corresponds to conflict avoidance, whereas the second method corresponds to a win–lose conflict resolution.
4. A final pattern had stages of focused and critical work followed by opposition. In this case, however, the opposition was resolved by *problem-solving* or *compromising.* This final pattern corresponds to the entire differentiation–integration sequence discussed in Chapter 1. Sambamurthy and Poole found that this fourth sequence resulted in better outcomes for their groups than did the first three sequences, consistent with predictions in the differentiation–integration model.

3.1.6 Final Thoughts About Stage Models of Conflict

Stage models highlight the ways in which parties' behaviors tend to perpetuate conflict cycles and illustrate how conflicts develop a momentum that leads interaction in constructive or destructive directions. This does not, however, mean that conflicts must inevitably follow the stages in these models. After all, the parties create stages through their interactions, and thus they may change direction. Parties may act in accordance with the episodic structure of the conflict they perceive *or* they may consciously choose to change the direction of the conflict. Chapter 8 discusses some general approaches to doing this.

Stage models of conflict depict how a conflict unfolds over the longer term. They give us the "big picture" of a conflict. But stages are generated through specific actions that the parties take. They are large-scale patterns that are made up of particular acts and responses that occur in immediate conflict interaction. What patterns does immediate conflict interaction exhibit and what factors shape it? One of the most important factors shaping conflict behavior is the interdependence among the parties.

EXHIBIT 3.1 • *Charting a Conflict*

It is sometimes helpful to chart the stages of a conflict. Think of a conflict you were involved in and, using one of the stage models, write the "history" of this conflict as a series of stages. If this is an ongoing conflict, what stage are you currently in, and what is likely to be the next stage? Looking at your history, what might you have done to change the direction of the conflict in a more productive direction?

CASE 3.1 • *Stage Models and the Parking Lot Scuffle*

The Parking Lot Scuffle exhibits clear stage structure. In terms of Rummel's model, there was no latent stage in this conflict. Because Tim and Jay did not meet each other until the accident, there was no incipient conflict. The triggering incident was the accident itself, which precipitated the interaction that led to the conflict. The discussion up to and through the scuffle was a balancing of power between Jay and Tim. They tested each other's positions and resolved and ultimately balanced power through physical violence. The end of the scuffle found the conflict in an unresolved state because issues, such as who will pay for the damage and whether Tim and Jay can work out a shared interpretation of the situation, were undetermined. At the end of the scuffle, the conflict subsided, but it may break out again later on when Jay and Tim must discuss the accident, responsibilities, and liabilities. A new triggering incident may start another cycle of power balancing, and the conflict probably will continue until the parties attain a settlement that both accept.

In terms of Pondy's model, Tim and Jay passed through the perceived and felt conflict stages very quickly and moved right into the manifest conflict stage. During this stage, they engaged primarily in distributive behavior and emerged into the aftermath stage following the scuffle. Their assessments of the episode are likely to be quite negative, which could create latent conflict in future encounters. They are likely to quickly go through the perceived and felt conflict stages when they meet, precipitating a manifest conflict once again.

Discussion Question

What does the stage model suggest Jay and/or Tim could do to break the cycle of conflict apparent in this case?

3.2 Interdependence

Interdependence is a central feature of our definition of conflict. In his groundbreaking work, Morton Deutsch (1973) noted that "the processes of conflict resolution that are likely to be displayed will be strongly influenced by the context within which the conflict occurs" (p. 10). Deutsch argued that the critical contextual feature of conflict situations—the one that makes the difference between cooperative resolution and potentially destructive competition—is the type of *interdependence* established between the parties.

Deutsch defined two basic types of interdependence: (1) *promotive,* wherein the persons involved in the conflict perceive that gains by either one will promote gains by the other, while losses will promote losses; and (2) *contrient,* wherein everyone perceives that one's gain will be the other's loss. Perceptions of promotive interdependence, Deutsch argued, tend to promote cooperative interaction, whereas perceptions of contrient interdependence tend to produce competition. Based on the work of White and Lippitt (1968), we would add a third type of interdependence, (3) *individualistic,* wherein members do not believe they are dependent on each other at all. It is characterized by a lack of common motives, autonomous behavior, rather indifferent attitudes toward others, and preoccupation with one's own affairs.

Deutsch identified several effects of promotive and contrient interdependence. When parties perceive promotive interdependence, they tend to stress mutual interests and coordinated division of labor, exhibit trusting and friendly attitudes, perceive similarity in their beliefs and goals, and communicate more openly and honestly. When parties perceive contrient interdependence, they tend focus on antagonistic interests and on constraining each other, exhibit suspicious and hostile attitudes, overemphasize differences, and communicate in a misleading and restrained manner. Studies by Deutsch and later researchers showed that eventually these consequences feed back to influence interaction, thereby strengthening the dominant tendency in the conflict: "cooperation breeds cooperation, while competition breeds competition" (Deutsch, 1973, p. 367).

The self-reinforcing cycle between perceptions of interdependence and conflict behavior creates an overarching *climate,* a shared sense of the situation that shapes how parties calculate their moves and interpret those of others. This climate shapes parties' assumptions about common interests and their perceptions of similarity or difference in their positions. It breeds friendly or hostile attitudes toward each other and affects their level of trust. This in turn, influences their communication, which further reinforces the climate, and so on.

This cycle is common in groups and organizations. For example, a manager and an employee with a bad work record are likely to enter a performance appraisal interview with the expectation that it will be an unpleasant, competitive situation wherein the boss rebukes the employee and the employee tries to evade responsibility. This contrient, suspicious climate leads both to interact mistrustfully and competitively to "protect" themselves. This reinforces the climate, which reinforces the interaction and so on, in a negative spiral. Similar positive spirals also work for promotive, trusting climates. Climate and its role in conflict will be discussed in more detail in Chapter 7.

One limitation of Deutsch's analysis is that it considers interdependence in either/or terms. Deutsch assumes that parties are *either* promotively interdependent *or* contriently interdependent (*or*, we might add, individualistic). In the Introduction, however, we noted that most conflicts involve mixed motive situations. That is, parties are interdependent so that some aspects of their relationships are potentially promotive and motivate them to cooperate, while other aspects are potentially contrient and motivate them to compete. Still other aspects of their relationships are individualistic. This presents us with a dilemma as we try to understand the effects on interdependence. How do we determine whether, on balance, a situation is promotive, contrient, or interdependent?

The solution to the dilemma lies in Deutsch's insistence that it is not *actual* interdependence but *perceived* interdependence that guides conflict behavior. Deutsch originally discovered the impact of interdependence through experiments in which he directly manipulated the interdependence of the parties. But he also realized that it was parties' perception of interdependence that made the difference, and that this would be the key in situations in which interdependence was not as clear as it was in the lab—that is, in the real world (See Case 3.2).

As conflicts unfold, parties look for cues to help them understand their interdependence. Probably the most important cues come from the communication and behavior of the other party. If Jack makes a move that seems aggressive and selfish to Jill, she is likely to decide that they are contriently interdependent (though of course she may not use that term). Contextual cues are also important. If we are meeting across the table from the other party, contrient interdependence and competition is implied by the spatial arrangement; if, on the other hand, we are sitting in two arm chairs at slight angles to each other, research suggests that this more likely to cue promotive interdependence (Burgoon, 2003). Also important are past experiences with the party, beliefs about conflict, conflict scripts, and other emotional and cognitive elements discussed in Chapter 2. Based on these cues, parties make judgments about their interdependence.

From this it follows that perceived interdependence may change over the course of the conflict. If, after some sharp interchanges, Jack apologizes to Jill and expresses his desire to reach a mutually acceptable agreement, Jill's perceptions of interdependence may change. She may adopt a "wait and see" attitude and search for cues that strengthen the case for promotive interdependence in Jack's future behavior. Perceived interdependence is shaped by interactions among the parties.

This does not mean that interdependence is solely a matter of perception. A married couple is interdependent in many ways, and these actual interdependencies produce many of the cues that shape their perceived interdependence. However, perceptions of interdependence—which focus attention on some interdependencies at the expense of others—act as a filter for actual interdependence.

Another limitation of Deutsch's argument is that it assumes both parties perceive the situation in the same way. That is, he assumes that if one perceives it as contrient, the other does too; if one sees the situation as promotive, the other also sees it that way. Parties' perceptions do often match. However, this does not have to be case. People often interpret the same thing differently. What might account for this divergence? The answer to this question can be found in tendencies toward reciprocity and compensation in human interaction.

CASE 3.2 • *Interdependence and the Parking Lot Scuffle*

At the beginning of the parking lot scuffle, Jay was very uncertain about the situation. He had not expected the moped to be in his parking place, and he jumped out of his car, trying to make sense of what had happened. When Tim registered his hostile comments, Jay perceived the situation as characterized by contrient interdependence. Jay attempted to bully his way through this barrier, probably because he interpreted Tim's remarks as indicating that Jay would be seen as a weakling if he gave in to Tim's attacks.

Tim's perception of the situation as contrient was triggered the moment Jay smashed into his scooter. He believed that Jay was at fault, but probably assumed that Jay would try to wriggle out of his responsibility. So Tim went right after Jay, seeking to force him to make restitution. As the interaction progressed, Jay seemed a greater and greater barrier to Tim, and Tim continued to apply pressure, which ended in the scuffle.

The climate in this case was competitive and threatening for both Jay and Tim. Tim immediately felt threatened because of the damage to his personal property—even more so because vehicles are often an important part of our personal identity in modern U.S. culture. He adopted a competitive approach that created a sense of threat and defensiveness in Jay's life-space. Jay responded with a competitive move by line 8, which further reinforced Tim's tendencies to compete.

Discussion Questions

- What factors created the perception of contrient interdependence between Tim and Jay?
- What common ground did Tim and Jay have, if any? Can a case be made that there was promotive interdependence in this situation?
- Is interdependence more reality-based or perceptually-based in this case?

3.3 Reciprocity and Compensation

Conversations unfold as each person takes a turn talking. With each turn the person makes a "move"—performs a behavior that has strategic significance. Any particular interaction is created through a particular sequence of moves as each participant takes a turn in response to the other's turn. Each move influences the next move, which in turn influences the following move, and so on, a phenomenon known as *mutual influence*.

Perhaps the strongest feature of mutual influence is the norm of *reciprocity*. According to several theorists, reciprocity undergirds all social exchange processes (Roloff & Campion, 1985). Gouldner (1960) suggests that the norm prescribes two things: "people should help those who have helped them, and people should not injure those who have helped them." As Roloff (1987b, p. 12) puts it, "a recipient of a benefit is morally obligated to return a benefit in kind."

Behavioral reciprocity is defined as the process of adaptation in which one party responds in a similar direction to another party's behaviors with behaviors of comparable functional value (Caughlin & Vangelisti, 2006; Burgoon, Dillman, & Stern 1991; Street & Cappella, 1985). The key to reciprocity is function. Because the same behavior may serve different purposes, reciprocity is more complex than simple imitation. For example, a joke may serve to reduce anxiety, establish rapport, or point out an imperfection in a non-threatening way. If party A tells a joke to defuse tensions, party B is said to have reciprocated if she engages in a behavior that also serves that function, such as laughing at the joke; party B need not tell a joke to reciprocate.

Compensation, sometimes also called accommodation (a term we reserve for a conflict style discussed in Chapter 4), is the corresponding process of behavioral adaptation in which one responds to a partner's behaviors with opposite behaviors of comparable functional value. For example, if one party attacks another, the second party would be compensating if he or she inhibits impulses to reacting negatively and instead engages in positive behavior toward the other.

Suppose party A initially makes dominant gestures and remarks in a conflict situation, while party B initiates equalizing messages. If A then reduces his or her dominance in response to B, this would be reciprocity. The same would be true if B increases dominance in response to A. By contrast, if B became submissive in response to the dominance of A, this would represent compensation.

Conflict interaction is often driven by reciprocity. In 1957 Leary described what he termed an "interpersonal reflex" to respond to hostile behavior with hostile behavior, leading to emotional escalation of conflicts. Burgoon et al. (1995) found that a predominant tendency in interpersonal interaction is to reciprocate negative behavior. In interpersonal relationships, complaints, defensiveness, and expressions of negative affect are often responded to in kind (Messman & Canary, 1998). Vuchinich (1984; 1990) analyzed conflict interchanges in fifty-two different families and found strong evidence of a symmetrical matching of conversational behaviors, particularly those expressing opposition. He found that the best determinant of any given move was the immediately preceding turn. Studies of children's conflicts suggest that an opposition move made by one child is likely to elicit a sequence of oppositional moves (Eisenberg & Garvey, 1981; Goodwin, 1982). Negative reciprocity has also been found in labor–management conflicts (Carnevale, 1986).

On a more positive note, Putnam and Jones (1982a, 1982b) found that bargainers generally engage in an attack–defend style of conflict, but uphold the norm of positive reciprocity when cooperative gestures are offered. They found that concessions offered in bargaining situations are frequently followed in kind. Gaelick, Bodenhausen and Wyer (1984) also found that positive behaviors and emotions were likely to be reciprocated in conflict interactions.

Escalation and de-escalation of conflicts are often a result of reciprocity. Each move, positive or negative, has the potential to establish a new, self-reinforcing sequence by initiating reciprocal responses. Mikolic, Parker and Pruitt (1997) summarized an impressive amount of evidence that aggressiveness and negative behavior in conflicts tends to escalate in a self-reinforcing pattern. Their study of responses to persistent annoying behavior in interpersonal conflicts found an escalating sequence of responses, starting with requests for compliance, followed by impatient demands, complaints, angry statements, threats, and abuse and physical aggression. Markey, Funder and Ozer (2003) also found that the more intense the interaction, the stronger the tendency toward reciprocity.

Positive moves are also likely to be reciprocated and move the conflict in more productive directions. In both intimate and labor–management contexts, cycles of positive responses, such as supportive statements and agreements, have also been found to occur, usually when the conflict has taken a fundamental turn toward a constructive direction (Donohue, Diez, & Hamilton, 1984; Gaelick et al., 1985). Indeed competent behavior in conflicts is in part defined as the ability to appropriately engage in actions that move the conflict in positive directions (See Exhibit 3.2).

EXHIBIT 3.2 • *Can Conflict Competence be Assessed?*

Some conflict theorists have offered ways of assessing whether the behavior people engage in during conflict can be judged as competent. This is an important question because it leads us to consider the major factors which influence people's perceptions of the behavioral choices people make when they address conflict in any situation. When do we see someone as acting admirably in conflict? When do we believe that someone has stepped over a line in reacting to an issue or is unable to manage the complexity of difficult conflicts as they arise? Cupach and Canary (1997) have offered a framework for thinking about how conflict behavior can be assessed—the conditions under which behavioral choices are viewed as competent or incompetent in dealing with conflict.

There are two broad criteria along which conflict behavior can be assessed: *effectiveness* of the behavior and *appropriateness* of the behavior.

- *Effectiveness:* conflict behaviors can be judged according to the impact or results they attain. Key questions to consider about the effectiveness of the conflict behavior include:
  - Do the conflict behaviors accomplish the desired goals of the person who enacts them?
  - Do the behaviors show an awareness of and address a range of goals simultaneously?
    - Instrumental Goals: the tangible outcomes or resources someone is pursuing in the conflict
    - Self-Presentation Goals: the personal image someone wants to preserve during and after the conflict
    - Relational Goals: the relationship status someone wants to preserve with those with whom he/she is in conflict

  - Do the behaviors address goals that the person believes are significant or important? Is the person making good choices about which behaviors are appropriate to pursue various goals?
- *Appropriateness:* conflict behaviors can also be judged as to whether they align with the norms and expectations for how people should deal with conflict
  - How are the conflict behaviors judged within a community, organization, or relationship in which they are enacted?
  - Do the behaviors violate ethical norms of the group of people who observe or are affected by the conflict?
  - Do the conflict behaviors transgress a community's consensus about what behaviors are justifiable, appropriate, or socially acceptable?

In assessing the conflict competency of behaviors, both of the above criteria come into play simultaneously. Behaviors that are effective may not be seen as appropriate (as, for example, when violent behavior is used in an attempt to change the behavior of a spouse in a marriage). On the other hand, behaviors that are seen as appropriate may not be effective in reaching personal goals (as, for example, when monetary rewards are promised to employees for changing their work behaviors, but the rewards have no effect on employee performance).

There are three factors that are known to influence whether someone is likely to engage in conflict behaviors that are seen as competent by the above criteria:

- *Knowledge:* Does the person have adequate knowledge about such factors as: what motivates people; what public and private rules

(continued)

EXHIBIT 3.2 Continued

exist that shape expectations about the acceptability of behaviors; when it is important to balance relational and instrumental goals?

- *Motivation:* Does the person have the desire or will to try to act effectively and appropriately? If people believe that they cannot balance effectiveness and appropriateness when they are in conflict, they sometimes lose motivation to try to sustain this balance when choosing conflict behaviors. They act to pursue goals without concern for appropriateness.

- *Skill:* Does the person have the communicative skill to enact behaviors that can simultaneously attain effectiveness and appropriateness? Balancing multiple goals and staying within acceptable norms of behavior is often challenging for people in stressful or difficult conflict situations. Competence takes a level of communicative skill that eludes some people, especially when they are engaged in vital conflicts that affect their futures or personal security.

Rigidity of the type described in Chapter 2 also contributes to negative reciprocity. Studies comparing distressed and nondistressed intimate couples, for example, have found differences in how repetitive the communication patterns are for these couples (Gottman, 1979; Ting-Toomey, 1983). Couples in the more distressed conflict relationships tend to interact in highly structured ways—their interaction tends to be built on more repetitive cycles and exchanges. This repetition is symptomatic of self-perpetuating interaction in which one party's move elicits a highly predictable response that in turn produces a predictable counter-response. In addition, these studies reveal the nature of these repetitive cycles. In distressed intimate couples, parties tend to exchange hostile and confrontive remarks so that common exchanges include one person complaining or confronting while the other defends (Ting-Toomey, 1983; Gaelick, Bodenhausen, & Wyer, 1985).

Negative reciprocity can also extend across conflict episodes. One common pattern in intimate relationships is the "demand/withdraw pattern" (Caughlin & Vangelisti, 2006; Roloff & Soule, 2002). In this pattern one partner confronts the other with complaints, criticisms, and demands, and the other withdraws, sometimes becoming defensive and sometimes passive. This pattern may extend through a number of episodes, becoming a sort of relational habit. At first glance, this pattern may seem to be accommodative, but scholars have concluded it amounts functionally to negative reciprocity in which neither partner gets what they want and the relationship deteriorates. Evidence suggests that the confrontational partner is more likely to be female and the withdrawing party is more likely to be male (Roloff & Soule, 2002). However, when the issue is important to them, there is evidence that males are equally likely to take the role of confronter as females are. While the confronter seems to be the one who initiates demand-withdraw, it really depends on where one draws the line. In a sequence of interchanges characterized by demand-withdraw-demand-withdraw-demand-withdraw, the demander is the initiator if we start at the first move, but if we happened onto the conflict in the fourth move, the withdrawer is most likely to be labeled the initiator. There is, indeed, reason to believe that withdrawing may sometimes spark demands (Roberts & Krokoff, 1990; Watzlawick, Bevin, & Jackson, 1967). Demand-withdraw, like all reciprocal patterns, is a system in which it is impossible to single out one or the other party as responsible.

As we might expect, negative exchanges sparked by reciprocity are associated with dissatisfaction with relationships (Caughlin & Vangelisti, 2006). For example, Gottman (1979; 1994) observed that in distressed relationships wives often match their husbands' initial moves and engage in one-upmanship, creating a highly charged and bitter interaction (See Case 3.3).

Compensation also plays an important role in conflicts. A compensating response to a negative act can break a destructive cycle and turn the conflict in more positive directions. Lukasik (2001) found evidence that adolescents who were deeply hurt by their friends during conflicts were likely to forgive their friend. In his study of family conflicts, Vuchinich (1987) found that about one-third of the attacks observed in family arguments was either ignored or given in to. Studies of satisfied couples indicate that parties often respond to negative acts like complaints by ignoring them, focusing on the nature of the complaint, and making positive statements to the other party (Roloff & Soule, 2002). In Chapter 8 we will discuss ways in which conflicts can be rerouted from destructive paths, and several of these involve compensation as a first step.

High levels of negative emotions make it difficult for parties to accommodate negative behavior (Rusbult, Drigotas, & Verette, 1994). To overcome the temptation to reciprocate negative behavior, optimism and a conviction that the conflict can be resolved are important. Johnson and Roloff (1998) found that the more optimistic parties were about the resolvability of an interpersonal conflict, the more likely they were to make positive statements and affirm their relationship with the other party. The accompanying Exhibit 3.3 discusses "Tit-for-Tat," a conflict management strategy that combines reciprocity and compensation to move a conflict in a positive direction.

CASE 3.3 • *Reciprocity and Compensation in the Parking Lot Scuffle*

Tim believed Jay was at fault for running into his scooter and expected Jay to pay for the damage. This type of behavioral and financial compensation is, of course, the norm in the U.S. when someone has been injured. However, Jay did not see the situation this way. He believed that it was Tim's fault for parking his scooter where it did not belong and so was not willing to engage in compensatory behavior.

Instead, Jay responded to Tim with questions and statements that were not exactly reciprocating Tim's challenges, but were clearly not compensating them. By turn 8 Jay is clearly reciprocating Tim's competitive behavior and the two are locked in a cycle of reciprocation that rapidly escalates the conflict, culminating in blows.

Discussion Questions

- Could Jay have compensated for Tim's aggressive behavior in a way that did not involve admitting fault or giving in to Tim's demands?
- Why do escalating cycles of competitive and aggressive behavior achieve the momentum that they often do?

EXHIBIT 3.3 • *The Tit-for-Tat Strategy*

A good example of judicious mixing of reciprocity and compensation is the *Tit-for-Tat* strategy. This strategy relies on tendencies to reciprocity in conflict interaction. To carry out this strategy you should initially match the moves of the other party. If the other party makes a competitive or hostile move, so should you; if the other party makes a cooperative or conciliatory move, so should you. This should go on for a few exchanges so that the other knows you are willing to respond in kind. If the moves you exchange are primarily cooperative, then Tit-for-Tat will tend to create a "virtuous circle" in which cooperation begets cooperation and an open, trusting climate develops. If the moves are primarily competitive, then you should switch to a cooperative move and repeat it several times, even if the other remains competitive. This gives the other a chance to reciprocate your cooperative approach and can switch the "vicious circle" of competition to cooperation.

Tit-for-Tat seems to work according to the following logic (Apfelbaum, 1974; Axelrod, 1984): By matching, you are demonstrating to the other that you will be responsive to his or her actions and therefore that you could be persuaded to cooperate, if he or she switches to cooperative moves. This encourages the other to exercise any impulses she or he may have to cooperate, to see if the partner can be induced to respond. If the other continues to compete, then when you switch to a cooperative move for a little while, you can check whether the other has interests in cooperation. If this "experiment" succeeds, then you have moved the conflict in a productive direction; if it fails, then you at least know that you tried and can then begin to think of other approaches.

Axelrod's (1984) research demonstrated that simple matching could generate cooperative behavior under a wide range of circumstances. Most striking, Axelrod's studies show that matching can induce even extremely competitive parties to cooperate. Axelrod cites four properties of matching tactics that tend to make the technique successful in inducing cooperation (1984, p. 20):

> avoidance of unnecessary conflict by cooperating as long as the other player does, provocability in the face of an uncalled for defection by the other, forgiveness after responding to a provocation, and clarity of behavior so that the other player can adapt to your pattern of action.

Axelrod's studies show that Tit-for-Tat can foster cooperation in large groups, even entire societies, provided that small clusters of individuals base their cooperation on matching and that they interact regularly. Once established on this basis, cooperation based on matching forms a very powerful pattern that persists even if others adopt competing tactics.

There is also evidence that if one party is slow to reciprocate cooperative behavior, the other is more likely to remain cooperative (Apfelbaum, 1974). Apparently, reluctant cooperation suggests conscious or deliberate intention and thereby implies a stronger commitment to cooperation.

We now turn to another important interaction process, issue framing. Just as reciprocity and compensation are shaped by, and in turn, contribute to emotion and social cognition in conflicts, interactional framing is influenced by and shapes psychological framing processes, in a self-reinforcing cycle.

3.4 Framing Issues in Conflict Interaction

In Chapter 2 we discussed the psychological processes of framing conflicts. The ways in which conflicts are framed is also influenced by conflict interaction. As parties interact, they give each other cues that may trigger certain types of frames. For example, if Sue condemns

Martin's behavior as unethical, Martin is likely to frame the conflict in terms of face-saving issues rather than taking an instrumental approach to the conflict. In this case Sue's move has cued the central issue Martin is likely to focus on as the conflict unfolds. If Sue suddenly shifts to a more compensating approach by stating, "I'm sorry, I was jumping to conclusions. Let's start over. Can you explain to me why you hired your nephew over the holidays?", Martin may shift his definition of the conflict to more instrumental and affiliative terms.

As the example illustrates, how a conflict is framed is influenced by the interaction among parties, and frames may shift as the conflict progresses (Keck & Samp, 2007). We know surprisingly little about this important phenomenon, but research on communication in negotiation offers some clues.

Research by Putnam and her colleagues (Putnam, 1990; Putnam et al., 1986; Putnam & Holmer, 1992) provides detailed evidence about framing in conflict interaction. They found that negotiators can differ in how they develop an argument about an issue on the table (Putnam et al., 1986; Putnam, 1990). One side in the negotiations might approach an issue by arguing about the harms of a current situation and how a particular proposal will address those harms. The other side might approach the same issue by attacking the possible benefits of a proposal. Of particular interest, they found that when parties start with different argument frames, the negotiations may be more likely to lead to creative problem-solving rather than compromising or trade-offs. It appears that when issues are argued from different frames, the parties develop their cases more fully and tend to search for more alternatives. It is not, then, that one frame wins, but that frames are altered and new frames are constructed by parties conjointly; frames on the issues emerge and develop in the interaction (Putnam & Holmer, 1992).

Putnam (1990) describes a pivotal interaction sequence in a contract negotiation between teachers and school administrators wherein the framing of interaction was central in determining the outcome. After considerable negotiation, the representatives for the teachers made several somewhat ambiguous comments about an offer on the table. Some administrators interpreted the comments to mean that the teachers might renege on an earlier concession. This was one possible frame for how the interaction was about to unfold, and was likely to prompt threats and accusations from the administrators, leading to destructive escalation. However, some of the administrators framed the teachers' comments differently; they heard the same comments but thought they were an inadvertent error or oversight on the teachers' part. Ultimately, the spokesperson for the administrators cast the moves as an error rather than strategic reneging. This allowed the teachers to correct the problem gracefully. (From all indications, the teachers *had* made an inadvertent error.) The teachers' move was framed in such a way that it encouraged the negotiations to proceed in a sequence of cooperative rather than competitive, escalating moves.

Reframing is not always mutual. One side in negotiations can reframe an issue and thereby influence the negotiation process as well (Brown, 1983). The decision to support a strike as a tactic in a labor–management dispute is often a troublesome and potentially divisive issue for workers. How striking is framed by the workers—what it means to them to strike—can have a powerful influence on whether the tactic is supported. Striking can be seen as "getting revenge" or striking can be seen as "principled behavior" (Donnellon, Gray, & Bougon, 1986). Reframing the meaning of striking during the process can influence the degree of support for adopting the tactic.

There is, then, a "dance" of framing in which each party advances its own interpretations of the issues and acts on them, the other party responds, and the parties move toward development of a shared frame, on the one hand, or toward divergent framings, on the other. When parties eventually converge on a shared framing, there is greater possibility for working together toward an integrative solution than if parties remain in their own worlds and operate out of different frames (See Case 3.4 on page 90).

Reframing of issues and problems is unavoidable as the parties discuss them. In many instances, people frame and reframe issues without fully realizing it. Reframing can redirect conflict interaction in either constructive or destructive directions. If parties want to control conflict interaction and direct it constructively, they need to be able to reframe issues and problems so that a wide array of alternative solutions can be considered.

Several moves that may influence framing of conflict issues have been identified. *Umbrellas* are issues one party introduces to legitimize grievances when the original issue is one that others would not normally accept as valid (Walton, 1969). For example, David may be angry at Brian because Brian received a promotion to a position David wanted. For David to express anger toward Brian because of Brian's promotion would seem petty. However, if Brian persistently comes to meetings late, David can legitimately chide him for that. David can then transfer his anger related to the promotion into an attack on Brian for always being late. The lateness issue serves as an umbrella for the anger generated by the real issue. People often do this in everyday conflicts: They are angry at someone and use the first legitimate issue that arises as an excuse to vent anger.

In *issue expansion* extra issues are attached to the conflict in order to increase the apparent distance between the parties' positions (Walton, 1969). As more and more issues are added, people see their interests as more and more incompatible. For example, assume David has lashed out at Brian for Brian's lateness. Brian could respond with a remark, such as "Well, you're not perfect yourself—your reports are always late!" David might then comment on Brian's sloppiness and Brian on David's jealousy, and so on, as the conflict develops into a real "everything but the kitchen sink" fight. In legal arenas, disputes may also be broadened by adding issues (Mather & Yngvesson, 1980–1981; Menkel-Meadow, 1985). For example, a dispute between a doctor and patient may be broadened into a complaint of discrimination against an entire group of people. In such instances, a single conflict is used as a test case for addressing a much broader social injustice or for protecting a group's rights.

Issue expansion may allow parties to save face by shifting attention to others' shortcomings, and enable them to point out that others share the responsibility for the conflict. However, issue expansion also can accelerate the conflict and create a perception that it is hopeless to try to work out a reasonable resolution because there are just too many issues to untangle.

Some moves redefine issues in ways that narrow and refocus the conflict. *Negative inquiry* involves asking the other party what he or she means by ambiguous statements in order to pin down the issues (Wilmot & Wilmot, 1978). The simple process of questioning can often encourage people to think through vague and judgmental statements and to reduce them to more objective terms that specify their needs. For example, in response to negative inquiry, the statement "You are sloppy" may change to "I want you to stop leaving the car such a mess."

Fogging also focuses issues but is more manipulative than negative inquiry (Wilmot & Wilmot, 1978). On hearing another's complaint, the party acknowledges only part of it, thus narrowing the "live" issues to those one party is ready or willing to address. For example, A might say to B, "This car is a mess. You are so sloppy!" B then fogs by replying, "It is a mess. I'm so sorry," shunting the sloppiness issue aside. Fogging focuses the issues, which may be useful for problem-solving and compromising. It can also be used in an avoiding style.

Fractionation (Fisher, 1964) can be used to promote integration. Fractionation involves breaking a complex conflict into component issues that can be dealt with singly or in sequence. In effect, it counteracts the complexity introduced by umbrellas and issue

CASE 3.4 • *Issue Framing and the Parking Lot Scuffle*

In turn 1 Tim framed the conflict by raising the issue of Jay's fault in the damage done to his bike. If Jay had gone along with this framing, the conflict would have taken a very different turn, with Jay possibly apologizing and agreeing to pay for the damage. Instead Jay offered a "counter-frame" by placing the blame on Tim.

The two frames are developed independently of one another in turns 1 through 7. Notice that Tim was pressing a case consistent with his framing, while Jay was responding with questions and statements that develop his own framing. In a real sense, Tim and Jay were talking past each other, because each has framed the conflict differently. There was a lack of engagement of the other party's issues by both Jay and Tim. The first engagement occured in turns 8 and 9. In turn 9, Tim challenged the implicit assumption in turns 2 and 8 that Jay's parking space is his territory and that Tim had trespassed, instead insisting on being compensated. Tim tried to establish the issue as damage to his bike, not whether Tim had any right to park in the space in the first place.

Jay's response in turn 10, asking Tim if he worked in the building, suggested that he is still focusing on the "rights" issue. If Tim did not work in the building, he certainly had no right to be in a parking space reserved for employees. Jay's response that Tim "has a problem," also attempted to turn Tim's accusation back on him. By charging that Tim is acting irrationally, Jay expanded the range of issues in the conflict. Adding the issue of Tim's problematic attitude, of course, was only likely to make Tim more angry and adamant.

Tim's response in turn 11 reasserted fault for the damage as the primary issue. Jay then tried to walk away. Not being willing to buy in to Tim's definition of the issues, Jay probably believed further talk was counterproductive. It is also possible that he was beginning to be fearful of Tim's "problem." Sometimes the issues we introduce reflect our fears as much as our thought about the situation, and Jay's statement at the beginning of turn 10 may have been stimulated by unease with Tim, rather than an attempt to "one up" Tim.

This case represents an abortive attempt at issue framing. Tim and Jay were never able to converge on a common issue or issues during their conversation. Their ability to confront the conflict and come to a resolution was hampered by this lack of common grounding.

Discussion Questions

- Can you think of other conflicts you have been in when you and the other party "talked past" each other by advancing different issues?
- Could issue framing have been done in a more productive way in this conflict? If you were in this conflict, how could you use framing to move the conflict in a more productive direction?

expansion by identifying specific, individual issues. Fractionation can be useful in setting an agenda for dealing with the conflict.

A good way to follow the progress of a conflict is to pay attention to the shifting patterns of issues. The redefinition, expansion, and narrowing of issues determine what parties work on and how the conflict ultimately turns out.

Microlevel interaction processes such as reciprocity, compensation, and framing are often discussed as though they occurred in a vacuum. It is important to consider the social context of conflict as well. The negotiators studied by Putnam and her colleagues were not just individuals, they were identified with union and management roles. These roles and the expectations that come with them were also an important part of the framing process. To understand the influence of social context on conflict interaction, we now turn to research on social identity, intergroup relations, and their impacts on conflict.

3.5 Social Identity and Intergroup Conflict

That conflict often arises between people of different nationalities, religions, races, ethnic groups, genders, or ages is not news. In Germany, the Nazis persecuted the Jews on the grounds that they were inferior to "Aryans"; in Iraq, the Sunnis and Shiites fight savagely trying to settle "age-old" scores; in the United States, whites persecuted African Americans because of their skin color; in some large corporations, women are cut out of management by the "old boys," who control the front office, and respond with legal charges of discrimination. The list goes on and on. In all these cases, differences between these social groups are the alleged causes of conflict. The conflict is presumed to stem from the group's characteristics, which makes it inevitable. The groups are seen as "natural" or traditional enemies.

There are at least two problems with this explanation of intergroup conflict. In most cases one or both groups have economic or political interests in the conflict; one or both stand to gain from the other's defeat (Billig, 1976). Intergroup differences may be used by parties to justify the conflict, but they are certainly not its ultimate or original cause. Second, usually several other groups are different from the conflicting groups, but they are not drawn into the conflict. The theories of natural differences have no explanation for why these particular groups are in conflict and the others are not drawn in (Oakes, 2003; Billig, 1976). To explain this, it is necessary to go beyond group differences and to consider social identity and intergroup interaction.

Although they may not be the ultimate or original cause of conflicts, intergroup differences often contribute to the persistence, intensity, and violence of conflicts. Few things are as troubling as a persistent conflict that feeds on group prejudices. Small wonder that sociologists and social psychologists have devoted a great deal of time to the study of intergroup conflict. In the United States, the study of intergroup relations can be traced back to the late nineteenth century when sociologists Robert Park and W. I. Thomas were concerned with the problem of how to integrate multiethnic immigrants into the American melting pot. One of the most famous works in this tradition is Gordon Allport's study, *The Nature of Prejudice* (1954). In Europe, similar ethnic tensions and the horrors of the first fifty years of the twentieth century inspired social psychologists, such as Henry Tajfel and Serge Moscovici (1976), to investigate the roots of group differences. This research has given rise to a huge body of studies on social identity and intergroup relations that yields some important insights for the study of conflict (Hogg, 2003; Oakes, 2003; Abrams, Hogg, Hinkle, & Otten, 2005).

The roots of intergroup conflict lie in the basic human need for identity. One source of identity is *social identity,* the sense of identity we get from belonging to a larger social group. This need fosters *social categorization*—a basic social process whereby people define themselves by identifying the groups they and others belong to (Hogg, 2003; Tajfel & Turner, 1979). Beginning in early childhood and continuing throughout adult life, a major factor in the definition of personal identity is the individual's perception of the social groups or categories he or she belongs to ("I am an American"; "I am a Minnesotan"; "I am a lawyer").

Identity, moreover, is defined not only by the groups to which a person belongs, but by the groups to which they do *not* belong (Rothbart, 2003). For example, many Americans define themselves both as being Americans and as *not* being Mexicans or Japanese or some other nationality. Members of management can draw their identity as much from being opposed to the union as from being a manager. Every organization and society can be described as a network of complementary and opposing groups. For example, in a typical American factory there might be groups divided between labor and management, line workers and staff, male and female, white collar and blue collar, to name just a few. Each group is defined not only in its own terms, but also with reference to its complementary or opposite group. Social categorization is the process by which people determine to what groups they and others belong, creating identification and oppositions among people.

The social categories forming the dividing points of organizations and societies differ from case to case and throughout history. Although men and women have always been important social categories in the United States, the nature of the category "women" and the relationship between the categories "men" and "women" have changed radically. Plus, the men–women differentiation is quite different in Japan, the United States, and Ghana. The importance of social categories also changes through history. During the 1920s, whether one was in favor of or against the legal prohibition of alcohol was an important distinction. Today, it is not even an issue. There is no one set of universal social divisions; they are socially defined and negotiated in each culture and subculture.

Communication plays an important role in social categorization. It is the medium through which people are taught categories. When children hear talk about general categories such as "boys" and "girls" or "blacks" and "whites," they are being taught social categories (Hogg, 2003; Operario & Fiske, 2003). For adults such categorizations come to seem like the natural order of things, and they readily learn and create additional categories. With each social category comes a characterization of what people in the category are like—their wants and needs, how they act, and so on. Of course, the characterization of each category differs depending on who describes the category. A member of the social group "women" is likely to describe the characteristics of men differently from the way a "man" would. However, communication barriers often prevent people in different social categories from "comparing notes" and recognizing the differences among their stereotypes of others. Blacks and whites, for instance, sometimes keep their theories about the other group to themselves, only discussing them with other blacks or whites. The process of group differentiation, discussed later, adds additional communication barriers that keep people from refuting social characterizations.

A person's style of communicating often serves as a marker of the social group to which he or she belongs. There is considerable evidence that characteristics of speech, such as dialect or accent, are used as indicators of the social category to which a person belongs (Fiedler & Schmid, 2003; Burgoon & Hoobler, 2002; Giles & Weimann, 1987; Giles & Powesland, 1975). For example, John's accent may suggest to Cho, a New Yorker, that John is a Southerner, and she may then attribute characteristics that she associates with Southerners (friendly, unsophisticated, conservative) to John.

When people accept social categories, they are likely to act toward those in other groups on the basis of characteristics or expectations that they attribute to the categories (Bourhis & Gagnon, 2003). This sets up a self-reinforcing cycle that preserves theories about other social groups (Hogg, 2003; Cooper & Fazio, 1979). For example, if people in group A, which generally don't care about politics, are taught that people in group B are politically conservative, those in group A may never raise the subject of politics in discussions with members of group B, because they dread boring political discussions. By so doing, they never give the people in group B a chance to show their true political beliefs. In turn, people in group B, who are actually somewhat centrist in their political beliefs, might think that the people in A are in agreement with them in their political agenda. That members of group A never talk about politics might confirm this for many group B members: since they are in agreement, there is no need to discuss politics. Thomas Scheff (1967) called this state of affairs *pluralistic ignorance*—each side is mistaken about the other, but neither is aware that it is mistaken. So both sides act on their "true" beliefs and invite behavior that confirms their views.

Consider the social category "gender," and its influence on expectations regarding conflict behavior. Most studies of actual conflict behavior show that men and women respond similarly in conflict situations, resolving conflict in similar ways both at work and at home (Nicotera & Dorsey, 2006; Chusmir & Mills, 1989; Turner & Henzel, 1987). However, there are robust differences in expectations about how men and women respond in conflict. For example, a study by Korabik, Baril, and Watson (1993) found that men and women did not handle conflict in similar ways, but were judged as being less effective when their behavior was not gender congruent (more competitive for men and more compensating for women). Research suggests that although men are generally thought to be more comfortable in conflict settings (Duane, 1989), using assertiveness and reason with greater effect in the workplace (Reich & Wood, 2003; Brewer, Mitchell, & Weber, 2002; Papa & Natalle, 1989) and approving of competition between parties (Baxter & Shepard, 1978), they are also more likely to avoid conflict (Roloff & Soule, 2002; Kelley, Cunningham, Grishman, Lefebvre, Sink, & Yablon, 1978). Women, on the other hand, are believed to react more emotionally in conflict situations and to be more flexible than men in conflict, adjusting their behaviors to meet the needs of the situation with greater skill (Reich & Wood, 2003; Yelsma & Brown, 1985; Kelley et al., 1978). Both men and women report engaging in more compensation when in conflicts with female partners (Berryman-Fink & Brunner, 1987). Such stereotypes are often self-fulfilling, creating differences in how we evaluate others.

What makes some categories salient in a particular situation? Garcia-Prieto, Bellard and Schnieder (2003) catalog several factors that can make social identities relevant. One factor is the *motivation* of the parties. Social identity is likely to be more salient if one or more of the parties has a need to enhance self-esteem, reduce uncertainty, or establish distinctiveness compared to others. In this case, drawing on membership in a social group can help meet these needs. For example, if Sue wants to establish her distinctiveness, she may identify with her profession as a nurse and communicate this identity to others who are not nurses. Doing so makes her feel special. A second factor that can make social identity salient is *awareness of difference.* A Latino man in a group of white men is likely to be aware of his identity as a Latino due to his minority status.

A third factor that can promote adoption of social identities is *others' reactions and expectations* about the party. Our nurse Sue is likely to identify with her profession when others ask her for medical advice. A fourth factor is the *existence of previous conflicts* among social groups. In Northern Ireland neighborhoods in the 1990s, it was difficult for anyone to not identify with either Protestant or Catholic factions. They had been in conflict for so long and the conflict was so intractable that taking sides was almost automatic. Each of these four factors makes it more likely that a particular social identity will be operative and gives us clues as to which identities to look for.

Intergroup conflict stems from a second process that complements social categorization—group differentiation. *Group differentiation* refers to the polarization between groups and the attendant stereotyping of other groups that trigger conflicts (Operario & Fiske, 2003). A wide range of events, including economic and political problems, natural disasters, wars, and population movements, can create conflicts of interest between groups. Conflicts can also arise due to the structure of society, as groups are put into opposition by historical traditions, the structure of economic opportunity, the nature of the political system, changing demographics, long-term shifts in economic fortunes, and other large currents. When this happens, groups tend to attribute responsibility for their problems to other groups and to unite against them.

This *we–they polarization* is produced by several communication dynamics (Abrams et al., 2005; Blake, Shepard, & Mouton, 1964; Sherif, Harvey, White, Hood, & Sherif, 1961). When groups are put into competition, there tends to be an increase in members' expressions of loyalty and commitment to the group. This behavior can be seen in rival street gangs who trumpet their "groupness" with colors, graffiti, secret signs, and steadfast obedience to their leaders' demands. It is equally evident in the fierce loyalty expressed by employees of competing firms, who will work long hours and devote themselves wholeheartedly to creating the best product or the winning bid. In-group messages also slant positions in favor of the group and demean the claims and validity of the other group. U.S. news coverage of the Iraq–United States situation in the recent Iraq War, for example, generally presented the U.S.'s side of the issues as reasonable common sense; the Iraqi view was generally presented as illogical, arbitrary, and without merit. The one-sided nature of the coverage served to reinforce Americans' perceptions of the correctness of the U.S. stance and to invalidate the Iraqi position. This general tendency to slant positions in favor of the in-group generally prevents reflection on the merits of the other group's claims (Abrams, et al., 2005).

Internal communication processes move the in-group toward a narrow, oversimplified view of the other group and contribute to the development of stereotypes—highly simplified beliefs about characteristics of other groups. In each case, all members of the other group are assumed to have the same threatening or undesirable characteristic. People who hold to the stereotypes may use them to interpret the behavior of a member of another group.

During the desegregation crisis that occurred in the Boston public schools during the late 1970s, newspapers reported the following incident (adapted from Cooper & Fazio, 1979, p. 153):

> A white girl who wanted to make a change in her program was using the wrong entrance to the high school, when a young black man touched her arm to get her attention. She screamed. The school's headmaster, Boston's title for a high school principal, was nearby and stepped in immediately, averting what he thought might have become a major incident.
>
> "He grabbed me," the girl said. "I was just trying to help her and tell her to use the front door so she wouldn't get into trouble," the boy said.

Stereotypical interpretations, such as this girl's, can promote strong reactions, heightening tensions between groups. Ironically, the stereotyper's expectations may be confirmed by the response his or her interpretations provoke from the other. Had the headmaster not stepped in, a violent confrontation between white and black students might have occurred. The whites would have come away with the conclusion that the black student had attacked the white student, and black students would have drawn the conclusion that they were always labeled as troublemakers, even when trying to help, due to the prejudice of whites.

Other communication processes heighten perceived disagreements between groups and separate their positions. Discussions in the in-group minimize similarities between the in-group and other groups and exaggerate differences between the groups' positions. For instance, news reports on Islam often emphasize its divergence from "Western" thought, downplaying the many similarities between Islam, Christianity, and Judaism. In a study of conflicts between line workers and office staff, Dalton (1959) found that the two groups heightened perceptions of differences between them by emphasizing differences in education level, social skills, and dress. Such claims serve to differentiate the groups and emphasize the chasm between them.

Polarization is heightened by suppression of disagreement in the in-group (Abrams et al., 2005). In-group messages minimize disagreements between members of the group and present a common front. Members who posit that the other group may have some valid claims or a legitimate position may be charged with disloyalty (Janis, 1972). This stance prevents members of the in-group from exploring possible common ground with other groups and preserves stereotypes.

These communication processes result in groups becoming strongly united against each other. As noted in the discussion of the psychodynamic perspective, Lewis Coser (1956) observed that this we–they relationship has useful functions for the in-group.

It creates high levels of cohesion and turns attention away from conflicts or dissatisfactions within the group. However, these dynamics also can create self-reinforcing cycles of polarization and hostility between the groups. If members believe the other group is responsible for their problems, hear only bad things about the other group, and are not permitted to test perceptions and beliefs, there is no way to improve intergroup relations. Members of the in-group, expecting the worst from the other group, are likely to act in a defensive or hostile manner toward members of the other group. In effect, the in-group creates a self-fulfilling prophecy whereby its worst fears about the hostility of the other group seem to be confirmed, justifying further polarizing communication (Hogg, 2003; Cooper & Fazio, 1979).

Once two groups have been in conflict for a time, they may develop intergroup ideologies to justify their positions (Volkan, 1994; Ross, 1993). *Intergroup ideologies* are organized belief systems that describe the differences between groups in terms that present the in-group in a favorable light and explain the conflict from the in-group's perspective. For example, in the ongoing Israeli–Palestinian conflict, each side has developed elaborate explanations of why it has *the* legitimate claims and has been wronged by the other side. These explanations provide each side with a ready stock of justifications for aggression toward the other and for both's unwillingness to make concessions.

Gouldner (1954) describes a similar case in a gypsum plant facing a strike. A history of confrontation between union and management led management to conclude that the union was simply trying to control everything that occurred in the plant. As a result of this belief, management saw no need to consider the legitimacy of any issues raised by the union because managers thought that under all of them was the hidden agenda of control. Management's lack of response to worker concerns contributed to a wildcat strike, which might have been averted if the managers had considered the issues on their merits. Intergroup ideologies solidify the conflict between groups because they are taken as unquestionable truth. New members and children are taught these beliefs with the result that they can see the other group only in terms of the ideology.

Together, the processes of social categorization, group differentiation, and intergroup ideology development define social reality so that members transfer general beliefs about other groups and their differences into conflict situations. These beliefs can funnel interpretations and actions to produce longer and more intense conflicts.

Differences in culture, history, and experience between groups can also create misunderstandings that heighten divisions. Shenkar and Ronen (1987, p. 268) discuss possible problems that can occur during negotiations between Chinese and U.S. citizens:

> The Chinese preference for restrained, moderate behavior suggests that one should avoid overtly aggressive behavior. The American task-oriented approach, which allows for the admission of differences in the positions of the parties to a negotiation so as to promote "honest confrontation" is viewed by the Chinese as aggressive, and therefore as an unacceptable mode of behavior . . . . The Chinese tend to prefer to make decisions behind the scenes . . . and this contributes greatly to American anxiety as to where they stand as discussions progress. These differences in cultural preference can cause serious misunderstandings that contribute to escalation of conflicts.

CASE 3.5 • *Intergroup Conflict Dynamics and the Parking Lot Scuffle*

Jay and Tim are from the same cultural group, so intergroup dynamics do not explain the Parking Lot Scuffle very well. However, if Jay and Tim had been from different groups—for example, were of different genders; had different sexual orientations; or were of different racial, ethnic, or national groups—these differences could have been salient. If they had, we would expect several dynamics described in this section to be set in motion.

We would expect that stereotypes about each group would surface and be woven into an interpretation of why Jay and Tim were reacting as they did. For example, if they were from different ethnic groups (say X and Y), then one might think of the other, "That's just how an X (or Y) would react here, always trying to get the upper hand." These simplified ideas would influence their attributions about each other and shape their behavior, perhaps making it more competitive than it would otherwise be. As they interacted, the we–they polarization would get in the way of understanding, further complicating efforts at constructive conflict management.

After the scuffle, Tim and Jay might talk about it with members of their own group. This would promote ideological processes by which members further polarize opinions about the other group. In turn, this would strengthen Tim's and Jay's current competitive orientations and undermine their ability to collaborate in later discussions.

Discussion Question

- Although Tim and Jay are not from different groups, the Parking Lot Scuffle contains several statements that might contribute to stereotyping. Can you identify some of these and explain how they might function in an intergroup conflict if Tim and Jay did belong to different groups?

Oetzel (2003) summarizes similar differences in American and Japanese styles that may lead to misunderstanding and conflict.

The intergroup conflict perspective reminds us that conflicts cannot be reduced solely to interpersonal terms. Larger social relations and the history of intergroup relations play an important role in many conflicts. Social identity and the group identifications that come with it is an important part of every person's identity, so it is inevitable that intergroup differences will be pulled into interpersonal conflicts. Indeed, sometimes people can be forced into a conflict by the structure of intergroup relations. In a community with racial problems, for example, it is difficult for people from different racial backgrounds to have an interpersonal conflict that is not in some way influenced by racial differences. The only sure way to prevent such conflicts is to change relationships between groups, which is quite difficult. Case 3.5 considers how social identity processes may have figured in the Parking Lot Scuffle.

Table 3.1 on page 99 summarizes some suggestions for questions to ask and measures that can be taken to work with conflict interaction. Chapters 4, 7, and 8 will present more extensive discussions of how to channel conflict interaction in productive directions.

EXHIBIT 3.4 • *Counteracting the Negative Impacts of Social Identity and Intergroup Conflict*

How can we create more positive intergroup relationships? To begin, we should be aware that stereotypes and negative attitudes between social groups are unusually durable and difficult to change. This is due, in part, to cognitive processes: once formed, beliefs about other groups become entrenched and dislodging them takes a good deal of counterevidence. Research suggests that counterevidence seems to make the stereotype more accessible in memory and therefore indirectly strengthens the stereotype (Dovidio, Kawakama, & Beach, 2003). Hence, it takes a lot of counterevidence to overcome the stereotype; the stereotype must be "overwhelmed" by counterexamples to change it. The durability of stereotypes and negative attitudes is also due to the within-group interaction processes just discussed.

The most common approach to reducing intergroup conflict is to bring members of different groups into contact (Brewer & Gaertner, 2003). The basic idea is that in-depth experience with members of other groups will show people that their stereotypes are unrealistic. Bringing environmentalists and business leaders together, for instance, will enable members of each group to see members of the other group as individual human beings like themselves, hence undermining engrained attitudes and stereotypes.

The "*contact hypothesis*" was originally advanced by the eminent social psychologist Gordon Allport (1954). His research indicated that contact will reduce intergroup prejudice most effectively if (a) it is handled so that it fosters "*social norms* that favor intergroup acceptance, (b) the situation has high 'acquaintance potential,' promoting *intimate contact* among members of both groups, (c) the contact situation promotes *equal status* interactions among members of the social groups, and (d) the situation creates conditions of *cooperative interdependence* [what Deutsch called promotive interdependence] among members of both groups" (Brewer & Gaertner, 2003).

Research has generally shown that contact under the conditions defined by Allport does create more positive attitudes toward members of the outgroup (Brewer & Gaertner, 2003). However, these attitudes do not necessarily translate to less prejudice or undermine stereotypes about other social groups as a whole. In some cases positive attitudes created by intergroup contact only attach to the specific people involved. They are regarded as exceptions, and the positive attitudes are not generalized to their group as a whole.

Brewer and Gaertner (2003) identify three routes by which contact can be used to defuse intergroup conflict. They call the first *decategorization*. This approach emphasizes seeing the other as a person, a unique individual, rather than as a member of a social category. So Jack might try to appreciate the unique qualities of Jill as a coworker, rather than presuming she holds the attitudes and behavioral predispositions of "accountants." You can take this approach yourself, although it is often easier if you have a coach or someone outside the conflict to help support you.

In the second approach, "*recategorization,*" parties emphasize common goals and interests, thus creating a new "category" around those interests. So Jack and Jill can emphasize their common identity as employees of XYZ Company, rather than as an "accountant" and an "engineer." This creates a common in-group identity that they both share. An important qualification of this approach is that the common goal and resulting common identity must be important to all parties. It cannot be some kind of "made up" category.

A third approach, *mutual differentiation,* recognizes the differences among social groups, but appreciates the strengths of the various groups and attempts to capitalize on them. Distefano and Maznevski (2000) outline three principles for mutual differentiation: Map, Bridge, Integrate.

First, parties explicitly *map* the important differences between their social groups, as well as similarities. Parties should try to understand the grounds for the differences and the value that characteristics of the other social group bring to the table. For instance, if we (stereotypically) map

EXHIBIT 3.4 Continued

men as more task oriented and women as more concerned with relationships, it would be important to acknowledge the advantages of each gender's perspectives. It is also important to map possible problems that might arise due to the differences, so they can be anticipated. For instance, due to their task orientation, men are more likely to try to hurry to a decision without considering how it will make parties feel.

Bridging is "communicating effectively across differences to bring people and ideas together." This involves fostering confidence in both parties that differences can be bridged and building motivation to overcome the problems that differences pose. In addition, bridging requires parties to use their maps of others to try to communicate in ways that reach the other. Continuing with our oversimplified stereotype, a man who is bridging to a woman might state a proposal and then offer his interpretation of its impact on relationships among those involved. Alternatively, he might simply state the proposal and ask her reactions. A final aspect of bridging is to establish some common ground among the parties around new ways of interacting.

Establishing norms of interacting that are acceptable to both sides is one way to do this.

Integrating requires parties to ensure that they work together toward a mutually acceptable outcome. This means that all parties must be able to participate on an equal basis and build on one another's ideas rather than debating them. They should also recognize that disagreements will arise and deal with them openly, a topic we will cover in much greater depth in subsequent chapters.

The Map-Bridge-Integrate approach obviously works best when the parties are in a long-term relationship and anticipate much future interaction. However, even a single party in a short-term relationship can employ these principles on his or her own to try to guide the interaction in positive directions.

As we observed in the section on intergroup conflict, because they are grounded in complex situations with long histories, dealing with social identity, stereotyping, group ideologies, and intergroup conflict is not necessarily easy. It is, however, essential, because like it or not, we are stuck with them.

TABLE 3.1   *Working with Conflict Interaction: Questions to Ask and Elements to Assess*

- What stage is the current conflict in? What triggers set it off?
- Has the conflict gone through repetitive cycles?
- What type of interdependence do the parties share?
- Are the parties reciprocating each other's moves? Is this moving the conflict in a positive or negative direction?
- How might you use compensation to "cool down" a conflict?
- Can you take advantage of cycles of positive reciprocation?
- How are issues developing? Are they expanding, contracting, or maintaining?
- How can you use the tit-for-tat strategy to move the conflict in a positive direction?
- Are social categories playing a role in the conflict?
- Can you avoid or refute stereotypes associated with social categories or encourage other parties to question their stereotypes?

3.6 Summary and Review

How do the stage models relate to one another?

Stage models describe how conflicts unfold over time. Rummel posits that conflicts pass through five stages: latent conflict, initiation, conflict behavior, balance of power, and disruption. This model, derived from studies of national conflict, is somewhat similar to Pondy's model of organizational conflict, which posits the following stages: latent conflict, perceived conflict, felt conflict, manifest conflict, aftermath. In both cases, conflict starts below the surface and then emerges into full-fledged struggle and then once again moves into a quiet period. Analyses of bargaining have tended to find three stages: distributive bargaining, problem-solving, and decision making.

Stage models depict the regular patterns during conflicts. These patterns form part of the context for moves and countermoves; the same behavior means different things during different phases. A competitive move means something different during Pondy's felt conflict stage, wherein it is a trigger that moves behavior into manifest conflict, than during the aftermath stage, where it might be seen as inappropriate because the conflict has been resolved (or at least has subsided).

Stage models have been criticized as too simplistic because actual conflicts have a greater variety of behavior patterns than the phase models depict. Their simplicity is sometimes useful, however, because they provide a simple set of milestones to help us in navigating conflicts.

What is the role of interdependence in conflict?

Our definition of conflict specified that it required interdependent parties. We distinguished three forms of interdependence: (1) promotive interdependence, which fosters cooperation; (2) contrient interdependence, which promotes competition; and (3) individualistic contexts, in which parties recognize little interdependence. Each form of interdependence creates a particular climate that shapes parties' expectations and their behavior toward one another.

Reciprocity and compensation: What are they and how do they affect conflict interaction?

Reciprocity is the tendency to respond to the other's behavior by matching it in form or function. Reciprocity of negative behavior can create vicious cycles that move the conflict in destructive directions. Reciprocating positive behavior can create virtuous cycles that move conflicts in productive directions. Reciprocity builds momentum in conflict interaction, and unfortunately negative reciprocity generally builds stronger momentum than positive reciprocity.

Compensation is the tendency to respond to the other's negative behavior with neutral or positive behavior. Compensation has the potential to reroute conflict from destructive to productive directions. Negative emotions make it more difficult for parties to accommodate.

Tit-for-Tat is a strategy that applies reciprocity and compensation in a judicious combination that has the potential to move conflicts in productive directions. By matching negative behavior, the party signals that he or she is willing to strike back. By compensating with positive behavior, the party signals that he or she would prefer a more productive approach and offers the other a chance to reciprocate the positive behavior.

Reciprocity and compensation shape conflict interaction at the microlevel and by so doing they contribute to larger patterns of conflict interaction. They help to define interdependence between parties and constitute larger phases and episodes of conflict. They also contribute to the threat-rigidity cycle and its positive counterpart that were discussed in Chapter 2.

How does framing operate in conflict interaction, and what is its relationship to the psychological framing of conflicts discussed in Chapter 2?

Framing of conflicts in interaction complements psychological framing processes. Parties attempt to influence which issues are in the forefront and how their moves are viewed by other parties. However, as with all interaction, framing is not fully under the control of any of the parties. The various moves in framing interaction influence psychological framing processes by giving parties cues for various interpretations. In turn, parties' psychological frames influence how they act toward each other, which further shapes framing interaction.

How do social identity and intergroup dynamics influence conflict interaction?

Many social divisions characterize society, including possible divisions between genders, socioeconomic classes, ethnic groups, and cultures. When these division points become salient, they can start a process of self-reinforcing polarization that can fuel conflicts. A we–they division that distances the parties and promotes stereotyping is created through communication processes of social categorization, group differentiation, and intergroup ideology formation.

Social categorization defines different groups and makes the divisions between groups salient. Group differentiation processes highlight the value of and similarities among members of the in-group and exaggerate the negative qualities of the out-group. Both in-group and out-group are portrayed as more uniform and cohesive than they actually are, and individual differences among members of each group are downplayed. Group ideologies are developed to explain the conflict in a way that favors the in-group and demonizes the out-group. Differences and grievances between groups are explained in terms of qualities and characteristics of the group's members and portrayed as inevitable and unchangeable. Other explanations of the conflict are downplayed, ignored, or refuted. The intergroup conflict perspective highlights the importance of social and cultural factors in conflicts and reminds us that conflicts cannot be reduced solely to the interpersonal level.

3.7 Conclusion

This chapter focused on patterns and dynamics of conflict interaction, and hence offers a complement to the chapter on the inner experience of conflict. Together, Chapters 2 and 3 offer a more detailed picture of the nature of conflict interaction and the factors that shape it.

Stage models represent the long-term patterns in conflicts. These models depict typical sequences of episodes of conflict interaction, showing the trajectory through which a conflict is likely to develop. Stage models suggest that conflicts may develop through repetitive cycles of alternating engagement and latency. There are clear connections between beliefs about conflict and conflict scripts and stage models. Emotion also plays an important role in the unfolding of the stages. Triggering events, for example, often arouse negative emotions such as anger and hurt, which fuel confrontations in stages of open conflict. Positive emotions may contribute to turning conflicts in more productive directions during open conflict. Negative emotions simmering during latent periods set the stage for future clashes, while positive emotions may promote integrative conflict management.

Interdependence, reciprocity and compensation, and issue framing are, in a sense, nested within conflict stages. The specific behavioral patterns that these generate constitute the episodes and larger stages we see in conflicts. The nature of interdependence among parties is an important determinant of conflict behavior and, hence, of how conflicts unfold. Promotive interdependence tends to create cooperation and thus is conducive to integrative resolution of conflicts. Contrient interdependence tends to create competition, and thus is conducive to destructive cycles. It is not the interdependence per se, however, that influences conflict, but parties' perceptions of interdependence and the degree to which they coincide. Parties' perceptions may diverge from the actual interdependencies, at least to some extent.

The specific moves that constitute conflict are patterned by reciprocity and compensation. Negative reciprocity tends to create destructive patterns and perpetuate cycles of conflict. Positive reciprocity and compensation tend to break negative patterns and move conflicts in productive directions. The framing of issues in interaction also influences the direction of conflict.

The nature of the interaction within a conflict stage differs, depending on the specific moves enacted in the stage. A latent conflict can be relatively mild or marked by bitterness and suppression of one of the parties. A triggering event may set off a rapidly escalating destructive cycle, or it may promote open discussion and attempts to negotiate a reasonable compromise.

The connection between microlevel moves and macrolevel stages or episodes is complex. Since stages are composed of moves, it is tempting to assume that specific actions taken by the parties add up to a stage and give it a particular character. However, as we have seen, the whole is often more than the sum of its parts. Parties can grasp larger patterns and when they do, their understanding of a stage or episode can influence the actions that they take. For example, assume Jake knows that Suzanne has hard feelings because of how they previously resolved a dispute. His knowledge of stage models suggests to him that Suzanne likely has built up anger during the ensuing period of latent conflict. In such cases, a triggering event may lead to uncontrolled escalation. In order to move the conflict in a more productive direction, Jake chooses to respond mildly to Suzanne's attack (i.e., to accommodate), thus short-circuiting the escalation. In this case, Jake's reaction is driven by the larger pattern of conflict stages, rather than by immediate considerations. Specific moves are not always independent of larger patterns, particularly those that fit into common scripts or beliefs about conflict.

This example also illustrates some ways in which the inner experience of conflict is related to the three microlevel processes. The type of interdependence among parties— promotive, contrient, or individualistic—influences attributions. If Jake and Suzanne have contrient interdependence, for example, Jake is more likely to interpret Suzanne's impending behavior as competitive, and this may lead him to take defensive measures, rather than his mild response. Jake's mild response, in fact, suggests that he perceives the situation as one in which promotive interdependence holds (or at least one in which it might be increased). Negative emotions such as anger may feed cycles of reciprocity, leading the conflict in negative directions. Jake's mild response is more likely based on an optimistic emotional state, and it is likely to foster Suzanne's positive emotions, further encouraging her to respond favorably to Jake's compensation. These are just a few of the numerous connections between emotion, social cognition, and behavior in conflicts.

When salient, social identity and intergroup conflict can strongly influence conflict interaction. When parties interact with each other on the basis of social identities, they rely on stereotypes and assumptions rather than treating each other as individuals. If the social groups in question have a history of conflict or enmity, assumptions of enmity are likely to be imported into the interaction and turn the conflict in destructive directions. Social identity and intergroup conflict are also likely to serve as emotional triggers and to shape social cognition.

In closing, let us return to the relationship between the inner experience of conflict and conflict interaction. We have argued that they mutually influence each other. However, there is also a long history of debate about whether human behavior is best explained on the basis of internal states and psychology or in terms of patterns of observable behavior and interaction. This is still an open question and one worth reflecting on. Which of the two types of explanations seem more fundamental to you?

Chapter 4 extends our discussion of conflict interaction by exploring conflict styles. A conflict style, such as competing or avoiding, incorporates a general expectation about how we should handle a conflict. It involves taking a particular attitude toward the other party and guides our behavior. Conflict styles offer us a "vocabulary" for talking about how we and others respond to conflict. They also represent strategic options available to us when a conflict looms.

4

Conflict Styles and Strategic Conflict Interaction

What is the best way to handle ourselves in a conflict? Should we stick to one approach, or be flexible? Should we let others have a say, or try to control the situation? Should we carefully plan how we will react, or improvise? And how do we avoid getting caught up in spiraling escalation or avoidance cycles?

A common recommendation is to plan your *strategy*. For example, many people rehearse what they are going to say during a confrontation. At one time or another, you may have found yourself talking to an imagined adversary—maybe your partner or boss—trying out different things and hoping to settle on a good approach. While useful, this advice overemphasizes the degree to which we can plan interactions. The key to an effective strategy is the ability to control the situation. However, as we've seen, conflicts are interactive, and often they move in unexpected directions. In the heat of the moment, it is often hard to stick to plans, even if we can remember them.

Rather than overemphasizing planning, we believe it is more productive to work on mastering various styles of conflict engagement so that you have some flexibility. The notion of *style* emphasizes a consistent orientation toward the conflict, an orientation that unifies specific tactics into a coherent whole, yet does not stress planning and foresight too much. Research indicates that most people have characteristic conflict-handling styles, which they tend to apply regardless of situational differences. You can, however, teach old dogs new tricks: people can learn new behaviors if they are aware of alternatives. Moreover, there is evidence that people change styles as disputes develop. Therefore, it is best to consider conflict styles as a repertoire of options that we can learn to apply. There will always be an element of strategy in the selection of styles, but it is important to keep in mind the emergent nature of conflict interaction and the surprises it brings. A conflict seems to be moving in a positive direction and then someone says the wrong thing and everything falls apart. Or in the midst of a heated dispute, one of the parties offers a compromise. In view of the unexpected twists and turns of interaction, about the best we can hope for is to be responsive to changes. Of course this still leaves all our questions open. How do we select an appropriate style? When should we change styles? What are the long-run consequences of various styles? How do we select the proper tactics to carry out styles?

4.1 Origins of Conflict Styles

Conflict styles were first articulated by scholars and consultants associated with the *human relations and human resources movements,* which had their heyday from the 1940s through the 1970s. This perspective assumes that the nature and quality of inter-personal relations in the workplace play a large role in determining employee motivation; satisfaction derived from work; level of absenteeism and resignations; management–employee relationships, and, ultimately, the productivity and success of the organization (Shermerhorn, Hunt, & Osborn, 2005). With its emphasis on human relationships, it is no surprise that conflict was a major concern of human relations scholars.

The concept of style originated with Blake and Mouton (1964) and Jay Hall (1969) who identified five distinct types of conflict behavior. Their classification is based on two independent conflict behavior components (Ruble & Thomas, 1976): (1) *assertiveness,* defined as behaviors intended to satisfy one's own concerns; and (2) *cooperation,* defined as behaviors intended to satisfy the other individual's concerns. These components combine to specify the five styles, which can be diagrammed as shown in Figure 4.1.

- A *competing* style is high in assertiveness and low in cooperation: The party places great emphasis on his or her own concerns and ignores those of others. This orientation represents a desire to defeat the other and compel him or her to do what the party wants. This style is sometimes also referred to as "forcing" or "dominating."
- An *accommodating* style is low in assertiveness and high in cooperation: The party gives in to others at the cost of his or her own concerns. Other writers have called this style "appeasement" or "smoothing." It is a self-sacrificing approach that may also be viewed as weak and retracting.
- An *avoiding* style is low in assertiveness and low in cooperation: The party simply withdraws and refuses to deal with the conflict. Parties who adopt this style may seem apathetic, isolated, or evasive. Another term for this style is "flight."

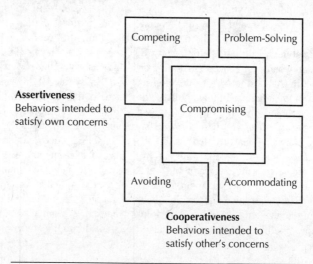

FIGURE 4.1   *Conflict Styles.*

- A *collaborating* style is high in both assertiveness and cooperation: The party works to attain a solution that will meet the needs of both parties to the conflict. In this orientation full satisfaction for all is sought. It has also been called "problem-solving" or "integration."
- A *compromising* style is intermediate in both assertiveness and cooperation: The party tries to arrange it so that both parties give some and "split the difference" to reach an agreement. In this orientation both are expected to give up something and keep something. This style has also been referred to as "sharing" or "horse-trading."

The five styles have proven to be a set of concepts for understanding conflict (see Case 4.1). They provide a common vocabulary and almost every major writer on interpersonal or organizational conflict has referred to the styles extensively (Nicotera & Dorsey, 2006).

Much research has been directed to defining and measuring conflict styles. Instruments include Hall's (1969) Conflict Management Survey, the Thomas and Kilmann (1974) Management-of-Differences (MODE) Survey, Rahim's (1983) Organizational Conflict Inventory-II, the Putnam and Wilson (1982) Organizational Communication Conflict Instrument, and the Ross and DeWine (1988) Conflict Management Message Style Instrument (see Nicotera & Dorsey, 2006 for a more detailed discussion of these). Each instrument identifies somewhat different styles or dimensions underlying conflict, but in general they reflect the five defined here. The instruments by Putnam and Wilson and Ross and DeWine specifically focus on communication behaviors in conflicts and are therefore of special interest.

CASE 4.1 • *Conflict Styles in the Parking Lot Scuffle*

You may wish to refer back to the original case on page 39.

From the outset Tim used a competing style, high in assertiveness and low in cooperativeness. This is indicated by his strong language, his demands for payment, and his refusal to consider Jay's point of view. Jay initially began with a collaborating style; he did not apologize or give in to Tim, which would signal accommodating or, possibly, avoiding. He attempted to develop an understanding of what happened that could be the foundation for problem solving. Tim's continued confrontations were answered with firm resistance in line 8. Here Jay clearly stated his unwillingness to accommodate ("Look, this is my spot.") and made an attempt to reframe the situation when he said, "You're lucky I stopped when I did." This signaled a continued attempt at collaborating that might have led to an integrative solution or a compromise had Tim followed this lead.

This in turn illustrates an important feature of collaborating: It does not necessarily mean that people are "nice" to each other. Often collaborating involves assertive moves that signal firmness and resolve. As indicated in Chapter 1, differentiation requires parties to acknowledge the validity of their differences, which sometimes requires one party to show the other that he or she will not be pushed around.

By line 10, Jay has abandoned collaborating and switched to a competing style ("You are the one with the problem. Do you work here?"). He may have concluded that Tim would never be reasonable and decided that the only way to obtain an acceptable outcome was to argue to a standoff. He may also intend to continue collaborating, in which case the point here was to further signal resolve and to register a mild threat that Jay could attack right back if he wanted to. Or Jay may have just been sucked into the confrontation through a matching

(continued)

CASE 4.1   Continued

process. Aroused by Tim's anger, Jay's aggressive impulses and anxiety about the situation may have provoked a "fight" response whereby Jay becomes just as competitive as Tim.

Whatever the case, by line 12 Jay lashed back at Tim and attempted to leave the scene—"Who in the hell do you think you are? *(Starts walking away.)*." Taken out of context, this move might appear to enact an accommodating or avoiding style. In this context, however, it seems to be part of a larger strategy to win through retreat. Jay snarled at Tim and tried to have the last word by walking away. As we have noted, there are variants of the five basic styles that identify different approaches to the same basic strategy.

Tim's reaction cemented the competition when he grabbed Jay. Jay continued with his retreat-and-win strategy, and Tim slugged him. Tim may have done this because he realized the situation was slipping away with Jay's impending retreat. Or, Tim may simply have been too incensed to "let go" of his attitude. If this was the case, he channeled his aggression into violence, which ended in the scuffle.

Discussion Questions

- How did the styles adopted by these two feed into the conflict?
- Could Jay have taken a different tact that would have resulted in a more productive conflict?

As the plethora of measurement instruments suggests, there are several different ways to conceive of conflict styles. The following sections attempt to sort out several different interpretations of conflict styles.

4.2 What Is a Conflict Style?

We have introduced conflict styles as a person's orientation toward conflict. But what exactly does this mean? Is a style a personal trait, which remains relatively constant over time, or is it instead a general strategy that can be varied at will?

Some scholars (e.g., such as Filley, 1975, and Moberg, 2001), discuss style as *the way a person usually responds to conflict*. In this view, styles identify *types of people or personalities*—the "tough battler," the "friendly helper," "the problem solver"—who are predisposed to handle all conflicts in the same way. This tradition has strongly influenced how the tests that measure a person's predominant style of conflict-handling behavior have been interpreted. Although the way the tests are scored allows people to fall under more than one style (for instance, people are often classified as compromisers and problem solvers), styles are interpreted as a relatively *stable aspect* of the individual's personality. Several studies have yielded some evidence that people develop habitual styles of responding to conflict that are fairly consistent across situations and time (Canary, Cupach, & Serpe, 2001; Gormly, Gormly, & Johnson, 1972; Jones & Melcher, 1982; Nicotera & Dorsey, 2006; Sternberg & Soriano, 1984). This view is somewhat misleading, however.

Although people typically have habitual ways of responding to conflict, they also have a capacity to change or adapt their behavior from situation to situation and over time in the same conflict. There is abundant evidence that people change their approaches as conflicts unfold (Canary, Cupach, & Serpe, 2001; Keck & Samp, 2007; Nicotera, 1994;

Phillips & Cheston, 1979; Sillars, 1980b; Papa & Natalle, 1989; Sambamurthy & Poole, 1992). In addition, the correlation between personality traits such as dogmatism, Machiavellianism (manipulativeness), neuroticism, extraversion, and agreeableness and conflict styles are typically low (Jones & Melcher, 1982; Moberg, 2001; though see Rogan and LaFrance, 2003, who reported substantial correlations between conflict style and verbal aggressiveness), suggesting that they are not firmly anchored in personality. People can and do adapt and change, and denying this capacity through the assumption of fixed styles denies an important human potential.

Taught to large numbers of people, this view could even be harmful. If people assume their styles are stable characteristics, they may not be motivated to change in order to break out of destructive patterns. If a supervisor assumes an employee is a tough battler and will always be one, he or she is likely to go into any disagreement with the employee with a belligerent "he's-not-going-to-run-over-me" attitude that greatly increases the possibility of destructive escalation. Alternatively, the supervisor may just give in to avoid the employee's wrath but later resent this act of submission. Neither response is a good one; not only do both responses increase the probability of destructive conflict and ineffective decision making, they also deny the worker's ability to change.

Assuming that the other person is inflexible by nature may also discourage parties from trying different approaches. The anticipatory attack the boss may make the employee respond as a tough battler as a defense, even though he would actually have preferred to discuss the issue quietly. Expectations about "how people are" too easily turn into self-fulfilling prophecies that can lead individuals to act toward people in ways that cause others to respond with the undesirable but expected behaviors. The attitudes freeze others into a mold that prevents the flexible and responsive behavior needed for effective conflict management. This problem is compounded when people believe they themselves have a characteristic personal style. "I'm a battler," they say and assume they cannot or do not have to be flexible because "that's just the way I am." Thus, conflict training programs and tests that purport to identify "characteristic styles" may escalate the very conflicts they are intended to help. People do fall into habits, but they can also change.

A second view of style defines styles as *specific types of conflict behavior* (Cosier & Ruble, 1981; Papa & Natalle, 1989). In this view, any behavior intended to defeat the other (for example, making a threat) is competitive, while a behavior designed to achieve a mutually acceptable solution (for example, restating the conflict in problem-oriented terms) is collaborative. In this view styles refer to categories of behavior, not types of people. This definition is an improvement over the previous one because it neither assumes nor encourages inflexibility. But it too has a problem: The same behavior can fall under different styles. A threat, for example, can be classified under competing, but it could also be classified under avoiding if it were intended to keep an opponent from raising a conflict ("I'll leave if you bring that up again"). Postponing a conflict is often advocated as a collaborative tactic because it gives both sides a "cooling off" period, but it can also be an avoiding tactic if used persistently. An offer to "split the difference" is certainly a compromise, but it can also be accommodating if what one offers is of little value and he or she does it simply to avoid losing. There is some validity in the definition of styles as behaviors, but another interpretation offers a more accurate conception of styles.

The third, and most useful, position defines styles as *behavioral orientations people can take toward conflict* (Thomas, 1975; Nicotera & Dorsey, 2006). In this view, a style is a general expectation about how the conflict should be approached—an attitude about how best to deal with the other party. A competing style is oriented toward defeating the other, toward achieving one's own goals without regard for others, and it dictates certain behavioral choices to achieve these ends. A collaborating style reflects an orientation toward mutual benefit; it favors moves that enhance cooperation and creative thinking toward this end. The definition of styles as orientations solves the problem of classifying specific behaviors under one style or the other—the same tactics can serve different intentions and attitudes. This definition is also true to the observations showing that people exhibit definite, consistent strategies during conflicts without denying their capacity to change. Choosing an orientation is making a decision about the principles that will guide one through the conflict, whether cooperative and/or assertive.

However, one limitation of the style concept is its focus on the individual. Style refers to the *orientation of the individual* during conflict; it reflects one person's approach independent of the other person. As we have seen, to understand conflict, it is not sufficient to stay at the level of the individual. The interlocking actions of all parties must be taken into account. Styles represent the "mind-sets" that parties have in the conflict, but what another person does often changes one's attitudes and intentions, often without the individual realizing it. Someone may go into a disagreement with a firm intention to problem solve, but if the other person betrays, or viciously attacks, or refuses to talk about the conflict at all, it is difficult to keep on problem solving. The other's reactions make one want to defend oneself, or strike back, or scream in exasperation, or withdraw completely. Conrad (1991) summarizes substantial evidence that the actual behaviors people engage in during conflicts differ from how they expect to behave. He attributes this largely to the influence of others' behavior. Canary et al. (2001) found that choice of conflict style was strongly influenced by the other party's stylistic choice.

To reflect style as behavioral orientations that interact with others' orientations, we have used the gerund (-ing) form for each style to indicate the *active process* involved in using a style. Styles are not something people simply put on and forget about, but something they must perform. Descriptions of styles will refer to the parties who carry out styles with the "-er" or "-or" suffix—a party using competing will be called a "competer"; a party who adopts an accommodating approach, an "accommodator"; and so on. This is purely for ease of expression and not because the styles are perceived as traits of the people who use them.

4.3 An Expanded View of Conflict Styles

At the beginning of the chapter we distinguished styles in terms of two dimensions: *assertiveness*—the degree to which the style attempts to satisfy the party's concerns—and *cooperation*—the degree to which the style attempts to satisfy the other party's concerns. However, Cai and Fink (2002) found that more than two dimensions were needed to adequately describe styles. Four additional characteristics of styles have been identified in previous research. Sillars, Coletti, Parry, and Rogers (1982) define *disclosiveness*—the degree to which a conflict style or tactic discloses information to the other party—as a basic dimension of conflict behavior. Disclosiveness encourages the creation of an open communication climate conducive to problem-solving. Styles also differ in *empowerment*—the degree to which they grant the other party some control or power. Some styles hinge on the party's control of the situation, others share control between two parties, and others give control to the other party. Hence styles can have an effect on the balance of power and its impacts on conflicts. *Activity* (Riggs, 1983) represents the degree of involvement with conflict issues. Parties' activity can range from very intense concern to apathy. Finally, styles can differ in *flexibility*—the degree of movement the party is willing to make in working out the conflict (Ruble & Thomas, 1976; Riggs, 1983). Some styles allow for considerable pliability in parties' positions, whereas others are quite rigid in their insistence that the initial position not be changed.

Thinking in terms of these six dimensions clarifies in more detail the differences among styles and enables us to discern variants of the styles, as Table 4.1 shows. So, for example, parties who adopt a competing style place a great deal of emphasis on their

TABLE 4.1 *Conflict Styles and Their Variants Rated on Six Dimensions*

				Empowerment			
Conflict Style	*Assertive*	*Cooperative*	*Disclosive*	*Self*	*Other*	*Active*	*Flexibility*
Competing	High	Low	Low to moderate	Yes	No	High	Low
Forcing	High	Low	Low	Yes	No	High	Low
Contending	High	Low	Moderate	Yes	No	High	Moderate
Avoiding	Low	Low	Low	Varies	No	Low	Low to moderate
Protecting	Low	Low	Low	Yes	No	Low	Low
Withdrawing	Low	Low	Low to moderate	No	No	Low	Moderate
Smoothing	Low	Low	Moderate	No	No	Moderate	Moderate
Accommodating	Low	High	Low to moderate	No	Yes	Low	High
Yielding	Low	High	Low	No	Yes	Low	High
Conceding	Low	High	Moderate	No	Yes	Low to moderate	Moderate to high
Compromising	Moderate	Moderate	Moderate to high	Yes	Yes	Moderate to high	Moderate
Firm compromising	Moderate	Moderate	Low to moderate	Yes	Yes	High	Moderate
Flexible compromising	Moderate	Moderate	Moderate to high	Yes	Yes	Moderate	Moderate
Problem-solving	High	High	Moderate to high	Yes	Yes	High	High

own concerns and little on those of the other party; they are not particularly disclosive or flexible; and they are highly involved in the conflict and attempt to maximize their control over the situation and to minimize control by others. In this section, we discuss conflict styles in more detail and spell out some variants of each style that differ in tone and tenor.

4.3.1 Competing

This style is marked by a primary emphasis on satisfying the party's own concerns and disregard of others' concerns. It is a closed style, low to moderate in disclosiveness; parties make their demands apparent, but often hide their true motives and any other information that might weaken their position. Competers are quite active and highly involved in the conflict. Competers aggressively pursue personal goals, taking any initiatives necessary to achieve them. Flexibility is generally low in the competing style. Competers attempt to avoid sacrificing any goals, instead using whatever effective means are available to compel others to satisfy their concerns. This requires that competers attempt to control the situation and deny others power or control. A notable exception exists when competers are working *within a team* against another team. Competitive people can be surprisingly flexible and cooperative with their teammates when engaged in a competition with an outside group (Carnevale & Probst, 1997).

There are two major variants of the competing style. In *forcing,* parties exhibit low flexibility and disclosiveness and simply try to get others to go along with them by virtue of superior power. There is no expression of concern or understanding for the other's position, nor any effort to build or to preserve a future relationship. The ways in which parties enact forcing range from rational yet unwavering demands to physical and verbal aggression. In a study of aggression in interpersonal relationships, Olson and Braithwaite (2004) described several forms of aggressive behavior, including shouting, throwing items, slamming a car door, pushing or shoving, throwing a drink on someone, and slapping or hitting. They noted, "physical aggression may not always be the *result* of ineffective conflict management, but, instead could be one of the first strategies employed" (p. 280, italics in the original). Crockett and Randall (2006) found that a poor relationship with family during adolescence was associated with the use of physical aggression and the use of threats during conflicts in adult relationships.

There are less aggressive but equally compelling tactics for forcing. Baxter, Wilmot, Simmons, and Swartz (1993) describe the "silent treatment" as a type of forcing intended to wear others down and compel them to deal with issues on the party's terms. Veiled threats and hostile jokes are indirect ways of bringing pressure on the other party. Manipulative tactics like self-abuse—doing violence to oneself as a means of compelling someone who cares to comply—and guilt-tripping can also serve a forcing orientation.

Contending is a "softer" form of competing. A contending style is somewhat flexible, as long as flexibility does not prevent the party from attaining his or her goals (Pruitt, Rubin, & Kim, 1994) and is also moderately disclosive. Contenders may try to explain why they are compelling others and express understanding and sympathy for others' feelings. A contending style is concerned with future relationships.

One strategy for contending is *toughness,* first introduced by Bartos (1970). A tough bargainer makes extreme opening demands, relatively few concessions, and small concessions when he or she does move. Through this approach, the party attempts to convey strength and determination and to discourage others sufficiently so that they will yield first, and there is evidence that it does so (e.g., Chertkoff & Esser, 1976). However, the tough party must be careful: if he or she is too uncompromising, the other party may respond with counterattacks or equal intransigence. In general, it seems best to convey an impression of "tough but fair" and to give on less important points.

Research indicates that using formal authority to compel others to accept a resolution to a conflict is more effective if the superior explains why the decision was made (Phillips & Cheston, 1979). Bies, Shapiro, and Cummings (1988) add that the explanation must be based on "objective" factors, such as company norms or budget constraints, rather than on the superior's preferences. This suggests that contending may be more effective than forcing in long-term working relationships. However, forcing is less time-consuming than contending, and it does not require the effort of maintaining a good relationship with others, which may be a low priority in some cases.

In general, competing styles tend to be favored when the outcomes of conflicts are important to them and when achieving an agreement through other means seems unlikely (Phillips & Cheston, 1979; Keck & Samp, 2007). Competing, especially forcing, is often advantageous when there is pressure to come to a resolution quickly, because competers can push their own agendas through.

It is important to bear in mind, however, that a competing style may create resentment that fosters future conflicts. This may be a significant problem if the cooperation of others is important in the future. Kurdek (1994; see also Crockett & Randall, 2006) found that couples reported lower levels of relational satisfaction if one or both parties employed personal attacks or lost control. More recent studies have also shown that people who use forcing styles are perceived as less interpersonally competent and less appropriate than those employing collaborating and compromising (Canary, Cupach, & Serpe, 2001; Lakey & Canary, 2002). The negativity that is sometimes associated with competing, particularly the forcing variant, has been shown in numerous studies to decrease relational satisfaction (Caughlin & Vangelisti, 2006). And as we will see in Chapter 5, use of a power resource in competing may ultimately undermine one's power base.

4.3.2 Avoiding

Parties who avoid conflict show low levels of concern for their own and for other parties' interests. Avoiding prevents issues from being aired, and since interests never come out it is difficult to address them. There is, of course, one exception: When parties use avoiding to escape from conflicts they fear they will "lose." But even in this case, issues remain unresolved and can resurface in the future. Avoiders choose a low level of activeness, sometimes bordering on apathy. They exhibit a low level of disclosiveness as well, because avoiding prevents parties from communicating about concerns or positions. An avoiding style varies in terms of the party's level of control, but it attempts to disempower others by denying them the possibility of dealing with the conflict.

The first variation of avoiding is *protecting*. The protecting style is used when parties are determined to avoid conflict at all costs. They are so concerned that the conflict will surface that they build a shell around themselves and deny that a conflict exists. In some cases protectors may respond to attempts to raise an issue with a strong counterattack designed to warn others off. A protecting style involves very low activeness and flexibility: Protectors do not want to work with the conflict at all and will accept no attempts to surface the conflict. Protecting is also low in disclosiveness. Protectors' motives for avoiding generally remain hidden.

A softer version of avoiding is *withdrawing*. In withdrawing, parties work to keep issues off the table, but they are somewhat more flexible than in the protecting style. One tactic that withdrawers use is *fogging*, whereby the party turns aside a criticism or attack by acknowledging only part of it. If Jill criticizes Jack, saying "You have ruined our chances to succeed by being so late with this report!", Jack may respond with "Yes, the report wasn't as good as it could have been." Jack fogs by not acknowledging his fault in delaying the report. Other tactics for withdrawing are to change the topic and to exit the conversation. Another approach to withdrawing is to argue that the issue at hand is not within the jurisdiction of the parties and should be referred to some one else. This is common in conflicts in organizations: by handing off the conflict to a superior or to another unit in the organization, the party tries to make it someone else's problem. Withdrawing is more subtle and flexible than protecting.

A third variation of avoiding is *smoothing,* in which the party plays down differences and emphasizes issues on which there is common ground. Issues that might cause hurt feelings or arouse anger are avoided, if possible, and the party attempts to soothe these negative emotions. Smoothers accentuate the positive and emphasize maintaining good relationships. Roloff and Ifert (2000) marshal evidence that the positive affect associated with smoothing is likely to diminish the negative impacts of avoiding.

Avoiding styles may be useful if chances of success with problem-solving or compromising are slight and if parties' needs can be met without surfacing the conflict. For example, avoidance has been shown to improve team effectiveness by eliminating a distraction that would otherwise derail progress on an issue (deDreu & Van Vianen, 2001). Sillars and Weisberg (1987) reported that some satisfied couples engaged in avoiding through "topic shifts, jokes, denial of conflict [and] abstract, ambivalent, or irrelevant comments" (p. 86). These couples used avoiding in order to fulfill their needs for autonomy and discretion.

Avoiding can also be effective if the party has a weak position or faces a formidable opponent. It may enable the party to save face by never raising the conflict. Avoiding may also be a useful approach if the party is not yet ready to face the conflict, and wants to postpone it until a more opportune time. In the midst of an emergency, for example, parties may agree to put their differences aside for the time being. Roloff and Ifert (2002) argue that avoidance may also be effective when used in cases where the issue is not considered to be particularly important.

However, avoiding leaves the issues behind the conflict unaddressed, and they may fester and eventually surface with destructive consequences. Wall and Nolan (1987) report that an avoiding style led to relatively low satisfaction among students describing their conflicts. And though it may work for some couples, avoiding can have negative consequences for others: Kurdek (1994) found that relational satisfaction was negatively related to the use of withdrawal strategies, in which one partner refuses to discuss the issues and tunes out the other. Avoiding can become destructive if issues are skirted—"walking on eggs" by mutual agreement. Avoiding can also impede development of relationships. As noted in previous chapters, successfully dealing with a conflict can enhance relationships and increase mutual knowledge. Finally, avoiding may worsen others' impressions of us. Gross, Guerrero, and Alberts (2004) found that parties rated partners who used nonconfrontational styles such as avoiding as inappropriate and ineffective. Lakey and Canary (2002) found that parties who behaved toward their partners in ways that the partners perceived were insensitive to their goals led partners to assess the party as having low levels of communication competence.

The protecting variant of avoiding may incur an additional disadvantage, because of its surface resemblance to forcing. It can anger others and encourage them to adopt a competing style. Protecting has an advantage over withdrawing in that it is not likely to make one seem vulnerable, whereas withdrawing may. However, withdrawing and smoothing are more likely to promote a good relationship with other parties than protecting. All three variations can be frustrating to someone who sees the conflict as important and wants to engage.

4.3.3 Accommodating

An accommodating style permits others to realize their concerns but gives little attention to the party's own concerns. Accommodators basically give in to others. Accomodation is sometimes intended to improve a bad or shaky relationship or to preserve a good one, especially when the issue is less important than the relationship. Accommodators are highly flexible; they are willing to accede to the other's demands and to change their own positions. Accommodators' level of activeness is low because they are not involved in the issues per se, but rather in their relationships with others. Accommodating involves a low to moderate level of disclosiveness; accommodators learn much about others' positions and concerns but generally disclose little about their own. Accommodators generally empower the other party and suspend their own control; they "go with the flow" of others' agendas. There are two variations of accommodating: yielding and conceding.

In *yielding,* parties exhibit apathy toward the conflict, show no concern with their own needs, and accommodate others entirely. Yielders are high in flexibility and low in activeness. They allow the other to control the situation and to define the outcomes of the conflict. The passivity of yielding does not encourage others to be concerned with the relationship. Yielders disengage themselves from the situation and go along with what others want.

A "firmer" version of accommodation is *conceding*. In conceding the party still accommodates others' concerns but is more involved in the conflict. Conceders maintain contact with the issues and accommodate in order to build a better relationship with others. Conceders may have a mixture of motives, including real concern for others and a tactical concern for building a relationship that may be useful in the future. Conceding generally is higher in disclosiveness than yielding because conceders are more involved in the conflict and others become aware of their willingness to build relationships. In some cases conceders may directly indicate that they are going along because they value the relationship. One way of viewing conceding is as an exchange in which the other gets what they want and the conceder gains future credit from the other that can be called in when needed.

Accommodating is a useful strategy when one is more concerned with future relationships with others than with the issues behind a conflict. Skillfully employed, an accommodating style can convey the party's understanding of others' needs, thus improving relationships. Accommodating is also useful when one party is weaker than another and will lose if the parties compete. By strategically choosing how he or she accommodates, the weaker party may be able to limit his or her concessions. For example, if Jill suspects that her boss is unhappy with the thoroughness of her reports and how punctually she turns them in, she might agree to make sure she gets them in on time to show her boss that she is complying, while diverting the boss's attention from the thoroughness issue.

One risk of the accommodating style is that the other party may take it as a sign of weakness and compliance. This may encourage the other to take a more competitive approach on the assumption that the accommodator fears confrontation. Like avoiding, accommodating through yielding may also have consequences for perceptions of the party by others. Recall Gross et al.'s (2004) finding that nonconfrontation was negatively related to partner's perceptions that the party's behavior was appropriate and effective. These negative impressions are not likely to occur for the conceding variant of accommodating. As noted in the previous section, Lakey and Canary (2002) found a positive relationship between other's perceptions that the party was sensitive to their needs and their impressions of the party's communicative competence.

4.3.4 Compromising

Compromising attempts to find an intermediate position or trade-off through which parties can achieve some important goals in exchange for foregoing others. Compromising involves moderate levels of assertiveness and cooperativeness because it requires both parties to give up some of their needs to fulfill others. Compromisers are moderate to high in activeness: In some cases, a great deal of energy and involvement are required to arrive at an acceptable compromise, while in others parties settle for compromise because finding an optimal solution seems unlikely. Compromising is in the moderate range of flexibility because compromisers are flexible enough to give in on some of their demands, but not so flexible that they will rework their positions to allow problem-solving or accommodating. Compromising involves moderate to moderately high disclosiveness: Compromisers let others know what they are willing to trade and their evaluations of other positions, but they do not always explain the reasoning or needs that underlie their offers. Compromisers attempt to empower both themselves and others, because shared control is essential to the give-and-take necessary for compromise.

One variation is *firm compromising,* which offers trade-offs, but exhibits limited flexibility of position and low to moderate disclosure. In this case, compromisers push other parties somewhat, showing a rather tough approach designed to motivate them to cooperate, hopefully on the compromiser's terms. Firm compromisers are highly involved in the conflict, working actively and taking the lead in hammering out the compromise. Recall the toughness strategy discussed as one means of competing. Bartos (1970) found that if two tough bargainers went up against each other, an optimal solution resulted. Each was firm and gave up some of their position (but as little as possible) in each round of discussions, and over time the parties reached a good compromise that met a good portion of their needs.

A somewhat more cooperative variation is *flexible compromising*. Flexible compromisers have less well-defined positions than their firm kin. They exhibit moderate to high disclosure because sharing thoughts and positions is an important requirement for the evolution of compromises from flexible positions. They search for possible tradeoffs as the discussion evolves. Flexible compromisers may be less actively involved in the conflict, in some cases following others' initiatives.

Sometimes—especially when there are two equally strong parties who are locked in an impasse—compromises are the best that can be achieved. Compromising can also enable parties to achieve a relatively fast resolution of the conflict. The tactic of *tacit coordination* is a good example of an approach to compromise that often yields quick results. In tacit coordination one party makes an offer based on a common norm that he or she believes the other is likely to accept. For example, we might offer to "split the difference" with the other in order to reach a compromise. Dividing things equally is a time-honored custom in the U.S. that is used to resolve conflicts between three-year-olds over a piece of cake, between seventy-year-olds over an inheritance from a sibling, and for all ages in between. Splitting the difference is so taken for granted as a measure of fairness that often the other party will accept it without further discussion.

However, compromise also carries disadvantages. As Filley (1975) noted in his classic book on conflict management, compromises often result in a low level of commitment from parties because they force parties to give up something they value. With the satisfaction of achieving some goals comes the bitterness of having to give up others. Compromising can also make the party seem somewhat compliant. If a party compromises, others may draw the conclusion that he or she is always willing to give up something to get something and bring this mindset to future conflicts or negotiations. This may lead to problems when the party is committed to a position and others expect him or her to compromise.

4.3.5 Collaborating

Collaboration is the conflict style favored by most scholars and practitioners, because its goal is to develop a solution that meets all of the important needs of both parties. In a successful collaboration, people are generally pleased and often enthusiastic about the resolution. It can be exhilarating to discover a creative solution through joint effort. Parties learn about themselves and new possibilities open up for the future. These favorable reactions energize people and contribute to effective follow-up and implementation of the solution.

For collaborating to work several conditions must be met:

- All parties must have a vested interest in the outcome.
- Parties must believe they have the potential to resolve the conflict in a way that satisfies all major interests.
- Parties must be willing to set aside hostility and grudges toward the other parties.

In an effective collaboration:

- The focus is on the issues and interests of those involved rather than on personalities.
- Parties are problem-minded rather than solution-minded, taking flexible rather than fixed positions; parties together search out the issues that separate them.
- Parties recognize that both sides have potential strengths and potential weaknesses and that rarely is one position completely right and the other completely wrong.
- Parties try to understand others' points of view as legitimate and recognize that meeting others' needs and interests is as important as meeting their own.
- Parties explore a range of options and evaluate them in terms of their strengths and weaknesses in addressing the issues and interests of all.
- Parties help each other preserve face, so that a change in position or viewpoint does not suggest weakness or capitulation.
- Parties attempt to "level the playing field" by minimizing the effects of status and power differences.
- Parties attempt to use argument and evidence to find the best possible solution rather than to argue for their own position or degrade other parties' positions.

Collaborators are highly concerned with both their own and others' needs. They are involved in the conflict, actively pursuing every issue to increase their understanding and probe possible integrative solutions. They are also flexible, not rigidly adhering to positions. However, this does not mean that collaborators give in to others: They are firmly committed to achieving their goals and do not sacrifice them. Collaborating works best when parties have high aspirations for the outcome of the conflict, firmly insist that their goals and needs be satisfied, but are flexible about the means by which this is done (Pruitt, 1981; 1983).

Collaborators are also moderately to highly disclosive. Collaborating requires a high level of information about the issues and about parties' needs, and this requires an open communication climate. Collaborating also requires parties to share control over the emerging solution. Hence collaborators attempt to empower others while not sacrificing their own power bases. As we will see in Chapter 5, this is most easily done when both parties have common power resources.

Issues and interests may evolve and change during collaboration. During the course of productive discussions, parties may gain insight into their own interests and conclude that what they originally thought they wanted was not what they really need. They may redefine their goals during the integrative process.

There is considerable evidence that collaborating yields positive outcomes. Experiments by Wall, Galanes and Love (1987) and Sambamurthy and Poole (1992) showed that acknowledging conflict and then openly addressing the issues at hand increased the ability of groups to achieve consensus and the quality of outcomes. In a study of new product development teams in organizations, Lovelace, Shapiro, and Weingart (2001) found that collaborative communication—as would occur in compromising and problem-solving—was associated with a team's innovativeness. Several studies of negotiations provide evidence that collaborative approaches led to more mutually beneficial outcomes (Brett, Shapiro, & Lytle, 1998; deDreu, Weingart, & Kwon, 2000; Weingart, Hyder, & Prietula, 1996).

A number of studies of work groups have found that conflicts that were (a) focused on substantive issues and (b) effectively resolved were positively related to group and individual performance (Poole & Garner, 2006). This effect was more pronounced in groups with high levels of interdependence among members, probably because conflicts are a greater hindrance when members must coordinate their work (Jehn, 1995; Janssen, van de Vliert & Veenstra, 1999). Alper, Tjosvold, and Law (2000) found that self-managed teams who took a cooperative approach to conflict—characterized by an emphasis on understanding all points of view, orientation to joint benefit, and finding a solution acceptable to all—had higher levels of effectiveness than those that were characterized by a win–lose orientation. Kuhn and Poole (2000) studied quality management teams in a government organization and found that those that developed norms favoring collaborative conflict management made more effective decisions than those that developed norms of avoiding or competing.

Collaborating also has positive consequences in interpersonal relationships. Kurdek (1994) found that relational satisfaction was positively related to the use of problem-solving styles. He also found that couples who used problem-solving were less likely to dissolve their relationships. Crockett and Randall (2006) reported that quality of young adult romantic relationships was rated higher in couples who discussed their problems rather than resorting to verbal or physical attacks.

The collaborating style is not without problems. It requires a great deal of time and energy. Creativity is not easy, and parties may have to spend a considerable amount of time exchanging offers and ideas before an acceptable solution can be hammered out. Hence, collaborating is difficult when there is little time or when there is urgent pressure to act immediately. Collaborating also encourages parties to get their hopes up, and this can cause problems. As we noted, goals are sometimes redefined and clarified during collaboration, and if one or more parties revises aspirations upward, it can create a situation in which interests cannot be satisfied. If a collaborating approach fails to deliver a timely solution, parties may give up on the process and switch to competing or some other style.

Power must be managed very carefully for collaborating to work. Collaboration presumes that parties are willing to suspend, for the time being, their use of power. If parties do not trust that others are willing to do this, then collaboration will collapse. Stronger parties, in particular, may be tempted to try collaborating for a while and then resort to force if they don't get their way. Indeed, parties with a stronger position may make only a show of collaborating and then justify use of force with the argument that they "tried everything short of force." The dynamics of power related to collaboration—and to conflict interaction in general—are complex and subtle.

4.4 Determining the Styles of Others

How do we sort out the styles that others use? On its face, this may seem to be a simple matter. The descriptions in the previous section distinguish the different styles and variants along a number of dimensions. However, behavior is often hard to read at the surface. For example, protecting (a variant of avoiding) and forcing (a variant of competing) may both be carried out through personal attacks on the other party. Studies of perception of conflict styles have shown that most observers have difficulty in distinguishing compromising from collaborating and avoiding from accommodating (Nicotera & Dorsey, 2006). Generally these studies tend to yield three conflict styles: (1) cooperative/integrative; (2) competitive/antagonistic/distributive; and (3) avoidance/accommodative (though Cai and Fink, 2002, report that their subjects were able to distinguish avoiding and accommodating).

That people have difficulty identifying and distinguishing conflict styles does not, in our opinion, reduce the value of differentiating the five styles and their variants. As the previous section indicates, there are clear differences in motivation and concern for the other party across the five styles, so they can be distinguished conceptually. The style typology offers us a variety of options to consider when we are engaged in a conflict. The styles also give us a reference point for diagnosing our own behavior and its possible consequences.

The difficulty that people have in distinguishing styles suggests that we should be cautious in drawing conclusions about others' approaches to conflicts. Appearances may be deceiving. Jameel, for example, may appear to be accommodating when he gives into Keisha's demand that he spend more time with her. But Jameel may actually be avoiding, because he fears that an open conflict will bring out complaints he suspects Keisha has about his unwillingness to commit to their relationship. Accurately ascertaining what style the other employs requires us to resist drawing quick conclusions and to be open to subtle cues. For instance, in giving in to Keisha, Jameel may make placating comments, such as "You know how much I want you to be happy." This comment suggests that Jameel is trying to reinforce his relationship with Keisha in an attempt to avoid addressing the larger issue of *his* commitment to the relationship. We do not mean to suggest you should always second-guess your judgments about others' styles, but it is important to be open to revising your reading of another person. One of the keys to effective conflict interaction is diagnosing other people's styles and responding appropriately.

4.5 Pairings of Conflict Styles

Some styles naturally seem to go together. If you look at Table 4.1, you'll see that competing—with high concern for self and low concern for other parties—and accommodating—with low concern for self and high concern for other parties—are complementary. The competer gets what he or she wants and the accommodator accedes to the competer's desires. Scholarship on communication in relationships has shown that this pairing of styles can be remarkably stable, as one partner assumes the dominant role in a relationship and the other assumes a submissive role (Fitzpatrick & Caughlin, 2002). This pairing of styles can be seen in how conflict is handled in traditional marriages, in the pecking orders seen in many friendship groups, and in the traditional superior-subordinate relationship in organizations. While it may seem that the accommodator would be frustrated, he or she may be gratified and rewarded by being able to help or satisfy the dominant partner. Over the long run, such relationships may prove to be unstable, because the less powerful party may eventually conclude that he or she is not going to get what he or she wants, or be unable to sustain the exchange.

Another complementary pairing of styles is competing and avoiding. This pairing occurs most often between parties who are formally committed to a relationship, such as a marriage or job. One party typically attempts to initiate a conflict, while the other avoids engaging. A well-known instance of this pair is the demand/withdraw pattern, which involves "one partner nagging, complaining, or criticizing and the other partner avoiding" (Caughlin & Vangelisti, 2006, p. 133). The withdrawal of the other, sparks further urgency in the first party to pursue the conflict, resulting in a self-reinforcing cycle that solidifies each party's intention to stick with their style. Demand/withdraw patterns have been shown to have negative impacts on relational satisfaction. There is also some evidence that a rigid pattern in which a husband demands and the wife withdraws is associated with abuse (Caughlin & Vangelisti, 2006; Gottman, Driver, Yoshimoto, & Rushe, 2002).

A somewhat surprising pairing is competing and collaborating. At first blush, one would think the competer would come out ahead by taking advantage of the collaborator. However, a steadfast collaborator can often find common ground with the competer and forge a mutually agreeable outcome. A competer's issues are usually out in the open, and this gives the collaborator an opportunity to find some way to meet both sets of interests. If the collaborator is firm and resolved and signals that he or she is trying to find a way to satisfy both, this may also win the respect of the competer and lead the competer toward collaborating. Cummings (Filley, 1975) found that when competers were paired with collaborators, a common result was mutual agreement, though competers still "won" in more than half the cases.

Symmetric pairings of conflict styles also occur. Avoiders often pair with avoiders to facilitate denial of a conflict. This pairing is also likely to be stable, as both parties prefer to hide the issues and prevent the conflict from surfacing. As mentioned previously, in some types of relationships, avoiding conflict can be related to satisfaction if the couple's philosophy is "let sleeping dogs lie," and they tolerate differences between them (Sillars, Canary, & Tafoya, 2004). At some point, however, not dealing with the underlying conflict is likely to cause problems for parties who collaborate in avoidance.

Two or more collaborators also form a stable pairing. While collaborators can often work well with others employing different conflict styles, when they meet with another collaborator, the stage is set for productive interaction. Collaborators challenge each other to innovate in an open field of possibilities. Although the results of this are not always brilliant, there is a likelihood that innovative and satisfying solutions will ensue during mutual collaboration. Jones and White (1985) found that groups composed of collaborators were more effective than groups of accommodators.

The final pair we consider are competing versus competing styles. Previously we noted that parties tend to match each other's moves. This tendency accounts for the fact that competing tends to breed competing. The symmetric competition sets up a self-reinforcing cycle that escalates the conflict until a stalemate results. In one of the few studies of sets of conflict styles, Cummings (reported in Filley, 1975) found that if both parties adopted competing styles the result was generally a stalemate.

4.6 Shifting Styles During Conflict Episodes

It is tempting to think of styles as more or less stable choices people make, but it is common for parties to change styles as conflict unfolds. Numerous studies have documented changes in conflict styles (Sillars, 1980c; Papa & Natalle, 1989; Conrad, 1991; Nicotera, 1994; Keck & Samp, 2007). Case 4.2 illustrates several styles two women adopt during a protracted conflict.

CASE 4.2 • *College Roommates*

Imagine yourself as Jill: At what points in your interaction with Rachel did your style change?

Jill, Rachel, Connie, and Tina decided to room together during their sophomore year at college. Jill and Rachel, best friends, decided to share one bedroom, and Connie and Tina the other. After a couple of months Rachel noticed that Jill and Tina spent a great deal of time together, doing laundry, fixing their hair in the same style, shopping and going out. Rachel had little in common with Connie and she was "a little hurt" that Jill had abandoned her.

More seeds for the conflict were sown right after Christmas break. Jill decided to try to lose some weight and went on an "oatmeal diet" in which her main food consisted of five bowls of oatmeal a day. Rachel did not think Jill needed to lose weight and teased her about the diet. Jill joined in the laughter and asked Rachel for nutrition advice. But Jill kept up her oatmeal regimen, and Rachel dropped the subject after about a week. During this time Jill and Tina continued to spend a lot of time together. Rachel reported being somewhat resentful because she had introduced Tina to Jill.

About a week later, Jill began to make sarcastic remarks whenever Rachel mentioned her diet. For example, Rachel walked into the kitchen and saw Jill standing and eating cottage cheese out of the carton. Rachel asked Jill if she was planning on eating the whole carton, and Jill replied harshly, "I will if I want to!" Rachel had meant this as a joke, but Jill's reply made her mad and she replied, "Do whatever the hell you want!" and walked out of the room.

Rachel gave Jill the silent treatment after the incident. Within earshot of Rachel, Jill complained about Rachel's behavior to the other two roommates. Rachel talked to Connie about the situation, but Connie did not offer much insight: She interpreted the whole conflict as a result of personal attacks between Jill and Rachel.

Rachel reported that she had decided to give up on her friendship with Jill. However, Jill felt differently and decided to confront Rachel.

Two weeks before spring term was over, Jill approached Rachel and told her that the two of them needed to talk. They went into the bedroom and closed the door. The following dialogue ensued:

Jill: What's going on between us?

Rachel: I don't know. What do you mean?

Jill: I mean why won't you talk to me anymore? You won't even say "Good morning" to me when you walk past me in the hall.

Rachel: I didn't realize I was supposed to talk. Sorry.

Jill: Were you planning on not speaking to me for the rest of the year and leaving without ever seeing me again?

Rachel: That was not what I meant to do . . . but I figured, why bother saying anything? Every time I open my mouth, I get a sarcastic remark back. I just didn't need that anymore, so I shut up.

Jill: I'm sorry, but I was hurt, and the way I handle it is by getting defensive and making sarcastic remarks. I didn't really mean to hurt you.

Rachel: Well, you did.

Jill: Well, you hurt me too, and I didn't know what to do.

Rachel: How did I hurt you?

Jill: I didn't like it when you made fun of my eating habits, like eating oatmeal five times a day. I also didn't appreciate it when you would make fun of my exercising or my big butt. How would you like it if I started teasing you about your thighs?

Rachel: Jill, I had no idea you were so upset about those remarks. Why didn't you tell me this a long time ago? It certainly would have saved a lot of hurt feelings and resentment.

Jill: I figured you would stop making them sooner or later. I thought you would realize you were hurting my feelings.

(continued)

CASE 4.2   Continued

Rachel: Jill, how could I? You were always going along with me and even making fun of yourself. Do you think if I had known I was hurting you I would have continued? I'm not that mean.

Jill: I know you're not, and I'm sorry I made so many rude remarks when I was hurt. I really want to get things straightened out between us. Doesn't our friendship mean anything to you anymore?

Rachel: Yes, it means something to me, but I didn't think it meant anything to you. I've been feeling really hurt lately by your behavior with Tina. I feel like you guys just run off and forget that I even exist. You are always doing everything together without including me. I figured she was just more important to you than me. Therefore, I would just finish out the year and go home and let you two have each other. I felt like I wasn't needed anymore.

Jill: I feel bad that you felt this way. I realize I have been spending a lot of time with Tina, but you've been pretty busy with your boyfriend. I didn't think you had much time for me either.

Rachel: Yes, I have been spending a lot of time with my boyfriend, but that doesn't mean I don't need your friendship too. We have been friends for quite a while, and it was hard for me to see you turn away like you did. I started spending so much time with my boyfriend because of that. Now, don't get me wrong. I realize what you and Tina have is special. However, that doesn't ease my pain at being rejected or excluded from everything you guys do.

Jill: I'm not rejecting you as a friend or picking Tina over you. It just so happened that Tina and I have a lot in common and we have fun together. This naturally leads us to spending more time together. We didn't really think you wanted to do everything with us.

Rachel: You're right. I probably wouldn't have. But, I felt like you didn't need me for a friend at all anymore.

Jill: Well, you're wrong. I still value our friendship, and I hope we can keep it going.

Rachel: I feel better for having talked it over, and I'm sorry for having hurt you.

Jill: I'm sorry too—I hope you can forgive Tina and me somehow.

Rachel: I think I can.

Discussion Questions

- Which of the moves or shifts in styles had the most impact on the ultimate direction this conflict took?
- Think of a conflict you have been involved in where the patterns of style changes were similar to the changes in this conflict.

Jill and Rachel use several different styles in this conflict. Jill starts with a forcing style during the kitchen incident, and Rachel responds with the protecting remark, "Do whatever the hell you want!" As often happens after protecting, Rachel moves into a withdrawing style, giving Jill the silent treatment. This type of withdrawing also contains elements of competing, because the silent treatment is often used to punish others and "show them how upset I am." During this period Jill continues forcing, talking to the other roommates about how unreasonable Rachel is being. Finally, Jill shifts to a collaborating style, telling Rachel that they have to talk. Rachel at first responds with protecting ("I didn't realize I was supposed to talk. Sorry."). Jill persists with collaborating, trying to get Rachel to talk about the issue openly. Rachel goes along with her, and the two have an open discussion about their problems. The discussion does not resolve the issue, however, and it ends with a compromise: Both apologize and Rachel says that she thinks she can forgive

Tina and Jill. However, this resolution is not wholly satisfactory—to Rachel, at least. She reports that she and Jill "have never been as close as they once were." In part, this is because Rachel and Jill do not work out a solution that addresses the sources of the conflict. Merely forgiving Tina and Jill is not the issue; Rachel wants Jill to spend more time with her, and it is not clear that Jill is willing to do that.

The styles change as the conflict unfolds. Shifts in styles are common when a conflict stretches over time. If one style does not "work"—as the collaborating style does not in the discussion between Rachel and Jill—parties often shift to a related style—compromising in this case. Another thing to notice is how Rachel shifts between protecting and withdrawing while remaining in the same overall style—avoiding. These shifts are common in the ebb and flow of conflict as parties bring issues to the fore and then back away from each other.

Putnam (1990) described a particularly interesting pattern of shifting styles. While it is common to presume that collaborators primarily engage in cooperative and open behavior, Putnam found that in many cases a mixture of competing and collaborating styles is more effective in inducing others to cooperate than a purely cooperative style. By competing, the party signals to the other that he or she is serious and is willing to use his/her power if necessary, and by collaborating, the party signals that he or she would like to resolve the conflict through problem-solving. This may dissuade the other party from competing or trying to take advantage, opting for a more positive approach as an alternative to escalating competition.

4.7 Selecting Conflict Styles

In choosing a conflict style, you should consider several factors. First and foremost, what are your goals in the immediate situation? Depending on whether your goal is to meet your own needs, help the other party meet his or hers, or satisfy the interests of both, different styles are more effective.

Second, you should consider the longer-term consequences of a style. Styles can improve or worsen relationships with others, and this may come back to help or haunt in the future. Then too, the styles that parties adopt may change them. If a style is used often enough, it may become a habitual tendency. So someone who accommodates often may develop a reputation for so doing, and others may assume they can get what they want by competing. Repeatedly seeing themselves accommodating, parties may come to see themselves as relatively weak, ignoring their unique resources and setting up a self-reinforcing cycle of accommodating behavior. Over the long term, conflict styles shape definitions of self. A final long-term consequence flows from the tendency to fall into patterns of complementary or symmetric styles. When this occurs, both parties become prisoners of each other's style. Because it is rare for one style to be appropriate for all situations, this inflexible interdependence can prevent parties from meeting their needs and cause long-term problems.

Third, you should consider the situation. One important variable is time. If there is a lot of time pressure, styles that require a good deal of consultation and creativity, such as collaborating, are not as likely to yield fruitful results. A second variable is the degree of trust you have in the other party. Disclosive styles that give the other person information about your preferences and how firmly you hold your position, for example, may give the other person an advantage over you and therefore are advisable only if you trust the other (or are willing to show trust in the other, in hopes of winning the other's trust). Some styles also leave you open to exploitation by others. Styles such also collaborating and accommodating may leave you vulnerable and are not advisable unless you trust the other person.

Finally, you should consider the ethical implications of selecting a style. Although no single set of values can be applied in all conflicts, you should assess your own values with respect to the styles. Some people are uncomfortable with styles that do not take others into account; this would indicate a preference for collaborating, compromising, and accommodating and a dislike for competing and avoiding. Others may believe it is very important to be assertive, favoring competing, collaborating, compromising, and the more active forms of accommodating and avoiding. All styles involve value choices. Although style choice is discussed from a situational standpoint, ethical imperatives can override concerns with short- and long-term effectiveness.

Exhibit 4.1 outlines a procedure for selecting conflict styles. It presents a decision tree for style selection based on several of the considerations outlined in this section.

EXHIBIT 4.1 • *A Procedure for Selecting Conflict Styles*

Building on existing evidence, we can propose a procedure for selecting conflict styles (Thomas, 1975; Musser, 1982; Ebert & Wall, 1983; Savage et al., 1989). The procedure takes the form of a *decision tree*—a diagram that supports the selection of options based on answers to a series of questions. The diagram presents a question to someone and, based on the answer to this question, the party traces different branches of the tree, which lead to other questions and branches, and finally to a recommended style. In the conflict style decision tree shown in Figure 4.2, the party would have to answer a maximum of five questions to arrive at a style selection. The questions are arranged in logical order, prompting the party to consider the factors that studies and common sense suggest are important.

1. *How important are the issues to the party?*   If the issues are important, the decision tree indicates that the party should pursue "firm" strategies that focus on realizing the party's interests; that is, forcing, contending, firm compromising, flexible compromising, and collaborating. If the issues are unimportant, however, less assertive strategies, such as yielding, conceding, smoothing, withdrawing, and protecting, are recommended because they can be less costly in time or energy.

2. *How important are the issues to the other?*   This question reflects the second dimension in the classic conflict style diagram—concern for others. If the issues are important to the other party, each party will benefit most by choosing strategies that take the other party into account; that is, flexible compromising, firm compromising, collaborating, yielding, or conceding. If the issues are not important to the other party, then it is more efficient to choose strategies that place less emphasis on the other party's needs; that is, contending, forcing, protecting, withdrawing, or smoothing.

3. *How important is maintaining a positive relationship?*   How conflicts are managed affects the long-term relationship between parties— their degree of trust and liking for each other

(continued)

EXHIBIT 4.1 Continued

and whether parties nurse grudges or hard feelings. In some cases, it is important to maintain a good relationship. This is true when you must work together in the future, or when the other party may control or influence your fate at some future time. In this case, it would be best to choose styles that build, or at least do not undermine, trust and positive feelings, such as, flexible compromising, firm compromising, collaborating, yielding, withdrawing, smoothing, conceding, and contending.

Alternatively, a good relationship may be impossible to maintain, and the party may decide that the best that can be done is to keep a protective guard up by maintaining a more formal relationship with the other party. The relationship between lawyers negotiating a divorce is an example of this. Both lawyers often try to maximize their clients' gains; there is little place for trust. Instead, they work on the basis of legal codes and professional practices that maintain decorum, foster progress on issues, and afford protection against cheating. In such cases, building or maintaining a relationship is not of concern, and styles that do not show concern for the other party may be adopted; that is, forcing and protecting.

4. *How much time pressure is there?* When time pressure is great, the best course is to adopt styles that are not time-consuming; that is, forcing, contending, flexible compromising, protecting, withdrawing, or yielding. When there is little time pressure, more time-consuming strategies may be better because they can promote deeper exploration of issues; these include smoothing, conceding, firm compromising, and collaborating.

5. *To what extent does one party trust the other?* Trust determines the degree to which one party is willing to let the other party control the situation. When trust is high, styles that empower the other can be used, including

collaborating, flexible compromising, firm compromising, conceding, and yielding. When trust is low, styles that protect one's own power are safer; that is, forcing, contending, protecting, smoothing, and withdrawing.

Answering the five questions leads the party through the diagram to recommended strategies. It is important to note that these are the optimal strategies for each case under the assumptions reflected in the choice rules. Although the rules represent some of the best evidence available on conflict styles, they do not exhaust all factors one might consider. As the decision tree diagram on the next page shows, in some cases not all questions are applicable. For example, time pressure is not relevant in distinguishing some styles. Also, there are a few "twists" to the general rules, as when firm compromising is a "low" trust strategy compared to collaborating in the very top branch of the tree. Although firm compromising is generally a trusting style, it protects the party relative to collaborating and is recommended when trust is low and collaborating is the other alternative.

To illustrate how the decision tree works, consider the following example:

Jack is a foreman for an industrial cleaning company. He really enjoys his work and has been with the same company, Acme Cleanzit, for twelve years. Recently his boss was replaced by a younger woman, fresh out of business school. Jack's new manager, Ms. Jorgensen, graduated at the top of her class, and while in school worked for the branch of Acme Cleanzit in her college town. Jorgensen has lots of new ideas and is quite impatient to try them out. She tends to lean toward using her authority to force issues. She has hinted that she expects Jack to help her implement her ideas and that she might have to replace any "problem employees". Jorgensen has the complete faith of top management at Acme, and Jack believes she will have management's backing in whatever she does.

Jack sees a conflict on the horizon. Jorgensen wants to try new water-pressure cleaning

(continued)

EXHIBIT 4.1 Continued

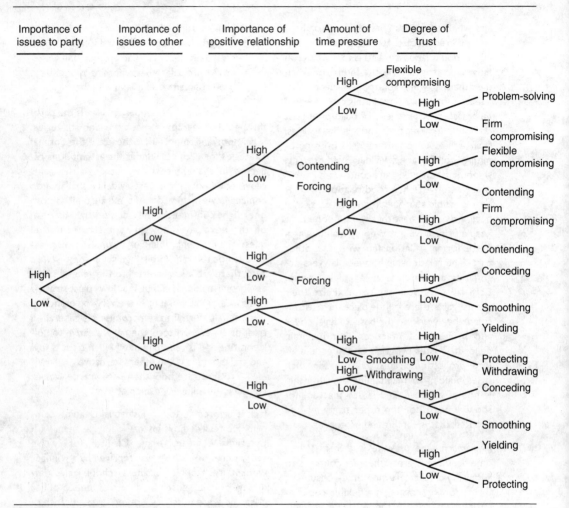

Importance of issues to party	Importance of issues to other	Importance of positive relationship	Amount of time pressure	Degree of trust

FIGURE 4.2 *Style Selection Decision Tree.*

equipment to replace the air-pressure equipment Acme Cleanzit has always employed. Jack has used water-pressure equipment in the past and does not like it. Although it cleans faster than air-pressure equipment, it breaks down easily and is somewhat dangerous to repair. He is afraid the rate of absenteeism and resignations will go up because the workers won't like the tedious process of repairing

the new equipment. Still, when the water-pressure equipment works, it does increase productivity, so he must concede Jorgensen has a point. When he receives her memo asking his input on water-pressure equipment, he writes her a memo clearly outlining his objections. After Jorgensen receives it, she brushes past him on her way out of the plant, saying, "We'll talk about this in the morning." It is

(continued)

EXHIBIT 4.1   Continued

clear to Jack that she is angry. While he has a couple of beers with fellow workers, Wilma and Joe, after work Jack finds himself rehearsing what he will say to Jorgensen the next day.

What Style Should Jack Choose?

In this case, the issues are important to Jack, so he should take the upward branch of the tree. The issues are also important to Jorgensen, so again he should take the upward branch. Unless Jack wants to lose his job, his relationship with Jorgensen should be highly important to him. Again he should take the upward branch. There is little time pressure, so the downward branch is most appropriate for this choice. Finally, it is not clear that Jack can trust Jorgensen, so the downward branch regarding degree of trust in the other is most appropriate, leading to the firm compromising style. This style encourages Jack to enter the discussion with clear and well-stated positions, and to demonstrate a willingness to move on views if he is truly convinced by Jorgensen. However, he should remain committed to having some of his important needs met, whatever the outcome of the discussions. This style takes the concerns outlined in the questions into account. Of course, other styles might also work, but they would not meet the criteria in the tree as well as firm compromising.

Consider a second example:

Cindy and John have been married for three years. As with many married couples, some of their worst fights stem from seemingly simple issues, such as how to decorate their house. They are in the process of redoing their recreation room, and John really wants to put up wallpaper with a hunting motif. Cindy does not like the idea of being surrounded by ducks and pointers while she watches tv and would rather have wallpaper with a modern design of some sort. However, she has found that with the right furniture any kind of wallpaper can look good, and she thinks she could probably live with ducks and dogs if it is really important to John. What is important to Cindy is that their relationship and

their faith in each other not be undermined by incessant arguments over "little things." As they sit together at breakfast, John once again raises the issue of the hunting paper, this time a bit testily.

What Style Should Cindy Adopt?

The best style in this case is conceding; it takes into account the importance of the issue to John, that it is not as important to Cindy, that their relationship is a high priority to Cindy, and that Cindy trusts John.

Some observations about the decision tree are in order. First, it is ambiguous in cases when some issues are important to the party, while others are not. The model confronts us with a dichotomous choice: It assumes issues are either important or they are not. In the common case where there are a number of issues, some important and some not, parties may try to switch styles when different issues are discussed, hoping to set up trade-offs. For example, if John adopts a firm compromising style when discussing his wallpaper and a conceding style when discussing furniture, Cindy may respond positively to his demands about wallpaper because she senses she can pick out furniture that will make even ducks and dogs look good. The combination of styles results in terms acceptable to both.

In applying the decision tree, it is also important to bear in mind that the answers to the questions may change over the course of the conflict. As emphasized throughout this book, conflict is an interactive process. As a result, earlier interactions can influence later ones. A party may begin a conflict episode with a firm conviction that his or her relationship with the other party should be preserved, but as the conflict unfolds, he or she may find that he or she no longer wants a relationship with the other party. If this happens, styles that were suitable at the outset of the conflict are no longer appropriate. It is important to monitor changing conditions to determine if conflict styles should change. It is also possible that a combination of two styles may be effective.

(continued)

EXHIBIT 4.1   Continued

Finally, the decision tree procedure is general and applies to a wide range of conflicts. However, this also means the tree may be less useful in particular situations. Savage and associates (1989) and Ebert and Wall (1983) lay out decision trees for negotiation tactics specifically adapted to organizational negotiations. Musser (1982) describes a choice tree for subordinate responses to conflicts with superiors. These procedures are tailored to specific contexts and can be highly useful in their intended settings.

4.8 Cultural and Gender Influences on Conflict Styles

4.8.1 Cultural Influences

The preceding points on stylistic effectiveness are limited to cultures that favor the confrontational model of conflict management. Indeed the subjects in most of the studies cited in the previous section were from U.S. or British cultures. Research in other cultures, however, suggests that different styles would be effective for the harmony and regulative models discussed in Chapter 3. The harmony model emphasizes avoiding, accommodating, and compromising over other styles (Kozan, 1997). Although problem-solving would be valued for its emphasis on the other party and cooperativeness, the need to confront the conflict when solving problems would make members of harmony cultures less comfortable with problem-solving than with the three styles just mentioned. Research on conflict styles in different cultures is still in its infancy, but evidence from studies of cultures with associative cognitive styles provides some support for this conjecture. Japanese subjects have been found to prefer avoiding or accommodating styles (Krauss, Rohlen, & Steinhoff, 1984). Studies of Arab (Elsayed-Ekhouly & Buda, 1996), Turkish (Kozan, 1997), and Jordanian (Kozan, 1991) subjects indicate that they prefer styles high in cooperativeness and concern for others over competition. Kim and Leung (2000) make a convincing case that the avoiding style has a fundamentally different, much more positive, meaning for people in harmony cultures than for people in confrontational cultures where most studies of avoidance have been conducted.

Parties using a regulative model would be predisposed either to avoiding or to competing in initial stages of the conflict and then to refer the conflict to some authority who resolves the conflict (Kozan, 1997). As noted in Chapter 1, relevant authorities would include a superior in the organizational hierarchy, a ranking family member, or a judge using a set of rules or laws. Depending on how the authority proceeded, resolution could occur through compromise or problem-solving or through a flat decision by the authority. In cases when the authority determined that one party was right and one wrong, the losing party would accommodate.

Appropriate styles thus differ depending on whether a culture employs a confrontational, harmony, or regulative model of conflict management. However, it would also be a mistake to assume that cultures are uniform. Local conditions and particular situations can override the general tendencies of a culture. Fry and Fry (1997) found that two adjacent Zapotec communities in Mexico had very different styles of managing conflict. In San Andreas (a pseudonym), there were high levels of aggressive behavior, homicide, wife-beating, and use of physical punishment on children. In contrast, La Paz (also a pseudonym) emphasized tranquility, respectful behavior toward others, reasoning with children, and harmonious relations in the family. The two communities also had very different images of themselves: "The people of La Paz perceived themselves as tranquil and respectful, whereas the citizens of San Andreas more ambiguously complain about jealous, aggressive, troublemakers in their basically good community" (Fry & Fry, 1997, p. 16). This study demonstrates that it is important to take local patterns and preferences into consideration, in addition to the more general culture.

Oetzel (1998) provided evidence of individual differences within cultural tendencies. A number of studies of conflict and culture have distinguished cultures in terms of the individualism-collectivism dimension. "Individualists value the goals, needs, and rights of the individual over the goals, responsibilities, and obligations of the group" (Cai & Fink, 2002), while collectivists reverse the emphasis and value the group over the individual. The U.S. and Australia are high individualist cultures, while China and Mexico are high collectivist cultures. A wide variety of studies have found that in general members of individualist cultures tend to prefer active styles that confront the conflict, including competing and collaborating, while members of collectivist cultures tend to prefer more passive styles such as avoiding or compromising. However, Cai and Fink (2002) raise a cautionary note about generalizing about cultures and conflict styles. They noted that conflict styles meant different things to individualists and collectivists. They also reported patterns of stylistic choices that differed from the findings of most other studies.

Oetzel (1998) found that an individual's self-construal—whether they see themselves as independent of others or interdependent with others in a particular situation—was a stronger predictor of conflict behavior in small groups than was culture. Culture and self-construal are clearly related to each other. Other things being equal, people brought up in individualist cultures are more likely to adopt independent self-construals, while people brought up in collectivist cultures are more likely to adopt interdependent self-construals. However, other factors also influence self-construal, including relationships to the other party, whether the situation encourages adoption of a competitive or cooperative orientation, and many other things. Oetzel found that self-construal was not strongly related to culture and, furthermore that a competing conflict style was related to independent self-construal and avoiding, accommodating, and compromising styles were related to interdependent self-construal. He also found that the collaborating style was strongly related to interdependent self-construal and weakly related to independent self-construal. These results suggest that individual and situational factors may override the influence of culture on style selection.

Cai and Drake (1998) report a similar pattern in studies of intercultural differences in negotiation behavior. Although differences were expected, when different cultures were directly compared in experiments, results indicated that factors other than culture had a greater influence on negotiation behavior. In one study on negotiation between U.S. and Taiwanese citizens, expected differences in facework behavior did not occur; instead, parties matched each other's face behaviors, and the strongest influence on behavior was negotiator role (buyer or seller). Other factors that influenced negotiations more than culture in other studies include authority, hierarchical position of the negotiator, age, and acquaintance level of the parties. Although these results are from controlled experimental settings rather than ordinary situations of intercultural contact, they suggest that we should be careful in assuming that people of different cultures will always act in ways consistent with their cultural upbringing.

In sum, while culture is likely to affect the choice of conflict style, there is no simplistic, cut-and-dried formula. It is just one of many factors that should be taken into account.

4.8.2 Gender Influences

The impact of gender on conflict styles has been the subject of much research. However, research shows that—at least for conflict styles—there is less difference than we might presume based on stereotypes of men and women. A number of studies have shown that males and females do not differ in terms of the tactics and styles they use in conflicts (Korabik, Baril, & Watson, 1993; Kluwer, deDreu, & Buunk, 1998; Watson, 1994; Nicotera & Dorsey, 2006), though a few (mostly older studies) have shown differences (Mackey & O'Brien, 1998; Rubin & Brown, 1975; but also see Brewer, Mitchell, & Weber, 2002). As Nicotera and Dorsey (2006) conclude, with respect to gender differences in conflict styles, "There is no *there* there. Conflict style is *not* driven by biological sex, regardless of how many studies try to find the effect; it simply is not there" (p. 312).

However, as we noted in the previous chapter, there are differences in how the genders are *expected* to think and act, and these expectations may influence how effective styles are. The stereotype is that women are expected to value relationships more than men and men are expected to focus more on tasks. In line with this, when women adopt competing styles (which focus on getting what they want regardless of the partner's wants), there is some evidence that they are evaluated more negatively than are men who compete (Korabik, Baril, & Watson, 1993). This is also consistent with a more general finding that because women are expected to be "nice and supportive" when they behave assertively, they violate social expectations and are perceived negatively by other men and women (Ivy & Backlund, 1994). Men who behave assertively are not judged negatively because this is consistent with what is socially expected of them.

4.9 Styles and Tactics in Practice

The preceding discussion may create the somewhat misleading impression that people can simply select and use whatever styles and tactics they think will work. When we consider styles and tactics in the rough-and-tumble world of "real conflict," however, things are often more complicated. It is one thing to sit and calmly deliberate about the choice of a style or tactic. It is quite another to have to deal with the reactions that styles and tactics provoke in others.

Case 4.3 illustrates how styles interact in a conflict episode. This conflict was not resolved because there was no successful differentiation phase to set the stage for integration. The issues and concerns each party had were never clearly defined. Mary tried to bring the issue out in the open, but Joan persisted in smoothing and withdrawing. In effect, Mary's contending style was neutralized by Joan's successful avoidance. Mary tried several times to shift her style toward compromising or problem-solving, but she was blocked when Joan persisted in avoiding the conflict. Mary could not involve both of them in a discussion

CASE 4.3 • *The Would-Be Borrower*

Imagine yourself as Mary: What style would you use as you respond to these issues?

A roommate conflict developed between Joan and Mary over the use of Joan's new car. When Joan talked to Mary about her anticipated purchase, Joan often said things such as, "It will be wonderful when we have a car." Mary interpreted Joan's use of the word "we" to mean that she might be allowed to borrow the car on certain occasions. When Mary's sister came to visit, Joan drove Mary's sister's car, and Mary figured this was a case of "share and share alike."

Joan began to shop seriously for a car during the two weeks before Thanksgiving. When Joan was about to make her purchase, Mary saw a new opportunity open up for her. Due to scheduling problems on her job, Mary was not able to go home for Thanksgiving. This would be the first Thanksgiving Mary had not been home. Mary asked Joan if she could use her new car to visit her parents, who lived about 120 miles away. Mary knew Joan would not need her car that weekend because Joan was going out of town with her parents for the holiday.

At first, Joan refused, but Mary persisted in raising the subject. Joan reported that she was "appalled that Mary had even asked." For Joan it was an issue of "invasion of personal property." As the tension over this question built, Joan began to use a withdrawing style: She gave Mary ambiguous, noncommittal replies and often simply did not reply at all. Mary had a more forceful, dominating communication style than Joan, and Joan saw avoidance as a way of sparing herself a direct confrontation with Mary. Joan assumed that a direct denial of Mary's request would provoke an emotional outburst, which she wanted to avoid at all costs.

In response to Joan's nonresponsiveness, Mary began to apply pressure indirectly, using a contending style. She pressed Joan to loan her car. Mary also had phone conversations with her parents within earshot of Joan in which she talked about the things they could do if she could get a car from Joan. Joan interpreted this as an attempt to make her feel guilty, and it worked. Joan felt a great deal of stress and turned to her family for support, which they readily gave. The interaction of the two styles set up a competitive climate and an impasse developed: Mary saw the issue as a question of a favor one would willingly do for a friend. Joan saw it as a question of whether Mary could infringe on her personal property.

Joan bought her car on the weekend before Thanksgiving and stored it in her parents' garage until it was insured. Mary mentioned her holiday plans with the car several times during the weekend and interpreted Joan's silence as acquiescence. The blowup occurred when an insurance salesman called on Joan. Mary had been giving Joan advice on insurance and was also present at the meeting. After discussing rates, the salesman asked Joan when she wanted her coverage to begin. Joan replied, "Thursday night at midnight"; therefore, the car would be uninsured on Thanksgiving Day and Mary could not drive it. Joan reported that this move was not premeditated: "I saw an escape hatch and I took it." The significance of Joan's shift to contending was not lost on Mary. She was shocked at "the devious way Joan had gone about it."

Mary reported that after the salesman left, Joan "just started babbling and babbling about nothing at all and getting really nervous." Joan shifted back to withdrawing after her one "trump." In the "twenty-minute scream-fest" that followed, styles shifted several times more. Mary asked Joan if she purposely started the insurance later to keep her from borrowing the car. Joan replied "Yes" and shifted back to other topics. After listening with half an ear for a while, Mary told Joan that she was "really ticked" with her. Joan replied, "I know you are. I knew you'd be like this. I knew you'd do this." Mary said that it would have been better if Joan had just told her "straight out." Joan replied that her mother had said that Mary should not be allowed to use her car. Mary was upset that Joan had told her mother: "Now I suppose you're going to tell your whole family what a rotten, miserable roommate

(continued)

CASE 4.3 Continued

you have!" Joan did not reply to this. Mary kept up her challenges, charging Joan with being selfish. Joan did not respond. Mary tried a normative justification, arguing that Thanksgiving is a special occasion. Joan did not respond. Mary asked Joan if the issue was that Joan thought she was a lousy driver. Joan replied that it was just too soon for someone to borrow her car. "Oh, so you don't want me to soil it before you can use it!" Mary flashed back.

When the shouting match ended, Joan did her laundry and remained in the laundry room for an hour, crying. Mary remained in their apartment, crying. When Joan returned to the apartment, the two did not speak until Joan approached Mary to show her a magazine article Mary had been looking for. This softened the mood somewhat but did not initiate conversation. Eventually, as they prepared for bed, Mary approached Joan: "Look, we've got to end this. I'm sorry I asked for your car. It's too soon for me to be asking. I should have realized this from other things you said." Joan replied that she was sorry she didn't give Mary a straight answer at

first. Mary was disappointed at Joan's answer because she expected an apology from Joan for not letting her use her car. Both women went to bed.

The two did not have much contact over the next few days. Mary reported feeling alienated from Joan: "It was a pretty terrible couple of weeks after that." The conflict was never really resolved, but it gradually faded into the background, and the two women resumed their friendship.

Discussion Questions

- To what extent do your options for approaching a conflict depend on the other person's behavior?
- Think of a situation in which you have wanted to use a collaborating style and found that the responses you received made it difficult or impossible.
- What styles would you have used if you were Joan or Mary? Might the conflict have turned out differently had the chosen different approaches?

unless Joan cooperated, and Joan did not. And even if Joan had wanted to discuss the issues openly, she was deterred by Mary's active persistence. Joan feared that she would not be able to hold her own in any discussion, so it probably seemed easier just to avoid. Her only forceful venture was the brief foray into competing when she set the insurance date. In anticipation of Mary's pressure, Joan quickly reverted to an avoiding style. The two were trapped in their respective styles; each style reinforced the other in a destructive self-reinforcing cycle.

The effectiveness of styles and tactics is dependent on others' actions. It is not simply a matter of selecting a tactic on one's own; another's reaction may reinforce or neutralize a tactic, or even cause it to "backfire." A party's ability to choose or change styles and tactics is also limited by what others do. In some cases, things get so out of hand that the parties are trapped, as Joan and Mary were. Only after a concerted effort can the direction of such conflicts be changed. The Would-Be Borrower case illustrates the interactive nature of styles and tactics and underscores an important point: Conflict interaction often acquires a momentum of its own.

This does not mean that selection of styles and tactics is a hopeless undertaking. People always have degrees of freedom that allow them to act in their own interests and to change situations for the better. However, there are limitations on what parties can control, and it is well to bear these in mind. The principles of conflict interaction discussed in earlier chapters offer useful resources for understanding the dynamics of styles and tactics.

4.10 Summary and Review

How do conflict strategies, styles, and tactics differ?

Strategies refer to a party's plans for a conflict, whereas styles refer to the general orientation that a party takes in a conflict, and tactics refer to specific behaviors a party engages in. A party adopting a competing style, for example, approaches the situation as a competition and chooses competitive tactics, focusing on attaining his or her goals and showing little regard for the other's goals. Styles are more flexible than strategies in that they do not require the party to plan out a definite set of tactics or behaviors. Strategies always involve the choice of one or more styles, but someone can enact a style without consciously planning a strategy. Planning ahead can be quite useful, but the fact that conflict interaction generally escapes the control of any single actor also points to the limitations of detailed strategies.

Is a person's style an unchanging characteristic?

Evidence suggests that people can and do change styles during conflicts. However, studies that measure conflict styles also suggest that people develop habitual styles that they tend to employ as their first tendency in conflicts. If we become aware of our conflict styles, it is possible to change them and even to choose them strategically. The main prerequisite for doing this is knowing how to enact different styles. That is why it is important to try styles and tactics that we do not ordinarily use.

What types of conflict styles are there?

The five classic conflict styles are competing, accommodating, avoiding, compromising, and collaborating. There are also variations within several styles, which represent different ways of carrying out the style. For example, forcing and contending are variations on competing.

Can conflict styles (and conflict behaviors) be described in terms of more basic dimensions?

Styles vary along a number of dimensions. Styles differ in terms of:

- *Assertiveness:* degree of focus on own goals
- *Cooperativeness:* degree of focus on other's goals
- *Disclosiveness:* degree to which information about the party's position or preference is disclosed to the other party
- *Empowerment:* degree to which one grants the other party some control or power
- *Activeness:* degree of one's involvement with one's own conflict issues
- *Flexibility:* degree of movement the party is willing to make to work with the other party in the conflict

These dimensions are useful because they give insights into the nature of the style or tactic. They also allow us to compare styles and tactics.

Is collaborating the best conflict style?

No style is always appropriate or necessarily superior to any other; it depends on the situation. In the discussion of problem-solving, a number of conditions for effectively using this style were listed. When these hold, problem-solving is the preferred style because it is most likely to result in productive conflict management. But the problem-solving style takes substantial time and energy on the part of all parties. Unless they are willing to commit to this, a less satisfactory outcome will result.

Studies suggest that other conflict styles may be more appropriate in particular situations. For example, forcing will be successful when time is short and when an organization's priorities must take precedence over individual preferences. Avoiding is likely to yield benefits if the other party is much more powerful and not inclined to compromise or problem solve. Moreover, effectiveness of styles varies across cultures. Different styles are likely to be effective for the harmony and regulative models of conflict than for the confrontational style emphasized in this book.

How do we determine the conflict style of another party?

Behavior often offers reliable cues as to the style of the other party. However, appearances can be deceiving, because the same behavior can be used to enact different styles. People are particularly prone to confuse accommodating and avoiding and also collaborating and compromising. When possible, it is a good idea to carefully observe the other party for a while before drawing conclusions about their styles.

Are some pairings of styles more likely than others?

Every combination of the five styles and their variants is possible, in principle. But some pairings of styles do seem to have a "natural" fit for each other. This includes the complementary pairs of competing–avoiding and competing–accommodating, and the symmetric pairs of competing–competing, compromising–compromising, and collaborating–collaborating.

Can parties change their styles as a conflict unfolds?

There is a good deal of evidence that people can and do change styles during conflicts. In some cases these changes may be strategically planned, but in other cases parties may shift styles in response to the other party's behavior or other aspects of the situation. In some cases they may not be aware of their shift.

How do I select an appropriate conflict style?

Several factors should be considered, including: How effective is the style likely to be in the situation? What responses will this style provoke? What will the consequences of the style be for long-term relationships among parties? Is the style ethical under the current conditions? The decision tree is available to help in choosing an appropriate style. It incorporates several questions that bear on the effectiveness of conflict styles.

How does culture influence conflict styles?

Scholars have identified general differences in the conflict styles preferred by different cultures. However, these are general tendencies, and individuals within any culture will vary as to which styles they prefer. Moreover, situational influences may override the impact of cultural preferences in the choice of conflict styles.

Do men and women differ in conflict styles?

Although it is sometimes assumed that men's and women's conflict behavior are quite different, research suggests differences are not this clear-cut. While early studies suggested differences, as research has accumulated, the bulk of the evidence suggests that there are few differences in conflict behavior between the genders.

4.11 Conclusion

This chapter has focused on the basic moves in many conflict episodes. The tactics described are used by parties to enact styles of conflict. Styles are general orientations toward conflict and represent the overall approaches that give tactics their meaning. As the discussion of variants on styles indicates, the five styles can be carried out in different ways, each giving something of a different flavor to interactions.

Styles alone are not sufficient to understand conflict, however. The other party's style influences how effective one's style can be and whether the party can even stick with the original style. So, at a minimum, the interaction of parties' styles and how these reinforce or cancel each other must be studied. Beyond this, we must recognize that descriptions of styles are not sufficient to fully capture what happens when parties enact a conflict. The communication processes discussed in previous chapters create a field of forces driving conflicts, and styles are used to attempt to navigate this field. Styles operate in a context set by other processes. For example, when face-saving is important, a competing style will be received differently than when parties are not attending to face. If people are caught in a spiral of escalation, a competing style may simply increase the escalation. But during periods of integration, brief use of the same style can contribute to constructive movement by increasing pressure for conflict resolution.

The selection of a style does not tell the whole story. Style choice has a major influence on conflict processes, but conflicts are also driven by the larger interaction context and by cycles of action and response, which are beyond any individual's control. It is important to neither underestimate or to overestimate the difference judicious style choices can make.

5

Power: The Architecture of Conflict

5.1 Power and the Emergence of Conflict

In Chapter 1 we note that conflict is sustained by moves and countermoves in interaction and that these are dependent on the power participants exert. As we will see, the degree of power participants can bring to bear depends on having the resources and the skill to use those resources effectively to act and to influence others. A good way to understand how power functions in conflicts is to examine the emergence of a conflict—the turn a conflict takes from a latent awareness of differences to actions and reactions that generate conflict interaction.

Whenever people are in some way dependent on one another, there are likely to be differences, and people usually become aware of the differences before any conflict-related interaction occurs. As we discuss in Chapter 4, several scholars have identified stages of conflict. You will recall the latent conflict stage in which a "consciousness of opposition" precedes conflict interaction and lays the groundwork for it. During this stage, parties may note differences that actually exist among them, or they may incorrectly assume there are differences when none exist. At this point, however, parties do not attempt to act on these differences.

Case 5.1A illustrates a group whose unified purpose is threatened by members' awareness of differences in priorities. Knowledge of real or assumed differences stems largely from parties' experience with each other.

Parties often know the stands others have taken in previous decisions and conflicts. They come to expect some parties to push for cautious or conservative choices and others to suggest or encourage major innovations. They know who are allies and who are enemies. Each party's stand provides a general sense of where he or she would like to see the conflict head. In assessing and planning their stands, parties try to forecast likely positions and anticipate where support or opposition will arise. When individuals foresee disagreement or incompatible goals this creates a consciousness of opposition.

CASE 5.1A • *A Raid on the Student Activity Fees Fund*

Imagine yourself as a magazine editor on this board whose publication may be threatened by the proposed budget cuts: What would be your likely response when you realize that there may not be sufficient funds to support all of the board's publications?

The Undergraduate Publications (UP) Board at a midsized university was responsible for overseeing five student-run publications: a weekly newspaper, an annual yearbook, and three magazines—a literary magazine, a political review, and a science journal—each published once a semester. The Board was created by the university to ensure comprehensive coverage of campus life and student accomplishments. Composed of two representatives from each of the publications (generally the editor and a senior staff member), plus a faculty advisor, the UP Board met monthly to discuss a wide variety of issues. Together they made decisions regarding advertising and editorial policies, selection of the following year's editors, hardware and software purchases for the Board's shared computers, and nominations of individual writers for national collegiate writing awards. In addition, the group collectively determined the budgets for each of the publications, working from a lump sum allocation made to the UP Board by the student government at the beginning of each semester. As these issues were discussed, Board members' assumptions about the relative importance of each of the publications became apparent.

At one Board meeting shortly before the semester's allocations were made by the student government, the faculty advisor mentioned that the university's administration was considering "raiding" the student activity fees fund to refurbish the student center. Because this fund is the sole source of money for the student government's allocation committee, it is possible that the UP Board budgets would be dramatically cut. After the meeting, members talked among themselves and with others about how the Board should handle potential cuts. Some members stated their positions explicitly as they discussed the consequences of eliminating one of the magazines, reducing the length of the yearbook, or other choices.

Through these discussions and through recollections of how individual UP Board members have felt in the past, members began to anticipate the suggestions that would be made to deal with the cuts. Because members sensed that preferences differed, an awareness of opposition mounted as the UP Board considered what it would mean to make any of these choices. The editors of the threatened magazines began to assess how much support from the Board they and their magazine had and who their potential advocates and opponents were.

Discussion Questions

- Why does the term "latent conflict" describe the situation that existed on this board?
- What could make this conflict move out of a latent stage and into an open conflict?
- What examples can you give of latent conflict stages in other situations (for example, family conflicts you have been involved in, neighborhood disputes, international conflicts you have followed)?

In this case study, the Undergraduate Publications Board has a prevailing sense of an issue arising; members recognize likely differences in viewpoints and share an uncertainty about whether these differences will need to be addressed. There is, in other words, a *perception* of potential incompatibility of goals or objectives. At this point, however, the conflict remains latent because there is no immediate stimulus for the members to act on their positions.

What might make the UP Board members act on their expectations? Returning to our stage models, a *triggering event* turns a "consciousness of opposition" into acknowledged conflict. Obviously, any number of events are potential triggers in this case: the student government president could announce that the UP Board's budget will be cut by twenty-five percent, a member who has been appointed as next year's editor of one of the publications may request a special meeting on the subject to plan accordingly, or a Board member may write a formal letter that argues strongly for the elimination of the science journal if publication cutbacks are necessary.

Once parties react to the trigger, conflict interaction can move through cycles of withdrawal, joking, problem-solving, heated arguments, proposals and counterproposals, and so on, in all their many forms. The triggering event signals a transition in the way parties think and act about the conflict. In the latent stage, they think in terms of possibilities, while conflict interaction confronts them with real threats and constraints. A triggering event alters people's response to differences and shapes the particular form conflict takes. To illustrate how moves and countermoves might vary as a result of a specific triggering incident, consider two scenarios that might unfold with the UP Board (Case 5.1B).

CASE 5.1B • *A Raid on the Student Activity Fees Fund*

Imagine yourself as one of the magazine editors attending a board meeting after the letter is written: What would be your likely response to each of the two scenarios?

Shortly after the faculty advisor mentioned the possibility of cutbacks to the UP Board's budget, a member of the group wrote a letter advocating the elimination of the science journal from the campus publications. This would fulfill cutback requirements without affecting other publications. The science journal was the clear choice, argues the letter writer, because it has the smallest circulation and has received no awards. As a result, two possible scenarios may occur.

Scenario #1: The letter is sent to the faculty advisor, with copies to other members of the Board. The members of the group assume that the letter will have no significant ramifications because the faculty advisor is not really a "player" in the group. The advisor reads the letter, acknowledges its receipt, and comments to the group as a whole that the issue will be discussed when the time comes.

Scenario #2: The letter is sent to the school newspaper, where it is published on the editorial page. The editor of the paper is the fraternity brother of two members of the allocations committee and has been known to use this connection to acquire special funding for the paper. In response to the letter's publication, some Board members request that a special meeting be called to discuss options for dealing with the cutbacks. Others write responses to the letter and submit them to the newspaper. Still others confront the letter writer and ask why such a proposal was offered when no cutbacks have yet been made.

Discussion Questions

- How would you account for the different responses to the same letter?
- What benefits does the triggering event have for the group?
- How did the following incidents act as triggering events: the Boston Tea Party; the bombing of Pearl Harbor; Rosa Parks's staying seated on a public bus; the 9/11 attacks; Hurricane Katrina?
- What kind of power was used in each of the above to make the triggering event have more of an impact?

It is tempting to think of triggering events in negative terms, as "the straw that breaks the camel's back." However, a triggering event also carries with it an important opportunity. As noted in Chapter 1, a critical requirement of constructive conflict management is thorough and successful differentiation of conflicting positions. Before they can move to an integrative solution, parties must raise the conflict issue and spend sufficient time and energy clarifying positions, pursuing the reasons behind those positions, and acknowledging their differences. By bringing the conflict out, a triggering event sets the stage for constructive resolution. It opens the possibility of clearing away problems and tensions that undermine relationships or group performance.

There is, of course, no guarantee that a constructive resolution will happen. As we observe in Chapter 1, uncontrolled escalation and destructive avoidance can also develop during differentiation. How the parties handle differentiation is the key to whether it becomes destructive or constructive. And how differentiation is handled depends in part on specific responses to the triggering event, which are shaped by parties' access to and use of power.

In both scenarios in Case 5.1B, the letter was a move that fractured the latent conflict stage; one party acted on behalf of his own goals and others responded to the move. Once the UP Board members recognized and acted on the latent issue, the conflict entered a new phase of open engagement. How they reacted to this trigger set the stage for how the conflict was played out. In the first scenario, others did not believe the letter presented much of a threat. As a result, it did not elicit a strong reaction, and it did not begin a chain of moves and countermoves aimed at settling the issue. Members recognized an issue had been raised, but there were no drastic countermoves because its consequences were neither immediate nor threatening. The letter "set the agenda" for future discussions. In the second scenario, the letter began a lengthy series of moves and countermoves that would not only determine how the Board would handle any cutbacks, but could also change the relationships among the Board members and alter its long-term climate.

Once a conflict is triggered, the moves people make depend on the power they can marshal. Parties' abilities and willingness to use power and their skill at employing it determine the moves and countermoves that will sustain the conflict. Power establishes the set of actions that individuals may use and sets limits on the effectiveness of other parties' moves. Each move reveals to others how willing a party is to use power and what kinds of power that party has. The response to the move reveals whether the use of power will go unchallenged.

The most important difference between the two scenarios is the difference in power of the Board member who writes the letter. In both cases the letter could easily be construed as an attempt to sway attitudes by getting a "jump" on others. Laying out one set of arguments before other positions or proposals are developed or stated could give the writer a great advantage. Despite their common objective, only the second letter had the potential to influence the outcome of the cutback decision. The author of the second letter was perceived to hold power and had been known to use it on previous occasions: other Board members knew that this individual had strong persuasive abilities, was a fraternity brother of members of the allocations committee, and was willing to go public with his options before raising them with others on the Board. In responding to the letter, members had to rely on their own sources of power, such as the right to request a special meeting about an issue and the ability to build alliances, to prevent the letter from firmly setting attitudes before a full discussion of the issue occurred.

The shift from latent conflict to the emergence of conflict interaction inevitably confronts the participants with the issue of power. During latent conflict, parties may have a sense of the sources of power people hold, and they may make estimates of how likely it will be for others to use power if the conflict surfaces. Once conflict interaction begins, however, each move and countermove confirms or challenges previous assessments of power. Individuals are caught up in an active process of testing and determining the role and limits of power in the conflict. But how, exactly, does this happen? The next section examines the nature of power more closely and points to several defining characteristics that make power a major influence on the direction conflict interaction takes.

5.2 A Relational View of Power

The everyday use of the term *power* misrepresents it to some extent (Bachrach & Baratz, 1970; Deutsch, 1973; Janeway, 1980; Clegg, 1989). Expressions—such as, "He holds enormous power" or "The purchasing department's manager has lost the power she once had"—imply that power is a possession. That is, it is something that belongs to an individual, which can be increased or lost, and which, by implication, can be carried away from a group or organization. In this view, power is a quality of the strong or dominant, and something the weak lack. This view, however, is misleading. Social philosopher Hannah Arendt (1969) points to the problem with this view when she states: "Power is never the property of an individual; it belongs to a group and remains in existence only so long as the group keeps together" (p. 44).

In Chapter 1 we defined power as *the ability to influence or control events*. What does it mean to say this ability "belongs to the group"? For one thing, it means recognizing that *social power stems from relationships among people*. Individuals have power when they have access to resources that can be used to persuade or convince others, to change their course of action, or to prevent others from moving toward their goals in conflict situations. These resources are controlled by individuals; it is easy to assume that the resources themselves equal power and that their owner therefore possesses power. However, this conclusion ignores the fact that any resource serving as a basis for power is only *effective because others endorse the resource* (Jewell & Reitz, 1981; Clegg, 1989). The resource only imparts power because it carries some weight in the context of relationships where it is used. The young child who throws a temper tantrum has power over her parents only if they are bothered (or touched) by the raucous fits and are willing to appease the child because the behavior is annoying (or heartbreaking). The boss who threatens to fire a worker can only influence a worker who values the job and believes his boss will carry out the threat. In both cases the second party must "endorse" the first party's resources for them to become a basis for power.

Parties can use a broad range of resources to exert power (Boulding, 1990; Dillard, Anderson, & Knoblach, 2003; French & Raven, 1959; Kipnis, Schmidt, & Wilkerson, 1980). Potential resources include special skills or abilities, time, expertise about the task at hand, personal attractiveness or likeability, control over rewards and/or punishments, formal position in a group or organization, loyal allies, persuasive skills, and control over critical group possessions (such as the treasury), to name a few. Anything that enables parties to move toward their own goals or to interfere with another's actions is a resource that can be used in conflicts. Communication skills, such as being articulate or being able to construct effective arguments, can be power resources in themselves. However, for a move to have an impact on another party's moves or on the outcome of the conflict, the resources it uses must be given some credence by others: either consciously or unconsciously others must endorse them. In this sense, power is always conferred on someone by those who endorse the resources.

At first glance, it would seem that the need for endorsement leaves an easy way out for weaker parties in conflict. Isn't it always possible to undermine the use of power by withholding endorsement of some resource? In principle, weaker parties always have this option. But the claim is misleading because the tendency to endorse power is deep-seated and based in powerful and pervasive social processes. At the most superficial level, we endorse power because the resources it is based on enable others to grant or deny things that are valuable. As Richard Emerson (1962) states: "[The] power to control or influence the other resides in control over the things he values, which may range all the way from oil resources to ego-support" (p. 11). This is an important, if obvious point, and it leads to a more fundamental issue: This control is exerted during interaction. One party makes a control bid based on real or potential use of resources, and the other party accepts or rejects it.

Perhaps the most critical aspect of this process is the other party's acceptance or rejection of the legitimacy or force of the bid; in other words, the other party's endorsement (or lack of endorsement) of the first party's resources and his or her ability to use them. This social process of endorsement is what underlies parties' perceptions of other parties' behavior as attempts to influence or control. If someone imitates the shape of a gun with his or her fingers, points them at someone else, and says, "Hand me your wallet," the "target" person may laugh at the joke, but he would not see this as a power move. If that same person picks up a gun and does the same thing, nearly everyone would see it as an attempt to influence or control. The party's endorsement of a gun as an instrument of force is a product of years of experience (education, television shows, firsthand encounters), which gives him or her an idea of its power.

At the same time, even the power that a gun confers is not inherent in the possession of the gun itself. Because power is relational, *the effectiveness of any resource is always negotiated in the interaction.* If the person at whom the gun is aimed tells the assailant to "Move out of my way," this is an attempt to withdraw endorsement of the assailant's potential power. The response may or may not succeed—that is the nature of any unfolding negotiation—but, as the interaction proceeds, the perception of power can change. It is interaction, then, that changes perception of resources and the power they can ultimately generate. The influential powers of intangible social resources, such as a good reputation or persuasive abilities, are built in much the same way: people must endorse them if they are to carry any weight. The tendency and willingness to endorse power stem from several sources, including preconceptions about what makes a person weak or strong, an aura of mystery, the judicial use of authority, and evidence of valued skills or abilities. Before these are examined in detail, consider the case of a unique and self-styled individual (Case 5.2, page 142).

CASE 5.2 • *The Eccentric Professor*

Imagine yourself as a student in this professor's class: Which of his characteristics might inspire you to respect him? How would your respect work as an endorsement of his power in the classroom?

In a large academic department, a professor became known as an exceptional intellect—a person who possessed unfathomable powers of insight and perspective. As a result of this perception, his colleagues and students often deferred to his judgment and looked to him to provide solutions to complex problems. In time, he came to hold the most powerful position in his college, choosing when he would teach and to whom.

The professor, Harold, was a prolific researcher and talented teacher. He held several advanced degrees from Ivy League universities and was a member of a wealthy, politically influential family. Perhaps his most singular trait was that he was fond of the unusual, the offbeat, the uncommon. He surrounded himself with objects and fashion from an earlier era, often wearing knickers, bow ties, and driving caps. He made it clear to anyone who inquired that he liked books and cats more than people. Because of his tastes, he kept to himself, shunning parties and all social gatherings. Harold maintained this interpersonal distance in his classes. He used seat assignments, a question period, forbade the wearing of hats or shorts in class, and never used first names, referring to students as Mr. and Ms. instead.

The first words of each of his lectures were delivered as he crossed the threshold into the classroom and he concluded precisely as the hour ended, his final sentence often punctuated by the bell. Not many months after his arrival on campus, he was asked to address the faculty as part of the college's colloquium series. His lecture, on thinking and learning, incorporated NFL training-camp films and analogies from the history of the stock market. In every conversation, from the important to the mundane, colleagues and students learned that Harold approached ideas and problems in unusual ways, from unusual angles. At first he was ridiculed and avoided, but he soon became an enigma to understand. And so the stories began.

He spent late evenings in the library and was seen carrying loads of books. When asked by one bold student what he was after, Harold supposedly replied that he was committed to having read a portion of every book in the library. After Harold worked for months on a computer algorithm, a colleague supposedly learned that he was to use the program to make all his important decisions, from buying a house to selecting a wife.

After receiving a national award for one of his essays, he chose not to attend the award ceremony, claiming that he would not fly or take a train. When beseeched to attend, he finally agreed and spent a week riding a bus to and from the faraway ceremony. Rumors spread that Harold had made a million dollars in the stock market and that he owned dozens of cats.

As the years rolled on, the stories grew and the mystery and power surrounding him deepened. His image as an eccentric intellectual, capable of performing extraordinary feats, was perpetuated by both students and professors caught up in the mystery of the man. In this way, Harold managed to gain considerable influence in his working environment, though in truth, he was more similar to his colleagues than dissimilar.

Discussion Questions

- Given the influence he held, what might undercut Harold's power?
- What might prompt resistance to Harold's power?
- In what ways do political candidates hold influence over voters that are similar to the ways in which Harold holds influence over his students?

The Eccentric Professor case illustrates four factors that influence endorsement:

5.2.1 Social Categorization

The social categorization process, discussed in Chapter 3, creates strong preconceptions about what types of people are usually powerful and what types are generally weak. Ranking executives, for example, are assumed by society to be wealthy, have connections, and be skilled in negotiation. Welfare mothers, on the other hand, are assumed to be poor and have little ability to get ahead in the world. An aura of competence and power attaches itself to the executive, something that the welfare mother does not have. Harold, being an Ivy League graduate with an upper-class background, might be ascribed by those around him with such characteristics as sophistication and worldliness. So it is with all social categories: Each tends to be associated with a particular degree of power, with certain resources, and with certain abilities use the resources available to them. These associations set up expectations that work in favor of or against endorsement of power moves by people from various categories: We endorse those we expect to be powerful and do not endorse those we expect to be weak.

These associations have several consequences. For one thing, they make the use of power easier for certain people and more difficult for others. A number of studies have been conducted on the effects of members' status outside decision-making groups on member behavior within groups (Ridgeway, 2003). Consistently, members with higher status in society—for example, doctors, lawyers, university students—are more influential than those with lower status—such as laborers and high school students—even if both members had exactly the same resources.

For example, a classic study by Moore (1968) had junior college students work in pairs to estimate the number of rectangles in an optical illusion. The experimenter led the students to believe that their partner was either a Stanford University student or a high school student. There was no difference in the ability of the students to estimate rectangles, but those who thought they worked with university students changed their estimates significantly more often than those who thought they worked with high school students. In other words, they allowed themselves to be influenced by "university" students and exercised influence over the high school students. The junior college students expected university students to be brighter and, therefore, to be better at the task. This assumption led the junior college students to endorse the university students' resources; the opposite assumption encouraged them to give less weight to the high school students' attempts to use their own resources. Whenever people from different social categories work together, similar preconceptions about their respective powers strengthen endorsement for some and weaken it for others.

Expectations about social categories not only shape members' perceptions of other parties' resources and abilities, but also influence their perceptions of themselves. People who belong to a respected social category generally expect to be powerful, and those who regularly receive endorsement for power moves, such as corporate executives, tend to see themselves as powerful and effective. They are confident when making future moves, and their confidence, in turn, is likely to lead to effective use of power, which reinforces their self-concepts. The same is true for those belonging to "powerless" categories. They expect to be ineffective and, therefore, generally give way before the more powerful.

Janeway (1980) argues that this is one of the major reasons women, minorities, and other low-power groups often take weak roles in conflict situations. They see themselves as having fewer resources than dominant groups, as being spectators rather than actors. Even though these groups have resources, including intelligence, social skills, and even sheer numbers, they do not realize their potential power. They believe they are weak and isolated and have little chance of competing with the "powers that be." In conflict, such people often do not assert themselves, and when they do, their efforts are not given the same weight of endorsement that people from powerful categories receive. Once again, there is a self-reinforcing cycle that serves to prove the weak are powerless and further strengthens other people's tendency to refuse endorsement.

Apfelbaum (1979) calls the socialization process that creates these perceptions of weakness *degrouping*. She argues that it is the most important mechanism by which the powerful maintain their positions. Here also is one of the roots of the common idea of power as a possession. If certain social groups are assumed to be consistently powerful, it takes only a small step to assume power is theirs by right; in other words, it is their possession. Because the process of learning social categorizations is gradual and extends over years, it is easy to lose sight of their flexibility and forget that all social groups are, to a great extent, created by those within and outside of them. If the social definition of who is powerful changes, patterns of endorsement, and therefore of those who can exert power effectively, can change radically.

When parties perceive another party as a member of a group rather than as an individual, they may act more forcefully or aggressively toward them (Pruitt, Rubin, & Kim, 1994; Reicher, 2003). This perceptual process is called *deindividuation* because it removes the personal and human characteristics normally associated with a party and replaces them with more global features. For example, it is not uncommon for people in conflict to refrain from using another party's name and to refer to him or her according to physical attributes or social roles, such as "that loud-mouthed boss" or "that aggressive lawyer." As the conflict and aggression escalate, so too does the degree of deindividuation. The opposing party may be identified by race or religion, denoting a more impersonal perception and label. Because people are seen as less human, the social inhibition on acting aggressively toward them disappears, or so we believe. Entire nations can get caught up in this pattern of deindividuation as a means to justify and absolve their citizens from being seen as aggressors. In every war in which the United States has been involved during the past century, examples of deindividuated names and labels for enemies, including the civilian populations, have surfaced. Such labels as "Krauts" and "terrorists" allow us to act aggressively without regulation or remorse.

It is important to acknowledge that often power differences attributed to social categories do realistically reflect inequalities in the social structure. The rich are attributed power, because money does indeed give them power. However, we would caution you against making absolute claims based on social structure, because in the give and take of interaction, power is to some extent "up for grabs."

5.2.2 The Mystique of Power

The use of power also carries a mystique that reinforces endorsement of moves by powerful members. Janeway (1980) explores the childhood and adolescent experiences through which people learn to use and understand power. The actions of adults are incomprehensible to children and so, Janeway argues, children attribute to adults mysterious, unfathomable powers. As the rich fantasy life of childhood gives way to the mastery of adulthood, people learn how power works, but the aura persists, dimmed perhaps but never extinguished.

In addition to childhood experiences, the historical connection between kings and queens and the divine contributes to power's magical aura, Janeway (1980) observes. As a result, "even today, it seems, the governed are ready to accept the idea that the powerful are different from you and me, and not simply because they have more power. We grant them a different kind of power that contains some element of the supernatural" (p. 77). In the Eccentric Professor case, Harold's unusual behavior and characteristics were both mysterious and fascinating to all of those around him. The perception that he was unique served to increase his prestige on campus. Mystique functions to reinforce existing power relations: "for the powerful, the magic aura offers a validation of dominance over and above the consent of the governed; for the weak, a defensive shield against feelings of inferiority and ineffectiveness" (Janeway, 1980, p. 126). After all, if power is a magical, unattainable possession, the strong must have special qualities and the weak cannot handle it and should not try. Kipnis (1990) notes that the supernatural mystique of power often carries with it reckless license: "Throughout history, we find a special divinity is assumed to surround the powerful so that they are excused from gross acts such as murder, theft, terrorism and intimidation" (p. 40).

The magical aura about power inspires a certain awe that facilitates its endorsement. It also tends to perpetuate power and weakness in the same hands over time. In groups, for example, more experienced, older members are often granted this aura or mystique. Although they may have more knowledge and information because of their longer stay in the group, the mystique assigned to them by newer members can linger and keep certain members in unwarranted influential positions.

5.2.3 Interaction

Interaction is the primary means through which endorsement is enacted. The response of other parties to a power move has a strong influence on an individual's endorsement. For example, if Harold, the eccentric professor, announces that hats and shorts are strictly forbidden in his classroom, and all members of the class obey without question, they are reinforcing one another's endorsement of the professor's authority. Each student observes the others obeying, and this lends additional weight to his or her own respect for Harold's authority. Assume, on the other hand, that a professor has been unfair in the past and that students have doubts about whether the professor deserves his or her authority. If one student refuses to go along with the professor's rules, it may very well undermine other students' endorsement of the professor.

How a power move is executed also influences its endorsement. Power involves the use of resources; successful power moves require skillful and appropriate use of resources. For example, when a leader or supervisor gives feedback and criticism to subordinates, it is more effective when (1) done privately rather than in front of co-workers, (2) positive points and improvements are discussed in addition to problems, and (3) raises or compensation increases are not tied to criticisms or the subordinate's attempts to solve his or her problems (Meyer, Kay, & French, 1965). A supervisor who follows these rules is more likely to gain the cooperation of subordinates, partly because this is a positive method of giving feedback, but also because the rules allow the subordinates to save face and do not push them into challenging the supervisor's authority. A boss who berates workers in front of their co-workers is more likely to face a challenge or, at least, create resentment that may emerge later on. Exerting power in a socially appropriate manner that follows the path of least resistance is conducive to present and future endorsement by others.

Exactly what constitutes appropriate and skillful use of power varies from case to case. Research offers a few general principles, but they are sketchy, at best, and do not add up to a systematic theory.

5.2.4   Legitimacy

Up to this point, we have emphasized what might be called the unconscious bases of endorsement. However, endorsements are often openly discussed and decided on. In these cases, parties value certain abilities, knowledge, or personal characteristics and explicitly support the legitimacy of the resource. A team might, for example, pride itself on always having sufficient information before reaching any final decision and compliment those who are most persistent in gathering and evaluating background material. One member could use this knowledge of the team's self-image as a basis for a move in a decision-making conflict. He or she could attempt to stop the team from adopting a solution by making the members feel guilty about not conducting an adequate search for information. In this instance, the powerful individual uses a resource that the team willingly endorses as a basis for a move. The move may or may not be successful and may or may not be intended for the good of the team, but it appeals to a resource that, as Arendt says, "belongs to the group."

5.2.5   Implications of Endorsement for Power

Recognizing the relational nature of power acknowledges the provisional and somewhat tenuous status of our resources. Regardless of how tight a hold a party may attempt to have on any resource, the resource is always used in the context of a relationship. It is the other party's view of the resource that makes it a basis for influence. Returning to the case of the eccentric professor, it may happen that Harold's ability to lecture unerringly and precisely for an hour is considered extraordinary by his students. They might look forward to class simply to see this feat performed. But if, over the course of the semester, students find reasons to leave class early, Harold's lecturing ability may wane as a source of power. If the other party's view of the resource changes, the basis of power shifts, redefining the possibilities for moves in the interaction. Because power is inherently relational, it is never entirely under one's control. The response to the use of power determines whether the resource that has been employed will remain a source of power as the conflict unfolds.

As parties use resources, their moves renew, maintain, or reduce the weight a resource has in the interaction. A clumsy move can weaken endorsement of a resource and confidence in the abilities of the user. A well-executed move can enhance endorsement of a resource. The skills of the user, the response of other members, and the eventual course that the conflict takes all determine whether a resource maintains or loses its endorsement. Even the nature of the resource itself is important because some resources (for example, money or favors) can be exhausted and others (such as physical force) allow no turning back once employed. The use of resources is an extremely complex process, and we will return to it throughout the rest of this chapter.

5.3 Power and Conflict Interaction

The use of power imposes constraints on others. A power move usually brings about a reduction of other parties' options by limiting the moves they can make, eliminating a possible resolution to the conflict, or restricting their ability to employ countervailing power. These constraints influence the direction the conflict takes; they make certain behaviors or styles desirable or, alternatively, impossible. They shape parties' perceptions of each other, kindling hope or desperation, cooperation or competition. As the conflict evolves and changes, so do the constraints under which participants operate. The other parties' responses to moves set further constraints, the responses to the countermoves set still further constraints, and so on, until the conflict is no longer wholly controlled by either party but is a collective product. It is greater than—and in a real sense out of the control of—any single person.

To illustrate the relational nature of power, the influence of power on conflict interaction, and the multiplication of constraints, consider the case of a research and development committee in a large corporation (Case 5.3 on page 148). This case is set in a corporate lab, but it could just as easily have occurred in other situations, such as a committee developing an advertising campaign, a team developing new software for a computer company, or a textbook selection committee in a university department. The case offers a clear illustration of the role of power in conflict interaction. During the early meetings members offered their reactions to various programs and tried to move steadily toward a final choice. Although there were differences of opinion about the programs in these early meetings, expertise and knowledge—resources used by members to exert influence and shape attitudes about the programs—were implicitly endorsed by the whole group. Members tried to articulate criteria for assessing the programs and to apply the criteria to the programs being considered. The moves parties made to keep a particular program under consideration were arguments based on knowledge and experience they had as researchers. Reasoned argument was the operating norm for the group, and as members worked together to make decisions through rational argument, they were, in effect, reinforcing the group's endorsement of expertise.

Once the group narrowed the list to two programs and a consensus did not emerge through reasoned argument, members began to use other resources. The manager gave a strong indication that he might be willing to use his formal authority to force selection of the program by turning to each project director and asking, "How upset would you be if I chose the program I prefer?" This move was significantly different from any move that participants had made before, and it broadened the scope of the conflict considerably. It overturned the assumption that influence would rest on logical argument and expertise.

CASE 5.3 • *The Creativity Development Committee*

Imagine yourself as a project director serving on this committee: What resources do you, and the other project directors, bring to the committee that could be a source of influence? What constraints, if any, do your resources place on Tom, the lab manager?

Tom was the manager of three research and development laboratories for a large chemical and materials corporation. He supervised general operations, budgeting, personnel, and proposal development for the labs. Each lab had several projects, and each project team was headed by a project director who was usually a scientist or an engineer. Tom had been a project director for ten years at another of the corporation's labs and had been promoted to lab manager four years ago. Although he had to transfer across the country to take this job, he felt he had earned the respect of his subordinates. He had been regarded as an outsider at first, but he worked hard to be accepted, and the lab's productivity had gone up over the last two years. Tom's major worry was keeping track of everything. His busy schedule kept him from close supervision over projects.

As in most labs, each project generally went its own way. As long as it produced results, a project enjoyed a high degree of autonomy. Morale was usually high among the research staff. They knew they were on the leading edge of the corporation's success and they enjoyed it. The visibility and importance of innovative research were shown by the fact that project directors were regularly promoted. It was in this milieu that Tom decided that productivity might be still further increased if research creativity were heightened.

Research teams often met to discuss ideas and to decide on future directions. In these meetings, ideas were often improved, but they could also be killed or cut off. Tom had studied research on decision-making, which indicated that groups often suppress good ideas without a hearing. The research suggested ways of preventing this suppression and of enhancing group creativity. Tom hoped to harness these findings by developing standard procedures through which idea development would be enhanced rather than hindered during these meetings. Tom asked four project directors if they would be willing to work with him to review the research and meet regularly over the summer to help formulate appropriate procedures. The four agreed to take on the task, and the group began its work enthusiastically.

During the first six weeks of the summer, the group met weekly to discuss relevant articles and books and to hear consultants. The group was able to narrow down a set of about fifteen procedures and programs to four prime ones. Eventually, two programs emerged as possibilities. However, as the list was narrowed from four to two, there was a clear split in how the group felt.

One procedure was strongly favored by three of the project directors. The fourth project director liked the procedure better than the other option but was less vocal in showing her support for it. In general, the project directors felt the procedure they favored was far more consistent with what project teams were currently doing and with the problems faced by the corporation. They believed the second program, which involved a lot of writing and the use of special voting procedures, was too abstract for working research scientists to accept. It would be difficult, they said, to use this procedure because everyone would have to fill out forms and explain ideas in writing before a meeting could be held. Because of the already heavy workloads, their people would not go along with the program. Researchers would ridicule the program and be prejudiced against future attempts to stimulate creativity.

Tom argued that the second program was more comprehensive, had a broader conception of problems, and would help develop more creative ideas than the first, which was a fairly conservative "brainstorming" process. Although discussion focused on the substantive nature of each program and its relation to the objective of creativity, the project directors knew that the program Tom favored was one he had been trained in at his former lab.

(continued)

CASE 5.3   Continued

Tom was a good friend of the consultant who had developed it. The project directors talked outside meetings about this friendship and questioned whether it was shaping Tom's attitudes. The climate of the group, which had initially been positive and enthusiastic, grew tense as issues connected to the power relations between the manager and project directors surfaced.

Although the project directors knew Tom could choose the program he wanted, the way in which the final choice would be made was never clarified at the beginning of the summer. The time that the project directors spent reading and evaluating the programs created an implicit expectation that they would have an equal say in the final choice. At the same time, the project directors had all worked at the lab for at least four years and had experienced firsthand the relative power of managers and project directors. They heard horror stories of project directors who had gotten on the manager's "wrong side" and been denied promotion or fired. When push came to shove, they expected the lab manager to have greater power and to be willing to use it.

At its final meeting, the group discussed the two programs for quite some time, but there seemed to be little movement. Somewhat hesitantly, Tom turned to each project director individually and asked, "How upset would you be if I choose the program I prefer?" One project director said he was uncomfortable answering. Two indicated that they felt they would have difficulty using the creativity program as it was currently designed. The fourth said she thought she could live with it. After these answers were given, Tom told the project directors he would leave a memo in their mailboxes informing them of the final decision.

Two weeks after this discussion, the project directors were told that the second program, the one the manager preferred, would be ordered. The memo also said that the other program would be used, on an experimental basis, by one of the eighteen projects. The decision caused considerable resentment—the project directors felt "used." They

saw little reason in having spent so much time discussing programs if Tom was just going to choose the program he wanted regardless of their preferences. When it began in the fall, one of the project directors told his team that the program would be recommended rather than required, and he explained that it might have to be adapted extensively to fit the unit's style. This director made this decision without telling the manager. Although the move was in clear violation of authority, he knew Tom could not visit the teams often and was therefore unlikely to find out about it. Another project director instituted the program but commented afterward that he felt he had not integrated it into his unit well. He questioned how much effort he had actually invested in making the program "work."

The incident had a significant impact on the way Tom was seen by the project directors. Several commented that they had lost respect for him and that they saw Tom as someone who was willing to manipulate people for his own purposes. This opinion filtered to other corporate project directors and scientists through the grapevine and caused Tom considerable difficulties in a labor grievance during the following year. In this dispute, several researchers banded together and defied the manager because they believed he would eventually back down. In addition, the project director who made the program optional for his workers served as a model for similar defiance by others. Once the directors saw that "optional" use of the program would go unpunished, they felt free to do the same, further reducing Tom's control. Eventually, Tom transferred to another division of the corporation.

Discussion Questions

- How do Tom's actions demonstrate the potential limits of the use of power?
- Can you think of organizational situations, such as corporate takeovers or strikes, where reactions to the use of power evoked more resistance than expected—and resulted in the removal of power?

The project directors anticipated that the manager, Tom, might exercise his right to choose the program. Although Tom's question was not the actual exercise of his right, it signaled the potential use of this power base to "resolve" the group's conflict. Tom was testing what impact the move might have if he disregarded the project directors' arguments and chose the program he wanted. In some ways, Tom's move was predictable. Research summarized by Kipnis (1990) suggests that people tend to use reason, logic, and simple requests until resistance occurs. At that point, beliefs about power guide the choice of tactics.

Tom's move marked a turning point in the conflict because it altered the resources members used. Tom moved from the use of expertise and knowledge, resources common to all members, to invoking his formal authority—a resource exclusively his. The project directors' response to Tom's move also invoked a new resource, their ability not to cooperate with their superior. The ability to run their projects independently was an "ace in the hole" for the project directors. Tom was responsible for productivity in all projects, and if his actions in this committee undermined the project directors' motivation or ability to work effectively, the outcome might reflect poorly on his ability to direct the labs and ultimately harm his reputation.

In suggesting that he might use his power, Tom elicited the threat of a similar use of power by the project directors. The project directors signaled their potential willingness to act on their own power in responding to Tom's move; Tom's move elicited a reciprocal use of power in the conflict interaction.

It is instructive to stop for a moment and reflect on what this countermove meant to the project directors. They were well aware of the power their manager could exert because they had all been in the corporation for many years. They held the manager–project director dichotomy firmly in mind and knew they had few resources in comparison to Tom. Moreover, because they themselves aspired to rise in the corporation, greatly admired the intellectual and political prowess of higher officers, and saw Tom's station as well beyond reach for the time being, Tom's acts held a certain magical aura for the project directors. The group operated in a fairly egalitarian and congenial manner, and this also reinforced the project directors' endorsement of Tom's move.

However, when Tom threw over the rational basis of influence and invoked the authority of his position, the project directors were jolted into considering countermeasures. They raised the argument of difficulty in using the program, but implicit in this was the threat that they would undermine it. They may not have consciously planned this threat. Their response was fairly weak because of the considerable endorsement they accorded to Tom's power. However, it carried the germ of an idea, and later, when their respect for Tom had waned even further, at least some of them would act on the threat.

The question–response exchange between Tom and the project directors illustrates how the use of power or, in this case, the indication of a willingness to use power, imposes constraints and thereby directs future moves in the conflict. When Tom asks for a response to the unilateral choice he might make, it reduces the range of appropriate moves his subordinates could make at that point in the interaction. It would not have been appropriate, for example, for them to comment on the relative academic merits of the two programs in responding to Tom's "How upset would you be . . . ?" question.

The question sought an indication of how willing the project directors were to employ the power they had. If, in response to the question, one of them had said, "I think the program we want has the following strengths . . . ," the statement would not have been an appropriate response to the question (although it might have been effective as a strategy to change the subject and avoid the question altogether). The question—along with Tom's direct focus—created a subtle but strong pressure to respond on the manager's grounds.

The question moved the discussion away from a consideration of the relative merits of the two programs; information and expertise were no longer bases for influence at that point in the exchange. Tom's move constrained the project directors' options in the interaction and actually directed them toward a reciprocal use of power. Any statement that would have been a conversationally appropriate response to the question (for instance, "I'll walk out of the meeting," "I'll be very angry and notify your supervisor," or "I'd get over it") is a comment about the project directors' ability or willingness to use their own bases of power. Tom's remark interrupted the group's present direction and turned the interaction toward a series of moves based on alternative resources: It was a classic triggering event.

Tom's final decision to choose the program he preferred and the response of the project directors to this move illustrate the importance of endorsement. In moving away from a form of influence that the group as a whole endorsed, Tom relied on his right as manager to choose the program he wanted. Although the right was a "given" in the situation, it did not necessarily have to be endorsed or accepted once that power was exercised. A bid for influence may not be successful if other members do not endorse the basis for the move.

The project director who decided to recommend rather than require the program and the director who said he did not use the program effectively did not fully endorse Tom's right to decide what program would be used. Although the project directors may or may not have been intentionally challenging Tom's power, in effect their responses were based on a belief that they had a greater say in how their projects were run than they had previously assumed. The project directors' decision questioned Tom's authority—his right to enforce the use of a program in the laboratories.

This does not mean that the project director did not fear reprisals by the manager. If Tom found out about this decision, he would either have to reestablish his power by imposing sanctions on the errant director or accept his diminished managerial role. It is likely he would have done the former. The project director was aware of this and gave credence to Tom's power, but he did so to a much lesser extent than he might have. After Tom's move, the project director saw him as unworthy of respect; he saw a way around Tom's power. The project director's original endorsement of Tom began to ebb.

The decline in endorsement of Tom's authority initiated in this incident continued through the labor dispute. Other subordinates saw that Tom could be defied successfully and heard disparaging remarks about him. They gossiped about "stupid" things they had seen Tom do and about his lack of respect for other project directors, there by eroding Tom's firm base of managerial respect. The project directors became more and more confident of their own resources vis-à-vis their manager. Tom's loss of endorsement points to some dangers of using strength.

5.4 The Use of Power in Conflict Tactics

Several researchers have developed extensive lists or typologies of conflict tactics or moves (for a particularly useful list, see Canary & Lakey, 2006; see also: Kipnis et al., 1980). The variety and range of these tactics show the many guises power can take in conflicts. Within this diversity, however, four distinct modes of power can be discerned.

1. Some tactics operate through the *direct* application of power: They are intended to compel others to respond regardless of what is wanted. These tactics bring physical, economic, and political resources directly to bear to force others to comply.
2. Other tactics involve a *direct and virtual* use of power: They attempt to elicit others' compliance by communicating the potential use of direct force. In direct and virtual use of power, parties openly display their resources and ability to employ them. Threats and promises are probably the best examples of this tactic.
3. Some tactics involve the *indirect* use of power: Someone may attempt to employ his or her power to shape interaction without ever making the use of power explicit. In the indirect mode, power or the potential to use it remains implicit and tacit.
4. Still other tactics may constitute a *hidden* use of power: In this mode, tactics use power to hide or suppress potential issues. The actual consequences of power are hidden because the issue is decided before it even develops or emerges.

Tactics may employ more than one mode of power. The particular mode(s) determine how open or explicit the influence attempt can be, the conditions it must meet to be effective, and the parties' general orientation and attitudes toward others. The modes in which a tactic operates indicate several important things about the tactic. First, they determine what skills and styles of behavior are necessary to use the tactic effectively. Making a threat, which involves direct, virtual power, requires a fundamentally different approach than does postponement, which uses power indirectly. Second, power modes shape the type of resistance the tactic is likely to meet. Different measures are necessary to counteract different modes of power. Finally, each mode has different effects on the endorsement of power underlying the tactic. For example, direct uses of power are much more likely to undermine endorsement than are hidden uses.

We illustrate the fundamental principles and processes involved in the "nondirect" power modes by considering three important and common tactics: *threats and promises* (direct, virtual power), *relational control* (indirect power), and *issue control* (hidden power). For each we outline how the tactic can be used, some conditions governing its effectiveness, and the likely points of resistance it can meet. Because the three tactics are "pure" examples of each category, the principles and problems enumerated here can be generalized to other tactics employing the same power mode.

5.4.1 Threats and Promises

In one form or another, threats and promises appear in almost every conflict described in this book. A *threat* is defined as an individual's expressed intention to behave in a way that appears detrimental to the interests of another individual, if that other individual does not comply with the request or terms. A *promise* is defined as an individual's expressed intention to behave in a way that appears beneficial to another individual, if the other individual complies with the request or terms. Threats and promises then are two sides of the same coin—one negative and the other positive (Kelley, 1965; Deutsch, 1973; Bowers, 1974).

Threats and promises are important not only because they are so common, but also because they are clear examples of the direct, virtual use of power to influence interaction. Threats and promises directly link resources—rewards and punishments—with influence attempts and therefore offer a clear illustration of the essential features of the implied use of power. Perhaps because of this, threats and promises were among the earliest tactics studied, and they have received more attention than any other conflict tactics of which we are aware (e.g., Tedeschi, 1970; Bowers, 1974; Gibbons, Bradac, & Busch, 1992). Although this research is fragmented, sometimes contradictory, and often hard to grasp, it can be put into perspective by considering threats and promises as aspects of power—as moves involving the skilled application of resources with an impact that is dependent on the endorsement of the influenced individuals.

It is obvious that effective promising or threatening depends on one person's control over resources the other person values. A manager in a large corporation can hardly threaten an employee with dismissal if the employee knows the manager has no authority to hire or fire; nor will employees believe the manager's promise of a raise if they know the manager has no clout "upstairs." However, effective influence does not necessarily stem from the person's actual control, but rather the other's perception that the person controls an important resource. A person's actual control over a resource becomes critical only if he or she has to carry out the threat or deliver the promise. The effectiveness of threats and promises is thus dependent on the individual's skill at convincing others that he or she has the resources and willingness to use them.

As in all power processes, the very act of threatening or promising can create or dissipate endorsement of the underlying resources. If a threat or promise is not carried out, it can suggest to others that the person does not have the necessary resources or the will to use them. This may in turn make others less likely to give credence to the person's resources and less likely to respond in the future. This development is particularly true of intangible resources such as authority. If the manager of a work team cannot carry out his or her promise to get a raise for them, the workers may lose respect and refuse to go along with the manager's future attempts to motivate or guide them (Bass, 2000, pp. 295–311).

Carrying out threats or promises also has consequences for their endorsement. As might be expected, actually carrying out threats may cause others to resent that person and may ultimately undermine his or her resources. Promises have a unique advantage over threats in that carrying them out actually enhances others' endorsement of the person's power. The use of promises tends to make the party seem more likeable, trustworthy, and considerate in the eyes of others. These perceptions reinforce the very credibility needed to pull off a promise effectively. In an effort to combine the greater compliance created by threats with the credibility reinforcement of promises, Bowers (1974) has suggested that most people use *thromises*—messages that convey both rewards and punishments simultaneously. If a manager says "We really can't take Friday off unless we finish this report today," she is conveying a rewarding offer in language often used for threats. By doing this, she may be able to enhance her employees' liking for her by indirectly offering a reward, yet constrain their behavior effectively. In addition, by indirectly indicating that she wants Friday off, she may increase the workers' identification with her and further strengthen her credibility and their endorsement of her authority.

The basic properties of threats and promises apply for all direct tactics. Most important, they depend on the person's ability to project the potential consequences of a direct move. This requirement makes the person's credibility critical.

5.4.2 Relational Control

During any face-to-face interaction, people constantly define and redefine their relationships. In describing how this process occurs, Watzlawick, Beavin, and Jackson (1967) have noted that every message carries two levels of meaning. Messages have a report aspect that conveys the content of the statement (in other words, the meanings people understand because they know the semantics of the language) and a command aspect that carries relational messages. A relational message is a verbal expression that indicates how people regard each other or their relationship (Burgoon & Saine, 1978). In effect, a relational message says "I see us as having this type of relationship." Relational messages are always bids. They attempt to define a certain type of relationship, but may or may not be successful depending on the listener's response.

There are as many possible relational messages as there are different types of relationships. These messages can convey implicitly that someone feels inferior or superior to another person, that he or she is irritated, likes someone, or sees the relationship as one in which it is all right to discuss very personal feelings. Any of these relational statements sends information about the way the speaker wants the relationship defined. If the listener responds with relational messages that accept the speaker's bids, the speaker controls the definition of the relationship. A group member who continuously refuses to take stands on important issues could be sending a relational message that says, "Don't see me as someone who will share responsibility for decisions made in this group." If other members allow this person to demur, they have accepted the relationship for which the recalcitrant person has bid. Alternatively, people who "guilt-trip" others are also bidding for a certain definition of the relationship. They want to induce a feeling of indebtedness in others and to establish a relationship in which others will go along because they feel obligated to do so.

Having one's definition of the relationship accepted is an indirect use of power that can yield considerable control in a conflict. Relational control is indirect because it sets expectations about what can and cannot be said in future interactions without any explicit statements or directives to other people. Relational messages are, by nature, implicit messages. We generally have a good sense of what our relationships with others are like without them having to tell us explicitly. We know whether someone likes or dislikes us, treats us as inferiors, equals, or superiors. Although there are instances when people overtly discuss and define their relationships, even these discussions carry implicit relational messages about what the relationship is like now that the participants have decided to talk about their relationship. A relationship between two close friends, for example, often changes dramatically when they talk about whether they love each other. The mere occurrence of such a discussion, regardless of the actual content of the conversation, says something about what the relationship is currently like. The discussion is a turning point in the relationship because the friends have signaled to each other that these types of discussions are now possible, or impossible, on a relational level.

Relational control is an important form of influence because people often accept previously defined relationships without question. Their understanding of a relationship sets a frame or context that defines what can or cannot be said in a conflict as long as that frame is in place. The parties' relationship may prevent certain moves from being used either because they seem inappropriate or because they are inconceivable given the nature of the relationship. That is, the relationship itself would have to be renegotiated for certain moves to be feasible.

Because relational messages are implicit, they are often problematic. First, they can be easily denied, misinterpreted, or reinterpreted. Comments that seem condescending or demeaning to one person may be viewed as helpful or assisting by others. Second, conflicts that escalate over trivial or inconsequential issues are often fights over the implicit relational messages and definitions that these issues carry. For instance, fights over who will do a trivial task may reflect an unsettled relationship issue. Typically, the relationship issue centers implicitly around who has the right to assign such tasks. As long as the relational issue goes unacknowledged, escalation over such minor problems is likely to continue. The same struggle exists in team interaction. Members commonly embed the expression of relational conflict, such as equity, workload, and status, in the task issues confronting the team (Simons & Peterson, 2000). Finally, the implicit nature of relational messages often masks the interactive nature of relational control. Like any use of power, relational control requires the endorsement of others. A relationship is not established until a relational bid has been accepted. Because relational messages are implicit, people often fail to recognize the ways in which they contribute to the definition of their own relationships.

Like other indirect tactics, relational control requires that the use of power remain undetected. If someone sees that there is an attempt being made to manipulate a relationship, the attempted control can be undermined (Tingley, 2001). Indirect tactics, on the other hand, are often particularly effective as a means of control because they go unnoticed. They gain their advantage before they are seen. Relationships are defined and redefined with every message that speakers send. As a result, relational moves are second nature. We do not reflect on whether we are accepting or rejecting a certain definition of a relationship each time one is offered.

5.4.3 Issue Control

In a classic effort to clarify several power-related issues, Bachrach and Baratz (1962; 1970) criticized the available sociological and political studies of power. They argued that power researchers were blinded to the most important and insidious use of power by their emphasis on observing the behavior of parties in conflict. This emphasis constrained them to study only direct, virtual, and indirect uses of power to control decisions and prevented them from considering hidden uses of power, which resulted in what they called *nondecisions*. A decision is a "choice among alternative modes of action" (1970, p. 39). It is arrived at through interaction among the parties and, hence, is shaped by moves involving the direct, virtual, and indirect use of power. A nondecision is the suppression or avoidance of a potential issue that might challenge or threaten the values or interests of one of the parties. It is a nonevent that never surfaces and results from the hidden use of power by one or more members. Power is hidden in this case because there is no opportunity to observe its operation. If an issue never even materializes and nothing happens, it seems as though power has never come into play when, in fact, it is responsible for the lack of action.

If you have served on a student council or other formal committee, you might have experienced hidden power in operation without realizing it. In such councils or committees it is often the case that the president, chair or other officers may quietly prevent an issue from being placed on the agenda or discussed in committee meetings. In many cases, members of the council or committee do not even know that the issue has been set aside. This represents an example of the exercise of hidden power. The officers can shape the group's actions and decisions without seeming to do so. In the same vein, the items that do make it to the group's agenda are often those that officers favor. Again, by shaping the group's agenda, the officers are subtly controlling the group.

Crenson (1971) illustrates "nondecision making" in a study of air pollution control in Gary, Indiana. He marshals impressive evidence that U.S. Steel prevented the adoption of air pollution standards not by directly opposing them, but by controlling the political agenda of the city. Because U.S. Steel was responsible for Gary's prosperity and had a powerful reputation, the issue simply was not raised for a number of years. When the issue finally did come up, the company was evasive. U.S. Steel did not take a strong stand for or against the issue, and most of the opposition was managed by community leaders with little connection to the company. As Crenson (1971, pp. 76–77) reports:

> Gary's antipollution activists were long unable to get U.S. Steel to take a clear stand. One of them, looking back on the bleak days of the dirty air debate, cited the evasiveness of the town's largest industrial corporation as a decisive factor in frustrating early efforts to enact a pollution control ordinance. The company executives, he said, would just nod sympathetically "and agree that air pollution was terrible, and pat you on the head. But they never did anything one way or the other. If only there had been a fight, then something might have been accomplished." What U.S. Steel did not do was probably more important to the career of Gary's air pollution issue than what it did do.

Its reputation for power and for benefiting Gary was sufficient to protect U.S. Steel from having to face the pollution issue for quite some time. Lukes (1974) and Bachrach and Baratz (1970) maintain that the hidden use of power is one of the most important and potentially dangerous power aspects precisely because it often goes totally undetected.

Issue control frequently occurs in face-to-face interaction. In many families, for example, some issues simply are not raised because one or both parents refuse to allow them to be heard. In families with domineering fathers or mothers, young children may not even try to voice their opinions because they know they will meet with strong disapproval. This prevents their concerns from becoming legitimate issues.

Two types of power resources come into play in issue control. First, parties may make definite moves that direct other parties' attention away from an issue. Control over what information people have access to is the most common means for accomplishing this. In his book, *Victims of Groupthink,* Janis (1972) notes that certain members of Kennedy's cabinet acted as "mindguards" to prevent the emergence of counterarguments against the CIA's plan for the ill-conceived Bay of Pigs invasion. The CIA had hatched a plan to invade Cuba with 2000 Cuban exiles, in an effort to overthrow Fidel Castro. This 1961 plan failed completely and embarrassed newly-elected President John F. Kennedy. Members of Kennedy's cabinet kept negative arguments against the invasion from being aired. As a result, the CIA's position was never challenged, which led to the ill-fated attack.

In other instances, people's attention is drawn away from conflict issues in more subtle ways. Bartunek and Reid (1992) and Fletcher (1999) illustrate, for example, how significant conflict issues in organizations never surface because they come to be cast as "personality conflicts" between members of the organization. Once seen this way, the underlying issues are often avoided.

The second type of resources involved in issue control suppress conflicts by creating fear of raising issues. One person's power and prominence may keep other people from even broaching a problem. Fear of the unknown—of whether raising an issue will create deep enmities with other members or upset the existing balance of power in the group—can also limit the issues raised. Even if there is no single overpowering person, people may fear an unpredictable collective reaction from the group if they transgress a strongly shared norm. Janis's *Victims of Groupthink* reports numerous cases where prestigious presidential advisors were subjected to ostracism, pressure, and even ridicule for disagreeing with the dominant sentiments of the cabinet.

There is also a skill factor in issue control. Because it operates tacitly, skillful issue control requires that the dominant person's power remains hidden. In the Gary pollution control case, U.S. Steel never openly agitated against the ordinance; to have done so would have aroused the community against it. As Pfeffer (1978) notes, this is one reason it is so hard to determine who holds power in organizations: Members do not want to divulge their strengths because they may become points of opposition for others.

Almost as effective, a dominant party may control issues by manipulating other issues indirectly related to the threatening issue. Pfeffer (1978) notes that one of the best means of influencing a decision is to control the criteria by which the decision is made. Because this is generally done very early in the decision-making process, its influence on the final outcome is often not apparent. Group leaders may shape members' evaluations by speaking briefly about what an effective decision might look like. These initial suggestions often have a strong influence on final decisions, despite the low-key manner in which they are delivered. Indeed, the frame or casting of the situation individuals offer may have a tremendous impact on what issues or ideas emerge in subsequent interactions (Putnam & Holmer, 1992).

As with all tactics based on hidden power, how issue control is managed can undermine or strengthen the endorsement of the controlling person's power. If control is flaunted openly, others may band together to counteract the person's dominance. Hence, working quietly and through indirect channels offers the greatest chance to preserve and strengthen endorsement. Issue control tends to perpetuate itself as long as it operates tacitly because it defines reality. It restricts people's thought processes and the alternatives considered and therefore rules out challenges to the power base that sustains it.

5.5 The Balance of Power in Conflict

There is widespread agreement among scholars of conflict that any significant imbalance of power poses a serious threat to constructive conflict resolution (Conrad & Poole, 2002; Folberg & Taylor, 1984; Rummel, 1976; Simon, Aufderheide, & Kampmeier, 2003; Walton, 1969). When one party can exert more influence than others because he or she holds greater power resources, or is more willing to employ his or her resources, the odds against reaching a mutually satisfying solution increase.

In the creativity development committee described in Case 5.3, the group initially acted under an assumption of equal power. The project directors believed the lab manager was holding his power in abeyance because he had called the group together to read, evaluate, and presumably select a new program for the lab. Interaction in early meetings was premised on the assumption of a balance of power. Members acted and reacted on the basis of their knowledge as researchers; because every member had experience with research, there was an assumption that all would have a say in the outcome. The project directors reported that it never occurred to them to refuse to use the program until after Tom indicated he might make the final choice himself. The shift from a recognized and self-endorsed balance of power to a state of potential imbalance when Tom acted on his managerial rights turned the course of the program selection away from the pursuit of a mutually satisfactory outcome. Tom asserted that he could make a choice that others would have little control over, and the project directors challenged that assertion.

Originally, Tom may have wanted to find a program on which the whole committee could agree; it is unlikely that he envisioned a split on the final options. Once the split occurred, however, the decision to act on a basis of power not available to project directors elicited their reciprocal use of power and triggered the beginning of a potentially destructive interaction. The relationship between Tom and his subordinates became strained; the quality of research could have been jeopardized, and the project directors' careers could have been threatened if Tom chose to retaliate.

When significant power imbalances exist, acting on those imbalances can escalate conflicts and promote the kind of destructive consequences no one on the creativity development committee believed were even remotely possible. Stronger and weaker parties in conflict are both in precarious positions as they make moves in a conflict interaction.

5.5.1 The Dilemmas of Strength

Power doesn't corrupt people; people corrupt power.

—William Gaddis

. . . control of other people's behavior and thoughts encourages the belief that those we control are less worthy than ourselves.

—David Kipnis (1990, p. 38)

Holding more power than others in a conflict is usually seen as a competitive advantage. However, the use of power in conflict interaction is often far more complex and self-threatening than is commonly assumed (Boulding, 1990). To demonstrate this complexity, we consider three dilemmas that the more powerful party in a conflict typically faces.

First, the moves that a more powerful party makes in a conflict are sometimes self-defeating because any source of power can erode once it is used. Because power must be endorsed by others in the group to be a basis for successful influence, using the resources one holds can prompt others to begin withdrawing their endorsement of those resources. Bachrach and Baratz (1970) suggest two reasons why this erosion tends to take place. First, they note that the use of power can cause "a radical reordering" of the values in the coerced person and undermine the power relationship (p. 29). The person who is the target of a power move may reshuffle his or her values so that the stronger party becomes less consequential.

This clearly happened in the creativity development committee case. The project director who decided not to require the program in his unit made a value decision about the relative importance of his role in the laboratory. He placed a higher value on his right to work as he thought best than on honoring his manager's right to assign the decision-making procedure. The project director had never considered counteracting his superior's orders before the summer committee met. It was Tom's use of power that prompted the project director to question it. Did Tom actually have the power of his position once he used it? In a real sense, he did not. The basis of his power eroded, in his subordinates' eyes, when he used the unique source of power he held in this situation. Tom still held the legitimate authority of his position, but that authority was weakened: The endorsement that gave it force over his subordinates was undermined.

Bachrach and Baratz also suggest that power may be exhausted because the constraint or sanction imposed by a powerful party "may prove in retrospect far less severe than it appeared in prospect . . ." (p. 29). The threat of power may be more effective than its actual use because the actual constraint may be more tolerable than was ever expected. Future attempts to influence the "weaker" party or gain compliance may fail because the power has been used once, and the weaker party has "lived through" its consequences. This is illustrated by the case of a new employee who is required to work alongside a powerful colleague (Case 5.4).

CASE 5.4 • *The Copywriters' Committee*

Imagine yourself as Jan: At what point would you have reacted to Rosa's behavior?

In the advertising department of a large company, a committee of all the copywriters normally approves the ads being released. One member of this committee, Rosa, often dominated discussions. Rosa was extremely forceful and had a habit of making cutting remarks about others who disagreed with her. Sometimes she shouted them down. This forcefulness initially cowed Jan, a new copywriter for the department, and she generally went along with Rosa's positions, however unwillingly. Jan finally decided to defy Rosa when Rosa attempted to revise an ad on which Jan had worked for several months. She attempted to refute Rosa's objections and received what she described as "a torrent of abuse" questioning her qualifications, competence, and loyalty to the department.

Jan reported that once Rosa's attack started, she realized it was not as bad as she had thought it would be. She recognized that Rosa was simply trying to manipulate her. Jan stood firm and, after some discussion, managed to work out a compromise in the committee. After this incident Jan was much less fearful of Rosa and became one of Rosa's leading opponents in the group.

Discussion Question

- How are the dilemmas parents face in disciplining children similar to the dilemma that Rosa found herself in?

Not only do powerful parties face the dilemma of losing power with its use, they also run a second risk—the risk of making false assumptions about the weaker party's response. Raven and Kruglanski (1970) suggested, for example, that stronger parties often anticipate that those in a less powerful position will resent the power they hold or dislike them personally. This assumption gives rise to an image of the weaker party as unfriendly or hostile. This image, in turn, encourages the stronger party to believe that an even tougher stand must be taken to defend against possible counterattack. The stronger party moves as if the weaker party intends to undermine or challenge his or her power base, regardless of the weaker party's actual intentions or feelings. In conflict situations, this assumption can quickly promote hostile escalation (Babcock, Waltz, Johnson, & Gottman, 1993).

False or untested assumptions about a weaker party are also likely when the more powerful party is successful. In research on how people explain their ability to influence successfully, high-status individuals who were able to change others' opinions were likely to believe that the change occurred because of ingratiation (Jones, Gergen, & Jones, 1963) or because the weaker party is not in charge of his or her own behavior (Kipnis, 1990). Stronger parties tend to believe, in other words, that others change their minds because they want to win the stronger parties' favor or because they are incapable of greater self-determination. Similarly, Walton (1969) suggests that in unbalanced power situations, the stronger party's trust in the weaker is undermined because the more powerful party may assume others act out of a dutiful sense of compliance rather than by choice (Pruitt & Rubin, 1986). This belief can encourage a stronger party to mistrust the behaviors of less powerful individuals and can prevent powerful parties from recognizing instances where others act, not out of a sense of duty, but because they see that the more powerful person is worthy of a receptive response. As Case 5.5 shows, power imbalances can exist in intimate relationships and undermine the stronger party's trust in the weaker.

CASE 5.5 • *Unbalanced Intimacy*

Imagine yourself as Tara: Is there anything you could do to enhance the trust you have in Ahmed's feelings toward you?

A college-aged couple (Ahmed and Tara) had been dating for almost two years, and, according to both of them, they had a fairly enjoyable relationship. They shared many interests, liked each other's friends and families, and had relatively few disagreements. Tara began to feel, however, that the relationship was unbalanced in a fundamental sense—Ahmed was an unusually insecure person. He felt that he was unattractive and was just plain lucky to have Tara interested in him. He often said that if she ended the relationship, it would be unlikely that he would ever meet anyone again. Tara likes Ahmed very much and wanted the relationship to continue. However, she also felt secure enough to think that if this relationship ended, in time she would probably meet someone else.

The difficulty for Tara was that she began to mistrust Ahmed's expressions of love for her. She said she could never be sure that Ahmed actually cared for her. She kept thinking that his feelings were simply based on his own insecurities rather than a real attraction to her. She ended up leaving the relationship because of these nagging doubts—doubts that ultimately stemmed from the much stronger position she held in the relationship.

Discussion Question

• What advice might a couples' counselor give to Ahmed and Tara?

A third dilemma of strength stems from the stronger party's ability to set the terms for reaching a settlement. In conflicts with significant differences in power, the stronger party frequently controls how destructive the conflict interaction becomes (Komorita, 1977). This control may stem not from the stronger party's power moves, but from failure to make de-escalation an attractive alternative to the weaker person.

A weaker party may have little motivation to stop destructive interaction cycles and begin searching for some workable solution to the problem, unless the stronger party demonstrates that this approach may be worthwhile. If the weaker party believes that compromising on an issue will mean "total loss" because the more powerful party can obtain "total gain" once the weaker party begins making concessions, the weaker party has little incentive to begin negotiating. If the more powerful party demands total capitulation, continued fighting or avoidance of the issue may be more attractive to the weaker party than an attempt to resolve the conflict through negotiation or problem solving.

In many conflict situations, it is easy for the stronger party to lay an implicit or explicit claim to a desired solution to the conflict and to create an impression in the weaker party that nothing short of that outcome will be acceptable. This impression can be enough to dissuade a weaker party from pursuing constructive approaches to the problem. The subtle ways in which a more powerful faction in a group can deter a weaker member from working on a conflict are illustrated in the case of a three-person office group (Case 5.6).

CASE 5.6 • *Job Resignation at a Social Service Agency*

Imagine yourself as a board member for this agency: What observations could you make regarding the relative power of the three employees?

A small social service agency employed three women to coordinate and plan projects that a large group of volunteers carried out. The agency was a fairly informal, nonhierarchical organization. The employees did not have written job descriptions; instead, an informal set of expectations about the agency's objectives guided their day-to-day work routines. The co-workers assumed that they had an equal say in the projects that were conducted by the office. None of them held the role of director or boss; all three answered to an agency board.

One of the workers, Kathy, was a single parent in her mid-forties who had worked at the office for a little over three years. The other two workers, Lois and Janelle, were in their early twenties, had just graduated from college together, and were good friends when they were hired. They had been at the office for less than a year. The younger employees had a great deal of

energy to devote to the agency, in part because they had few personal commitments outside work that would direct their time or attention elsewhere, and in part because they had a well-developed and somewhat idealistic view of the path they wanted the agency to follow. Kathy, on the other hand, found it difficult to support and raise a child while working. Also, because she had been working at the agency for three years, she did not have as much enthusiasm for her work as Lois and Janelle. The job had become more routine for her and was primarily a way of making ends meet.

Over a period of several months, Lois and Janelle became increasingly dissatisfied with Kathy's work at the agency. They felt she did not complete project reports on time or in sufficient detail, and as a result they tried to complete or revise a considerable amount of her work. They felt that Kathy had a different perspective on what their jobs entailed and what the goals of the agency should be. They were frustrated by the additional work they were forced to do and by their

(continued)

CASE 5.6 Continued

belief that Kathy was not allowing the agency to change and move in new directions.

A fairly short time later, Lois and Janelle became more vocal about their dissatisfaction with Kathy's work. Although they would occasionally give specific criticisms about her performance, the larger issue of how much say they would have in moving the agency in new directions brought them to a quick, defiant stand against Kathy. The issue that "Kathy is not doing her work right" quickly became "we want Kathy out." Kathy was aware of her co-workers' feelings and realized that they had different conceptions about the agency and their roles in it. On a day-to-day basis, however, she tended to avoid confronting the issue as much as possible. When questioned about her work, she would typically respond with a question that mirrored the resentment and hostility of Lois and Janelle: "How could I do all that when I've been trying to deal with a sick child at home all week?" Kathy felt that the two women had very little

understanding of her situation. She knew that the two younger workers saw her as a "bad person," and she felt they did not seek the kind of information that would allow them to see why her view of the job and agency differed from theirs.

Lois and Janelle eventually confronted Kathy with the problem by bringing it up to the agency board. They told the board that, in their view, Kathy was not fulfilling her job requirements and that she was resisting efforts to improve the agency. When questioned about the situation, Kathy tried to defend herself, but soon became conciliatory. Feeling enormous pressure from the two other workers, Kathy resigned from the agency within a few weeks after the board meeting.

Discussion Question

- As a board member, what could you have done to try to resolve the agency conflict constructively?

Because this office had little organizational structure and few direct lines of authority to evaluate performance formally, the two newer workers at this agency developed a considerable power base. Their friendship and similar views about what the agency should be doing made the pair a strong coalition, capable of making Kathy's situation unbearable. In taking an early hard-nosed stand and concluding that Kathy had to leave, they provided no incentive for Kathy to change her behavior. It is surprising that Kathy did so little to change in the face of her co-workers' criticism because, as a self-supporting parent, she needed the job badly. Although the two newer employees may have had a valid criticism of Kathy's work, their belief that Kathy had to leave the agency was, in effect, a demand for total capitulation. Kathy became convinced that there was little reason to work through the issue. Even if the board had decided she should stay on, it would have been difficult for her to work closely with the other employees. The women had the ability to pressure Kathy to resign and, by leaving the impression that they indeed wanted this outcome, they discouraged any initiatives to work on the conflict constructively.

5.5.2 The Dangers of Weakness

One way to analyze a conflict is to define parties' needs and determine which of the needs are incompatible. In the social service agency case, for example, the needs of the two newer staff people were basically twofold: to move the agency in new directions and to have the office run efficiently, while maintaining an equal division of labor among the three workers. Kathy's needs centered around the necessity of balancing a difficult home life with a demanding job. This general concern lay behind her need to continue with established programs rather than begin new ones and to work at a slower pace than her co-workers at the office. Although the issue spread fast and became highly personalized, the "problem" underlying this conflict centered around the apparent incompatibility of these two sets of needs. A collaborative or problem-solving orientation to this conflict would have set the participants in determined pursuit of a solution that could have met both sets of needs simultaneously. However, problem-solving approaches to conflict are premised on an assumption that participants recognize the legitimacy of each other's needs. When the needs themselves are held in question, there is no reason for the participants to search for some way of satisfying those needs.

In a situation where power is unbalanced, the greatest danger for weaker parties is that their needs will not be viewed as legitimate, that they will not be taken into account when the conflict is resolved. When more powerful parties discount weaker parties' needs, the solutions they seek, such as firing Kathy, are ones that by definition are unacceptable or unsatisfying for other parties. This is more than just a case of the stronger person's needs winning out over those of the weaker. The stronger person can often determine what needs are relevant through his or her ability to define what the conflict is about—in other words, to exert issue control.

The social service case provides an excellent example of the effects of issue control on weaker parties. When the issue was brought before the board, it was defined as a conflict over whether Kathy would or could hold up her end of the agency's work and adapt to its new directions. This put Kathy in a defensive position. Several possible alternative definitions were not considered: The conflict could be (1) over whether the agency should expand, (2) over whether fair and reasonable demands were being made of Kathy, or even (3) over quality-of-life issues (Kathy claimed the job took away family time, and the two new members wanted the work to play a big role in their lives). Each of these definitions implies a different focus for conflict interaction than the definition presented to the board. Definition 1 defines the conflict as a problem common to all three members concerning the agency's goals, whereas definition 2 questions the behavior of Lois and Janelle, and definition 3 reorients concerns to external issues such as members' overall satisfaction and life plans.

Clearly it would have been easier for Kathy to respond to any of these issues than to the issue presented before the board, but they were not raised. Lois and Janelle used their power and momentum to press their attack before the board and, by "getting the first word in," set an agenda to which Kathy had to reply. Kathy had little choice but to attempt to defend herself, and this response no doubt made her look bad in the eyes of the board and undermined her already shaken confidence.

A danger of weakness is that stronger parties may be able to define the terms and grounds of the conflict in their own favor (Sheppard, Lewicki, & Minton, 1992; Geist, 1995). Even the language a powerful party uses can have a significant impact on the way an issue is perceived or it can be used to legitimize and maintain the status quo (Giles & Wiemann, 1987; Conrad & Ryan, 1985). This type of definition not only puts the weaker party at a disadvantage, but it may also hurt both parties by resulting in an ineffective or harmful solution.

The more powerful party often only understands one side of the conflict, and his or her grasp of the underlying causes may be imperfect. As a result, the definition of the conflict advanced by the stronger party may not state the problem in terms that would lead to an effective solution. For example, in the social service agency, Lois and Janelle defined the conflict as Kathy's lack of cooperation. This definition pressured Kathy to resign. The social service agency lost Kathy's experience and talent and had to pay for hiring and training a replacement.

The outcome might have been different had the situation been defined as a conflict over whether the agency should expand. This definition recognizes both sides' concerns by emphasizing the agency, not the members. Although the same issues would probably have come out—Kathy's lack of energy, Lois and Janelle's desire to innovate—they would have been discussed in terms of a common issue, and much of the pressure would have been off Kathy. Perhaps, if managed correctly, a problem-solving approach could have generated solutions all could have lived with, while preserving Kathy's talents for the agency.

A second danger of weakness is its tendency to become self-perpetuating and self-defeating. As mentioned before, weak parties tend to perceive themselves as powerless; they exhibit "learned helplessness." These perceptions can discourage parties from attempting to resist or make countermoves to a powerful person's moves. The end result is a reinforcement of the powerful person's control and further proof of the weak person's impotence (Kipnis, 1990; Kritek, 1994). This process simply reproduces both parties' positions. Research on dating partners (Roloff & Cloven, 1990) supports this self-perpetuating tendency in unequal power relationships. There can be a "chilling effect" on the expression of conflict when perceived power differences exist between dating partners. When one party feels that the other has superior alternatives to the current relationship, the weaker party is less likely to express conflict issues. Weaker parties who are influenced by the chilling effect are reluctant to raise issues because they fear that conflict escalation might damage the relationship further and put it at risk. Similarly, research on marital partners (Kelley, 1979) suggests that the more dependent partner attends more to the care of the relationship than the less dependent partner. The effect of such moves by less powerful parties is to preserve and reinforce existing power structures in relationships.

People who are convinced that they have little influence and who are threatened are more likely to commit acts of desperation. As noted in the previous section, sometimes the weaker party may be convinced that he or she has little to lose by resisting, and a serious attack—one that threatens the existence of the relationship or organization—may appear to be the only course with a chance of success.

For example, in a charity fund-raising committee, one man with very little power faced the loss of the money necessary for the survival of his "pet" project, a community development loan corporation. If the project fell through, the member stood to lose his job as director of the corporation as well as his position on the committee. Believing the committee was about to veto his project, the member threatened to go to the local newspaper and state that the committee gave no support to the local economy. This would arouse a great deal of controversy around the committee and possibly hurt its major fund-raising drive, which was to begin in two months. The committee ultimately forged a compromise that gave the project partial funding, but the member's move caused considerable anger.

The committee's cohesion was undermined, and the project was canceled two years later. The desperation of weakness can motivate "absolute" acts with the potential to destroy relationships or groups or lead to worse retributions later on.

5.5.3 Cultural Differences in Values Concerning Power

The preceding discussion assumes that maintaining equality is an important value. Although it is certainly important in most Northern European–derived cultures, equality is not a central value in all cultures. Hofstede and Bond (1984) define power distance as a characteristic of cultures that reflects the "extent to which the less powerful members of institutions . . . accept that power is distributed unequally" (p. 419). The higher the power distance in a culture, the more its members accept unequal distributions of power. Ting-Toomey (1999) notes that power distance is low for Austria, Israel, Denmark, Ireland, Sweden, Norway, and Germany. Canada and the United States are moderately low on this dimension. Power distance is high in Malaysia, Guatemala, Panama, the Philippines, Arab nations, India, West African countries, and Singapore.

In these latter cultures, lower power parties do not expect to be part of the decision process, and the value of respect between parties of different status is taught from a young age. Ting-Toomey (1999, p. 71) observes:

> People in small power distance cultures tend to value equal power distributions, equal rights and relations, and equitable rewards and punishments based on performance. People in large power distance cultures tend to accept unequal power distributions, hierarchical rights, asymmetrical role relations and rewards and punishments based on age, rank, status, title, and seniority. For small power distance cultures, equality of personal rights represents an ideal to work toward in a system. For large power distance cultures, respect for power hierarchy in any system is a fundamental way of life.

Parties in high power distance cultures are likely to employ either the harmony or regulative models of conflict management rather than the confrontative model. For both models, and especially for the regulative model, balancing power is not as important as other considerations. Hence, power imbalances do not influence conflict interaction as strongly in these cultures as they do in cultures that favor a confrontative model of conflict management.

5.6 Working with Power

5.6.1 Diagnosing the Role of Power in Conflict

There are a number of barriers to accurate diagnosis of power relationships. For one thing, people are often unwilling to talk about power or to provide honest and accurate assessments of their own or others' power for several reasons. Given our culture's emphasis on democracy and equality, the open use of power is not socially sanctioned. Parties may be unwilling to admit that they use force or that a group is controlled by only a few members because they believe it makes them look bad. Furthermore, because power depends on endorsement, powerful parties often try to keep their power unobtrusive in order not to alienate those they influence. If weaker parties cannot see the power, or if they do not understand how it works, they can do nothing to upset the present balance.

Additionally, many moves, such as issue control, use power indirectly, and it is hard to determine who has influence. Finally, power and endorsement processes depend on relationships between parties rather than being properties of individuals, so it is often hard to determine where the source of power is. If power stems from relationships, it is misleading to try to identify a particular person who holds power. The more important question may be who assents to the use of power or who withholds endorsement.

These barriers make the assessment of power a complex process for which there can be no set formula. It is best to try several approaches. One way to assess power is to *determine the possible power resources in the situation and identify who holds them.* This involves identifying both obvious resources, such as status, knowledge, personal attractiveness, or formal authority, and more subtle sources of power, such as confidence or the ability to predict another's behavior. A second, complementary approach is to *identify power through its effects.* Those whose preferences consistently win out and who are accommodated by other members are generally those who control resources and use them effectively. A third indicator of power is *conservatism.* If power is relational, then changes in existing relationships generally alter the balance of power, while stability preserves it. People who are against changes are likely to believe they will lose by them. These are often the people who hold substantial power under the status quo.

None of these three indicators is foolproof, but they are a good starting point. Judgments about power ultimately rest on knowledge of relationships among parties, their particular history, and the nuances that signal dominance and subordination. Diagnoses cannot be programmed and must be continually refined.

Another important diagnostic tool in analyzing power is the *ability to recognize when parties draw on unique or shared power resources as a basis for influence in conflict.* Parties can attempt to influence a conflict by drawing either on the unique resources they hold or on sources of power commonly available to everyone and explicitly endorsed as a legitimate basis for influence. When parties use unique power sources, integration is more difficult and escalation more likely. Each move premised on unique sources of power "tells" others that an attempt may be made to resolve the issue by means not available to everyone. This message can promote escalation by prompting other parties to use their own resources to counter moves they cannot reciprocate.

The creativity development committee case (Case 5.3) provides an illustration of people moving from the use of shared to individual resources. In the early meetings, parties' actions were contained by boundaries that the group as a whole accepted. The project directors and the manager drew from a set of resources they all shared and saw as a legitimate basis for changing opinions and determining possible outcomes. When Tom indicated that he might make the final choice based on his position as the lab manager, the emphasis shifted to the unique sources of power that individual parties held.

Similarly, in the Job Resignation case (Case 5.6), the conflict drew on unique power bases. The two newer staff people used their friendship and agreement on agency policy to move against Kathy. Kathy drew from her seniority and experience as an older worker to justify her position in response to the challenge she faced. The three women never developed an implicit agreement about what resources could be used to influence each other. There was no mutually-endorsed set of resources that could be used to work through the conflicts over the quality of work and the long-range objectives of the agency. In making moves based on their unique sources of power, parties worked on the problem from their own standpoints and discouraged give and take on common ground.

To safeguard against the dangers of unbalanced power, then, parties need to forestall power moves based on unique resources. But how do parties promote the use of shared power? Although there is no cut-and-dried answer to this question, research and practice suggest some guidelines.

5.6.2   Fostering Shared Power in Conflicts

Three primary conditions encourage reliance on shared power in conflicts. First, *if all parties are in agreement on the primary goals of the relationship, group, or organization, unique sources of power are less likely to be used.* A shared sense of purpose gives members a common orientation, which encourages interchanges on common ground (Mansbridge, 1990; Larson & LaFasto, 1989). A common goal gives the group a center that encourages members to identify with each other. When they identify, members are likely to think in similar terms about how to influence each other. They are not as likely to resort to unique resources that could underscore potential divisions among them.

Classroom teams formed to complete a project assignment often fail to attain a common goal or purpose. Some students see the team's major aim as education; they accept the premise that going through the trials and tribulations necessary to complete the term project will be a good learning experience. For these students, the general purpose of the team is to learn how to collectively carry out assigned tasks. Other students do not buy into this educational objective. Their goal is simply to complete an acceptable assignment that meets the basic requirements for the course and to get a good grade without expending too much effort.

Differences over how the project should be accomplished, how often they should meet, or how much time should be spent on each task are ripe for escalation into full-blown conflict. Without a shared goal, parties are likely to feel disconnected from others and to turn to unique sources of power. When all parties buy into the same goal, there can still be considerable debate over how long meetings should run and so on, but the team is working toward the same conception of success as it tries to reach agreement on issues. In terms of power, a shared goal forms a basis for common effort that encourages members to operate on the same level when they try to influence each other (Jehn & Chatman, 2000).

In the Job Resignation case, the three women never reached agreement about what the primary goals of the agency should be. There were implicit differences that the two factions never tried to resolve or meld into one shared mission for the office. As a result, differences over an issue, such as what constituted quality work at the agency, were "settled" when members turned to the unique sources of power they held. Sticking to the shared definition of their problem—should the agency expand?—might have helped the three women to identify common goals.

A second condition conducive to a shared power base is *the group's or organization's willingness to make power resources accessible to all members.* A resource truly shared by the membership is an attractive alternative to unique sources. If, for example, knowledge of the history of the organization is endorsed as an important resource for influencing decisions, settling differences about policy matters, and so on, then all members—even new people—must be given access to this knowledge. New members, of course, will be less influential than others at first because they do not enter the team with a full history in hand.

However, if the relevant information is made available on a decision-by-decision or issue-by-issue basis, newer members can draw on the same sources of influence that long-standing members use. In some teams, this is done through formal channels such as orientation sessions, training in skills valued by the group, and written histories.

Even when all information is available and access is given to all members in principle, certain members may consistently be more influential than others because they are more skillful. Some members may be more powerful than others because they are better able to articulate positions the team recognizes as appropriate or consistent with its direction. Ensuring access to all does not mean that all members will be equally able to use a resource. Some members may be able to apply the resource more quickly or insightfully as new issues arise, and therefore their power, their ability to influence the direction of conflicts, will appear to be greater. The difference is, however, that the power these members exercise is legitimate because the group as a whole continues to endorse the resources regardless of who uses them.

The importance of equalizing the power resources available to all members is clear in the Job Resignation case. In their coalition, Lois and Janelle had a source of power unavailable to Kathy. If Lois and Janelle had not taken advantage of their alliance and had instead tried to deal with Kathy one-on-one, they might have been able to work out a more constructive solution. From one-on-one conversations, Lois and Janelle might have been able to understand Kathy's needs and feelings better. They might also have seen her potential and the problems that kept her from contributing. Kathy, on the other hand, might not have been intimidated by the united front of Lois and Janelle and might herself have seen the merits in their case. Once each side understood the other's needs and problems, working out a solution would have been easier. Moreover, once Kathy was assured that the other two would not use their superior power to force her, she might have become less reactive and more willing to work with them on improving the agency.

A third condition underlies the first two: *The group should recognize that its members are the source of power and that they participate continually in the exercise and renewal of power.* The group must work to see through the myth of power as a possession to the process of endorsement necessary for any move to be effective. It must acknowledge that this endorsement occurs in members' interaction and that therefore, as Janeway (1980) argues, all power is grounded in *community* among members. This is what democratic nations try to do in their constitutions, and this is what groups must do to build a shared power base. However, just as governments often have trouble remembering their popular roots, so too do groups and teams have trouble remembering the roots of their power.

As noted, the endorsement process operates to hide the source of power from members. Long socialization, the mystique of power, and subtle interaction processes veil members' roles in endorsement. To achieve a balance of power, groups must adopt structural measures to counteract these forces (See Table 5.1). Groups have done this in a variety of

TABLE 5.1 *Working with Power: Measures to Take to Manage Power Constructively*

Diagnosing Power
- Determine possible resources available to parties and who holds them.
- Identify power through its effects.
- Identify conservatism—where the system resists change—often a sign of power structures.
- Look for unique versus shared power resources.

Fostering Shared Power
- Ensure all parties have shared goals.
- Develop common bases of power that all parties have access to.
- Reach agreement on norms concerning what types of power can be used and how it can be used.
- Make parties aware of how endorsement of power resources works.
- Encourage lower power members to band together as a counterweight to higher power members.

ways, including rotating leadership regularly, appointing "process watchers" to comment on members' moves and group interaction, setting up retreats and evaluation periods to help members discuss power-related problems, and forcing their leaders to adopt a nondirective style. Whatever the specific steps, these moves tend to be effective because (1) they make members aware of their community and their responsibilities to the group and to each other, (2) they emphasize admitting all members into discussions on an equal basis, and (3) they deemphasize the prominence of any particular individual.

This section has emphasized the need to develop shared power bases. This is meant as an ideal or goal to strive for, not as the only effective or justifiable use of power. Some groups have such deep-seated discrepancies that weaker members have no choice but to develop and use unique power bases. In such instances, the use of force or countervailing resources may be the only way to check or get the attention of the controlling members. The literature on teams and organizations is full of examples of groups with authoritarian leaders who became so oppressive that members saw no choice but to band together and to rebel. A forceful countermove was the only way these parties could get their message heard. Unique sources of power can be used beneficially, but in the long run doing so is likely to create unstable situations. One side may topple the other, but, in time, the toppled side is likely to strike back. Moving to a shared power base greatly enhances the likelihood of a constructive and mutually beneficial solution.

In one sense, these suggestions are preconditions; they must be in place in a group if members can hope to develop shared power resources and to use them as a basis for moves in any conflict interaction. In another sense, these suggestions offer long-term intervention strategies; they are areas that the group can work on to establish general expectations for how it operates. They can govern what members consider doing when they try to sway each other's thinking about issues.

What happens, however, when these preconditions have not been established or when someone uses unique resources in a conflict that is particularly important to him or her? Although no intervention is foolproof, several approaches may help prevent escalation in such instances.

First, it may be helpful if people discuss their likely reaction to the use of unique resources. For example, members might acknowledge that they will see people who uses seniority to justify job assignments as "out for themselves." Open discussions can effectively raise the group's consciousness about power moves. It can help the group learn that certain resources will change conflict interaction dramatically. It also alerts the group to possible dangers or pitfalls that might result.

A second approach is aimed at developing structural changes in interaction when power moves are based on unique resources. One of the most effective tools for changing the influence of power in conflicts is to increase people's awareness of the role they play in creating and sustaining others' power. If members become aware of how their endorsement is shaped by social categorization, the mystique of power, and their own interaction, they are well on the way to seeing through the existing power structure.

The value of this type of "consciousness-raising" is illustrated by the support groups that spring up in professions undergoing rapid change and coping with the struggles that result. These groups, ranging from female executives in male-dominated corporations to nurses and medical orderlies attempting to have more input in hospital decisions, give their members a chance to share problems and fears and to give each other advice. People help each other understand how those dominant in their professions maintain their positions. They also work out ways of being more effective and build resolve and courage to face difficult situations. They encourage members to question what was previously unquestionable—the taken-for-granted relations of authority and obedience, strength and weakness. Formal support groups are not the only thing that can serve this function: A conversation over dinner or after work can generate important insights. Just realizing one is not alone and sharing experiences are often important steps.

As Janeway (1980) observes, in addition to awareness, mutual support is another way for weaker members to counterbalance stronger ones. People generally associate coalitions with open shows of strength and solidarity, as in a union vote, but such displays may be ineffective in many contexts. "Raising the flag of defiance" can threaten stronger people and cause them to overreact, sending the conflict into an escalating spiral. Those who have greater resources stand to lose if the current balance tips in a new direction, and they will resist such moves. A coalition is more likely to be successful in moving a conflict in a productive direction if it is unobtrusive. The pact between people should not be openly displayed, and, if possible, any coordination or support should not be obvious. In addition, a coalition is more likely to turn conflict in a productive direction if it aims for a balance of power than if it tries to win. If the powerful people's interests are not threatened, and if they do not face serious losses, they are more likely to cooperate with efforts to achieve a balance of power.

5.7 Summary and Review

What is power?

Power is the ability to influence or control events. It depends on resources parties can employ to influence others and attain their goals. A wide variety of resources can serve as sources of power, including material resources (money or strength), skills, likeability, and formal position in a group or organization.

What gives resources their empowering nature?

Resources are not valid in any absolute sense. The effectiveness of a resource as a basis of power depends on its endorsement by other parties. If a resource is not valued or validated by others—or if they do not believe the party's use of the resource is legitimate—then the resource will not motivate them to comply. Even direct physical violence cannot necessarily force someone who does not endorse it to comply.

How does the process of endorsement work?

Endorsement is negotiated in interaction. This negotiation is influenced by four factors: social categorization, the mystique of power, legitimacy attached to certain resources, and the degree to which resources are used skillfully in interaction. Because it is produced in interaction, the endorsement of power differs across situations and may change during an episode. These differences tend to remain hidden, and the fact that power is produced through the collaboration of all parties is obscured by the tendency in U.S. culture to avoid open discussion of power in interpersonal relationships.

The effective power in a given situation is a product of the give-and-take in which parties employ resources to place constraints on each other. One party's constraint is answered by another party's countermove, and the resulting web of constraints gives the conflict direction by favoring certain moves and making other moves less productive. Each move—or power bid—places a certain resource into play, and the four factors mentioned in the previous paragraph influence whether the bid is accepted or not. When bids are accepted, the resource is endorsed for future use, and bids that are rejected decrease the endorsement of the resource.

How does power operate when a conflict tactic is employed?

Power may operate in four distinct modes. *Direct power* employs resources to compel others to comply in an open power move. *Direct and virtual* uses of power imply the potential use of direct power, but do not actually put the resources into play. *Indirect power* moves use resources to influence interaction, but do not make the use of power explicit. *Hidden power* is employed to frame or limit the discussion of issues behind the scenes; tactics that use this mode of power keep issues from being contested and predetermine the outcome of conflicts.

Some tactics use more than one mode of power. We discussed three that exemplified more or less pure modes of power. Threats and promises employ direct, virtual power. To use them skillfully, a party must make the threat or promise credible. Relational control employs indirect power by defining the nature of the relationship between the parties, thereby making certain moves likely and constraining the use of other moves. The endorsement of indirect power depends on its remaining under the surface—hidden from view. If one party senses that the other is trying to manipulate him or her, the relational messages that define and constrain behavior become less effective, and the relationship itself—the key resource in relational control—may be endangered. Issue control employs hidden power to set the agenda for a conflict, enabling some issues to be raised and suppressing others. As with indirect power, hidden power needs to operate under the surface and in the back rooms. If it is brought into the open, issue control is generally viewed as improper manipulation, and endorsement of this channel of power decreases.

Why is the balance of power among parties important?

Imbalances of power result when parties possess different resources that are endorsed at different levels. For most cultures in the United States, maintaining equality of opportunity is valued. When parties do not have equal control over the situation, several problems can result. Although being the stronger party may seem desirable, it creates certain dilemmas. Using the very resources that contribute to strength may undermine their endorsement due to the resistance and resentment of weaker parties. Stronger parties also tend to assume that the weaker party is complying only because he or she is forced to. This creates a sense of distrust of the weaker party and encourages the stronger party to continue forcing, further undermining the relationship between the two. Imbalances of power also encourage the weaker party to give up on cooperative solutions, effectively guaranteeing repeated cycles of forcing. A continuing imbalance of power may encourage the weaker party to feel powerless and devalue his or her resources. This further cements control of the stronger party because his or her resources are endorsed by the weaker party, who also "dis-endorses" his or her own resources.

It is important to note that balancing power is not a key value in cultures with high power distance. In such cultures, the dynamics of power in conflicts are likely to be quite different.

How can we work productively with power in conflicts?

The first prerequisite to working with power is to understand how it operates in the situation. Indicators of who has power and the impacts it has on the conflict include who controls power resources and might use them, conservatism, and the effects of power. One important aspect of power is whether the parties have unique resources. Once parties (and third parties) understand how power operates, they can move to change the situation.

How can parties foster shared power?

Shared power is more likely when: (a) parties are in agreement about broader goals, and a shared sense of purpose overarches the conflict; (b) key sources of power are accessible to all parties, rather than distributed unequally; and (c) parties understand their own role in the creation of power and actively work to manage how power is used in the conflict.

Several steps may be taken to encourage a move toward shared power from a situation in which unique sources of power are used. First, parties can openly discuss their reactions to certain power moves, indicating which sources of power are acceptable to them and which are threatening or negative. Second, parties can change the structure of the situation so that certain types of power resources are encouraged and other resources disallowed. Third, weaker parties can support each other to resist a more powerful party with the goal of reaching a stalemate that can promote discussion or structural changes.

5.8 Conclusion

Power is the architecture of conflict interaction. The moves and countermoves in a conflict are based on a party's ability and willingness to use power. Power moves are based on resources people hold that serve as a successful basis of influence. These resources can range from material goods to time, physical attractiveness, communication skills, and other talents. Power must be viewed as a relational concept because in order for resources to be a basis for influence, the resources must carry the endorsement of others. Power is thus always conferred on people by those who endorse the resources, and it is conferred through interaction.

At first glance, the relational nature of power seems to suggest that weaker parties in a conflict always have a way out. They can withdraw their endorsement if more powerful parties apply pressure. There are, however, strong social forces that encourage or sustain the endorsement of various forms of power. Whatever the distribution of power may be, its balance is critically important in determining the direction of conflict. When power is unbalanced, the stronger and weaker parties both face dilemmas as they make moves and step through difficult conflict situations. Stronger parties can exhaust their power by its use, consciously or inadvertently set settlement terms that encourage continued escalation, and make faulty assumptions about the likely response of a weaker party. Weaker parties may have to live with a definition of the problem that ignores their real needs because they have no hand in determining what issues get addressed.

6

Face-Saving

Imagine that you are so absorbed in texting your friend while walking to class that you fail to notice a stairwell. Suddenly, you are off-balance, falling on what should be level ground. Thanks to superior coordination skills, you keep from going head over heels down the steps, but you do jerk and jump down the jagged cement. Your belongings fly into the air, but you make a remarkable recovery, landing on both feet and catching your cell phone before it hits the ground. Just as your nerves and heart settle, you notice that a group of your classmates is watching. In fact, it is obvious from the expressions on their faces that they have seen the entire embarrassing event.

A million thoughts race through your mind. What do you say or do? Do you walk on and ignore them? What about the things you dropped? You are struck by a sudden desire to say something intelligent, something that reflects you are not the clumsy boob you appear to be. Instead, you stoop down to pick up your things. You look at the steps and curse them, as if they were human and had consciously decided to trip you. With a newfound composure, you turn to your classmates and say, "What are you looking at?" You immediately realize this is a silly question, so you add, "I was texting and didn't see the steps." They laugh. You turn red. One onlooker says, "Hope you didn't break your cell." He probably meant it as a joke to ease the moment. Somehow, though, this joke stings. They turn and walk away. Half-jokingly, you vow to hate these people for the rest of your life. You are amazed at how bitter you feel. Hours later, you wonder what the big deal was. How could you have gotten so flustered and bent out of shape over a simple misstep and comment?

The answer lies in what scholars, and now practitioners, commonly refer to as *face*. Face is a central theoretical concept used in a wide array of disciplines and is defined in as many ways. Yet most definitions concur that "face" is concerned with identity needs. People have identities or public images they want others to share. Although the attributes vary, people want to be seen by those they encounter as possessing certain traits, skills, and qualities. They constantly position themselves in interaction with others (Harre & Van Langenhove, 1999). In short, *face is the communicator's claim to be seen as a certain kind of person.* As one scholar in the area puts it, face is "the positive social value a person effectively claims for himself [*sic*] by the line others assume he has taken during a particular contact" (Goffman, 1955).

The concept of face can be traced to fourth century B.C. China. The Chinese distinguish between two aspects of face, *lien,* and *mien-tzu* (Hu, 1944). *Lien* stands for good moral character. A person does not achieve *lien,* but rather is ascribed this quality unless he or she behaves in a socially unacceptable manner. To have no *lien* means to have no integrity, which is perhaps the most severe condemnation that can be made of a person. *Mien-tzu* reflects a person's reputation or social standing. One can increase *mien-tzu* by acquiring social resources such as wealth and power. To have no *mien-tzu* is simply to have floundered without success, an outcome that bears no social stigma.

6.1 The Dimensions of Face

Although scholars generally concur that face is a universal characteristic of being human, there is less agreement as to the common identities or "face wants" people share. Brown and Levinson (1978; 1987) propose the most popular view in their theory of politeness. *Politeness theory* conceives of face as something that can be lost, maintained, or enhanced and must constantly be attended to in interactions. Specifically, the authors propose two dimensions of face: *Positive face* refers to a person's desire to acquire the approval of others; *negative face* is the desire for autonomy or to not be imposed on by others. Conflict may arise because many communicative acts, especially instances of social influence, are face-threatening. For example, a request to "get busy with that report" may interfere with the hearer's negative face wants or the desire for autonomy. According to the theory, the degree to which face is threatened by a request is a function of three factors: the social distance between the parties, the relative power of the parties, and the intrusiveness of the request or act. The greatest potential face threat is found when there is greater social distance between the parties, the listener has more power than the speaker, and there is a great degree of imposition placed by the communicative request or act. We refer to the theory as "politeness" because the degree of face threat is thought to determine how polite a speaker will be. Brown and Levinson propose that people use five general strategies to perform a *face-threatening act* (FTA), represented in Table 6.1.

The strategies and examples in Table 6.1 are presented from most to least polite. The most polite strategy is to *avoid* the FTA completely—the speaker makes no request.

TABLE 6.1 *Politeness and FTA Strategies*

	Example Request: Begin Fixing the Dinner Meal	
Politeness	*FTA Strategy*	*Example*
High	Avoid—do not perform	No request is made.
	Going off-record	I'm really getting hungry.
	Negative politeness	I know you are busy, but could you start cooking dinner?
	Positive politeness	You are such a good cook. I can't wait until you start dinner.
Low	Bald on-record	Would you fix dinner?

Source: Adapted from Brown and Levinson (1978).

The next strategy is called *going off-record*. This is when the FTA is performed in such an ambiguous manner that it could be interpreted as some other act by the hearer. Going off-record is stating a request indirectly or implicitly. The third strategy is the use of *negative politeness*. This strategy attempts to mitigate the threat to the hearer's negative face by giving him or her autonomy. *Positive politeness* is the fourth strategy—the speaker performs the FTA with attention to positive face needs (the want of approval). The least polite strategy is a *bald on-record* FTA with no attempt to acknowledge another's face wants. Politeness theory contends that speakers employ the strategy that fits the situation. The more serious the FTA, the more polite the speaker will attempt to be.

Lim and Bowers (1991) extend the Brown and Levinson concept of positive face (the desire for approval) because it compounds two different human face needs: the need to be included and the need to be respected. The need for inclusion, they maintain, is the need to have one's person and personality approved of, whereas the need for respect is the need to have one's abilities and skills approved of. As a result, Lim and Bowers distinguish between three types of human face needs: the want to be included or *fellowship face,* the want that one's abilities be respected or *competence face,* and the want not to be imposed on or *autonomy face*.

6.2 Face-Loss as It Relates to Face-Saving

When face wants are not addressed during interaction, one or both of the parties may experience a loss of face. People are said to *lose face* when they are treated in such a way that their identity claims are challenged or ignored. Given the strong need to maintain a favorable image, face-loss can lead to an impasse in interaction and exacerbate or create conflict between parties. Goffman (1955) describes several face-loss consequences. First, face-loss often causes a party to be momentarily incapacitated or confused. The shock that one's identity is facing attack sometimes takes a moment to adjust to. Second, the party may feel shame or embarrassment. This feeling is often accompanied by a host of common symptoms that reflect this social distress, including blushing, sweating, blinking, fumbling, stuttering, and general nervousness (Sharkey, 1988). Third, the party may feel inferior or less powerful. In sum, face-loss is an unpleasant experience, seen from the eyes of the harmed party as social humiliation. Not surprisingly, research shows that parties are willing to retaliate and sacrifice rewards at great costs when they perceive the threat of humiliation (Brown, 1977).

Face-saving behaviors are defensive attempts to reestablish face after threats to face or face-loss. In other words, face-saving is what a person does to regain the image he or she believes has been dismissed. The remainder of the chapter explores the consequences of face-saving strategies for parties in conflict.

6.3 A Threat to Flexibility in Conflict Interaction

Continued change is often a good sign in conflict. Changes in a person's positions and styles, as well as more general shifts in the climate and emotional tenor, indicate that a person or group is successfully resisting tendencies toward rigid perpetuation of conflict interactional patterns. They also decrease the likelihood that the parties will lock into the destructive cycles that trained incapacities often produce. As uncomfortable as it sometimes is, parties should be encouraged by change because it usually means that others are still working on the issue and that a breakthrough is possible. Change requires energy; the use of energy to move the conflict interaction in new directions suggests that there is still some level of motivation to deal with the unresolved issue. Any signs of stalemate or rigidity can easily paint the first gray shades of discouragement on a colorful, although difficult and emotionally draining, conflict.

The emotional side of conflict is intimately connected with a party's flexibility. As noted in Chapter 1, every move in conflict interaction affects relationships, liking or disliking for each other, mutual respect or lack of respect, beliefs about each other's competence, and a score of other beliefs and feelings. Face-saving is an attempt to protect or repair relational images in response to threats, real or imagined, potential or actual. It can limit a party's flexibility in taking new approaches to the conflict issue. In addition, because of its relational consequences, face-saving often carries an emotional "charge" that can greatly accelerate destructive escalation or avoidance in conflict. Like the effects of trained incapacities, face-saving issues often redefine conflicts. Once face-saving becomes a concern, parties' perceptions and interaction patterns can lead to a progressive redefinition of the conflict, which changes a potentially resolvable difference over some tangible problem into an unmanageable issue centering on the relationships between the parties and the images they hold of themselves.

Before exploring face-saving in detail—its causes and its consequences—it is useful to consider a few illustrations. Cases 6.1 through 6.3 (pages 178–180) show three diverse conflict situations wherein the ability to be flexible and to change approaches, positions, or interaction styles are in jeopardy. At the heart of each case lies a concern with saving face.

- In Case 6.1, a university professor became increasingly concerned about the way students would be likely to see her if she changed her mind about a decision she had recently made.
- In Case 6.2, a group feared that an outspoken, quick-thinking member would have trouble backing off from a position once she took a stand on an issue. To the group's surprise, she had little concern about being seen as "wishy-washy" and changed stands once a better argument was made by other members.
- In Case 6.3, three staff members felt their face was threatened by one person who "took charge" without the team's endorsement.

In each of these cases, some form of face-saving was a central concern and could have undermined the parties' ability to successfully deal with the conflicts. In the grade dispute, the professor had taken a stand on an issue and was reluctant to move from that position because she might be seen as indecisive or unsure of herself. When she reconsidered her decision, she recognized that the student may have had a good case and that she may have been too harsh in enforcing her no make-up policy. As she entered the meeting where the conflict was to be addressed, however, there was a great likelihood that her current beliefs on the problem would not be stated unless something was done to ease her concern about the image she might acquire by following her inclinations. Part of her reluctance to

CASE 6.1 • *The Professor's Decision*

Imagine yourself as the English professor: Why might you be so concerned about your image?

An English professor at a Midwestern university was called by the academic appeals referee and told that a student in her introductory writing course had filed a grievance about a grade he received last semester. The student was given a "D" in the class because he did not take the final exam in the course. On the day of the exam, the student had left a message with the department secretary saying that he was ill and would not be present for the test. Although the professor received this message, the student did not get back in touch with her until after the grades had to be submitted. When the student did get in touch with the professor, he told her that he had three other final exams scheduled that same week and had decided to take those tests to stay on schedule rather than making up the English final immediately. He said he had thought he would be able to contact her again before the grades had to be reported, but, as it turned out, he was too slow in doing so. On hearing the student's explanation, the professor had decided to stick with her earlier decision to give him the grade he received without any points on the final. The student's grades on the earlier tests and writing assignments were good enough that if he had received a "B" on the final exam, he would have finished with a "B" in the course.

After receiving the call from the appeals referee, the professor began to question her decision. Originally she had felt justified in taking a tough stand because she had stated a very clear policy about missing tests and assignments early in the term. However, realizing that she might have been somewhat dogmatic in this case, she was leaning toward allowing the student to take a make-up exam and using that score to recompute his final grade. But as she entered the meeting with the appeals referee and student, she became increasingly concerned about changing her mind. She knew that word travels fast among students, and she was worried that soon she would have a reputation for changing grades or class policy when the right pressure was applied. She was also increasingly bothered by the student's decision to register a formal complaint against her in the college.

Discussion Questions

- How could an understanding of the professor's concern for her future image assist the appeals referee in this case?
- Can you think of examples of conflicts in which you felt someone's concern about image contributed to his or her inflexibility?

CASE 6.2 • *The Outspoken Member*

Imagine yourself as Rhonda: Why do you think you are so willing to change your position? What is the image of yourself that you are protecting?

A group of twelve leaders and activists in the antipollution movement of an eastern city began meeting to discuss strategies for dealing with an attack on water standards that was currently being made in their area. A local business executive was mounting a campaign that could have jeopardized water and waste treatment standards if it gained sufficient support. The group of

twelve met to determine what could be done to counteract the business campaign and to coordinate the efforts of environmentalists who wanted to work on the project. They saw their main task as building an effective alliance of people in town who wanted to work for environmental quality at this crucial time.

The people in the group were from a wide variety of backgrounds and professions: Some headed smaller civic organizations, some were students, one worked for a local newspaper, one was

(continued)

CASE 6.2 Continued

an elected city official. One member, Rhonda, was an attorney in her thirties and a long-time activist in local politics. She was outspoken, and took the floor several times early in the first meeting. She spoke in a loud and confident tone of voice, and came to the meeting with well-developed ideas about what the group should do. She was able to argue her position clearly and forcefully while other members still seemed to be thinking about what the current situation was like and calculating what should be done as an immediate plan of action.

When Rhonda made a strong case for what the group should do in the first part of the initial meeting, the climate in the group grew uneasy and tense. Several people looked at each other uncomfortably, and most people seemed hesitant to speak. The group seemed to be "holding its breath" and anticipating that Rhonda would be difficult to work with. Although she was obviously bright and had good reasons supporting her suggestions, members feared that Rhonda had set ideas and would not budge from the proposal she had just articulated so forcefully. The group worried Rhonda would feel as if she had lost face if she moved away from her stated position.

After several people made comments that were not related to Rhonda's proposal, one man in the group began pointing to possible complications and problems with Rhonda's suggestion. She listened intently, and when he was finished speaking, Rhonda said that she really had not thought of the points he had raised and that she agreed they posed a serious set of problems. She asked the man if he had an alternative suggestion, listened to it, and then shortly began arguing for it. She made stronger and more well-reasoned arguments for the man's proposal than he himself had made, and Rhonda was able to clarify questions other people in the group had about the proposed plan without dominating the interaction or intimidating people further.

The group soon saw Rhonda as one of its most valuable members. She could carry a line of thought through for the group and lay out a well-reasoned set of arguments for a stand she was taking, but at the same time, she was not hesitant to turn 180 degrees on an issue if new information or evidence was presented that she had not previously considered.

Discussion Questions

- What are the dangers of assuming that someone would be threatened if you argued with them?
- Can you describe a situation where you felt someone was not changing a stated position even though you felt he or she had had a change of mind?

CASE 6.3 • *The Controversial Team Member*

Imagine yourself as one of this case's three staff members: In what ways is your face threatened by your co-worker? Why would you want to talk to your supervisor?

Four staff members in a personnel office at a large computer corporation were assigned to a rather demanding recruitment project in addition to their regular job of interviewing and placement. They were asked to design and implement an effective program for minority recruitment and placement within the corporation. The project was viewed as one of the top priorities for the department, and the workers knew that the success or failure of the project would have a significant impact on their advancement in the organization.

About a month before the project was due, one of the team members asked her immediate supervisor if they could meet with him.

(continued)

CASE 6.3   Continued

The supervisor agreed, but when the team arrived, only three of the four members were present. The team had not asked the fourth member to attend the meeting with the supervisor. The problem the team faced was that the fourth member repeatedly made decisions and completed tasks that all team members had not endorsed. The three staff members felt that these decisions and actions were threatening the quality of the entire project.

The fourth member was a man who had been in the personnel office a year longer than the other three. He felt he had more knowledge and experience than the other staff members, and he made this point on several occasions. He also told them that he did not want this project to interfere with the time he needed to complete his normal work routine, and so he was willing to make certain decisions about the project on his own to move things along faster.

Although the three felt intimidated by their co-worker's outspoken and evaluative style, they also felt that he was bright, hardworking, and did have some experience that they lacked. In most cases, however, they felt this additional experience was unrelated to the current assignment. They saw the man's concern about the project taking time away from his normal work as pure arrogance; they all had the same work schedule to complete

each week and needed to find time to work on the recruitment project.

The team felt particularly insulted because, on several occasions, the man did not show up for meetings that had been scheduled. He did not let the group know that he would not be attending nor did he offer any explanations for his absence afterward. He also made no attempt to get information that he held to these meetings. Thus, the team's work was often delayed. When he was present, meetings were tense and antagonistic, and the motivation of the team had plummeted because of the problem.

When the supervisor asked the team if they had discussed their reactions openly with the "problem" person, the three members said they had not. They had wrestled with the idea but decided that the issue was just too emotional to air openly. They were, however, mad at the co-worker, felt intimidated by him, and wanted the department management to hear about the problem.

Discussion Questions

- Is there a "downside" to having face concerns addressed by someone who is not directly involved in the conflict?
- In what ways does "gossip" sometimes function as an attempt to receive face support?

move also stemmed from an already existing threat to face: The image she had of herself as a fair professor had already been called into question publicly by the student's decision to contact the college official.

In the environmental group, the face-saving issue was anticipated by members who heard Rhonda make forceful arguments early on. A tense and uneasy climate arose because most members assumed Rhonda was strongly committed to her position and would be inflexible. There was a general sense that Rhonda would be a "problem," if the group challenged her suggestions. The group was surprised and relieved to find that Rhonda's intellectual and verbal abilities could provide information and clear reasoning for them without being tied to her self-image. If no one in the group had run the risk of questioning Rhonda's initial stand, because of the fear of embarrassing her, the group could easily have become dissatisfied with the decision-making process but remained silent, perhaps eventually splintering into pro-and anti-Rhonda factions.

Face-saving was certainly a concern of the staff on the personnel project as they entered the supervisor's office. Although the team feared the emotional strain and potential long-range consequences of raising the issue with their co-worker, they felt he had treated them unfairly. They were made to feel as if their input on the project was unnecessary or even harmful. At least part of their motivation for contacting the supervisor was to restore face: They did not want to think of themselves as incompetent; nor did they want to see themselves as people who would accept unfair treatment without resistance. If the supervisor agreed with their accusations and assessment of the situation, their face would be restored.

When face-saving becomes an issue, it threatens parties' ability to remain flexible and shift their modes of conflict interaction. Face-saving reduces flexibility and the likelihood of change in group and interpersonal conflict situations for two reasons. First, the emergence of a concern with saving face inevitably adds another issue to the conflict. The additional problem tends to take precedence because it stands in the way of getting back to the main issue (Penman, 1991; Wilson, 1992). Energy and attention are drawn away from the central issue and are spent on peripheral matters; work may stop on the issues that count most as people deal with the threat to face. In each of these three cases, face-saving added issues to the conflict that diverted attention—and interaction—away from the central concern, or exhausted the parties before an adequate resolution was reached (Table 6.2).

In the grade dispute in Case 6.1, for example, the main conflict was over the professor's policy on make-up exams and her decision to enforce that policy in the current situation. The professor's reputation as indecisive or soft was really a secondary, although related, issue. In the environmental group, members' attention started to shift from a concern with how the group should go about protecting water standards to how the group was going to deal with a member who appeared to be dogmatic and would likely be threatened by criticism. In the personnel project team case, the central conflict was over decision-making rights in the group. By not addressing this issue, the three workers added a face-saving concern: They felt unjustly intimidated by the man and spent considerable time trying to feel better about the situation and attempting to decide whether they had somehow helped elicit the man's arrogant behavior. These additional issues can easily displace the team's focus if they remain salient concerns or if the members fail to address a face-saving issue that is influencing members' behaviors.

TABLE 6.2   *Possible Consequences of Face-Saving in Conflicts*

- Reduces parties' flexibility
- Adds an issue to the conflict
- Turns attention away from more tangible concerns
- Increases the likelihood of impasse
- Encourages an all-or-nothing approach to resolution
- Prompts parties to turn to outside people to address concerns

Besides multiplying issues, face-saving makes inflexibility likely because face-saving concerns usually include the real possibility of a future impasse in the conflict. Motives to save face are difficult to alleviate in conflicts and tend to foster interaction that heads toward stalemates and standoffs. After examining face-saving in a variety of formal bargaining settings, Brown (1977) notes that issues related to the loss of face are "among the most troublesome kinds of problems that arise in negotiation" (p. 275). Several factors contribute to the tendency for face-saving issues to head toward impasse.

Face-saving issues often remain highly intangible and elusive because people are reluctant to acknowledge that their image has been threatened. People can sense that something is going wrong and that positions seem to be tightening, but the face-saving motive may never be raised explicitly. To acknowledge a threat to one's image is in some ways to make that threat all the more real. One can maintain a desired self-image despite what others think as long as one can somehow deny what others think. To openly state what the threat may be and risk confirmation of the belief is in some cases to remove the possibility of denial. Therefore, the threat to one's image may be real and may be influencing the conflict interaction, but it often lies beneath the surface where it will go unrecognized or unaddressed.

The professor in the grade controversy, for example, might go through the entire meeting with the student and appeals referee without raising the issue of her image or without noting that she felt put off by the student's decision to contact the referee about the matter. Although these concerns may never surface, they could prompt her to make strong arguments in favor of her original decision, even though she now doubts its fairness, or to make unreasonable demands on the student before moving from her initial stand. An effective third-party appeals referee might anticipate these face-saving concerns and make suggestions that alleviate them but not require that the issue be stated explicitly (Shubert & Folger, 1986). Often the mere presence of a third party allows someone to move from a position without losing face because they can attribute any movement they make to the other party: "I never would have settled for that if the appeals referee hadn't pushed for it" (Pruitt & Johnson, 1970; Brown, 1977).

There is another reason why impasses are likely outcomes of conflicts complicated by face-saving issues: Conflict interaction becomes highly vulnerable to an all-or-nothing approach to resolution when face-saving issues arise. A gambler who loses all evening at a casino table may feel a need to bet big at the end of the night to restore face with those who have watched him or her struggle for a missed fortune. When an issue becomes heavily steeped in establishing or protecting face, it is often easier for participants "to go for broke" or walk away than to remain in a situation that, in an important sense, undermines their self-concept or sense of self-worth. Face, in many instances, is seen as an issue on which no compromise is possible. Personal honor and a commitment to oneself can take precedence over any continued involvement with or commitment to the relationship.

The staff who worked on the personnel recruitment project were all too willing to let the one man make decisions for them even though his behavior insulted and upset them. The members expected further embarrassment if they brought the issue to the man's attention; they thought he would defend himself by pointing to his own experience and chide them for ignoring their daily work tasks to work on this project. Rather than risk the confrontation and a further affront to their self-image, members were willing to walk away from the issue, even though it meant continued frustration with the project.

6.4   Conflict Interaction as a Face-Saving Arena

Face-saving messages are concerned with an image the speaker tries to maintain or re-establish in the interaction. Because this image depends on other parties' reactions, any attempt to save face is an attempt to negotiate the speaker's relationship with other parties in the conflict. Face-saving messages offer information about how the speaker wants and expects to be seen in the exchange. As we noted in Chapter 5, this type of *relational comment* (in other words, "This is how I see you seeing me" or "This is how I want you to see me") is carried by any message a speaker sends (Watzlawick et al., 1967). In the case of face-saving messages, however, the relational comment is more salient because it is under dispute; the face-saving message is a defensive response to a perceived threat. The speaker has reason to believe that his or her desired image will not be accepted by other members. As a result, the speaker feels a need for assurance or confirmation and engages in various behaviors, such as those in our examples, to "restore face." It is difficult to proceed without resolution of the face problem and will often be dominated by this problem until the speaker feels satisfied that enough has been done to establish the desired image. It is clearly the speaker's perception of how others are taking him or her that determines when the face-saving issue is lifted from the interaction.

If a person rushes into an important meeting fifteen minutes late and says, "Back-to-back meetings never seem to work out," the comment carries a face-saving message. It asks the group to see the person as someone who is so busy that he or she may have to overschedule meetings and end up being late at times. This relational message serves a face-saving function because it supplants a potentially threatening image others could hold; it asks people not to see the speaker as someone who is inconsiderate of others' time or is unconcerned about what may go on at the meeting. Being busy, hardworking, or overtaxed is a positive image; being inconsiderate, slow, or careless is an image the person wants to avoid.

In an insightful analysis of face-saving work in everyday interactions, Goffman (1967) describes how people try to conduct themselves in social encounters to maintain both their own and other parties' face. Goffman emphasizes that the mutual acceptance of face is "a condition of interaction not its objective" (p. 12). Interaction ordinarily proceeds on the assumption that the faces people want to project are, in fact, the ones that are accepted as the exchange unfolds. There is a noticeable strain or a recognizable problem when face maintenance becomes the objective rather than a precondition of interaction. Even in ordinary interaction, then, people feel a need to amend the situation when a face-saving issue arises so that the exchange can unfold without the concern.

In group conflict there is a noticeable difference in interaction when face-saving issues arise and become the objective of the interaction. There is a shift away from group-centered and group-directed interaction toward interaction focused on the experience of the individual member and his or her relationship to the group. Conflict interaction is group-centered when all parties take into account their membership within the group and continuously recognize that any movement made on an issue must be made with other parties in the conflict. Individual positions and stands can be argued, and indeed must be, if adequate differentiation is to occur. However, members never lose their identities and concepts of self when interaction is group-focused; the commitment to self and the sense of personal identity become secondary to the awareness that the conflict is a shared experience and that change or movement in the direction of the conflict will be *with* other members.

The emergence of face-saving as an issue undercuts the group-centered focus in conflict interaction. When face-saving becomes an issue, individual concerns begin to outweigh those of the group or the substantive issues in the conflict. The commitment to establishing a desirable self-image takes precedence over the sense of belonging and cohesion that exists when members more fully "step into" the group.

Face-saving produces a qualitative change in the nature of the group's conflict interaction. When interaction becomes individually focused, one person steps into an "official role" that he or she holds as an individual. Obviously, such a role is always available to each member but it can easily remain dormant while members try to sustain group-centered interaction. The role of the member as an individual raises concerns about what the person looks like to the group, what impact that person in particular is having on the outcome of a decision, what place he or she holds in the group's power structure, and so on. In a sense, the individual adopts an authority position and wants to be seen as the authoritative representative of an image he or she wants to maintain or a role he or she wants to play in the group's process. This separation lays the groundwork for the inflexibility discussed previously.

The following example, which is an actual transcript of a discussion among four graduate students, illustrates a turn from group-to individual-centered interaction. The students in this discussion were given a topic as part of a class assignment. Believe it or not, their task was to clarify Plato's conception of truth. In the interaction just prior to this segment, the students, who were from the same department and knew each other quite well, joked about the seriousness of the topic and were somewhat eager to go off on a tangent before leaping into the task at hand. As this segment of interaction begins, Kathy asks Peggy about her research on gender differences in people's thought patterns. The group recognizes that the question is somewhat off the assigned topic, but they are more than willing to pursue it and delay their discussion of truth. The group eventually ties the issue of gender research back to the main topic, but that part of the exchange is not included here. Watch for the turn the interaction takes toward individual-centered interaction.

Kathy: (*to Peggy*) Are you doing any more work on differences in male thinking?
Peggy: (*answering Kathy*) Uh, hum.
Dave: I have an article.
Peggy: Collecting data as a matter of fact.
Dave: I have an article that is so good. This is off the subject, but let's talk about it for a few minutes.
Peggy: That's right, let's forget truth. I'd rather talk about males and females than truth.
Kathy: Mhmmm.

Gary: Mhmmm.

Dave: Candice Pert is into, got into, pharmacology and is now in neuroscience. She is the discoverer of what's called the opiate receptor in the brain. Those are the brain cells that opium has an effect on. The ones they're attracted to.

Peggy: Hmmmm.

Dave: And they've, they've gone from opium receptors to ah, Valium receptors, to any tranquilizer. And she's working now on a marijuana receptor, that the cells hit. And it's so neat . . . (*Some laughter while Dave is talking; Gary mimes something and Kathy makes a comment under her breath and laughs.*)

Dave: (*laughing slightly*) Now wait a minute, wait a minute. This is fascinating. (*General laughter*)

Gary: I've already heard it, so I'm spacing off on my own here.

Dave: She made this discovery when she was a grad student.

Kathy: Then there's hope for me yet. (*General laughter*)

Peggy: (*pointing to the back of her head*) Ah, here are my opiate receptors.

Dave: She's first author, and her male mentor and advisor and teacher is second author.

Peggy: Hmmmmm.

Dave: There was an award given called the . . .

Kathy: (*interrupting*) And he got it, right?

Dave: (*continuing*) The Lasky award, which is seen as a stepping stone to ah, to a Nobel prize, and ah . . .

Kathy: What do opiates have to do with men and women?

Dave: Now wait a minute.

Peggy: (*jokingly*) Wait, wait—have patience, have faith.

Dave: Here's . . . here's your politics in it to start with.

Kathy: All right.

Dave: She was first author on this paper when this Lasky award was given; it was given to four men.

Kathy: Mhmmm.

Dave: And she was invited to the awards ceremony. That's the extent of it. And she talks about it a little bit.

Peggy: Oh, marvelous.

Dave: But in the interview she talks about the—you know—I can be known as a scorned woman here, but I've done some other things since then that are really important to me. And she, she uses the analogy of the brain as a computer. And although she doesn't talk about what we would commonly call software, that's what you learn, she really, she's looking at what she calls the hardwiring. The circuitry in the brain. And the differences in male/female circuitry.

Peggy: And she's found some?

Dave: She's found some possibilities. Some probable areas. Now there are differences, there are some other differences that are not just male and female. There are differences, say, between what we would consider healthy, normal personalities and, say, schizophrenia.

Peggy: Mhmm.

Dave: (*There's a three-second interruption here as someone enters the room, then Dave continues.*) Ah, you look at the evolution of language instead of being male-oriented and thinking that men had to learn how to use language so that they could coordinate hunting down a large animal. It was women who were the ones who were staying home.

Kathy: (*sarcastically*) To get them out of the cave.
(*General laughter*)

Peggy: To talk to the walls.

Dave: Yeah, you know talk to walls, talk to the kids.

Peggy: Well, that's interesting. I'd like to read that.

Dave: And from the beginning. Yeah, it's really fascinating because there are detectable differences in male and female brains.

Kathy: Hmmm (*makes a face*).

Peggy: Yeah, I'd like to read that.

Dave: (*to Kathy*) You act like I'm being chauvinistic.

Peggy: No.

Kathy: No, I'm just, I'm . . .

Dave: (*interrupting*) Oh boy, this is terrible.

Gary: She'd act a whole lot worse if you were being chauvinistic.

Kathy: Do I act like you're chauvinistic? Yes.

Dave: You made a face.

Kathy: (*laughing*) I'm trying to see inside my brain to see if there are any differences. That's all.

Dave: Differences. What, from mine?

Kathy: Yes.

Dave: But how can you see mine?

Kathy: Oh, I don't know. I can't see in mine either. Let me be successful here first. No, I was thinking of brains, young Frankenstein, you know.

Dave: (*laughing*) Oh, yeah.

Kathy: Twelve years dead, six months dead, freshly dead.

Dave: Yeah, yeah.

Kathy: Sorry, Dave, I'm just not on that level today.

Dave: No, no.

Peggy: Well, I think there are some very definite differences in language use and that would be some clue as to why. I've always talked about it being culture, socialization, and that sort of thing, but, ah . . .

Gary: I wonder if there's a change coming in that with the revolutionary changes in men and women's roles in society—they're now becoming different—and if that will have an effect on this too.

Peggy: Go back far enough and actually you can see that the species will evolve differently. . . .

Initially, the group's interaction in this exchange consisted primarily of offering and evaluating information about research on gender differences. Although Peggy did not elaborate on her research when Kathy asked her about it, Dave's comments about the brain's sensitivity to drugs held the group's interest and prompted continued interaction on this topic. It became the focus of questions and jokes in the group, and it also raised the issue of how sexual politics becomes involved in research. Dave's summary of the article he had read and his commentary about the possible implications it might have for understanding the evolutionary development of male and female language use set the stage for the turn toward individual-centered interaction that took place in this discussion.

After Dave says "Yeah, it's really fascinating because there are detectable differences in male and female brains," the next twenty speaking turns are focused on Dave's image in the group. These comments deal with Dave's relationship to the group rather than with the topic that had surfaced and engaged the group as a whole. Kathy's facial response to Dave's statement made Dave concerned about whether Kathy or the other group members saw him as a chauvinist. Peggy, Gary, and Kathy all attempt to reassure him, although sometimes lightheartedly and perhaps unconvincingly, that he is not seen as a chauvinist because of the way he summarized the article and reacted to it. In the main, the group handles the face-saving concern by joking about the article, becoming somewhat ludicrous (with the references to young Frankenstein's brain) and finally treating one of Dave's major points (about the possible value of an evolutionary explanation for language differences) seriously. When Peggy and Gary make their comments in the last three speaking turns in this segment, the interaction is turned back to a group focus. The interaction is no longer focused on Dave's experience in the group and the way he is seen by others. Dave lets his concern about his image drop, and the group continues with an exploration of the merits and problems with research on gender differences.

Because people are always concerned about their self-concepts and roles within a dyad, group or organization, conflict interaction tends to teeter somewhere between group and individual emphases. It is possible to achieve a healthy balance that eases the basic antagonism between individuals' commitments to themselves and the need or desire to work in the group or dyad. Needless to say, this balance is difficult to maintain when conflicts occur.

Conflicts provide an arena where the balance is easily tipped toward the concerns of individual members, making face-saving likely to occur. Several factors, in combination, may lead the group away from group-centered interaction once conflict arises. First, as we note in Chapter 1, differentiation can lead to a focus on the individual over the social unit. Parties arguing for a position in front of others may be hesitant to leave their initial positions once they make a public statement. Second, attribution processes and reactions to uncertainty foster a tendency to point the finger at others and assign responsibility for the emergence of the conflict to a single individual or faction. The accused are put in the paradoxical position of, on the one hand, having to defend themselves against the charges, thus giving continued prominence to their individuality, while, on the other hand, needing to move the interaction toward a group focus if real progress toward reaching a resolution is to be made.

Third, as we observed in Chapter 5, parties in conflict often turn to unique sources of power during conflict interaction. Any move based on unique power sources gives prominence to the characteristics of individuals in the conflict and promotes countermoves that are also based on unique sources of power. When parties use unique sources of power to try to influence others, they put an important part of themselves on the line. If the move is not successful, their image, not the image of the whole group, is threatened and may need to be redeemed through the use of threats, force, or deception.

In sum, conflicts are likely arenas for establishing and defending parties' images of themselves. These concerns can easily turn interaction away from constructive work on the conflict issue and toward secondary, but troublesome, issues that stem from the individual's relationship to the group. When these concerns arise, they tend to promote inflexibility in interaction and prevent the group from approaching the conflict from new directions.

Although these destructive tendencies are likely, it should be noted that there may be times when a turn toward individual-centered interaction is useful or necessary. Some individuals may need certain images of themselves confirmed, even though the images may not have been questioned by other people in the group. Someone may, for example, have a strong need to know that his or her contributions are valued by other people. To fulfill this need, the interaction would have to center on the person's relationship to the group. This in turn could serve a useful function, *if* it provides valuable feedback about a member's performance or an incentive for someone to continue with his or her work and involvement in the group. In most cases, this type of interaction occurs outside conflict situations, so it rarely becomes problematic.

6.5 Face-Saving Frames in Conflict Interaction

Three general ways of framing face-saving can be distinguished. Each reflects a different interpretation the party trying to save face might assign to the situation. These interpretations act as "mind-sets" to promote defensive, face-saving behavior. Each frame has recognizable symptoms that distinguish it from the others and each requires different corrective measures. Two of these frames have been studied by researchers who focused on competitive contexts such as negotiation and bargaining settings: resisting unjust intimidation and refusing to step back from a position. They have been alluded to in the earlier cases, but deserve more explicit attention because they pose a serious threat to constructive conflict interaction. We also discuss a third frame that has not been studied by previous researchers: suppressing conflict issues. This frame is unique to more informal conflict settings (like most work or group decision-making contexts) where the interaction is premised, at least initially, on the assumption that people will act cooperatively to make decisions and settle differences. Few researchers have studied these noncompetitive contexts.

6.5.1 Resisting Unjust Intimidation

Brown (1977) and others (Deutsch & Krauss, 1962) have suggested that face-saving often results from a need to "resist undeserved intimidation in order to guard against the loss of self-esteem and of social approval that ordinarily results from uncontested acquiescence to such treatment" (Brown, 1977, p. 278). When people feel they are being treated unfairly or pushed in a way that is unjustified, they are likely to make some attempt to resist this treatment. Interaction can turn toward a defense of one's self-image as the individual tries to establish that he or she will not be intimidated. It carries an "I don't have to take this" or "Any fair-minded person wouldn't stand for this" message to the other party.

When this frame is taken, it always carries two components. First, there is an accusation that others are in fact treating the person unfairly or aggressively. In some cases, the other party will recognize (although perhaps not admit) that there may be some grounds for the accusation. The other party's response in this case is likely to be a defense of his or her behavior or accusation. For example, in a local health department, an assistant administrator conducted several surprise inspections that made employees very nervous and defensive and came near to causing a labor dispute. When one supervisor confronted the assistant administrator with this problem and challenged her fairness, she refused to discuss the issue. Her responsibilities, she argued, forced her to "tighten up the ship" and to increase work quality by whatever methods she had available.

In other instances, the accusatory face-saving frame can take other parties by surprise and elicit either an initial defensive response ("We never did that to you") or avoidance because people are unaware or do not believe they have attacked. This type of face-saving message requires some type of reaction because it carries an accusation. The accusatory nature of the frame makes it a force that redirects interaction. Even the indirect response of active avoidance means that the parties have decided to allow future interaction to be influenced by the unacknowledged but real effects of an issue that they had decided to ignore.

The second important component of this face-saving frame is the sense of adamant resistance it conveys. The speaker suggests, in effect, that "business as usual" cannot continue until the concern has been addressed. This sense of resistance often accompanies messages sparked by a perceived threat (Gibb, 1961). Such messages have the potential for altering the climate of the relationship or group, as we'll see in Chapter 7. Once this type of face-saving frame is settled, others may feel that it is no longer safe to allow the interaction to continue in the present direction or to suggest new questions or issues for discussion. The defensive party has claimed the right to define the immediate topic of conversation until he or she is satisfied.

Others can challenge this frame, but the move would be immediately recognized as a challenge and thus contribute to an air of threat; it would increase the chance that the relationship would be adversely harmed or that the group may splinter. Messages that suggest unfair treatment, such as those sent by the workers in the personnel department, may also imply that people are not committed to one another. It hoists a warning flag signaling problems with trust and responsibility. If this issue is not met head-on, the parties may have difficulty sustaining an image that they are committed to each other.

Face-saving framed as unjust intimidation can have destructive consequences. In one case, a woman who had planned to leave a job in a food distribution company for unrelated personal reasons decided to stay on six months longer to "fight it out" with her uncooperative co-workers. She did not want to leave with the feeling that she had been driven away. In Case 6.3, the three intimidated workers spent considerable time and effort trying to feel better about themselves. This time could have been spent on the project if the issue had been addressed at an earlier point.

When this framing goes unaddressed, it is also common for the threatened party to contact an outside party for help, hoping that a neutral outsider might understand and perhaps exonerate him or her. Although a third party can help in many instances, if the person trying to save face contacts the outsider, it may subvert any legitimate effort to mediate the problem. The parties have to recognize the problem and agree on a need for outside help before any intervention is likely to be successful.

Finally, if this frame is not confronted, the parties trying to save face often feel a need to explain the causes behind the unjust or intimidating treatment. Because others have not supplied any reasons or denied that they intended to intimidate, the party may make unfounded attributions about the causes of other parties' intimidating behavior. These unchecked attributions can shape the comments the party makes from that point on and lead to a more serious set of impenetrable problems. For example, in the food distribution company mentioned before, three people were involved in the conflict, including the woman who stayed on for six months to "fight it out." All three incorrectly assumed that the others hated them and were attacking them for reasons of personal incompatibility. Actually, all three were merely responding to the others' aggressive behavior, and their responses fed on each others', thereby escalating the conflict.

The key to alleviating concerns that emerge from this face-saving frame lies in parties' abilities to give feedback without eliciting further animosity. Parties who feel they are being unjustly treated or intimidated must be able to state their perceptions in a way that does not prejudge others or discourage them from explaining their behavior. Escalation and standoffs are likely when criticism is handled poorly as a face-saving issue is addressed. Although many prescriptions have been given for constructing feedback, most discussions of constructive criticism stress that feedback must be timely (Maurer, 1994). In other words, it should be offered at a point that is both relevant and the least disruptive. It should also be centered on descriptions of the party's own feelings rather than assumptions about what others intend—for example, "When you didn't show up for the dinner, I felt put down"; rather than "You wanted to teach me a lesson by not showing up for our dinner."

Face-saving concerns that stem from the unjust intimidation frame can be managed best if the parties have set aside time for regular evaluations of the process. Setting aside five or ten minutes at the end of each meeting or day for evaluation can allow people to raise issues early before they become impasses and to give positive or negative feedback to each other without interfering with work or other obligations. Resentment and hostility are less likely to build and affect other issues if the parties know time has been set aside to address relational issues or concerns about interactions.

6.5.2 Refusing to Give on a Position

A second face-saving frame is based on parties' fears that they will compromise a position or stand they have taken on some issue (Pruitt, 1971; Brown, 1977). People often remain committed to a stand or solution even in light of convincing refutations, not because they still believe it is the best option but because they believe moving away from that position will harm their image. This frame emerges when someone believes that reversing his or her stand, or stepping back from a position, is unsafe.

There are many reasons why this may be a real fear for people involved in a conflict. In their analysis of the forces governing commitment to decisions, Janis and Mann (1977) suggest that people may remain committed to an undesirable decision because they believe that they will look indecisive, erratic, or unstable if they retract or reverse their choice. "To avoid perceiving himself as weak-minded, vacillating, ineffectual, and undependable, the person turns his back on pressures to reconsider his decision and sticks firmly with his chosen alternative, even after he has started to suspect that it is a defective choice" (p. 283). For example, Epstein (1962) reports that novice parachutists, fearing loss of face, often go through with their decision to jump even though their desire to skip what may seem a dangerous and senseless endeavor increases as the time for the jump approaches.

Janis and Mann also suggest that there is a certain momentum behind reaching a decision or articulating a position in public. This momentum stems from the difficulty of reversing a decision once it is made or retracting a position once it is stated. It simply takes more work and effort to explain why one has changed one's mind than it does to stick with a previously stated position. The destructive consequences of leaders being overly identified with their stated viewpoints and with their organizations in general have been well documented (Finkelstein, 2003). Having personal identity linked too closely to professional identity is a road map for rigidity and its negative effects.

Goffman (1967) discusses a similar motive for this frame. He indicates that people's fears of moving from a position can rest on a belief that they will not be taken seriously in the future if they step away from a position they have taken. In this case, the party believes that his or her credibility will suffer if he or she gives ground on an important issue or decision. The party fears that his or her ideas or suggestions will be overlooked or considered less seriously or given less weight in the future.

6.5.3 Suppressing Conflict Issues

In situations that assume parties should be able to reach agreement without conflict or that people can handle any conflict without seeking outside help, we may strongly discourage others from admitting that a conflict exists or is beyond our control. If a party attempts to acknowledge the existence of a conflict or to raise the possibility of seeking third-party assistance, he or she may lose face in the eyes of others. The person may be seen as someone who causes problems or is eager to find fault with the way the other parties operate. This threat may deter people from engaging in adequate differentiation, and it may promote prolonged and destructive avoidance of an issue.

Given this frame, if someone decides to raise an issue, conflict interaction can turn in a negative direction. A turn toward inflexibility and stalemate may be imminent if the person feels his or her image must be defended at all costs ("I don't care whether this hurts you or not, I think we need to address it"). These complications may mean that the parties cannot differentiate successfully or that integration is unattainable.

Academic appeal referees at colleges and universities are assigned the task of mediating disputes that arise between students and faculty about grades, financial aid, discrimination, enactment of departmental or university policies, and so on. One referee at a large university reports that students are often reluctant to raise conflict issues and, as a result, conflicts are not addressed until the issues have gotten out of hand. Students are often hesitant to raise concerns with a third party because they fear loss of face in the eyes of their mentors. In university settings, student–faculty relationships are premised on a cooperative assumption: Students (especially graduate students) and faculty are expected to work and learn together to advance knowledge in their academic fields. When a conflict arises over issues such as grading or interpretation of departmental policy students feel that if they take the issue to a third party (even one the university endorses), they may threaten or destroy their relationship. Students fear that the faculty will see him or her as someone who is unwilling to work through difficulties cooperatively and is trying to make the professor look bad in the eyes of a representative of the institution. Third parties who work in this context need to address face threats and help restore an atmosphere of cooperation so that the relationship can continue after the specific issue has been resolved.

In these types of conflicts, the threat to face stems from a fear of being seen as someone who is willing to jeopardize a good relationship by bringing a conflict out in the open. This fear is almost inevitably founded on a belief that the very emergence of conflict is always harmful or destructive.

6.6 Face-Giving Strategies

After exploring the destructive nature of face-saving, this chapter now turns its attention to how people help others avoid taking such extreme measures. This section examines the dynamics of face-giving.

Face-giving refers to the strategic moves that support the other party's image or identity claims. To fully grasp how people "give face," we must first examine how people orient to face in everyday interaction.

Goffman (1957) identifies two strands of face-orienting, or face-giving, strategies: corrective and preventive practices. As the names imply, *corrective practices* are what people do after a face-threatening act or loss of face. Face-saving strategies are corrective practices. In contrast, *preventive practices* are what people do to avoid threats to face. Preventive practices are either defensive or protective. Defensive strategies involve actions to prevent threats to one's own face. For example, people often ask the hearer to suspend judgment by using disclaimers, such as "Now some of my best friends are professors, but. . . ." Protective strategies consist of actions that prevent or minimize threats to another party's face. For example, people often provide normative accounts for others, such as "The traffic must have been horrendous. I'm surprised you got here so fast."

Defensive strategies can be seen as alignment actions (Stokes & Hewitt, 1976). *Alignment actions* are verbal efforts to resolve discrepancies between people's conduct and cultural expectations. Essentially, these actions or messages align a person's behavior with cultural norms. For example, imagine you are late to a very important meeting. Just as you slink into the room, the group pauses and your colleagues turn to greet you. Feeling that your absence has clearly violated expectations, you say, "I'm really sorry. My car would not start." Such an alignment message demonstrates that you are not eccentric and allows you to manage your social identity in the group (Table 6.3).

Researchers have identified several types of alignment actions used in everyday speech (Cupach & Metts, 1994). The largest group of alignment actions falls under the rubric of accounts. *Accounts* are reason-giving descriptions that presume one of the parties has committed an offense. They serve as devices to make failure or inappropriate behavior sound reasonable (McLaughlin, Cody, & Rosenstein, 1983). In addition to descriptive

TABLE 6.3   ***Working with Face-Saving: Types of Face-Giving Alignment Actions***

- Account: gives reasons for a behavior
- Apology: expresses regret
- Quasi-theory: provides adages, simplistic explanations
- Excuse: admits action, denies responsibility
- Justification: admits responsibility, denies consequences
- Disclaimer: asks for a suspension of judgment
- Counterclaim: denies negative intentions
- Conversational repair: corrects or restates a conversational error
- Remedy: offers a reparation to an offended party

reasons for behavior, common accounts include apologies, quasi theories, excuses, and justi-fications. An *apology* expresses regret over an earlier action. Statements—such as "I'm sorry," "I will never do that again," "What can I do to make up for this?"—acknowledge re-sponsibility and express remorse (Fraser, 1981). When speakers use apologies they presume that others recognize that a failed and face-threatening event has occurred. *Quasi-theories* are simplistic formulas or adages used to explain away complex situations. "Boys will be boys" and "We had a falling out" are examples of quasi theories.

The most common accounts are excuses and justifications, which attempt to shift the burden of accountability. When people admit that their actions may be wrong or inappropriate, but deny responsibility, they are employing an excuse. *Excuses* such as "I didn't feel well," "I couldn't resist," and "The phone was busy" readily acknowledge a mistake but resist responsibility because of mitigating circumstances (Shaw, Wild, & Colquitt, 2003). Researchers classify excuses into three types: (1) statements that deny harmful intent, (2) statements that deny volition and assert lack of bodily control, and (3) statements that deny the party performed the action (Tedeschi & Riess, 1981). Whereas excuses focus on responsibility, justifications focus on the consequences of the actions. *Justifications* are statements in which the party admits personal responsibility but denies negative consequences, usually by relating the action to some socially accept-able rule of conduct such as higher authority, self-defense, company policy, or situa-tional norms. Statements such as "It was necessary in the long run" and "If we had held the meeting, it would have been a disaster" are examples of justifications. They claim a behavior was appropriate given the circumstance.

Other types of alignment actions include disclaimers, counterclaims, conversational re-pairs, and licenses. *Disclaimers* ask the hearer for a suspension of judgment to prevent a neg-ative typification (Hewitt & Stokes, 1975). Statements, such as "I realize you might think this is wrong but. . . ." and "This is only my opinion but. . . ." defeat in advance doubts and unfa-vorable reactions. *Counterclaims* are devices used to deny unfavorable intentions (Stutman, 1988). People intuitively know that a speaker with persuasive goals is considered less trustworthy by others. When one party may benefit from a persuasive exchange, such as dur-ing sales encounters, the hearer naturally becomes more resistant to messages he or she re-ceives. As a result, when people pursue persuasive goals they often deny that intent by stating the opposite. Because they counter the perceived goal of the message that follows them, these devices are called counterclaims. Statements such as "Now I'm not trying to persuade you but. . . ," "I don't want to change your mind but. . . ," and "This isn't an excuse but. . . ." deny unfavorable intentions.

When people make conversational errors, they often attempt to revise what was said with corrections, restatements, or requests to ignore earlier actions. Statements such as "Oh, I didn't mean that" and "You get the just, ah, gist" serve as *conversational repairs*. Repairs serve as "detours" and "time-outs" for people to correct utterances they have employed (McLaughlin, 1984). Interestingly, what gets repaired may not appear wrong or in need of correction; sometimes only the speaker perceives that a conversational misstep was made.

A *remedy* is often proposed to make reparations to an offended party. This sometimes occurs even when the offense is unstated or unknown. For example, imagine a scenario where, at the beginning of a joint assignment, a co-worker mistakenly misplaces a file that may be useful for the project. Even though the other has neither requested the file nor knows of its disappearance, the co-worker feels guilty. The co-worker then begins to offer a series of remarks that can be seen as remedies: "I think I should keep a list of all files that move through the office." "My organizational skills are not up to par. I should probably seek training." "It's time I reorganized my desk." Remedies, like other alignment actions, signal that a party is attempting to preserve face.

Grice (1975) maintains that people follow four implicit rules or maxims during conversations. Speakers cooperate with each other by (1) offering accurate or truthful information, (2) maintaining economy in speech by being neither too brief nor too lengthy, (3) offering relevant and topical points, and (4) refraining from overly obscure or ambiguous speech. When speakers anticipate breaking one or more of these rules, they often employ licenses to forecast the rule violation (Mura, 1983). *Licenses* give the listener notice that a violation will occur or is occurring but that the infraction is necessary or unusual. For example, a speaker who breaks the rule of speech accuracy may qualify the statement: "I love your new car. I don't know much about cars." Words and phrases, such as "in fact," "actually," "really," and "of course," are often used to signal qualification. After being verbose and breaking the rule of speech economy, a speaker may say "I told you everything so that you could decide for yourself." A license used for breaking the rule of relevancy might sound like this: "I went off on a tangent because I need a plan for tomorrow." Breaking the rule of not using ambiguous speech might be followed by: "I know that sounds confusing, but it's really not." As alignment actions, licenses serve to defend the face of the speaker by reframing the rule-breaking event.

The devices used to prevent threat to one's own face can also serve as flags or markers that attention to face wants is desired. At the very minimum, such markers signal that the hearer is experiencing or anticipating a threat to face, and further challenge will result in a face-saving strategy. Protective strategies basically consist of the same alignment actions. The only difference is that we align for the other party. When people preface statements or evaluations with any of the alignment actions, they are essentially protecting the face of others. Consider the possible ways a superior might protect the face of a subordinate while communicating that an improvement in work quality is needed. One might use an excuse: "You have been working hard the last few weeks, but let's talk about where this effort gets you." One might use a justification: "With all the assignments I throw at you, it's no wonder I have noticed a problem with quality." Or a disclaimer might be used: "Heaven knows quality is impossible to define, but. . . ." The options are diverse and plentiful. The key point is that protective strategies provide the listener with a means to protect face.

Goffman (1955) maintains that all interaction is potentially face-threatening; whenever people interact, they are making identity claims. Tracy (1991) notes that these claims may be quite general as opposed to personalized and specific. For example, in a grocery line we often want to be seen as patient; in a car, that we can drive with skill. Because people care deeply about how they are perceived almost all the time, there is always some potential for a threat to face.

Inadvertently, people walk on each other's identity claims. Social situations involve tensions between cooperation and competition, between one's and others' face. Even in situations where it is in the best interest of the speaker to cooperate, people employ messages that are threatening and antagonistic (Craig, Tracy, & Spisak, 1986). The need to protect another party's face is ever present. Related research suggests that some people seem to be better at face-giving than others.

A broad body of research on communication has been aimed at understanding how communicators design messages that promote relational harmony and facilitate goodwill between parties. This work can loosely be described as investigating *person-centered* speech—any communication intended to support, comfort, or otherwise confirm the hearer can be considered person-centered. Such speech consists of prosocial behaviors and displays a willingness on the part of the speaker to verbally express his or her thoughts and feelings in a way that takes the other into account. Essentially, researchers conclude that this message design is driven by an ability and by a desire on the part of the speaker to adapt his or her communication to the hearer to achieve one or more strategic goals (Applegate & Delia, 1980).

To engage in person-centered speech, research demonstrates that the speaker must possess an ability to take on other perspectives; *perspective-taking* suggests a skill to adopt the psychological viewpoint of the other. It allows the speaker to anticipate the behavior and reactions of others. Perspective-taking presumes that the motivations, intentions, and feelings of any individual are unique. Moreover, it presumes that the character of each situation is equally original. Once a speaker understands the psychological viewpoints of others, he or she can then adapt his or her communication to achieve any of a number of strategic goals, such as task (persuasion, instruction, entertainment) or identity (credibility, social status, intent). Of the many strategic goals a speaker might pursue, person-centered speech highlights the importance of relational maintenance. Hence a focus on the unique characteristics of others, or the situation, to promote the relationship is highly personal or person-centered.

In contrast, many communicators assume the identities of others, and the meaning of their actions, can be understood in terms of assigned roles, contexts, and topics. Communicators working from this mode need not understand other parties' perspectives, nor adapt to other actors. Instead, they focus on the assigned roles of the participants, the authority that inheres in those roles, and the norms surrounding such role relationships. This is known as *position-centered speech,* which expresses feelings through nonverbal channels rather than elaborating them through verbal codes. Such speech often appears to focus on the topic or the task at hand at the expense of others parties' feelings. It is not that communicators who use position-centered speech are insensitive to others, but rather that they assume individual identities, such as image or motivation, can be dispensed with by following fixed rules of social conduct.

Whereas person-centered speech promotes relational harmony and facilitates goodwill between parties, position-centered speech encourages defensiveness and caution. Communicators who employ person-centered speech generally exhibit the following patterns:

- Speech that is more indirect so as to lessen the degree of imposition placed on the hearer, but not to the point of inhibiting understanding
- Use of face-sensitive messages that attempt to protect the desired image of the hearer
- Ability to align other parties' behavior to situated norms
- Reliance on information-seeking through questions
- Refraining from overt evaluations and attacks on other parties' self-concepts
- Sensitive use of challenges, directives, and demands

There is a good deal of variation across cultures in the propensity to engage in face-giving interactions. Ting-Toomey (1999) notes that parties from collectivistic cultures are oriented more toward giving face and avoiding face-threatening incidents than are members of individualistic cultures. So in Asian, African, and Latin American cultures (collectivist), face-giving is expected and more common than in American and Australian cultures (individualistic).

Oetzel et al. (2001) found that self-construal—the individual's feeling of interdependence with or, alternatively, independence of, others—was strongly correlated with facework concerns. An independent self-construal was positively associated with saving face, while an interdependent self-construal was positive associated with giving face. These are the same patterns that would be expected in individualistic and collectivistic cultures. Oetzel et al. argue that individuals within each culture differ in self-construal and they provide evidence that this individual level variable predicts better than the cultural level variable individualism-collectivism.

6.7 Working with Face-Saving Issues

The key to diagnosing face-saving issues successfully lies in parties' abilities to recognize its symptoms in interaction. When face-saving occurs, the interaction becomes centered on a secondary issue rather than on the substance of the conflict. The substantive problems that parties must resolve are buried by statements and reactions indicating resentment or by arguments that defend individual positions but do little to advance parties' understanding of the problem. Because the face-saving issues are related to the more substantive problems, they can come to dominate the interaction before parties realize it.

For example, parties may defend alternative positions in what appears to be a heated debate. They may do so, however, only because they feel that if they back away from their positions, they will not have credibility in future discussions or decisions. In this case, the most pressing issue, the one that has the greatest influence over the interaction, is "How will others treat someone who changes his or her mind?" However, the content of the discussion remains focused on a substantive point, disguising the face issue. If parties fail to realize that a secondary issue is driving an interaction, face-saving can produce destructive escalation and seriously threaten relationships.

Establishing climates that prevent face-saving concerns from emerging is probably the most effective means of eliminating their destructive influence. The climate within a team, organization, or relationship plays a critical role in determining whether face-saving concerns will emerge and become problematic. People have shared expectations about whether it is safe to move away from a stated position, whether conflict issues can be raised without threatening the relationships, and whether someone's feelings of unjust treatment can be discussed openly. Although establishing a constructive climate is something people can work toward, using methods discussed in Chapter 7, difficult interventions are needed when a constructive climate has not been established or when some event calls the climate into question. For example, when something happens that makes parties unsure about whether they can step back from a position and still be seen as credible, even the most comfortable atmosphere can begin to disintegrate.

The absence of credible explanations can lead people to react. In fact, research has shown that the absence of reasonable explanations is linked to a decrease in cooperation (Colquitt, 2001), increased levels of retaliation, such as litigation and theft (Wanberg, Bruce, & Gavin, 1999), and withdrawal and interference (Shaw, Wild, & Colquitt, 2003). So, during conflict situations people become explainers. Parties are quick to elaborate on exactly what they did, why they did it, or why it was unavoidable, so as to dampen any potential assault on their competence. The most common of these explanations are excuses and justifications. Individuals judge decisions, for example, by comparing what happened to what might have been (Folger & Cropanzano, 2001). Research suggests that when confronted with questions about what happened, the choice between excuse and justification is critical. Whereas excuses demonstrate that a mitigating circumstance made the decision necessary or unavoidable, justifications demonstrate that the decision was appropriate in light of the circumstances. In re-examining decisions made to protect face, excuses are preferred over justifications because they are seen as more reasonable by those on the outside looking in. Excuses create a reasonable climate where honest mistakes could have been made. Justifications sound honorable in that they accept full responsibility, but they challenge integrity by suggesting the decision wasn't that bad after all. So to prevent face issues from coming to the forefront, it is important to enable parties to explain themselves without becoming defensive, yet at the same time, maintain quality and rigor of thought.

Interventions that attempt to stop the destructive effects of face-saving must recognize that face-saving centers around the negotiation of one's image. The alignment actions that people use to prevent loss of face serve as flags or markers to the other party that attention to face wants is desired. When you hear an alignment action, bells and whistles should go off. These devices signal that the hearer is experiencing or anticipating a threat to face. Further challenge will result in a face-saving strategy. At this point, the use of protective strategies to align the other party's actions may help to prevent their face-saving measures.

The face-saving frames discussed in Section 6.5 threaten to impose an undesirable image on the speaker. Consider the following statements, which various face-saving frames imply:

- *Resisting unjust intimidation:* "Don't see me as someone who accepts unfair treatment or intimidation."
- *Stepping back from a position:* "Don't see me as someone who is indecisive" (and therefore easily defeated or weak).
- *Raising unacknowledged conflict issues:* "Don't see me as someone who is willing to cause problems by raising conflict issues."

Each of these statements reflects a guess that the party has made about other parties' likely reactions, and each indicates that the person feels threatened by the image he or she assumes others will assign. However, each statement is founded on an assumption about other parties' interpretations and reactions, which can either be confirmed or refuted by subsequent events. The interaction that occurs when face is an issue is always a negotiation; it is an attempt to settle what image others can assign to someone.

Interventions that treat face-saving as a negotiation process may have the greatest chance for success (Ting-Toomey & Kurogi, 1998). Three steps can be taken to help facilitate this process. First, reducing defensiveness may prevent continued escalation. A person trying to save face always perceives a threat—the threat of having an undesirable image assigned to him or her by others. Defensiveness is a likely reaction to perceived threat (Gibb, 1961). People feel they must be on guard because a mistaken move on their part can result in some undesirable consequence. Research by Rapaport (1960) and other work summarized in Chapter 7 suggest that defensiveness can be reduced by having an opponent indicate an understanding of another party's position and by recognizing some area of validity in the other party's position. Parties can show that they understand why another party feels unfairly treated or worried about appearing weak or indecisive; they can also recognize ways in which the belief may actually be legitimate. If the parties have handled similar incidents poorly in the past, acknowledging these can show a sympathetic understanding for the person's concern. Acknowledging a party's position as legitimate and indicating an understanding of it do not ensure that the issue can be settled easily, but they do allow for the possibility of an open discussion as the negotiation unfolds (Roth, 1993).

Second, the negotiation of a face-saving concern can be facilitated if the parties open the door for an exchange of concessions on the issue. Pruitt (1971) demonstrates the importance of letting both parties in a negotiation tell each other, either implicitly or explicitly, that an exchange of concessions is possible and safe. The parties need to know that there will be some reciprocity if one side begins making offers. Although face-saving issues are not the same as formal bargaining situations where offers can be made in increments, it is useful to think of the negotiation of a face-saving issue in the same general terms. Take as an example the face-saving situation where someone is hesitant to step back from a position. The party who is concerned about losing face needs some assurance that moving away from a position is safe and that it will not reduce his or her credibility. Comments, or reactions that confirm credibility and give parties a way out are likely to reduce their concern for face.

CASE 6.4 • *The Productivity and Performance Report*

Imagine yourself as Ron's supervisor: What cues did you pick up that enabled you to handle this situation successfully?

Ron, an office worker, was assigned the task of putting together an extensive report that described the productivity and performance of people in various divisions of a corporation. When the report was printed, a copy was sent to each division head for his or her inspection before it was distributed generally in the corporation. One division head called the research office after reading the report and was irate about an error that he found in the description of his department. He saw the mistake as a significant problem that could cause considerable damage to his division's reputation and future.

The complaint was discussed by several supervisors in the research office before it reached Ron. When he was told about the error, Ron became very defensive and argued that the information that appeared in the report was accurate. It was clear to his supervisor that the information was in error and that Ron was trying to save face. Ron was defending his position, not because he firmly believed that it was correct, but because

acknowledging that he had made a mistake could mean that he would be seen as incompetent.

The approach Ron's supervisor took in handling this situation was to point out that compiling the report was an immense and difficult task because the information had to be drawn from so many different sources. Often it had to be inferred from sketchy notes or letters that various people in the departments submitted to the records office. The supervisor congratulated Ron for putting together a report that had 10,000 pieces of correct information. These comments allowed Ron to admit the error because they reduced the threat of his being seen as incompetent. More important, they allowed Ron and his supervisor to begin discussing possible ways that the error could be handled so that the irate division head would be satisfied and accurate information about the unit would be disseminated.

Discussion Question

- Identify a specific situation in which a disputant is more interested in face issues than in moving ahead cooperatively. What suggestions would you make?

In Case 6.4, a supervisor in a large recordkeeping office at a corporation recently dealt with a difficult face-saving issue by trying to reassure an employee that it was safe to move away from a position. Signaling that an exchange of concessions is possible is important in other face-saving situations, although the way signaling occurs would be different. The party trying to save face because of perceived unfair treatment is often preoccupied with making this known. Broadcasting perceived slights can take precedence over any desire to discuss issues per se. To address this, others must provide some assurance that the issue of mistreatment will not be lost or forgotten if the party stops emphasizing it, which is often more difficult than it may appear at first glance. If a person feels that he or she has been treated unfairly in the past, believing that others actually want to address the issue may be difficult.

A party who raises a conflict in a situation where parties typically avoid potentially divisive issues—or actually believe that none exist—may also show a concern for face. This party may believe that others see him or her as the cause of the problem rather than as someone who raised an issue that needed to be addressed. At least one other party must step forward and say that he or she believes it is an important issue to discuss, or the person who raised the issue may become defensive, assuming others hold him or her responsible for the conflict.

TABLE 6.4   *Working with Face-Saving: What You Can Do to Counteract Its Negative Impacts*

- Diagnose the type of face-saving that is occurring.
- Do not presume you understand the other party; test any assumptions you make.
- Reduce defensiveness by:
    - Establishing a constructive climate.
    - Recognizing some valid points the other party has made.
    - Expressing understanding for the other party's position.
    - Expressing sympathy for the other party.
- Enable parties to account for their actions and accept their accounts.
- Use face-giving strategies.
- Exchange concessions.
- Stress consequences of the substantive issue to turn attention away from face issues.

If defensiveness cannot be reduced, or if parties cannot facilitate negotiations through an exchange of concessions, a third step can be taken to help stop the possible destructive effects of face-saving interaction: One or more parties can stress the consequences of not settling the substantive issue. This tactic is frequently advocated as a way to sharpen conflict, so that members will become more motivated to deal with the issue (Walton, 1969; Stulberg, 1987). When face-saving is an issue, increasing tension by pointing to the consequences of an unresolved conflict can encourage a party who is concerned about face to care more about the substantive issue than the potential threat to his or her image. It can, in other words, help direct the interaction away from a personal focus toward a substantive focus.

Benjamin Franklin was an early proponent of face-giving in his discussion club with fellow tradesmen, known as the Junto, and he gave us some good advice for setting up nonthreatening situations. Franklin's first rule was to display humility during conversations and to put forth ideas through suggestions and questions, using (or pretending) naïve curiosity to avoid contradicting people in a manner that could offend them. In the discussions held by the Junto, Franklin observed: "All expressions of positiveness in opinion or of direct contradiction were prohibited under small pecuniary penalties." Franklin later tried to bring a similar approach to the Constitutional Convention (without the monetary penalties!), and he is remembered as a moderating force in the deliberations of the founding body. Table 6.4 provides some strategies for counter-acting the negative impacts of face-saving.

6.8   Summary and Review

What is face?

Face is a communicator's claim to be seen as a certain type of person; the positive social value a person claims for himself or herself. Two dimensions of face can be distinguished. Positive face refers to a person's desire to gain the approval of others. This dimension has two subcomponents; the need to be included and the need to be respected. Negative face refers to the desire to have autonomy and not be controlled by others.

How does one lose face?

People lose face when their identity claims are challenged or ignored by others. Mutual acknowledgment and cooperative maintenance of face is one of the major concerns in everyday interaction. Challenges to face, which can occur during conflicts and other non-routine episodes, are unusual and threatening. A threatening experience can drive conflicts in negative directions. Face-saving behavior represents attempts by the party to save or to restore face, and it is a major source of inflexibility in conflicts.

How does face-saving affect issues in a conflict?

When face is threatened, saving face may supplant substantive issues for one or both parties. When this happens, unrealistic conflict (defined in Chapter 1) is likely to predominate. Face-saving also inhibits a group-centered approach to a conflict in which parties try to work out resolutions that are satisfactory for the group as a whole. Parties become individually focused and are concerned primarily with their own image and status; this promotes destructive conflict.

How is face-saving framed in conflict interaction?

Three basic frames for face-saving occur during conflicts, depending on which interpretation the party places on the face-threatening behavior. First, parties may frame their actions as resisting unjust intimidation. In such cases, people are concerned that they will be seen as weak and treated unfairly, and their behavior is oriented toward fair treatment and not giving into a threatening party. Second, parties may refuse to back down from a position, for fear they will compromise a prior stand on an issue. In this frame, parties adamantly defend their positions in the face of resistance. Third, people may frame their behavior as an attempt to suppress potentially damaging conflicts. In this case, parties are afraid to confront a conflict that they believe may result in a humiliating defeat. The face-saving frames involve different behavioral patterns, and each must be handled differently. To avoid damage due to face-saving, it is important to recognize how it is framed and to address the concerns implicit in that frame. For example, when parties see themselves as resisting unjust intimidation, this can be counteracted by behaving fairly and equitably and signaling respect and autonomy to others.

What is face-giving?

Face-giving occurs when parties support other parties' face claims and work with them to prevent loss of face or to restore face. Corrective and preventive face-giving can be distinguished: Corrective face-giving occurs after loss of face, whereas defensive face-giving is intended to prevent loss of face in the first place. Studies of interaction moves, called alignment actions, have uncovered a number of moves that give face, including accounts, apologies, quasi theories, excuses, justifications, disclaimers, counterclaims, conversational repairs, and licenses. These moves are not only used to give face—parties who use them are sometimes signaling their sensitivity to face concerns.

How does person-centered speech contribute to face-giving?

Person-centered speech is communication intended to support, comfort, or otherwise confirm the hearer. As such, person-centered speech gives face and support to parties' attempts to maintain or to restore face. Perspective-taking skills make engaging in person-centered speech more likely.

6.9 Conclusion

Face-saving concerns are, at base, concerns about relationships. When interaction becomes centered on these concerns during a conflict, people negotiate how they will see each other. Each message and response establishes whether a desired image will be allowed to stand in the eyes of others. Because these images are closely tied to parties' self-concepts, face-saving interaction has a strong influence on how comfortable people feel and how successful the parties will be at resolving conflicts constructively.

Teams and relationships often benefit when the role of individuals and their sense of self become the focus of interactions. Relationships can be improved and people can feel better about themselves because others have confirmed self-images they value. When the need to save face emerges, however, interaction can head toward destructive escalation because a party may feel his or her self-image is under attack. Uncertain that a desired self-image is accepted by others (or certain that an undesirable image has been established), a person seeks confirmation of a new relational image. If the acceptance of this bid is problematic, moving on from the issue can be difficult. Attempts to redirect the topic or shift back to group-centered or person-centered interaction can be thwarted by feelings of resentment or a preoccupation with the other party's resistance to changing his or her view. When face-saving issues go unresolved, making any decision or addressing any issue can be a highly volatile task. Unsettled issues about self-images can be played out in other more substantive contexts with potentially disastrous effects for the relationship, group, or organization.

7

The Context of Conflict Interaction

Nothing in life stands alone, singular and independent of everything else. All things oc-cur in some context, and it is the context in which they occur that gives them a large part of their meaning. We now turn to the context of conflict, the final piece of the puzzle we are assembling.

Webster's Third New International Dictionary (1986, p. 492) defines "context" as "the interrelated conditions in which something exists." The context of conflict encom-passes such a vast array of conditions that it is literally impossible to completely cover them. So we will focus on three elements of context that are particularly important in conflict: the histories of the parties, the climate of the social situation in which the conflict occurs, and the nature of the surrounding organization.

Parties bring personal and relational histories, which shape the issues in the conflict and the nature of conflict interaction. Based on previous experiences and the goals and as-pirations they have forged, parties have particular agendas of issues that matter to them and, hence, are likely to be the subject of conflict. Based on previous experience, parties are also predisposed to prefer some styles of managing conflict and to object to others. These expectations exert a strong influence on conflict interaction.

Conflicts are also influenced by the general atmosphere of the social situation, that is, by the situational climate. Climate is a generalized belief concerning how things will go in a conflict. It centers on beliefs concerning the nature of interdependence among the parties and associated beliefs about trust, supportiveness and power. Climate is not a natu-ral phenomenon, but instead is created and sustained by the participants in the relation-ship, group, or organization.

The final element of context is the organization in which the conflict unfolds. Organizations develop habitual ways of handling conflict, formal and informal dispute resolution systems. The specific norms and practices governing dispute resolution in the surrounding organization constrain how the conflict can be handled.

History represents the aspects of conflict unique to the individuals and their relationship, while climate represents the immediate social context for the conflict. The organizational context represents the impact of the larger social system within which the conflict occurs. All of these are mediated through and in turn influence conflict interaction. In subsequent sections we explore each in turn.

7.1 History

Our previous experiences obviously have a major effect on everything we do and say, and this is certainly true for conflict. History exerts its influence on conflict in several ways.

Our upbringing has a powerful influence on how we respond to conflict. In Chapter 2 we discuss psychodynamic theory, which argues that early life experiences leave a strong persistent mark on us, even if we are unaware of it. Our experiences with conflict in childhood and adolescence can shape how we respond to conflicts later in life. For example, Bippus and Rollin (2003) found that parties' attachment style, the approach to relationships individuals develop through their interactions with primary caregivers as infants and children, was related to their conflict management style. Bippus and Rollin studied pairs of friends and had each subject fill out an attachment measure and asked each friend to rate the other's conflict style. They found that securely attached individuals—those with positive views of themselves and comfortable with intimacy and relationships—used compromising and collaborating styles significantly more than insecure individuals. Crockett and Randall (2006) found that the quality of relationships adolescents had with their families influenced how they handled relational conflicts as young adults. Specifically, those whose adolescent family relationships were high quality were more likely to engage in collaborating and less likely to use force in relational conflicts, than were those with low-quality family relationships. Gayle and Preiss (1998) found that memories of an unpleasant conflict experience could affect workplace relationships, if the conflict remains unresolved. Bower (2007) summarizes a number of studies that showed that negative experiences with significant partners earlier in life transferred to current conflicts.

Our personal history also shapes what we want from life, our goals and aspirations. These define the issues, large and small, critical and trivial, that are at the heart of conflicts. If we have long aspired to attain an important goal such as a promotion at work or a loving relationship with "that perfect one," and someone else interferes, a conflict is almost certain to erupt. Personal history may also make us sensitive to more trivial issues. A friend once told one of the authors about an international, six-hour flight she took, where a child drummed his feet on the back of her seat. When she changed flights and was seated in front of another child, she dreaded more drumming. Fortunately, there was none. However, if that child had kicked her seat, she was sure she would have snapped. Everyone has a list of needs, goals, and projects—some relatively permanent and others that change with the situation—that can be a source of conflict. In every encounter with others, the intersection of these lists defines the possibility of incompatibilities.

Relationships, too, have histories. The previous encounters we have with others—both conflictful and nonconflictful—give rise to issues for future conflicts and also expectations about how the other will behave. Recall the beliefs about conflict and conflict scripts described in Chapter 2. We develop similar beliefs and scripts about conflicts with others, and these play a role in how we engage in conflicts. The serial arguments described in Chapter 1 offer a good example of this. Couples who engaged in serial arguments reported that they could predict how the next episode would go; before it began, they already knew that the outcome would be unsatisfactory (Roloff & Soule, 2002).

Finally, at a more global level, social groups have histories. The intergroup conflicts discussed in Chapter 3 often take generations to develop and generate long-standing issues that may insert themselves into interpersonal conflicts. An African American and a Northern European American in conflict may also entertain race-related issues imported from the long, ignominious history of racial discord in U.S. society. These issues persistently lurk between parties from different social groups, and if group identities become salient, they add fuel to the fire.

As the preceding discussion illustrates, history can influence conflicts in many different respects and on many different levels. How are we to make sense of the different ways in which history may influence a particular conflict or the parties involved?

One useful framework for so doing is Coordinated Management of Meaning Theory, developed by Pearce and Cronen (Pearce, 1976; Pearce & Cronen, 1980). Coordinated Management of Meaning (CMM) theory is concerned with how individuals organize, manage, and coordinate their meanings and actions with one another. The theory proposes that the interpretation of a conversation or message is shaped by the context or nature of the relationship between the parties as well as the self-concept and culture of each individual. Because each individual inevitably brings a unique history of experiences and meanings to any conversation, meaning will always be somewhat idiosyncratic or unique. The more individuals share similar or complementary worldviews, self-concepts, and understandings of their relationships, the more likely they are to arrive at similar interpretations of conversations and messages. CMM Theory provides a framework for explaining both how parties attribute meaning to a message, conversation, or relationship, and how parties then come to coordinate both their meanings and actions in the course of a conversation. Meanings are important because they lead to decisions about what action to take and what action to avoid.

The theory proposes that individuals organize meanings hierarchically, using one level of meaning to determine meaning on another level. The seven levels of meaning, shown in Figure 7.1, on page 206 range from the broad and abstract to the concrete and specific. The hierarchy can be viewed as an inverted pyramid or triangle. At the bottom of the triangle is a specific message within a conversation. The hierarchy demonstrates the many layers of meaning that we coordinate to create coherence in interpreting specific messages and actions. It also gives us a picture of how different aspects of history and context influence parties' perceptions and interpretations of conflict interaction. Starting from the top, the first two levels of meaning are broad-based, cumulative ways of viewing the world and one's self.

Cultural patterns refer to a socially shaped framework for viewing the world and one's roles and actions within it. This broadest context acknowledges the influence of one's particular cultural experience and how it shapes how all experience is viewed and interpreted. The second level, *life scripts*, refers to an individual's expectations of how his or her life will unfold based on his or her past and present experiences. For instance, as a student your expectations may include completing this course, which will contribute to your earning a degree, which will lead to a better job, and will enable you to buy a home.

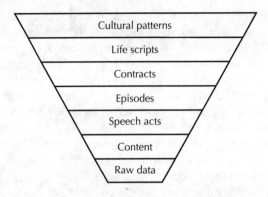

FIGURE 7.1   *Coordinated Management of Meaning: Hierarchy of Interpretive Contexts*

Life scripts are more complex than the "movie script" metaphor implies. An individual's interpretation may refer to the entire life course up to now, or to the events of the past year, depending on which the individual takes to be relevant. Typically, future-oriented scripts are rather simple, because we see the future in terms of general outlines, not the details we have about the past.

The next level of meaning concerns the specific individual or individuals with whom one interacts at a particular point in time—*contracts* define and specify expectations of the particular relationship based on the kinds of episodes that occur within the relationship. *Episodes*—the next level of meaning—focus on the particular interaction taking place at a particular point in time. They define the kind of activity that occurs between individuals based on the kinds and sequencing of messages being exchanged. More specifically, the next three levels focus on a particular message that a speaker has produced in the flow of interaction: *Speech acts* identify the intent of the speaker ("What is the speaker trying to do by saying this to me?"), whereas *content* is the decoding of the substance of the message, and *raw data* concerns the audio and visual signals that are immediately apprehended by the senses.

CMM Theory offers one way in which to understand how the various types of history affect parties' interpretations of a conflict. Social identity processes operate at the cultural level and also influence the individual's life script. Personal life history affects life scripts and also contracts, since our life scripts affect what we expect from relationships. Previous relational history between parties affects the contract level primarily.

An individual coordinates meaning by using one level in the hierarchy to aid in the interpretation of meaning at another level. For example, if the intent of the speaker is unclear (speech act), then the receiver relies on the nature of the episode, the kind of relationship, and his or her life script and culture to help identify the likely intent. This logical relationship between levels produces constitutive rules for determining meaning. *Constitutive rules* stipulate how meanings at one level determine meanings at another level. For example, if one party says to another, "You have not been treating me fairly," what this means would depend on the nature of their relationship (for example, manager–employee, husband–wife) and the nature of the interaction episode (job review, intimate dinner) to determine what this message "counts as." Generally, parties move to the next higher or lower level of the hierarchy first and then to higher or lower levels still if uncertainty remains. In some cases they may also skip levels.

This interpretation then leads to action. Relying on regulative rules formed by one's culture, self-concept, relationship, type of episode, and speaker's intention, one determines an appropriate response. *Regulative rules* specify what acts are appropriate given the nature of the relationship, the episode, and what the other person has said. Do you respond to the charge of unfairness with a justification that you have not been treating your employee unfairly? Or do you apologize to your romantic partner? So, constitutive rules are means for identifying the meanings of relationships, messages, and so on, whereas regulative rules identify what action to take given these meanings. In this way, both meaning and action are interrelated. Case 7.1 shows how the Parking Lot Scuffle, Case 2.1 (see page 39), can be interpreted using CMM Theory.

CASE 7.1 • *Coordinated Management of Meaning in the Parking Lot Scuffle*

Refer back to Case 2.1 on page 39 to refresh your memory on the scuffle.

According to CMM Theory, each individual inevitably brings unique experiences and meanings to any conversation; hence, meaning will always be to some degree idiosyncratic. The more individuals share similar or complementary worldviews, self-concepts, and understandings of their relationships, the more likely they are to arrive at similar interpretations of conversations and messages. The lack of a common context in the Parking Lot Scuffle portends that interpretations of what is said will be especially problematic.

In this case, we do not have data concerning the individuals involved and their perceptions, so we must infer from their actions how they might see the situation. Furthermore, the parties are strangers, so they are more likely to see the situation differently and not to understand one another's perspective.

Tim aggressively confronted Jay over the accident. This strong opening may reflect a life script that included a self-concept of standing up for himself to avoid being pushed around by others. In addition, as strangers, Tim and Jay's relational contract was one totally defined by the situation of the accident, and each must use extraneous information to predict how the other might

act. Given that Tim told us that he cannot afford to have a moped fixed and that we know Jay has a parking space whereas Tim does not, it is possible that Tim perceived Jay as a higher-status person who may treat him poorly. These conclusions may produce the regulative rule that if one is in a threatening situation with a higher-status person, then one must stand up for oneself so that advantages will not be taken. Note how Tim continued to focus on the damage done to his scooter and how Jay must pay for it.

What counts as appropriate behavior in this situation is up to the participants. Because the nature of the relationship during the episode is relatively unfamiliar, other regulative rules specifying appropriate action are also unclear. Constitutive rules are also contested. Both Jay and Tim struggled over how to interpret their speech acts, as displayed in lines 10 and 11, when Tim demanded that Jay explain what employment had to do with the accident. Only general cultural patterns helped them interpret many of their remarks and questions (see also Case 2.4, which deals with how culture affects the scuffle). In fact, it appears as though Jay may be slow on the uptake, taking questions in lines 1 and 8 at face value rather than as challenges.

It may be that the participants have created a rule system that encourages the use of escalating

(continued)

CASE 7.1   Continued

tactics. The redundancy of tactics in the episode supports this conclusion. Tim repeatedly threatened Jay, using a wide variety of speech acts. Jay, on the other hand, who seemed to be on the defensive during the episode, repeatedly resorted to questions and justifications. Almost as if the episode is written to music, each accusation or threat by Tim increased in intensity, while each question by Jay responded with rising force. This result may suggest that Tim and Jay created a repetitive pattern of caustic actions. From this vantage, we can see the same patterns emerge line after line as participants respond to each other's actions in the same way. In any case, CMM Theory would suggest that the Parking Lot Scuffle was more a conflict over how to coordinate necessarily ambiguous meanings than a conflict about the moped accident.

Discussion Questions
Analyze your own behavior in a recent conflict using CMM concepts.

- What expectations did you have?
- What meanings did you assign to the other person's actions?
- Can you identify the source of those expectations and interpretations?

The parties' meanings and actions become coordinated with one another as their rules become intermeshed. However, it is important to note that *coordinated* does not necessarily mean that individuals agree on the meaning of what is going on. Rules can be shared as individuals share meanings on a variety of levels. But rules may also differ, yet yield coordinated action. Consider the young college student who complains that he hates going home on the weekend because as soon as he enters the house his father starts interrogating him about his personal life at college. The son feels that he is independent and no longer needs to report to his father. The father, he believes, should respect his privacy. When his father asks him questions, he feels that he is treating him as a child and does not trust him. If the father were asked for his interpretation of these visits home, he would explain that he wants to be a good father and maintain a close and caring relationship with his son; therefore, he tries to show his interest and caring by asking about his son's life at school. The more his son withdraws, the more he feels he must persist because he does not want their relationship to deteriorate and become distant. And, of course, the more he persists, the more the son withdraws. The result is a very well-coordinated conversation, one in which the participants do not even suspect that the event has a different meaning for each of them.

CMM Theory provides a basis for identifying and understanding how the same event can have different meanings for the parties involved and how these meanings affect their actions. The theory explains why participants sometimes seem vulnerable to escalating moves in interaction. According to CMM, people act according to the interpretive rules they use. Through interaction, participants create an interlocking rule system, which is considered interlocked because the *rule-guided behavior* of each party is interpreted and responded to by the rules of the other. In other words, each action becomes the condition of the next rule-guided interpretation. Because the type of interaction participants produce is a function of the rule system they create, certain patterns can be self-sustaining.

Although most episodes vary widely, in some cases, people become so enmeshed in an episode as to be "out of control" (Cronen, Pearce, & Snavely, 1980). In these situations, the rule system created by the participants produces unwanted repetitive patterns (URPs). The same patterns emerge again and again as participants interpret and respond to each other's actions in the same way. Once this pattern is established, we expect it to occur over and over. It is natural to make similar choices based on what we think our partner is likely to do (Berk & Anderson, 2000). Such repetitive patterns for participants are difficult to recognize and hard to break, as the father-son example just mentioned shows.

CMM Theory also suggests one way in which intergroup differences may influence conflicts. As social categorizations and stereotypes become salient through the processes discussed earlier, they highlight elements of contracts, life scripts, and cultural patterns that focus on group differences. Once these are activated and important to parties, they influence interpretation of episodes, speech acts, and content. For example, if a male manager and female employee get into an argument and one registers a comment about the other's gender ("that's just what I'd expect from a man [woman]"), gender groupings would be highlighted. Subsequent remarks would be very likely to be interpreted in light of prevailing cultural beliefs about gender or gender-related parts of the parties' life scripts. In a real sense, the conflict becomes as much about gender as about the original issue because the framework of meanings emphasizes intergroup conflicts between genders.

7.1.1 Working with History

How do we understand how history influences a conflict? After all, history is such an extensive subject that it almost paralyzes our ability to analyze its impacts on conflicts. The CMM hierarchy can help us to understand other parties' perspectives on a conflict. It operates on the simple assumption that not all of the parties' history is relevant to every conflict. Only specific portions of history are activated. Some portions are already nurtured by the parties and they bring them to the conflict. For example, an old grudge might be the first issue raised in a conflict. Other portions emerge in the course of the conflict interaction. If one party makes a threat, the other may well respond with defiance, and then the threat itself may become an issue in the conflict. CMM Theory suggests that the key to understanding the behavior of others is to consider the relationship among levels in the hierarchy.

To understand where the other party in the conflict is coming from, consider how episodes, contracts, life scripts and cultural patterns in the other party's life may contextualize his or her speech acts and content. A manager we knew (we'll call him Ahmed) once reassigned a task that had been the responsibility of one employee (Reza) to another (Iftekhar). Reza repeatedly tried to keep control of the task, consulting with Iftekhar and sometimes fighting with him over how to do it. Ahmed confronted Reza about her behavior and she pleaded with him to have the task reassigned to her. When Ahmed refused, Reza began a covert campaign to undermine his authority, talking him down to other employees and going to his superior to complain about the reassignment.

After a great deal of difficulty with Reza, Ahmed realized that this task was important to Reza because it was part of her life script: she saw mastering this task as an important stepping stone to another job, and by reassigning it Ahmed had inadvertently thwarted her plan for self-improvement. Ahmed would never have come to this realization had he not

TABLE 7.1   *Working with History: Measures that Turn Conflicts in Productive Directions*

- To understand other parties' issues or actions, jump up the hierarchy to the episode, contract, life script, or cultural pattern levels to contextualize speech acts of content.
- Confirm your interpretations by moving back down the hierarchy to determine if other issues or actions are consistent with them.
- Consider multiple levels together to contextualize conflicts.
- Analyze your own issues and behaviors in light of the hierarchy of meaning.

been able to step back from the immediate conflict and consider the broader meaning of the task for Reza. He confided his interpretation to Reza, and after a long and productive discussion they agreed that Reza and Iftekhar would share responsibility for the task and that Reza would also train Iftkehar in doing it. This allowed Reza to add another important qualification to her resume.

Often we are so embroiled in the immediate give-and-take of a conflict that we focus only on content and speech act levels, and perhaps on the episode. By jumping up to the higher levels we can often clarify the deeper meaning of issues and actions. (See Table 7.1.)

In the same vein, we can use the hierarchy to understand our own issues and conflict behavior. We seem so transparent to ourselves that it is easy to forget that layers of history underlie every issue we have and every action we take. Sometimes, unbeknownst to ourselves, we are driven by things we are not aware of. Have you ever been angry at someone and thought it was due to something that they had just done, but later on realized that a totally different, older issue was the source of your anger? Very often, things are more deeply motivated than we presume at first. For example, one partner in a relationship, Dirks, always smoothed over conflicts with his partner Hans. He told Hans this was because Hans was so forceful it intimidated him. But on reflection, Dirks recognized that he had once lost a cherished relationship because of too many arguments, so Dirks had (without telling Hans) implicitly made part of his contract with Hans that he would not fight with him.

Self-clarity is very important to effective conflict management. If we do not know what we really want from a conflict, it is difficult to collaborate or compromise effectively. If we are not aware of the sources of our conflict style or of particular moves we make, it is difficult to adapt or respond appropriately to others. If we are not aware of what drives us, it is difficult to help others understand us. Whenever you find yourself wondering where you are coming from or why you did something, you can use the hierarchy to reflect on your behavior.

To this point we have focused on what each party brings to the conflict, including their personal, relational, and cultural histories. Now we turn our attention to the specific context that parties enact in their interaction, the climate of the situation.

7.2 Climate

People often speak of "getting the feel of" a situation or "learning the ropes." Managers, labor leaders, and politicians observe an "air of conflict" or "a mood of compromise" among their employees, colleagues, or opponents. Planners and consultants assess the "climate for change" in the organizations or teams they try to influence. These people respond to the general, global character of the situation, to what has been called the "climate" of the situation. *Climate* represents the prevailing temper, attitudes, and outlook of a dyad, group, or organization. As the meteorological name implies, social climate is just as diffuse, and just as pervasive, as the weather.

Climate is important in understanding conflict interaction because it provides continuity and coherence to mutual activities. As a general sense of a relationship, group, or organization, climate enables members to ascertain their general direction; what it means to be part of the group; what actions are appropriate; how other parties are likely to react; and what other information is necessary to guide parties' behavior and to help them understand the social situation. In The Columnist's Brown Bag (Case 1.1, page 33), the open and relaxed climate encouraged participants to exercise their curiosity and to be receptive to each others' comments. Questions, answers, and discussion flowed freely and spontaneously for most of the session. When the questioner challenged the editor, the atmosphere grew tense, and participants became hesitant and defensive.

The challenge seemed out of place, given the openness of the previous discussion. It introduced great uncertainty and some hostility into the proceedings. People reacted to the challenge as a violation of appropriate behavior, and this colored subsequent interaction. Eventually, rather than risk escalation of the challenge and permanent collapse of free, relaxed exchange, the leaders chose to terminate the session. By evoking certain types of behavior and discouraging others, the open climate gave the discussion direction and held it together. It united the diverse styles and concerns of individuals by providing a common ground for acting together and for reacting to a "crisis."

Implicit in any climate is an attitude toward conflict and how it should be handled. Climate constrains and channels conflict behavior; it lends a definite tenor to interchanges that can accelerate destructive cycles or preserve a productive approach. During the brown-bag session, the questioner's challenge was hastily cut off because the group was in "guest speaker mode," which implied a respectful and friendly attitude toward the editor. The challenge raised the specter of open and prolonged disagreement and potential embarrassment of the speaker. The group's open, non-evaluative climate made the challenge seem inappropriate. Rather than allow disagreement to ripen, those in charge were eager to end the session. Interestingly, the reaction of others to the challenge contributed to the sudden shift from an open climate to a tense and evaluative one, even though this is the last thing they would have wanted. The interplay of concrete, specific interactions and generalized climate is a critical force determining the direction of conflicts. A large part of this section explores this relationship.

In Chapter 3, we discussed a major theme that defines the climate in conflict situations: the type of interdependence members perceive. Recall that there were three types of interdependence: promotive (cooperative), contrient (competitive), and individualistic. As parties work out the type of interdependence they have, they answer questions related to motivation in the conflict, such as: Can we gain if we cooperate, or will one's gain be another's loss? Can I expect others to take a competitive attitude? Will my needs be met if I "go with the flow," or do I need to take a competitive approach to get what I want? Can we shift this apparently competitive situation to one more conducive to cooperation and integration?

Clearly, trust and supportiveness are closely related to interdependence. The promotive, contrient, or individualistic climate suggests answers to questions related to trust: Am I likely to be taken advantage of if I open up to others and try to engage in problem-solving? Does the apparently friendly and cooperative approach of others really hide either competitive or "every man for himself" approaches? Is it safe to express my true feelings about this conflict, or should I hide them? Will there be tolerance for disagreements and different points of view?

Interdependence also has important implications for parties' beliefs about how power will be used in the conflict. The three types of interdependence imply very different answers to critical questions related to power: Will this come down to a power play, or can we use open discussion, negotiation, and problem-solving to resolve the conflict? Will the existing power structure determine how the conflict turns out, or is there a possibility of opening things up and addressing the needs of low-power participants?

Finally, the climate of interdependence is also related to the cohesiveness of a dyad, group, or organization. The climate helps parties address questions such as: Does this relationship have a long-term future, or will it dissolve in the near future? Do I and other parties feel some degree of ownership for this team? Am I really committed to this relationship (or organization or team)? Do others feel committed?

Table 7.2 summarizes common beliefs associated with promotive, contrient, and individualistic climates. Note that these climates tend to foster a package of related and reinforcing beliefs about the context of the conflict.

Case 7.2, Riverdale Halfway House, provides an illustration of how climate develops and operates in a work group. It will serve as our main example in the remainder of this section.

A quick perusal of Case 7.2 indicates that a contrient (competitive) climate prevailed after George replaced the previous director. George and Carole were each trying to protect their own "turf." Relationships among employees were distrustful and employees did not feel safe expressing themselves. Parties dug entrenched positions and assumed they were right—that it was up to others to mend their ways. Employees protected themselves and showed little concern for others' feelings. Although emotions were expressed to some extent (at least by George), they were perceived as levers for manipulation and not as a means for deeper understanding.

Power figured regularly in day-to-day interaction. George used his directorship to berate staff members. His attempts to circumvent Carole and her opposition created a climate in which the use of power in a competitive fashion was taken for granted, with predictable consequences. Just such an assumption about George kept Carole from confronting him about the issues that were undermining their relationship.

George believed the employees were out to get him and that they did not respect his authority. The other employees were resistant to George and regarded him as an opponent who would try to defeat them by browbeating them and by using his authority. Members perceived different factions with opposing interests. There also seemed to be a general feeling that, although the employees of Riverdale were committed to the organization and Riverdale had a future, there was not much common ownership of the organization or its problems. An important reason the staff at Riverdale was unable to manage its conflict was because members believed raising the issues again "wasn't

TABLE 7.2 *Climates of Interdependence and Their Implications for Trust, Power, and Cohesiveness*

Type of Inter-dependence	Trust and Supportiveness	Power	Cohesiveness of the Social Unit
Promotive (Cooperative)	Parties can trust one another. Opening oneself up to others will be supported. True feelings can be expressed safely.	Use of power is likely to be downplayed in favor of collaborating. Shared power resources will be favored. All parties will work toward an acceptable solution together.	The social unit has a future. There is common ownership of issues, and equality is emphasized. All are committed to the social unit.
Contrient (Competitive)	Parties cannot trust each other if their interests differ. It may not be safe to open up or express feelings openly because they may be used against us.	Power is likely to be used. Unique sources of power will be favored. Higher-power parties will attempt to force or pressure lower-power parties to accept their preferences.	The social unit may not have a future; its future depends on high-power individuals. There may be common ownership of issues, but there are differences in the status and importance of members. Some parties are more committed than others.
Individualistic	Parties cannot trust one another because it's "everyone for themselves". Others will not be interested in or concern themselves with your true feelings.	Power is likely to be used. Unique sources of power will be favored. Higher-power parties will attempt to force or pressure lower-power parties to accept their preferences.	There is not much future for the social unit. There is little common ownership, and there are differences in the status and importance of members. There is little commitment to the social unit.

CASE 7.2 • *Riverdale Halfway House*

Imagine yourself as Carole: How much of an impact do you perceive yourself having on the organization's climate? How would you describe and explain the change in climate that occurs? How might descriptions and explanations be different for different people in this group?

Riverdale Halfway House is a correctional institution designed to provide low-level security confinement and counseling for male youth offenders. It houses about twenty-five second- and third-time offenders and for all practical purposes represents the last stop before prison for

(continued)

CASE 7.2   Continued

its inhabitants. Residents are required to work or look for work and are on restricted hours. Counseling and other life-adjustment services are provided, and counselors' reports on a prisoner can make an important difference in both the length of incarceration and the conditions of release. Because the counselors are also authority figures, relationships between staff and prisoners are delicate and touchy. Staff members are subjected to a great deal of stress as the prisoners attempt to manipulate them.

The staff of Riverdale consists of a director who handles funding, general administration, and external relations with other agencies, notably the courts and law enforcement offices; an assistant director who concentrates on external administration of the staff and the halfway house; three counselors; two night caretakers; and an administrative assistant who handles the books and paperwork. The director, George, was the newest staff member at the time of the conflict. The assistant director—who had applied for the director's slot that George filled—and the three counselors had been at Riverdale for at least a year longer than George. They described George's predecessor as a very "charismatic" person. Prior to George's arrival, relations among the staff were cordial, morale was high, and there was a great deal of informal contact among staff members. The staff reported high levels of respect for all workers under the previous director. Workers felt engaged by an important, if difficult, task that all worked on as a team.

With George's arrival, the climate at Riverdale changed. Right before he started, the staff changed offices and rearranged furniture, leaving the shoddiest pieces for George, who regarded this as a sign of rejection. He believed the staff had "gone around him" and had tried to undermine his authority by rearranging things without consulting him. He was hurt and angry despite the staff's attempts to explain that no harm was meant. Added to this was George's belief that Carole, the assistant director, resented him and wanted his job. Carole claimed she did not resent George, although she did fear that he might have her fired. She tended to withdraw from George in order to avoid conflict. George interpreted her withdrawal as a sign of further rejection, which reinforced his suspicion of Carole.

The staff felt George was not open with them, and that he quizzed them about their work in a manipulative fashion. Several staff members, including Carole, complained that George swore at them and ordered them around; they considered this behavior an affront to their professionalism. George's attempts to assert his authority also angered the staff. In one case, he investigated a disciplinary problem with two staff members without consulting Carole, who was ordinarily in charge of such matters. George's investigation did not reveal any problems, but it embarrassed the staff members (who had been manipulated by prisoners) and made Carole feel George did not respect her. George admitted his mistake and hoped the incident would blow over.

Ten months after George arrived at Riverdale, the climate had changed drastically. Whereas Riverdale had been a supportive, cohesive work group, it was now filled with tension. Interaction between George and the staff, particularly Carole, was formal and distant. While the staff had to some degree pulled together in response to George, its cohesiveness was gone. Informal communication was down, and staff members received much less support from each other.

A consultant was called in to address the problems. As the third party observed, "the staff members expected disrespect from each other." They felt stuck with their problems and believed there was no way out of their dilemma. There was no trust and no sense of safety in the group. Members believed they had to change others to improve the situation and did not consider changing themselves or living with others' quirks.

The staff wanted George to become less authoritarian and more open to them. George wanted the staff to let him blow up and shout and then

(continued)

CASE 7.2 Continued

forget about it. There was little flexibility or willingness to negotiate. As Carole observed, each contact between herself and George just seemed to make things worse, "so what point was there in trying to talk things out?" The consultant noted that the staff seemed to be unable to forget previous fights. They interpreted what others said as continuations of old conflicts and assumed a hostile attitude even when one was not present.

The third party tried to get the group to meet and iron out its problems, but the group wanted to avoid confrontation—on several occasions, scheduled meetings were postponed because of other "pressing" problems. Finally, George found another job and left Riverdale, as did one of the counselors. Since then, the staff reports that conditions have improved considerably.

Discussion Questions

- At what points in this conflict could a significant change in climate have occurred? What alternatives were available to staff members at these points?
- To what extent do you feel that this group's climate was inevitable?

worth the hassle" and would only worsen an already unpleasant situation. The group's cohesiveness had been so disrupted by its problems that members feared they would not be able to do their jobs if the conflict advanced any further. The Riverdale case offers excellent illustrations of some important points about climate that can now be explored in more detail.

7.2.1 More Detail on Climate

Climate can be defined more formally as the relatively enduring quality of a social unit that (1) is experienced in common by members, and (2) arises from and influences their interaction and behavior. Here we employ the term "social unit" to refer to dyads, groups, and organizations, because the points we make apply to all. Several aspects of this definition require explanation and can be illustrated from the case.

First, climate is not solely psychological—it is not an intangible belief or feeling in members' minds. Climate is a quality of the social unit itself because it arises from interaction among members. For this reason, a climate is more than the beliefs or feelings of any single individual (Fink & Chen, 1995; Poole, 1985). The climate of Riverdale was hostile and suspicious not because any particular member had suspicions about or disliked another, but because of how the group as a whole interacted. Members were hostile and suspicious toward each other, and these interchanges built on themselves until most group activities were premised on hostility.

This is not to say that individual perceptions of climate are not important. Parties' perceptions play an important role in the creation and maintenance of climate because these perceptions mediate the effects of climate on their actions. However, climate cannot be reduced to the beliefs or feelings of individuals. Various individuals in the Riverdale case had different perceptions of the hostile situation. George thought the group was hostile because Carole wanted his job and the staff resented him. Carole felt the hostility was because George cursed at her and went around her in making decisions. It is clear that neither George nor Carole had the "correct" or complete view, but they were reacting to a common situation. Their beliefs and feelings represent a particular sampling and interpretation of experiences in the group.

George's and Carole's perspectives on Riverdale's climate can be viewed as individual interpretations of the group's climate. However, individual perceptions provide only a partial picture of the climate itself. A social unit's climate is more than any individual's perceptions and can only be identified and understood if the unit's interaction as a whole is considered (Poole, 1985).

This can be understood by considering a second feature of the definition, that climate is experienced in common by members. As the preceding paragraph suggests, because climate emerges from interaction, it is a shared experience for the parties. This implies that there should be some common elements in members' interpretations and descriptions of the group, even though there will be differences in specific details and concerns. Therefore, the staff at Riverdale all agreed that the group was tense, hostile, and hard to manage. Although each person focused on different evidence—George on the furniture incident, Carole on George's cursing—and had somewhat different interpretations, a common theme emerged; the consultant was able to construct a unified picture of the climate from the various members' stories. Common experiences do not mean identical interpretations, but they do mean a unifying theme.

Third, because climates are products of interaction, no single person is responsible for creating a climate. In the Riverdale case, it would be easy to blame George for creating the hostile atmosphere but closer consideration shows that all the others contributed too. The counselors rearranged the furniture without considering that George might be insecure in a new job. Carole withdrew when George confronted her, which prevented an airing of the issues and possibly increased his suspicions. The hostile atmosphere at Riverdale was so pervasive because most members acted in accordance with it. Their actions reinforced each other and created an expectation of hostility in most interchanges.

Climates are also relatively enduring; that is, they persist for extended spans of time and do not change with every simple change in interaction. In some social units, the same climate may hold for months or years. At Riverdale, for example, before the previous director's departure, the climate had been promotive, and it took a good deal of interaction among George and the staff to redefine the climate. Once established, however, the contrient climate built for ten months before a consultant was called in. Of course, the operative terms here is "relative." In some cases, a climate may have a shorter life, as in the brown-bag discussion of Case 1.1, where a challenging, hostile climate supplanted the generally relaxed climate after only an hour.

Both long- and short-lived climates represent periods wherein definite themes and directions predominate in a social unit's interaction. The "life span" of a climate is determined by the relative stability of the interaction that generates and sustains it (Poole & McPhee, 1983; Poole, 1985). In some social units, the climate is firmly established in fundamental assumptions of group operation and therefore changes very slowly because interaction patterns change slowly as well. In other cases interaction can shift the underlying assumptions of the group rather quickly, as in the brown-bag discussion. This is particularly true when those involved are relative strangers. Because climate reinforces the patterns of interaction from which it arises, the longer a climate holds, the more en-trenched and enduring it is likely to become (Poole & McPhee, 1983). Climates are changed by changes in interaction that "break the spell" and reroute the interaction.

7.2.2 Climate and Conflict Interaction

In all interaction, and particularly in conflicts, one of the key problems parties face is their uncertainty about how to act and about what the consequences of their actions will be. Even if it is a dreary rehash of a long-standing argument, each conflict holds the potential for change, for better or worse, and uncertainty always hangs over its course and outcome.

There are two ways in which individuals can respond to this uncertainty. First, they can let "nature takes its course," and follow their natural psychological and interaction-based processes for reducing uncertainty, as detailed in Chapters 2 and 3. These chapters described a number of processes, including falling back on beliefs about conflict or con-flict scripts, making attributions (often erroneous) about the causes of conflict and using these to predict future behavior, relying on matching and accommodation, or by becoming rigid, responding to all conflicts in the same way regardless of circumstances. Each of these, or a combination, represents ways of responding to conflict that do not involve much adaptation on the part of the individual.

The second means to cope with uncertainty is to try to diagnose the situation so that we can react in an appropriate manner. Because the complexity and emergent nature of interaction render exact prediction impossible, parties must project their actions and esti-mate how others will respond to them. This projection can occur consciously (as when we plot out a strategy in response to the situation), or it can be unconscious (as when we recognize the nature of the situation and react to it unthinkingly), but it always involves estimations and guesswork about the future. Climate is indispensable in this process.

Parties use their sense of climate to gauge the appropriateness, effectiveness, or likely consequences of their behavior. The prevailing climate is projected into its future and enables us to project the impacts of various moves or styles. At Riverdale, for exam-ple, the firmly entrenched climate of hostility and suspicion led Carole to expect hostile interactions with George, and therefore she came into situations with her guard up, tended to interpret most of George's actions in an unfavorable light, and to act in a hostile or defensive manner toward George.

Unable to predict the specifics of a conflict, parties use their general impressions of a situation (in other words, of its climate) to generate specific expectations about how things should or will go. Because climate is so diffuse and generalized, it is difficult to trace the particular reasoning involved in these projections; for this reason, it is often thought of as intuition.

Climate also plays an important role in understanding others, an important supple-ment to the hierarchy of meaning discussed in the previous section. Climate provides cues to help us to interpreting others' intentions. For example, at some point early in the con-flict, Carole decided George intended to undermine her authority and maybe even force her to leave Riverdale. As a result, she was uncooperative and withdrew whenever George confronted her, answering what she perceived as hostility with hostility. Carole may have been right or wrong about George; that she drew conclusions at all was enough to stimulate her hostile behavior. As discussed in Chapter 2, however, several biases can influence the attributions parties make about others during conflicts, so climate may be contributing to misunderstanding.

Individual actions, each guided by climate, combine and build on one another to impart a momentum in the social unit. At Riverdale, for example, individuals picked up on the hostile climate, and their defensive and unfriendly actions thrust the group into a tense spiral of hostile exchanges. This process can also have beneficial effects. Friendly and responsive actions encouraged by an open climate also tend to create a chain reaction and to give the conflict a positive momentum. In particular, studies of trust have found a bias toward assuming cooperativeness on the part of others once trust has been established (Zand, 1972; Deutsch, 1973). The influence that climate exerts on individual behavior translates into a more encompassing influence on the direction of the unit as a whole.

Because each party acts on an interpretation of climate based on observations of others (and their reactions to him or her), the prevailing climate has a *multiplier effect*—it tends to reproduce itself because parties orient themselves to each other and each orients to the climate in projecting his or her own acts (Fink and Chen, 1995). For example, friends tend to be cooperative because they assume that is "the way things should be" between friends. When one party sees the other being friendly and cooperative, this reaffirms the relational climate and probably strengthens the inclination toward cooperativeness. Because this happens for everyone, the effect multiplies itself and becomes quite strong.

The multiplier effect, however, can also change the climate under some conditions. If one party deviates in a way that "breaks" the prevailing climate, and other parties follow the lead, the nature of conflict interaction may change. If the change is profound and enduring, it can result in a shift in the overall climate. Take the cooperative relationship among friends in the previous paragraph. If one party selfishly starts to press her interests, the other may conclude that he must do the same. Once individuals begin to act only for themselves, the underlying assumptions may shift to emphasize competition and taking advantage of others or individualism. This reflects a radical shift in the relational climate, the result of a single party's shift multiplied through the actions of the others. Obviously, this is a very complicated process.

Sustained as they are by interaction, climates are vulnerable to temporary shifts due to temporary alterations of interaction patterns. These shifts can be beneficial, as when a couple with a serious relationship problem declares a temporary "truce," or they can present problems—for example, when a normally harmonious group is disrupted by a "no holds barred" fight between two members. The shifts, however, are also vulnerable to the reassertion of the former climate. The longer the climate has been sustained, the deeper its grooves are worn, and the more likely the traditional quality of the social unit is to reassert itself. It is only by hard work that a temporary improvement in climate can be institutionalized.

As this chapter has shown, climates are created and maintained by particular events in interaction. However, because climates are generalized and diffuse, it is easy to forget this. Parties are often aware of a change in the tone of the team or relationship soon after a critical incident occurs. It is hard, for example, to miss the connection between an insult and increased tension. However, if the tension persists and becomes a part of the prevailing climate, the climate tends to become second nature. It is easy to forget that climate depends on how individuals interact and assume that things are "just that way," that the enduring qualities are independent of what parties do. Because they are so diffuse and generalized, and because they tend to be taken for granted, climates are often somewhat difficult to identify. Exhibit 7.1 describes some ways in which we might diagnose the prevailing climate of a situation.

EXHIBIT 7.1 • *Identifying Climates*

Climates are diffuse and implicit, and so it takes some art to identify them. Our discussion implies several guidelines for the diagnosis of climates:

1. *Climate themes are best identified by observing the entire social unit for an extended period.* Although exchanges between key members—for example, George and Carole at Riverdale—can play an important role in the team or dyad, they must be generalized and influence other parties' interchanges to become part of the unit's climate. To become a relatively enduring feature of a social unit, interchanges "with the same feel" must occur repeatedly and be recognized as characteristic by members. This implies that climate themes should permeate interaction and that those that are most enduring and significant will tend to emerge most frequently over time.

2. *Focus on interaction.* Talking with people is a critical part of diagnosis. The consultant gets most of her initial ideas about Riverdale by interviewing the staff involved in the conflict. However, members' ideas will always be somewhat biased. One may be angry at another and therefore attempt to cast that person in a negative light by claiming he or she causes problems. In other cases, people bias their accounts to make themselves look good. In the Riverdale case, neither George nor Carole was aware that their behavior contributed to the conflict; each blamed the other and believed the other had to change to resolve the conflict.

Individual oral or written accounts are thus "contaminated," and they should not be the sole source of evidence on climate. If observations based on interaction are consistent with reports, then the conclusions in the reports can be trusted, at least to some extent.

However, if interaction is inconsistent with reports, the inconsistency itself can be an important source of information about the organization, team, or dyad. One of the authors was working with a citywide charitable group to try to resolve arguments over its budget. The secretary of the group had confided that he believed the president always favored funding proposals from groups in which she had special interests. However, on observing several meetings, the consultant noted that the president was fairly objective, whereas the secretary pushed his interests very strongly. This suggested that the secretary had trouble monitoring his own behavior and had projected his personal tensions and biases onto the president, who was threatening because she stood in the way of his priorities. The consultant took the secretary aside to discuss the problem, and, for a while, the secretary was able to take his biases into account. (The group later reverted to its old bickering, however, because of problems in following the third party's advice.)

(continued)

EXHIBIT 7.1 • Continued

To obtain a valid reading of climate, it is valuable to cross-check individual oral or written accounts, minutes of meetings, other historical records, and actual observations. This has a particularly important implication for those trying to diagnose their own relationships or groups: They need to talk to other members, and to outside observers, if available, to get their views. One's own views represent only one perspective and may yield biased perceptions. There is no privileged vantage point; even the external observer can be subject to misperceptions: All views must be cross-checked to identify climates accurately.

3. *Use indirect evidence.* Parties may not be aware of the climate, so it is also necessary to utilize whatever indirect evidence we can get concerning climate. Metaphors that are explicitly expressed in the interaction are a particularly good source of insight into climate. Often metaphors incorporate unconscious associations capable of telling us more about the social unit's sense of itself than anyone's account.

For example, one college department we are acquainted with described itself with a "family" metaphor. Members repeatedly referred to the department family, and potential new hires were told the department was like a "big family." In line with this metaphor, several faculty members filled the slots reserved for father, mother, uncle, and aunt. Even the problems and conflicts in the faculty related to issues of authority and independence often associated with parent–child or parent–parent relationships. Patterns of conflict behavior in the department reflected the family metaphor to some extent: the "father" tried to take charge of the situation, and the "mother" tried to soothe those involved and sympathized with them. The "children" were rebellious but unsure of themselves and tended to buckle when the father applied pressure. Because the precise details of meaning are only implicit in a metaphor, parties will often use metaphors, whereas they would not provide an explicit description carrying similar meaning. This makes metaphors valuable as a means of understanding a relationship, group, or organization.

In failing to realize that they themselves hold the key to maintaining or changing the climate, parties thereby become controlled by the climate. Like the employees of Riverdale, parties may assume they have to keep acting as they do because there is no alternative. This assumption is responsible for the tendency of climates to reproduce themselves rather than to change. In the next section, we discuss how to change and improve climates and their impacts on conflict.

7.2.3 Working with Climate

Much of the previous discussion has focused on how a climate is generated and sustained in interaction. However, interaction can also change climates. One bit of advice often given to lower-status members is simply to be more assertive, to speak up when issues concern them, and to resist interruptions. This advice is sound, for the most part. To shift the climate of Riverdale in a less competitive direction, Carole might have discussed her feelings about being passed over for the director position with George. By confiding in George, she might have taken a first step to building trust and changing the climate to a more promotive footing.

Consider Case 7.3, "Breakup at the Bakery." How might the bakery employees change their climate?

This section advances three measures for changing climate. Earlier analyses of climate clearly imply a first principle: Small, cumulative changes in interaction can eventually result in significant changes in climate. For example, in team or organizational contexts, many people report that their first feeling of belonging to their social unit occurred when members began using "we" when talking about activities. This subtle difference signals a change in identification from "individual" to "member;" it promotes a more relaxed climate in the

CASE 7.3 • *Breakup at the Bakery*

Imagine yourself as an employee at this bakery: Why would you be reluctant to share your emotional reactions with the others?

A group of seven people had established and run a bakery for two years when a severe conflict emerged and threatened the store's existence. Two workers, Joe and Juanita, had been in a committed intimate relationship for several years but were now going through a difficult breakup. Neither Joe nor Juanita could stand being around one another, but neither could afford to quit his or her job. The bakery needed both members' skills and experience to survive financially.

Over three months the climate in the workplace grew more and more unbearable. Workers had to deal with the tension between the couple while working under daily time pressures and the constraints of having a minimal staff. Many believed that they could not work effectively if the situation got much worse. Important information about bakery orders and deliveries was not being exchanged as workers talked less and less to each other.

The group decided to call in a third party to help improve the situation. In discussing the problem with individual staff members, the third party realized that the workers strongly resented having to deal with the "relationship problem" at the bakery. They felt they were being forced to choose sides in the conflict or risk losing the friendship of both. At the same time, it was painful to see two friends endure a difficult emotional trauma.

Although the staff members were eager to share these feelings with the third party, almost nothing had been said to Joe or Juanita about their conflict. The staff was not willing to discuss the emotional issues because they seemed highly volatile and might lead to the breakdown of the work group. The climate had prevented them from expressing emotional reactions, which might have helped the couple understand how their breakup was affecting everyone. As a result, tension heightened and the bakery was about to go under. The third party was able to increase members' feelings of safety, and eventually all were able to talk about the problems.

Finally, at one tension-filled meeting, another member, Karen, openly stated that she felt uncomfortable and that she wanted to talk about Joe and Juanita's problems and their effect on the group. In the ensuing discussion, many issues and feelings emerged. Members were relieved to talk openly, and both Joe and Juanita were able to unburden themselves and get support from the group. The tension between Joe and Juanita did not subside as a result of Karen's intervention (in fact, it continued until Joe left the bakery), but the group's climate improved markedly and members were better able to cope with their co-workers' relationship problems.

Discussion Questions

- To what extent can one person improve the supportiveness within an organization through communication and action?
- Could this group have shifted the climate without the help of a third party?
- Do you think that climate is necessarily affected when some co-workers have an intimate relationship?
- What were the risks that Karen took?

group by indicating to members that others are well disposed toward them and that they are on common ground. In the Bakery, members might have tried to shift the climate in a more promotive direction by raising the emotional issues between Joe and Juanita. For example, in a tense meeting, one member might have said, "Joe, are you okay with our decision? You seem a bit tense about it." Without explicitly surfacing the conflict, the members could attempt to bring the tension out gradually and also to signal that they will not put up with it. This would at least let the group move forward, even if Joe and Juanita do not address their conflict directly. Exhibit 7.2 offers some specific ways in which we can use communication to build promotive, cooperative climates.

EXHIBIT 7.2 • *Creating Constructive Climates*

As you can probably guess, a promotive or cooperative climate is most conducive to integrative conflict management and problem-solving. Competitive climates are useful during differentiation, but it is important to shift to a more cooperative climate to move into the integration stage. Exactly how do we cultivate a promotive, cooperative climate?

One useful set of guidelines comes from Jack R. Gibb's classic article, *Defensive Communication* (Gibb, 1961). Gibb addresses the problem of how to prevent defensive behavior of the type that fosters competitive climates. He distinguishes defensive and supportive behavior. A *defensive* posture is one in which parties perceive or anticipate threats. A defensive person devotes a great deal of energy to protecting himself or herself and focuses on defeating the other party. Defensiveness prevents one from listening fully to other parties' messages. The defensive person often distorts or misinterprets messages to confirm his or her own sense of threat and danger. Moreover, defensiveness causes the person to behave in a way that makes others defensive too. Gibb comments that "defensive behavior, in short, engenders defensive listening, and this in turn produces postural, facial, and verbal cues which raise the defense level of the original communicator" (p.141). Conversely, a *supportive* posture tends to produce accurate communication and to reinforce supportive behavior in others. Supportive behavior gives a conflict its best chance to move in a productive direction.

All this should sound pretty familiar in light of earlier discussions. Defensive behavior correlates with a contrient, competitive climate, while supportive behavior correlates with a promotive, cooperative climate. However, Gibb takes this one step further and describes how to communicate in order to produce a supportive, as opposed to a defensive, climate. He discusses six categories of behavior on which defensive and supportive climates contrast.

According to Gibb, a defensive climate is produced by communication that is *evaluative*, whereas a supportive climate is encouraged by *descriptive* language. For example, the evaluative statement "You are messy and inconsiderate!" might be reframed as the descriptive message "Your things were scattered around the living room this morning." No one likes to be judged, and evaluative language implies judgment. Once a judgment is made, the one judged cannot try to reason with it; it is final. The only option is to reject the judgment, thereby erecting barriers between the parties. Evaluation also implies that the communicator does not grant legitimacy to the person's arguments or position. By contrast, descriptive language leaves the field open for discussion. The one judged can explain that the room is not really cluttered by his or her standards.

Descriptive statements tend to open up dialogue, whereas evaluative statements tend to close off communication, leaving resistance or avoidance as the primary options. The wording of statements

(continued)

EXHIBIT 7.2 • Continued

plays an important role in determining whether they are evaluative, but nonverbal communication is also important. As Gibb (1961, p. 142) puts it:

> Anyone who has attempted to train professionals to use information-seeking speech with neutral affect appreciates how difficult it is to teach a person to say even the simple "Who did that?" without being seen as accusing. Speech is so frequently judgmental that there is a reality base for the defensive interpretations which are so common.

A second characteristic of communication that encourages defensiveness is that it is *controlling*. Speech that attempts to control often fosters resistance, especially in conflict situations. This can be contrasted with supportive communication, which is more *problem-oriented*. Rather than trying to get someone to do what the speaker wants, problem-oriented messages try to define a problem on which both can work. So instead of saying "Stop talking so loudly!" which attempts to tell the other what to do, we might say, "You are talking too loudly and this is making it hard to hear Jack," which designates this as a problem to be dealt with. The accused can dispute the definition of the problem, or explain why he is talking loudly, or apologize, but the choice is left to him based on the way the statement is phrased. Of course, the history of a relationship influences whether a statement will be taken as controlling or not. Even statements phrased in a problem-oriented fashion may be perceived as controlling if one party has used them to manipulate the other party in the past.

Third, defensive climates are promoted by statements that seem *strategic*. Supportive climates are promoted by *spontaneous* messages. "When the sender is perceived as engaged in a stratagem involving ambiguous and multiple motivations, the receiver becomes defensive" (Gibb, 1961, p. 145). If a message that seems to be a sincere request on the surface is really a tactic to get us to do something we would not otherwise want to do, we are likely to react defensively. Deception promotes reaction.

On the other hand, if "what we see is what we get"—if the other is sincere and open—then one is likely to respond more spontaneously as well. People are not always reluctant to give others what they want, but they may be reluctant to be maneuvered into doing so. Of course, this puts us in something of a dilemma if we are trying to influence the climate of a situation. Can a message be strategically spontaneous? Is spontaneity a strategy that is available to us?

A fourth speech characteristic that creates defensiveness is apathy toward us by the other party. If another's speech is *neutral*, it often conveys the message that they do not care about us. On the other hand, *empathetic* speech styles, which indicate true concern for others, promote supportive climates. To create a supportive climate it is important to acknowledge the legitimacy of others parties' emotions and needs—to empathize with them. This does not imply agreement with others parties' demands, merely acceptance of them as real, legitimate concerns.

Defensiveness can also result when other parties' messages convey a sense of *superiority* in position, power, wealth, intelligence, family background, education, or physical attributes. Gibb reasons that such statements cause defensiveness because they cause the listener to "center upon the affect loading of the statement" rather than its content. "The receiver then reacts by not hearing the message, by forgetting it, by competing with the sender, or by becoming jealous of him" (Gibb, 1961, p. 147). To promote a supportive climate, it is important that sender and receiver perceive common ground, a shared, problem-solving relationship. Communication should convey *equality* between the parties. Although differences may exist between sender and receiver, it is important to attach little importance to them in the situation.

Finally, defensiveness is encouraged by messages that seem *certain* and dogmatic. Statements that assert they are the final word on an issue leave others with little control over the interaction and may provoke resistance. Anyone who has talked in a

(continued)

EXHIBIT 7.2 • Continued

dogmatic "know-it-all" way has experienced the reactions to certainty that create a defensive climate. Messages that convey the attitude that one is willing to experiment with ideas and to change one's position are more likely to create a supportive climate. So ideal messages should have a *provisional* quality. Rather than saying "You are always late for meetings," it may be better to say something like, "It seems like you've been late quite a bit lately." A less absolute and more provisional message encourages others to think over your comment and leaves room for a constructive response.

It is difficult to manage our communication along all six dimensions summarized in Table 7.3. However, a more supportive style can be learned. To start, you might try to write down what you said in a case when someone else became defensive and evaluate this according to the six categories. Think of how you might rephrase your comments in a more supportive fashion. There is no guarantee that adopting a supportive communication style will cause others to be supportive as well; however, it offers the best chance for success and is well worth trying.

TABLE 7.3 *Working with Conflict: Measures to Move Climate in Productive Directions*

- Create a constructive climate by modeling your communication after the guidelines given in Exhibit 7.2.
- To generate a more constructive climate:
  - Make small changes in your communication, using the six types of behavior that promote supportive climates, as specified by Gibb.
  - Openly discuss aspects of the climate that trouble you.
  - Create a critical incident in a bid to change the climate. It is important to time this move carefully and to be sure to choose an issue that will be salient to other parties.

Moves that depart from the patterns implied in the prevailing climate function as bids for change. If parties follow up on these bids, the bids may eventually become "institutionalized" and could potentially alter the climate. A study by Lindskold, Betz and Walters (1986) showed that clear and unambiguous changes in behavior could quickly change climates from cooperative to competitive or vice versa. More often, however, bids are rejected. Sometimes others simply fail to support an action that departs from accepted patterns, whereas in other cases dominant individuals actively suppress a bid for change. When parties look back at successful bids for change, they often identify them as turning points.

A second tactic for working on climates is to openly discuss aspects of climate that trouble parties. Much of the climate's influence on interaction depends on parties' inability to recognize it. If they can bring its effects out in the open and consciously move to counteract them, climate can be used to channel conflict interaction in constructive directions. Often this consciousness raising is done by one insightful person.

There are also formal procedures for evaluating a social unit's climate and functioning (Auvine, Densmore, Extrom, Poole, & Shanklin, 1977). Self-evaluation questionnaires on which members of teams or organizations rate their own and others' performance and weaknesses are often used (see Johnson & Johnson, 1975, for several good forms). Questionnaires provide a structured and legitimate way to raise criticisms and open them up for discussion. This "survey–feedback" process can be used to set goals for changing a social unit's interaction and, ultimately, its climate (Case 7.4).

CASE 7.4 • *The Expanding Printing Company*

Imagine yourself as an employee of this company: What fears might you have of having consultants come in to assess the organization's climate?

A small but prosperous printing company had been experiencing tremendous growth in a relatively short period of time. New equipment, expanded services, new employees, and expansions in sales territories and clients were just some of the changes that accompanied this growth. Older employees noticed a gradual change in the working climate in the company. What had once been a playful, relaxing atmosphere had quickly become somber and tense, at least in the eyes of several outspoken critics of the changes. Open conflicts became more frequent. For the first time, employees began to hold informal gripe sessions. Verbally aggressive behavior among employees was no longer kept behind closed doors. Perplexed, the company's president turned to a team of communication consultants to assess the situation and recommend strategies for improving the climate.

The consultants conducted in-depth interviews with the president and a select number of employees to discern their perceptions of the company. This interview process was guided by a series of questions geared toward understanding the working climate—for example: (1) What kind of people work here? (2) Do people respect each other? (3) How do they show respect or disrespect? (4) What is the leadership like in this organization? (5) How are decisions made in the company? (6) What types of conflicts surface with regularity? (7) How does information travel through the company? (8) What role does the grapevine play in disseminating information?

After reviewing the information obtained through these interviews, the consulting team elected to survey the entire organization with a self-report instrument measuring sixteen dimensions thought to be important to the working climate. This instrument assessed dimensions, such as work space, performance standards, managerial structure, job pressure, and employee morale. Within days of administering the survey, the consultants led a "town meeting" to report the results.

The meeting allowed employees to share opinions about the change openly and to compare perceptions. They discussed key issues uncovered through the interviews and the climate measure. Although the president of the company resisted competing views at first, she soon began to listen and inquire about the employee feedback. With the help of the employees, the consulting team had identified three issues central to the company's climate.

First, employees believed that the expectations and standards for performance were too low, especially for new recruits. The president was flabbergasted. The employees wanted higher performance standards for everyone—something the President had been sure they would resist. Second, employees were concerned for their physical safety. They were worried that new equipment and expansion in the same physical space would create poor working conditions. Third, many employees felt that the opportunity to participate in decisions was reduced as more employees were added. This resulted in frustration and struggles over many of the new decisions passed along during the recent changes. The consultants, the president, and the employees drafted a set of policy and procedural changes that addressed these and other issues. A follow-up survey a few months later reflected a much healthier organization, a company with a working climate described in one report as "robust."

Discussion Questions

- Were consultants really necessary in this case?
- What kinds of things, if any, could the president have done to "manage" the climate of the organization effectively during this period of time?
- Imagine yourself as the consultants. Why would you take the approach that you did, and ask the questions that you did?
- What kinds of resistance were the consultants likely to meet from the employees?

A third tactic for altering climate is to create a critical incident that shifts the entire direction of the climate. Recall the example in Chapter 1 (page 33) of the faculty brown-bag discussion wherein the student suddenly challenged the speaker: The climate shifted from congenial to tense. Critical incidents break up climates, either because they make members more aware of themselves or simply because they are so striking that members unconsciously pick up on them and perpetuate new patterns. Once interaction patterns are changed, they generalize to climates, and if they are changed for a long enough period, the prevailing climate changes. Parties can attempt to create critical incidents to alter unfavorable climates. Several considerations must be taken into account to do this effectively.

For one thing, timing is critical: people must be able to recognize propitious moments for acting on the climate. Bormann (1972) gives a good example of the importance of timing. In the groups he studied, he found a certain point in discussion at which one member would venture a favorable comment or joke about the group. In cases where others responded with more favorable comments or followed up on the joke, the group generally developed an open, inclusive climate. When people let the favorable comment drop, the group usually took a much longer time to develop cohesion, if it did so at all. Timing is vital; if the critical moment passes, it is gone and there may not be another chance.

Along with timing, salience is also important. The move must hold the parties' attention if it is to serve as a watershed. The student's attack on the brown-bag lunch speaker captured the attention of other people; thereafter, they were reacting to the student's move and their reactions reinforced the tension his statement originally interjected. There are many ways of enhancing the salience of a move—including raising the volume of your voice, using colorful or symbolic language, being dramatic, or saying something surprising. Used properly, these tactics increase the probability that the move will prove effective.

Finally, a party who aspires to create a critical incident should have credibility and respect in the eyes of other parties. The actions of a respected group member, for example, are likely to receive attention from others and therefore have a good chance to influence the interaction. In addition, making an effort to change climate can be interpreted as manipulation; moves of a respected and trusted member are unlikely to be rejected as self-serving.

Of the three approaches for changing climate, creating a critical incident is the most uncertain. It is difficult to do, and it has the potential to backfire—others may reject the person who attempts to maneuver the climate. When effective, however, the critical incident tactic gets results quickly, and it can be initiated by a single person. Small, cumulative changes and open discussion are more certain to work but are also problematic. Small changes operate piecemeal through day-to-day interaction; it is easy therefore to lapse back into old patterns. To use this technique successfully requires a clear sense of purpose and patience. It does not work quickly and is of limited utility in situations where climate is causing an immediate crisis in a social unit or relationship. Open discussion works much more quickly than cumulative change, but it can add fuel to a conflict by introducing a new issue: People satisfied with the present climate may side against those who are dissatisfied. The emotions associated with discussions of power relations or supportiveness may generalize to the conflict and intensify disagreements on other issues. In using any of the approaches discussed here, it is important to be aware of possible problems and take measures to circumvent them.

7.3 The Organizational Context

In addition to the context enacted within the conflict situation, there is also a wider context represented by the organization or social situation within which the conflict occurs. Here we focus on the specific influence of organizations on conflict. When conflicts occur in organizational contexts, conflict style and the moves parties can make are not always a matter of individual choice. The structure and culture of organizations or social units also affect which conflict styles are preferred and their effectiveness. A conflict in an organization with procedures that emphasize strong management control will be quite different than one with looser, more participative management. In the former organization, a supervisor is likely to be involved in managing the conflict, while in the latter, parties may be left to themselves.

Ury, Brett, and Goldberg (1988) argue that the structure and culture of organizations influence the development of their dispute resolution systems, their preferred ways of managing conflicts. Some organizations have formally established dispute resolution systems, such as a grievance procedure or a mediation office, and others rely on ad hoc systems, such as making it part of the manager's job to handle conflicts that disrupt the work process. Some conflict resolution systems are formally provided by the larger community—for example, the courts or community mediation services. (See Exhibit 7.3.)

Three types of dispute management systems common in U.S. organizations have been identified by Ury, Brett, and Goldberg (1988): Interest-based, rights-based, and power-based. *Interest-based systems* attempt to find a resolution that satisfies the parties' underlying interests or needs. One example of a formal interest-based system is the dispute mediation services that are increasingly being adopted by large organizations. For example, one large university has an Office of Dispute Mediation where parties can file formal cases that go through a multi-step conflict management procedure. Other organizations, such as the one in The Productivity and Performance Report Case (Case 6.4, page 199) have cultures that encourage people to adopt interest-based approaches on an informal basis. Interest-based systems tend to favor the problem-solving and compromising styles.

EXHIBIT 7.3 • *What Type of a Dispute Resolution System Does an Organization Have?*

How do we determine what type of dispute resolution system holds in a given case? Ury et al. recommend asking the following questions:

- What do people do if they have a complaint?
- With whom, if anyone, can they bring up an issue?
- What happens when disputes are negotiated? Do the parties search for solutions that meet the needs of all sides? Do they go to authorities? Do they openly compete or use threats, intimidation, or other power tactics?
- How frequently do negotiations break down? What do parties do when facing a breakdown?
- Is there a formal program or set of rules or procedures parties can use when a dispute occurs?

Rights-based systems attempt to establish which party is right based on independent standards accepted as legitimate and fair by the parties. Some standards, such as the legal code, are formally established, while others are socially accepted norms, such as seniority or equity. The most familiar rights-based system is the courts of law, as when an employee sues her employer for discrimination on the basis of gender. Participating in this system requires the assistance of an attorney because its procedures are so technical and complex. However, a parent who cuts a piece of cake in half to stop an argument between two children is also using a rights-based system.

Managers are also called on to use rights-based dispute resolution. Jameson (2001) reports that supervisors were the most commonly relied on third party for disputes among workers. Rights-based dispute resolution systems tend to promote the contending form of the competing style and the protecting form of the avoiding style. Parties make their best cases to the adjudicator—whether judge, parent, or manager—and rely on him or her to make the call.

Finally, in *power-based systems,* parties attempt to coerce others into doing what they want. Examples of power-based systems are strikes by workers and lockouts by employers, a manager ordering an employee to do a task the employee finds unpleasant, and fistfights among teenagers. Power-based dispute resolution tends to occur in the absence of interest- and rights-based systems; it is the "default" mode of conflict resolution in most organizations. The Undergraduate Publications Board in A Raid on the Student Activity Fees Fund Case (Case 5.1A, see pages 137–138), is an example of a system in which power is the primary means of managing conflict. In power-based systems the competing, avoiding, and accommodating styles are most common.

It is important to note that a resolution system can differ for different types of conflict and for different parties. Union members, for example, may make heavy use of grievance procedures, whereas managers may prefer to use power-based systems when dealing with employees.

The three dispute resolution systems are not entirely independent of one another. Rights-based systems often evolve to correct for the problems and abuses of power-based systems; for example, the labor mediation system may evolve because of the harms caused by strikes and labor–management conflict. Rights-based systems also require the use of power to enforce decisions. A court's verdict or ruling has the force it does precisely because it is backed up by police and/or other government agencies who will compel parties to honor the court's decision. Interest-based dispute resolution systems are often established as alternatives or supplements to rights-based systems. Mediation, for instance, is commonly offered as an alternative to a trial in divorce on the grounds that it offers both parties a chance to satisfy their interests; a decision by a judge or jury often favors the interests of one side over the other.

Ury, Brett, and Goldberg (1988) estimate that in most organizations the use of the three dispute systems resembles a pyramid, with a majority of conflicts handled through power-based approaches, a significant portion through rights-based approaches, and a smaller portion through interest-based approaches. In organizations that do not have formal interest-based systems or organizational cultures that encourage interest-based approaches, power-based and rights-based conflict management are prevalent. Even in organizations with formal dispute resolution systems, power-based approaches are common.

To use formal dispute resolution systems, parties must request or apply; however, there are barriers to bringing a conflict out into the open. Parties may fear being labeled as troublemakers if they formally complain or as incompetent for not being able to manage their own affairs. Those with power may avoid formal systems because they believe they can get their way in any case and that the formal system may not decide in their favor.

Ury et al. recommend that organizations try to "invert" this pyramid so that most conflicts are resolved according to interests, a significant portion according to rights, and only a small portion through the use of power. This may require establishing not only a formal dispute resolution system based on problem-solving, but also changing the organization's culture and employees' attitudes. Organizational dispute resolution practices generally develop gradually over the years and are grounded in deep-seated thought and action habits.

Ury et al. report the case of Bryant High School, which implemented a mediation program to help students manage conflicts more constructively. Bryant had experienced building tensions and violence, some between students and some between students and teachers. A major barrier to the success of the mediation program was students' lack of communication, negotiation, and problem-solving skills. One girl put it this way: "All I ever wanted to do was fight. If someone said something to me I didn't like, I didn't think about talking, I just thought about fighting" (Ury et al., 1988, p. 34). A climate of confrontation and violence was deeply embedded in Bryant's culture, and students and teachers there had learned that competing was the primary mode of conflict management. To remedy the situation, the school undertook a major training effort, providing workshops and classes in problem-solving and nonviolence techniques to more than 3,000 students and staff. The idea was to develop attitudes favoring nonviolent dispute resolution and motivation among students, teachers, and administrators to use the mediation system. After several years of training at Bryant, the mediation program was used for a significant number of conflicts, and violence was reduced. Bryant's program worked because school officials were willing to undertake a prolonged program to change the school's culture, climate, and attitudes.

7.3.1 Working with Organizational Dispute Resolution Systems

The dispute resolution systems in an organization can favor certain approaches to conflict, and it is important to bear this in mind when selecting a style. In a power-based system, competing is the preferred mode, and parties who want to adopt problem-solving or compromising styles will find the going tougher than they might in an organization where interest-based systems are more common. Parties who adopt problem-solving or compromising styles may be seen as weak or vacillators in power-based systems, and others may seek to take advantage by forcing their own solution on the conflict.

Rights-based systems tend to favor competing styles too, but of a different sort. In rights-based systems parties take their arguments to an authority who makes the decision. The competition in this case does not depend on marshaling resources, such as the support of others or even physical strength, but rather it depends on who can make the best argument that appeals to the rules of the system. Employees in a rights-based system often have little incentive to work out conflicts themselves; instead, they polarize and make the best case they

TABLE 7.4   *Working with Conflict: Measures for Using Organizational Dispute Resolution Systems to Best Effect*

- Determine which type of organizational dispute resolution system is in force for the type of conflict you have: interest-based, rights-based, or power-based. Learn how to operate within this system.
- If you do not believe the current dispute resolution system is appropriate or fair, try to "change the venue" by moving the conflict into another system. Most organizations have more than one dispute resolution system.

can to their superior, a judge, or other authority. Problem-solving, with its emphasis on open communication and consideration of others' interests, can place parties at a disadvantage in a rights-based system because it gives important information to the other parties.

This does not mean that parties have to go along with the prevalent approach to resolving a dispute. They can try to "change the venue" of the conflict by moving it into a different dispute resolution system. An employee who is being browbeaten by co-workers can shift from a power-based to a rights-based system by taking the problem to a supervisor or filing a grievance. Conflicts can be taken from power- and rights-based systems into an interest-based system by applying for mediation when this is an option. People also can make styles that are not favored by a system work, but this requires determination and some skill. For example, an employee may need to adopt a competing style initially in order to resist a co-worker's attempts to force her to go along with his preferred work schedule. Once the co-worker realizes that forcing is not going to work, he may seek a compromise or problem solve, even in a workplace where power-based approaches are commonly used. (See Table 7.4.)

7.4 Summary and Review

How does the coordinated management of meaning theory contribute to our understanding of the context of conflicts?

CMM Theory helps us to understand how history plays a role in conflicts and how individuals create and sustain meanings during communication processes. It proposes a hierarchical model with several levels of meaning: from highest to lowest they are cultural patterns, life scripts, contracts, episodes, speech acts, content, and raw data. When people try to understand communication at one level, they use other levels as context. For example, a joking comment is likely to mean one thing in a friendly conversation episode, but quite another during a conflict episode. The levels are used to specify two kinds of rules that govern communication. Constitutive rules indicate what an act stands for or indicates in a particular context, whereas regulative rules specify appropriate actions in that context. Parties use the two types of rules to interact. Each party invokes a particular set of rules as he or she interacts, and these may or may not be consistent. How the rule sets of the parties mesh determines how the interaction goes. If inconsistent rule sets are used, coordination becomes difficult and interaction may break down, or, in some circumstances, go out of control. The CMM hierarchy can help us to understand the deeper meaning behind the other party's issues and actions. It can also help us to understand ourselves better.

What is climate?

Climate captures the overall feel of the situation for parties. It is experienced in common by members of a dyad, group, or organization and is a product of interaction. It also influences interaction because it shapes the attributions parties make about each other, their predictions about how interaction will unfold in the situation, and the behaviors they engage in.

How can we describe the climate in a social unit or interpersonal situation?

Climate can be described in terms of three types of interdependence in a situation: promotive (cooperative), contrient (competitive), and individualistic. Each climate has implications for supportiveness and trust, power, and cohesiveness of the dyad, group, or organization. These elements do not exhaust the variety of possible conflict themes, but they do represent the areas most commonly found in climate analyses.

How does climate affect conflict interaction?

Climate shapes interaction by facilitating parties' prediction of how the episode will unfold and their interpretations of other parties' words and deeds. Through this, it influences how parties act. As we saw in Chapter 2, interpretations are also influenced by attribution processes, which tend to favor competitive over cooperative orientations. It is important to understand the influence of attribution processes because they make it more difficult to establish a cooperative climate and tend to dampen the impact of cooperative climates.

How does interaction affect climate?

Climates are the product of interaction. Climatic themes shape conflict interaction, and conflict interaction moves in a cyclical fashion to shape climates. This multiplier effect can set climates in place by influencing parties to act in a way consistent with the climate, thus reproducing the climate. However, this same cycle leaves an opening for those who would like to change the climate. Changes in interaction and critical incidents can alter climates by creating new behavioral precedents and by making parties aware of undesirable ruts into which the team or dyad may have fallen. Changes in interaction set up new expectations for the future and raise new issues that may persist and change the climate if sustained by people's actions.

Climate and interaction influence each other on at least two levels. At the most elementary level, climate influences individual actions, which in turn have a role in building climate. At a second level, a temporary climate may overshadow the general prevailing climate of an organization. For example, a sharp fight may break out in a generally cooperative organization, temporarily creating a competitive climate with little supportiveness for people.

What are some tips for identifying climates?

Climates are best identified by observing an entire social unit or dyad for an extended period of time. This observation should focus on their interactions because this is where climates are enacted. The descriptions of promotive, contrient, and individualistic climates suggest what to look for in interaction. Themes that constitute climate are often found through identifying the metaphors used in a group. Finally, your own feel of or intuition about the climate is a useful guide. Climates are often felt more than directly spelled out.

What can parties do to change a climate?

At least three things can be done to change climates. First, one can undertake small changes in interaction; if parties are persistent and consistent in these changes, they often generalize to change the climate as a whole. A second tactic is to discuss troubling themes openly. When troubling aspects of climate surface, parties often realize that they were all bothered by them and can then act together to deal with them. It is also useful to discuss the themes that are useful and constructive so that parties can continue building on them. A final option is to intentionally create a critical incident that alters the climate in "one fell swoop." This is a riskier strategy, but in some cases it can be used to good effect.

How do we create a constructive climate?

A supportive climate is one in which people feel safe and valued. It can be contrasted with a defensive climate in which parties perceive threats to their interests and identities and do not feel valued. Supportive climates can be created through communication that is: descriptive rather than evaluative, problem-oriented rather than controlling, spontaneous rather than strategic, empathetic rather than neutral, equal rather than superior, and provisional rather than certain.

How does the organizational context influence conflict?

While there are many ways in which organizations can influence conflicts, we have focused on the formal or informal procedures and norms organizations have for managing conflicts, organizational dispute resolution systems. Three types of systems can be distinguished, interest-based, rights-based, and power-based. Each type of system favors specific styles of conflict management and incorporates particular norms about what is and is not acceptable behavior in conflicts. More than one type of system may hold in the same organization, and often there are different types of systems for different types of conflicts.

7.5 Conclusion

With our attention given to the conflict unfolding in front of us, we often neglect the impact of context. This chapter has attempted to understand the impacts of three elements of context—history, climate, and organizational environment—on conflict interaction and outcomes. We have also considered concepts and models that can be used to understand the nature of contexts and how they affect the directions conflicts take.

Context is a vast topic and so our treatment of it is necessarily incomplete. Other things that might have been considered include, aspects of the physicial context of the conflict, such as where it occurs (in your office, for example, or in the other party's office), nonverbal elements such as seating arrangements, the role of social issues of the day in defining the issues that arise, and other aspects of social structure, such as family or relational norms.

"History is just one damned thing after another," a wit once commented. So it is with our life histories. So much has happened in our individual experiences, in our relationships, and among social groups we belong to, that it is difficult to sort out what should be relevant to a conflict. But each of us brings certain concerns based on history to our conflicts. The hierarchy of meaning defined by CMM Theory is one conceptual tool we can use to give us ideas about what aspects of other parties' histories may be relevant to a conflict. It can also be used to give us insights into our own, often-murky motivations in a conflict.

Composers often describe the emotional tenor of the piece they have written in a short phrase above the first measure of the sheet music. Phrases such as "*allegro agitato,*" "*appasionato,*" or "tenderly" are instructions that tell the performer what mood the piece should convey to an audience. Climates are much like these musical instructions. They do not specify the "notes," the specific behaviors members undertake; instead, they give an indication of the expected tone or temper for interaction, whether promotive, contrient, or individualistic. Climates reduce people's uncertainty about how to act and about how to interpret other parties' actions by providing a simple, general idea—a feel—of the situation and of whether things are right or wrong, appropriate or out of place. This is particularly important in the uneasy uncertainty of conflict; the general temper of the situation surrounding a conflict is a critical determinant of whether it takes a productive or destructive direction. A hostile, tense climate can make escalation inevitable; a cooperative climate can turn the same situation toward problem-solving. As the "composer" of its own interaction, a dyad, group, or organization can change the instructions on how behaviors will be played out and interpreted. These shifts in climate come as the people hear their own changes in emotional pitch; they will have a strong influence on the direction conflict interaction takes.

Organizations also orchestrate our behavior. The various organizations in which a conflict occurs—be they businesses, schools, libraries, churches, or clubs—develop preferred modes for handling conflict and tend to channel conflicts into these modes. One can try to play different notes, but the tendency of others to follow the organization's lead may make these different tunes sound off-key. To sustain an alternative method of handling conflicts requires us to find ways to harmonize our approach with those favored by the organization.

8

Managing Conflict

This chapter builds on the insights of Chapters 1 through 7 and discusses how you can manage your own conflicts. Self-management is the optimal approach to managing conflict, because the solutions you work out together are often more appropriate and effective than those made by outsiders. If the solutions "fit" all parties well, then you are more likely to follow through on them and, hopefully, avoid relapses back into the same conflict all over again.

This chapter could also be titled, "How to Collaborate." The most effective way of managing conflicts is to engage in mutual collaboration with the other party, a process we have sometimes referred to as "problem-solving." As we observed in Chapter 4, sometimes collaboration is not feasible, or we have motives other than to work out a mutual solution, so conflicts can also be managed through compromise or one of the other styles. Collaboration, however, remains the gold standard. If it is done well, collaborating is the one approach to conflict that has the highest probability of yielding an outcome that will result in satisfaction and prevent eventual relapse back into conflict. It sets the stage for moving forward with the other party.

As the normative model described in Chapter 1 indicated, to effectively work through conflict, parties must first differentiate and then make the transition into integration, while avoiding spiraling escalation or rigid avoidance of the conflict. This chapter is organized around this model. First we consider differentiation and how it can be managed so as not to lead to escalation or avoidance. Then we lay out a model for conflict management that moves from differentiation through integration. Finally, we consider some special techniques for working through various stages in the problem-solving process.

8.1 Review of the Normative Model for Conflict Management

Before proceeding, it will be useful to review differentiation and integration. Recall that in the differentiation stage, parties express their differences, staking out positions and criticizing others and their positions. Differentiation is quite useful, because if it is handled properly, the parties realize they have differences, that all sides are serious and that, therefore, some type of mutually acceptable resolution should be reached. However, as we have seen, things do not always go this way. Differentiation can sometimes be quite sharp and can spiral out of control into an escalating cycle of conflict. Differentiation may also be threatening to parties, and rigid avoidance can result instead of real differentiation.

Differentiation is an essential precursor to integration, because unless differences are thoroughly understood and appreciated by all parties, it is impossible to come to a solution that satisfies the parties' interests and deals with their incompatibility. If differentiation is handled properly, at the end of this stage parties will:

- Have a preliminary understanding of each other's issues, interests, and positions.
- Acknowledge the legitimacy of each other's issues, interests, and positions, even if they do not agree with them.
- Realize that the differences cannot be resolved without working together.
- Have some motivation to resolve the conflict, even if that motivation is only the knowledge that the other party will continue to resist and prolong the conflict unless a mutually acceptable resolution is worked out.

This list makes it evident that differentiation contributes some very important elements to collaboration. Without it, parties would not have the knowledge or motivation necessary to engage in collaborative problem-solving. When all or most of the four functions of differentiation have been fulfilled, the parties are ready to move into the integration stage.

In the integration stage, parties:

- Further explore their issues, interests and positions and improve their understanding of the problems underlying the conflict.
- Search for and acknowledge common ground or tradeoffs that they can capitalize on to attain a mutually acceptable solution.
- Identify and analyze possible options.
- Move toward a solution that, ideally, meets everyone's needs, but at least is one all parties can live with.
- Commit to implementing the solution and to keeping their part of the bargain.

If the integration stage is not properly handled, there is a high likelihood that the conflict will reemerge in the future. And even after integration has occurred, there is a need to monitor the parties' behavior to ensure they are abiding by the agreements.

To work with conflict, then, it is necessary for parties to differentiate, but keep things under control. At some point, they must make a transition from differentiation to integration. Managing that transition is important, but also rather tricky. It is to this that we now turn.

8.2 Navigating Differentiation

We have used two nautical metaphors to describe the movement through the two stages of conflict. In Chapter 1 we likened it to tacking a boat against the wind. The metaphor implies that we can use the tendencies toward escalation and avoidance to nudge the process in a productive direction. Tendencies to escalate can be used to sharpen the conflict and stimulate parties to take each other seriously and attend to each other's issues. The complementary tendency to pull away and withdraw from the conflict can be used to dampen the escalation and keep the conflict moving toward integration. A second metaphor we use is sailing between Scylla and Charybdis, two mythological monsters. In navigating differentiation, we must sail between the two negative tendencies of differentiation, avoiding both, to make progress toward a positive resolution of the conflict.

This is not to say that competing should be avoided altogether during differentiation. Actually, it is often quite useful. A competing approach signals the importance of an issue to others. The general assumption is that people will not forcefully pursue a goal unless it is meaningful to them. So being willing to fight for something shows others that it is a priority and helps them realize that they should try to understand the competer's issues.

Competing also has another useful function. By persistently competing parties demonstrate resolve. Sometimes a party will engage in uncollaborative behavior such as trying to wait you out, avoidance, or even competition in the hope that you will give up and go away, or even give in. By engaging the other party sharply, a competing style demonstrates that you must be reckoned with. As we noted in Chapter 3, the costs to the other party of engaging in a competition may also motivate him or her to shift to a more collaborative approach, and the more resolve you show, the more the other party is likely to assume these costs will persist or even increase as time goes on.

As Putnam (1990) showed, effective conflict management and negotiation often involves a combination of competing and collaborating. The competing behavior sharpens the conflict and signals commitment to positions, while collaborating moves the parties toward a mutually acceptable position.

So, the challenge is to differentiate without developing so much negative momentum that spiraling escalation or rigid avoidance occur. In the preceding chapters, we discussed strategies and techniques for dealing with problems introduced by emotional, cognitive, and interaction processes, by power, by face-saving, and by the context of conflict. These are summarized in the tables near the end of each chapter. Following this advice will help you deal with specific problems that might occur during differentiation or that might rear their heads during integration. But there are also some strategies and techniques that specifically deal with differentiation.

8.2.1 Framing Problems or Issues

How we state our problems, issues, or positions makes a difference. It is important to cultivate a promotive, cooperative climate during differentiation, and the ways in which we frame problems and issues contribute to this. This is best accomplished by placing primary emphasis on the problem or issue itself and not on the people involved. One of the classic sources on conflict and negotiation, Fisher and Ury's (1981) *Getting to Yes* puts it as follows: Focus on the problem, not the people. If we state our issues as problems without blaming the other party, the other party is much less likely to become defensive. The attention of all can then be on the problems before them and not on defending themselves or feeling blame or guilt.

Gordon (1970) has advanced a useful model for stating problems:

> "I have a problem. When you do X, Y results, and I feel Z."

This may seem a little formulaic, but note what this model does. First, when we state a problem this way (*"I* have a problem . . . "), we are taking *ownership* of it, rather than putting it off on the other. This is likely to reduce the blame the other would feel if we had stated things differently, for example, saying "You drive me crazy!" In this case, the statement points the finger at the other, setting the stage for defensiveness.

By *describing the specific behavior* the other party engages in (X), we avoid evaluating the other party. If we say, "When you interrupt me," it puts the focus on the behavior, something that is specific and also something that can be changed by the other party. If, on the other hand, we say "Your interruptions are so rude!" the other party will understand the behavior but also feel evaluated, which is likely to lead to defensiveness and perhaps some pushback.

Outlining a specific, observable consequence of the behavior helps the other party understand what results from his or her behavior. For example, to continue our interruption example, the party might say, "When you interrupt me, I do not get to contribute my ideas, which might help us do a better job." The party may well not be aware of the damage his or her behavior does, or of the possibilities not yet explored.

Finally, *stating how the behavior makes you feel* helps the other party understand its consequences for you. This also reinforces your ownership of the problem, because they are your feelings.

Here's a full example:

> "I have a problem. When you were complimented on our presentation and didn't acknowledge my contribution to it (X), it made me feel angry (Z). I don't believe I was given proper credit, and this makes me wonder if I should work as hard next time (Y)".

This model for stating problems is likely to foster the supportive climate as discussed in Chapter 7. It is descriptive, problem-oriented, and conveys equality. It is strategic, rather than spontaneous. However, if you convey your message in an open way and leave yourself open to explanations, the other party should see your strategy as supportive rather than manipulative. This model is not particularly empathetic, but again, if you convey openness to discussion, you can show empathy in other ways.

Formulas like this may be awkward, and you should not feel constrained to follow the model provided here. It is simply important that all four elements be present in your communication of the problem.

This manner of stating problems is meant to situate the problem "out in the open" between you and the other party so that you can discuss it in a collaborative fashion. It leaves the other party a number of options for responding, rather than backing her or him into a corner. The other party can consider changing behavior or finding a way to help assuage your negative feelings. He or she can also explain the behavior from his or her point of view, so that you can understand it better. Finally, the other party can reject your problem and refuse to change.

It is important to be persistent in stating your case. If rejected, do not back down. You do not have to be confrontational, but you can be firm and resolute. Insist that the issue is important and should be addressed. If the other party still refuses to recognize the issue, at least you know you tried before taking other routes.

In any discussion of problems or issues, it is important to ensure that you have understood the other person's point of view. As the discussion of attributions in Chapter 2 showed, there is a tendency to assume that our own points of view are more valid than those of the other party. Attribution processes also encourage us to place blame on others, while not assigning it to ourselves. And these tendencies are heightened when social identities are salient and the other party is from a different social group. It is important to keep these tendencies in mind and try to correct for them.

A helpful tactic is to reflect on the other parties' statements to see if you understood them properly. This is done by phrasing what you believe the other party is saying in your own terms and asking him or her if your understanding is correct. In response to the previous problem statement, we might say:

> "So what you're getting at is that you think I don't acknowledge your contributions to the project adequately. Do I understand you correctly?"

This gives the other party a chance to explain further. It also prevents you from acting on incorrect assumptions or incorrect information. Finally, it has the benefit of giving you some time to collect yourself. It is difficult to be confronted with a problem, and if we feel threatened or hurt, and these feelings flood us, we are likely to react in a counterproductive way.

8.2.2 Cultivating a Collaborative Attitude

How we approach differentiation also has a strong influence on how the conflict unfolds. A positive, constructive attitude toward disagreement and differences can build confidence that the conflict does not have to get out of hand and can be faced constructively.

Tjosvold (1995) advanced a model of *constructive controversy,* which posited that "open discussion of opposing views is most critical for making cooperative situations productive." This somewhat surprising view argues that conflict is essential to effective cooperation. Underlying it is a positive attitude that from the conflict can come improved outcomes and better relationships.

If we combine the premises of Tjosvold's model with those of another, Hall and Watson's classic "rules for consensus decision-making" (1970), we can suggest the following principles for constructively engaging during differentiation:

- Avoid arguing for your own position. Present your position as clearly and logically as possible, but consider seriously the reactions of the group in any subsequent presentation of the same point.
- Avoid win–lose stalemates in the discussion of positions. Discard the notion that someone must win and someone must lose; when impasses occur, look for the next most acceptable alternative for both parties.

- Avoid changing your mind *only to avoid* the conflict and to reach agreement. Withstand pressures to yield that have no objective or logically sound foundation. Strive for enlightened flexibility; avoid outright capitulation.
- Avoid suppressing conflicts by resorting to voting, averaging, coin flipping, and the like. Treat differences of opinion as indicative of an incomplete sharing of information and viewpoints and press for additional exploration and investigation.
- View differences of opinion as both natural and helpful rather than as a hindrance to decision-making. Generally, the more ideas expressed, the greater the likelihood of conflict, but the richer the array of resources as well.
- Search to understand the other parties' perspective. Do not presume your position is the correct one. Listen to others' arguments with an open mind.
- View initial agreement as suspect. Explore the reasons underlying apparent agreements; make sure that people have arrived at similar solutions for either the same basic reasons or for complementary reasons before incorporating such solutions into an agreement or decision.
- Work for mutual benefit, and see yourself and the other parties as "in this together."
- Show respect for the other parties in everything you do. Avoid embarrassing or insulting them.

These principles encourage parties to air and to address differences rather than to come to agreement quickly. They counteract the tendency to come to premature convergence on a single solution and reliance on objective standards where none exist. Hall and Watson and Tjosvold have tested these procedures and found that groups trained in these attitudes produced better answers on problem-solving tasks and in team performance than did untrained groups. In part this can be attributed to a "synergy bonus" from the procedure: It allowed groups to make use of all their members' skills and knowledge.

The attitude reflected in these principles is useful in all stages of conflict, but particularly so in differentiation. In the face of problems and the hostile and negative statements often expressed during differentiation, this attitude offers clear-headed hope that if the parties work together, they can reach a creative solution that acknowledges the needs of all. It offers others a chance to see in the conflict the potential for great improvements in the current situation.

8.2.3 Moving from Differentiation to Integration

Managing the transition from differentiation to integration is a critical move in productive conflict management. How to best do this depends on the situation. In some cases both parties are exhausted by competition and tired of its costs. In other cases, tensions are so great that parties can barely stand it. In still other cases, parties who have been steadfastly avoiding conflict are only too aware of this and want to move ahead and deal with the issues. In these cases, parties are likely to welcome a suggestion that they talk and try to resolve the conflict. A conciliatory move by one party is very likely to be accepted by the other party.

There are, however, times when it is not clear whether the other party would entertain a move toward collaboration. When this is the case, one strategy is to test the waters, yet not expose yourself too much. If the other responds positively, then you can gradually develop a collaboration.

One famous model for how to do this is *experimental integration*. The key to experimental integration is to make a conciliatory or cooperative move, yet not let your guard down so that the other party can take advantage. If the other party responds in a positive fashion, then you can answer with more integrative moves and eventually move into full-fledged integration. The approach is experimental in that the conciliatory or cooperative move is an experiment—it tests how the other will respond. If there is no real conflict, the other should respond cooperatively, and you can then signal back with another cooperative move, and so on, to gradually bring about integration.

The best-known method for experimental integration is Charles Osgood's Graduated and Reciprocated Initiatives in Tension Reduction strategy (GRIT) (Osgood, 1959, 1962, 1966; Lindskold, 1979; Kramer & Carnevale, 2003), which was developed for conflicts between nations, but can easily be adapted in more modest form for interpersonal conflicts. The specific points in the GRIT strategy are as follows (based on Lindskold, 1979):

1. The climate for conciliatory initiatives needs to be set by making a general statement of intention to reduce tension through subsequent acts, indicating the advantages to the other party of reciprocating.
2. Every unilateral move should be announced publicly prior to making it, indicating that it is part of a general strategy.
3. Each announcement should invite reciprocation from the other. Reciprocation need not come in the form of the same move but should be a conciliatory step of some sort.
4. Each initiative must be carried out as announced without any requirement of reciprocation by the other.
5. Initiatives should be continued for some time even if the other party does not reciprocate. This gives one a chance to test the party's sincerity and also puts pressure on the other party.
6. Initiatives must be unambiguous and permit verification.
7. Initiatives must be risky and vulnerable to exploitation, but they also must not expose the party to a serious and/or damaging attack.
8. Moves should be graded in degree of risk to match the reciprocation of the other party. Once the other party begins to reciprocate, the initiator should reciprocate with at least as risky or slightly more risky moves.

The first three points make the initiative clear and may put pressure on other parties to comply with the conciliatory gesture. Points 4 through 6 make it clear to the other party that he or she has the freedom to respond or not, and that this is not a trick or maneuver. Point 7 is crucial because it gives the party the security to attempt the experiment. The party stands to lose if the other takes advantage of the move, but the move does not expose his or her position so much that the other party can win the day. Finally, point 8 represents an attempt to gradually increase cooperation. Etzioni (1967), for example, shows how Kennedy and Khrushchev followed a pattern similar to GRIT to bring about the thaw in East–West relations that followed the Cuban Missile Crisis. Other evidence supporting the effectiveness of GRIT is summarized by Kramer & Carnevale (2003).

This strategy can be adapted to interpersonal conflicts by omitting point 2, which is only necessary when parties communicate to a broader audience. It tries to capitalize on reciprocity, as discussed in Chapter 3, to move the conflict in a positive direction.

Another approach to experimental integration is the *reformed sinner* strategy (Pruitt & Kimmel, 1977). In this strategy, the party initially competes for a period of time and then shifts over to cooperation. If the other party responds cooperatively, the party continues cooperating, but if the other competes, the party shifts back to competition. In experiments and field studies this strategy has been shown to be effective in inducing the other's cooperation. Of course, for the strategy to work, there must be an incentive for the person responding to the reformed sinner to cooperate rather than exploit the weakness. Thus, the reformed sinner must maintain a "stick" and be prepared to use it again if the "carrot" does not work.

Why does the reformed sinner strategy work? One explanation points to the respect that such a strategy wins for the party. By initially competing, the party demonstrates an ability to punish the other party. Voluntarily giving up the punishment possibility and exposing oneself to the other generates respect and also a sense that the party must be sincere in his or her offer of cooperation.

The second explanation is simpler than the first and goes hand-in-hand with it: It posits that once the other party has experienced the negative consequences of competition, sudden cooperation will be attractive and motivate the other to cooperate. If this explanation is valid, it implies that the party should take care to make the other recognize the disadvantages of competition and the advantages of cooperation.

Once the conflict has been "tamed" somewhat, and parties have begun to fulfill the functions of differentiation, a more formal procedure for working through the conflict can be employed. The next section outlines this procedure.

8.3 A Procedure for Managing Conflicts

This section outlines a procedure to finish differentiation and move through integration effectively. This procedure, a synthesis of several problem-solving and conflict resolution models (Filley, 1975; Gouran & Hirokawa, 2003; Scheidel & Crowell, 1979; Straus, 2002; Whetten & Cameron, 1998), is designed to structure parties' interaction as they work toward a mutually acceptable solution. It is also designed to counteract some of the errors or problems that can result from the conflict dynamics discussed in previous chapters.

The procedure has five steps that build logically on one another. As much as possible, parties should go through the steps in order, keeping deliberations on each step separate:

1. *Issue Identification:* The parties define and explore the issues underlying the conflict. This involves addressing the following questions:

    - *What are the issues?* Parties share their perceptions of the key issues in the conflict and their own positions. They also share their perceptions of how others see the key issues; this often helps parties clarify misunderstandings.
    - *Are we motivated to do something about the issues?* Parties must develop a shared sense of the need to address the issues. This does not mean that all issues must be important to all parties. Some issues may fall within the scope

of discussion because they are very important to one party and are recognized by the others as legitimate.

- *How do we feel about the issues?* Parties share their feelings about the conflict and their reactions to others' behavior. In answering this question it is important that both sides accept others' feelings because feelings cannot be right or wrong—they must simply be accepted. Parties cannot be forced to change their feelings; they must change them of their own accord. Nor does this mean that emotion should take over the process. Rather, it reflects the recognition that airing emotional reactions helps parties to understand one another.

- *What are the root causes of the conflict?* Parties attempt to identify the causes of the problems or issues underlying the conflict. Often the immediate conclusions that parties draw about the causes of the conflict are shallow and hasty. Some research and reflection can often allow parties to see more fundamental problems that must be solved for the conflict to be resolved.

  In one example of this, two co-workers in a clothing resale shop had a long-standing conflict over scheduling their hours. They repeatedly attempted to work out a mutually acceptable schedule, and repeatedly found themselves shouting at each other's intransigence. After some consideration, they finally realized that the problem was not their lack of consideration for each other, but rather the fact that the shop was understaffed and stayed open too long for the two of them to handle. They spoke to the owner, who agreed to take some of their hours himself.

  It may prove impossible or impractical to establish root causes, due to the time and expense involved. If this is the case, then the solutions should address the immediate issues. However, we would encourage you to try hard to identify root causes. If you do not, any solution you develop may just be temporary patchwork.

At the end of this step, parties should have a mutual understanding of the issues they will address. If there are many issues or if issues are complex, it is a good idea to try to subdivide them into sets of related issues. Trying to tackle very large issues can lead to discouraging results.

While the questions are logically ordered, you do not necessarily have to address them in the order presented. Some cycling back and forth among the questions is often necessary to develop an adequate sense of the issues that must be addressed.

It is, however, important to finish this first step before proceeding to other solutions. Issues and problems should be defined without discussion of solutions. If solutions are introduced at this point, they tend to shape definition and analysis of the issues so that they emphasize features corresponding to the solution. To continue our example, the two shopworkers initially approached the conflict with the idea that if they could just work out an acceptable schedule, they could resolve their conflict. Starting with a preferred solution led them to assume their issue was scheduling, initially blinding them to the fact that the real issue was an insufficient number of workers, and that the owner was also a party to their conflict.

2. *Vision:* In this step parties develop a vision of what the future will be like if they fully resolve their conflict. In so doing they address the following questions:

   - *What would the relationship/group/organization be like if we resolved this conflict?* Parties envision what things would be if the conflict was addressed effectively. This can be done by focusing on how resolution of the conflict would change things. Or it can be through envisioning what things would be like without this conflict altogether.
   - *How would we feel if we resolved this conflict?* Parties envision how they will feel when the conflict is effectively resolved. This also involves envisioning how they would feel about each other if there were no conflict.
   - *What other things could we accomplish if we did not have to deal with this conflict?* Parties envision what they would do with the time and energy they currently devote to the conflict if it were resolved. It is important to consider not only the time spent on the conflict itself, but the time spent thinking and brooding about the conflict and its effects. This gives parties an opportunity to think about other possibilities and opportunities that would open up if the conflict were managed effectively.

   Limiting our focus to issues or problems tends to give our thinking a negative cast. That is, we concentrate on identifying what is wrong, and try to address it. Developing a vision, by contrast, concentrates our attention on a positive future in which the conflict has been addressed and the issues resolved. A vision provides energy and positive motivation to work on the conflict.

   Trying to develop a vision may seem to be a diversion of time and energy away from managing the conflict. Recall from Chapter 2, however, what important forces hope and optimism can be. In the process of problem-solving there may be discouraging periods, and a hopeful vision can give us the energy we need to keep working.

3. *Solution Generation:* Parties generate a wide variety of possible solutions. This may require some research and considerable thought. It is important to develop as many options as possible. Often the most obvious solution is not the best one, as the case of the shopworkers shows.

   It is important to resist the temptation to evaluate solutions at this point. This tends to inhibit contributions and reduce creativity, because parties may become fearful that they will be evaluated negatively for their ideas or that their ideas will be rejected without serious consideration.

   One useful technique for solution generation is *brainwriting,* a variant of the classical brainstorming procedures. In brainwriting, parties are asked to silently write their ideas down for several minutes. Then, just as in regular brainstorming, parties alternatively state their solutions, which are recorded on a display that all can view. No evaluation of solutions is allowed. If someone else's idea suggests a new one or a variation of an existing idea, then parties are encouraged to add to the list (this is sometimes called "piggybacking," since the new idea rides on a previous one).

4. *Solution Evaluation and Selection:* Parties evaluate possible options and select a final solution. This may involve combining elements of several options. It may also involve having parties trade off so that one gets what he or she wants for one issue and the other is satisfied with the outcome on another issue in exchange. Fractionation of issues, discussed in Chapter 3, is often useful in generating trade-off issues, because it breaks large issues into smaller ones that can be dealt with separately.

A useful technique for solution evaluation is the *two-column method.* For each option, parties generate their own individualized lists of pros and cons. These may be shared publicly or they may just be reference points for negotiation over the final solution.

5. *Implementation:* The parties plan how to put the solution into effect and determine how effectiveness will be evaluated. It is important to follow up later to make sure all parties have met their obligations and no unforeseen problems have arisen.

Sometimes, work in a later step encourages us to rethink earlier work. For example, the generation of options might spark new thoughts about how issues could be defined. In that case the process cycles back to rework issues and then revise vision and options, if necessary. It is important to be flexible when using this process, because every conflict and every set of parties are different.

It is helpful to maintain the constructive attitude discussed in previous sections throughout the problem-solving process. It will greatly enhance your ability to carry out each step effectively. In the next section we discuss two additional procedures, one for defining problems and goals and the other for facilitating discussion and exchange of ideas. These may be useful in specific steps of the conflict management procedure.

EXHIBIT 8.1 • *How Can We Manage Extreme Conflict?*

The terrorist attacks on September 11, 2001, forever changed America's view of its own vulnerability and the nature of conflict in a world of global differences. For those interested in the study of conflict, one fundamental question rose from the ashes of that dreadful day: What moves individuals and groups toward extreme remedies such as violence and acts of terrorism? Of the many approaches to that question, one stands out for its commonsense value.

Eidelson and Eidelson (2003) suggest that individuals and groups can hold dysfunctional beliefs that are both self-perpetuating and destructive. Five beliefs stand out for their potential to lead to horrific violence such as terrorism: superiority, injustice, vulnerability, distrust, and helplessness. When these belief domains are present in individuals or groups, the capacity for extreme remedies against others exists.

Superiority is the belief that a person or group is better than others in special ways. When holding this belief, people feel as if they deserve or are entitled to special treatment. Societal rules and laws are often thought not to apply fully in light of the status these people hold. *Injustice* is the belief that the individual or group has been mistreated by specific others or by the world at large. The sense of unfairness from this "treatment" becomes the center of sense-making and a debilitating or immobilizing preoccupation. *Distrust* is the belief that others are truly out to get an individual or group

(continued)

EXHIBIT 8.1 Continued

and intend to do harm; hostility and malevolent action lurks around corners and can be interpreted as such by the simplest of acts. Those who distrust expect to be humiliated or abused at any moment. *Vulnerability* is the belief that the welfare or position of a person or group is in the hands of powerful others, that dangers exist virtually everywhere. An exaggerated sense of defenselessness is a sign that fear of vulnerability is in play. *Helplessness* is the conviction that even carefully crafted plans will result in dismal failure. Individuals believe nothing they do will make a difference, while groups feel powerless or at a distinct disadvantage compared to other groups.

In a world of varying socioeconomic means and cultural and religious differences, one or more of these belief domains is not uncommon, especially toward those outside the culture we ascribe to. When each of the domains exists in a person or a social unit, savage acts of violence toward others can occur in conflict situations. When social realities clash, tactics that usually work to alleviate conflict, such as compromising or collaborating, can actually make matters worse (Pearce & Littlejohn, 1997). So what can be done to manage conflicts that arise from such beliefs? The answer seems to be to confront the foundations of expected violence before it begins. Of course, this is not an easy proposition. How can we dramatically challenge the core beliefs of individuals and groups around the world?

There is no simple answer to this complex dilemma; however, in addition to reframing, two ideas appear to be more promising than others. First, these belief domains are steeped in rational thought, albeit dysfunctional in bias. Keeping "real" data in front of people goes a long way toward diluting the five critical beliefs. What facts, evidence, and information can we muster to show and prove that people are not vulnerable, helpless, or superior? What actions can we take to reduce the feelings of distrust or injustice that others feel? Whether at a national, local, or individual level, when faced with these beliefs in people or in groups, we can use rational thought to disarm the strength of such distorted reality.

Second, it is important to do the unexpected (McRae, 1998). The very nature of these five beliefs is to assume the worst, to see a pessimistic reality at odds with one's own worldviews. Sometimes we need to engage in the least expected, positive actions as a contrast to the deeply held convictions that people are out to harm or humiliate. As in the ancient lesson of holding sand in one's hand, the harder you squeeze, the more sand you lose. We are told that athletes learn this same lesson under wet conditions—one has to hold a football or baseball loosely, not firmly, when it is raining or snowing in order to control it. By doing the opposite of what's expected, a new way of seeing a problem may emerge.

8.4 Additional Useful Techniques

A key barrier to managing conflict is that parties may not be able to agree on a problem definition. One option is to use a complex definition that includes all issues and then try to come up with a solution or a package of solutions that resolves most or all of them. Another option is to try to reframe the conflict to develop a shared definition.

In response to this need, Volkema (1981, 1983) developed the *Problem–Purpose Expansion (PPE) Technique* to help parties recognize and transcend narrow thinking in their framing of issues and problems. Volkema argues that the effectiveness of any conflict management strategy depends on how parties formulate the problems they face. Problem formulation has at least two effects on conflict. First, it channels parties' thinking and can severely limit the range of solutions considered. In the Creativity Development Committee (Case 5.3, page 148), the major problem was expressed as "selection of the best possible procedure for making decisions in the research meetings." This formulation of the problem constrained members to search for a single procedure to be used by all project teams, which eventually worsened the conflict. How this problem was formulated implicitly ruled out several solutions that would have allowed members to work on common grounds, such as adopting two procedures and testing each in half of the project teams or adopting several procedures and allowing the project directors to choose whichever they liked best. As we have seen, people tend to converge on solutions prematurely, and an overly narrow problem formulation encourages this.

Second, problem formulation also affects parties' motivation when a conflict emerges. How the research committee formulated its problem set up a win–lose situation once members became divided over the two candidate programs. Because only one program could be adopted in this approach, a win–lose fight became inevitable, with the manager ultimately forcing his preferred solution.

Volkema shows that problem formulations vary along a continuum from narrow to broad. For the Creativity Development Committee, the formulation, "Selection of Tom's procedure for the project teams," would be the narrowest scope possible because it focuses on a single solution and specifies what must be done. The alternative problem formulation, "Selection of the best possible procedure for making decisions in the research meetings," is broader than the first. Note that the second formulation admits a greater number of possible solutions than the first because it does not specify which procedure should be chosen and opens up a range of possibilities. The second formulation also focuses attention on a different set of actions than does the first. With the first formulation, parties are likely to focus on how they can get project teams to like Tom's procedure. With the second, they are likely to concentrate on searching for alternative procedures and choosing one.

A still broader problem formulation than the second would be: "Selection of the best possible procedures that can be used by the teams." Broader still is: "To make the best possible decisions in the project teams." Both of these formulations open up a wider range of possibilities and imply different actions than do the first two (indeed, the fourth opens up the possibility of discarding the procedures altogether, if members agree it is impossible to find a good one).

Volkema argues that some levels of formulation promote more creative and effective solutions than others. Exactly which formulations are best varies depending on the parties, the nature of the conflict, the surrounding environment, and other factors. In general, it is difficult to identify the best formulations. However, this chapter's earlier discussion of trained incapacities suggests one way to identify which formulations are not desirable— namely, those that promote trained incapacities.

Identification of the problem formulations being used in a conflict is a complex process. For one thing, problems are not always explicitly stated. Sometimes, in fact, people consciously avoid clear problem statements in an attempt to keep conflicts suppressed. In such cases, problem definitions can be inferred by listening to discussions. Figuring out the definition is fairly easy once one is familiar with some examples of problem formulations. An additional complication is introduced by the fact that problem formulations may change as the group works on an issue. In the Creativity Development Committee (Case 5.3), the problem was initially "selection of the best possible decision-making procedure for the project teams," but over time it shifted to "should we adopt the manager's preference?" which implied confrontation. Clearly, these shifts reflect significant occurrences in the conflict and changes in the relationships among members. Indeed, several researchers have proposed that decision making is nothing more than a series of redefinitions and reconceptualizations of problems leading gradually toward narrow solution statements (Lyles & Mitroff, 1980; Poole, 1983). It is important to be sensitive to these shifts and their implications for the direction conflict takes.

The PPE Technique has two basic parts. The first is a format for stating the problem: an infinitive + an object + a qualifier. For example, if the problem is presently thought to be "how to convince the residents of a neighborhood that a sidewalk should be installed along their block," the problem might be stated as:

to convince neighbors that a sidewalk is needed

Infinitive + Object + Qualifier

This statement of the problem then serves as the basis for brainstorming a set of possible solutions (see Table 8.1 for possible solutions associated with this formulation of the problem).

The second part of PPE expands the first problem statement by reformulating it, allowing for a second round of brainstorming that generates a set of different solutions. Reformulation is done by asking: What are we trying to accomplish by this?

- *We want* (most recent formulation) . . . to convince neighbors that a sidewalk is needed.
- *In order to* (reformulation) . . . get neighbors to pay for the sidewalk installation.

The group might decide it wants to convince neighbors that a sidewalk *is needed* in order to get neighbors *to pay* for sidewalk installation. This process is then repeated to generate a whole set of formulations and solutions (see Table 8.1). Comparison of the levels can enable parties to recognize the narrowness in their thinking and the trained incapacities that may be operating. By making parties aware of different formulations, PPE can disclose the values and assumptions underlying a current way of looking at a problem and suggest innovative viewpoints.

TABLE 8.1 *A Hierarchy of Expanded Problem Statements*

Problem Statements	Possible Solutions
To convince neighbors that a sidewalk is needed (What are we trying to accomplish by this?)	Gather data; hold public hearings; go door to door
To get neighbors to pay for sidewalk installation (What are we trying to accomplish by this?)	Go to the Transportation Department; sue neighbors; introduce a resolution at City or Town Hall
To get a sidewalk installed (What are we trying to accomplish by this?)	Pay for sidewalk yourself; install sidewalk yourself
To make the area where a sidewalk would go passable (What are we trying to accomplish by this?)	Level off area; build walkway
To make pedestrian traffic safe	Reroute auto traffic; partition off part of street; stop auto traffic for pedestrians; put up caution signs for autos

The PPE technique can also be used when the problem in question is "about" a relationship or group itself rather than about something people might do. For example, in the Riverdale Halfway House (Case 7.2, page 213), the problem was formulated as how "to resolve the animosities between George and Carole." PPE might lead to other formulations conducive to constructive dialogue, such as how "to clarify lines of authority at Riverdale" or how "to create a more supportive climate at Riverdale." In both cases these broader reformulations change the focus of the problem from Carole and George to the group as a whole and provide a common problem that the entire group can work on.

PPE tries to jolt people out of their well-worn, unreflective channels and encourages them to consider new ideas. As Chapter 6 noted, a surprising or startling move can also do this. A former chair of the board of General Motors is reputed to have said during a particularly docile meeting, "Well, it appears as if we're all in agreement. Why don't we all try to work up some conflicts over the weekend so when we come back on Monday we'll be able to think this proposal through thoroughly?" The chair's statement was designed to surprise the other members and jolt them out of their premature agreement. When members return to their task they may well do so with greater concentration and renewed vigor.

A second technique useful for conflict management is to find a common goal that both parties value, commonly called a *superordinate goal*. The Robber's Cave experiment of Sherif and associates was one of the first studies of this technique (Sherif, Harvey, White, Hood, & Sherif, 1961). They created two opposing groups of summer campers, the Bulldogs and the Red Devils. When the two groups had to work together on the common goal of solving several emergencies, between-group conflict was reduced. Numerous subsequent studies have supported the utility of superordinate goals (Hunger & Stern, 1976; Pruitt & Rubin, 1986; Schofield & Euric-Fulcer, 2003). To be effective, the goal must have high appeal for both parties and accomplishing it must be beyond the capabilities of any single party. In addition, competition and conflict among parties over other issues must be set aside. So a couple who often argues about how much to spend on redecorating their house may pull together when threatened by a financial crisis. The common goal of weathering the storm overcomes their perceived differences. As this example illustrates, a superordinate goal need not be something both parties want; it can also be something they want to avoid or a common enemy. From time immemorial, political leaders have used the perception of threats from without to unite factionalized nations.

The superordinate goal tactic is one of the most reliable integrative tactics, but it does not work under all circumstances. If the parties fail to attain the superordinate goal, the goal may lose its attractiveness and competition will ensue (Hunger & Stern, 1976; Worchel, Anderoli, & Folger, 1977). Given their previous conflict, the parties are likely to blame each other for the failure. Then too, finding a superordinate goal does not resolve a preexisting conflict, as the example of our redecorating couple shows. Once the couple is in the clear again, or if they fail to get out of their financial crisis, bickering over redecorating could easily resurface.

The tactic will also fail if each party does not have a clear and distinct role in attaining the superordinate goal (Deschamps & Brown, 1983). They must have a clear idea of how their efforts fit together or they may lose their sense of identity. If this happens parties are less likely to be attracted to cooperating with each other. It is also worth noting that parties may have trouble discovering or recognizing superordinate goals when hostilities run high. A "cooling off" period is often necessary before the superordinate goal can be used to promote cooperation (See Case 8.1).

CASE 8.1 • *The Psychological Evaluation Unit*

Imagine yourself as Laura, one of the psychiatrists: How might the climate of this group affect the way you engage in conflict?

The Psychological Evaluation Unit at a large hospital was composed of three psychiatrists, a psychologist, and two social workers. The unit was purposely designed as a multidisciplinary cross section, with competent professionals from all "helping" areas: psychiatry, psychology, and social work. Each profession had to exert its influence if the unit is to function properly. The unit emphasized a high level of professionalism for its members and, because of this, presentation of oneself as a professional was very important. The unit was charged with diagnosing disturbed patients and with running a training program for newly graduated doctors interning at the hospital.

The unit was created at a time of budget surplus for the hospital. The services it provided were originally provided by staff psychiatrists, but the unit was created to consolidate diagnostic techniques and leave the staff psychiatrists free for therapy. However, there has been a budget crunch set in the last year and the hospital board was looking for services and units to cut. Because the evaluation unit was new, it was high on the list of departments to be scrutinized. Members were worried about the unit's survival and most decisions were made with an eye toward making the unit look good, (or, at least, not look questionable) to outside observers.

The psychiatrist who headed the committee, Jerry, chaired most meetings and represented the unit in the hospital bureaucracy. He was a "take-charge" person, and the psychologist and social workers were intimidated by his forceful style. He tried to be open, but, partly due to his strength and partly due to uncertainty about their status in the unit, the other three had relatively little input in group discussions. The other two psychiatrists, Alberto and Laura, sometimes provided a balance, but they were not as aggressive as Jerry and therefore tended to be overshadowed. Alberto and Laura were aware of Jerry's take-charge tendencies and had tried to encourage the psychologist, Paul, and the social workers, Megan and Liu to speak up. However, all tended to hang back in the face of Jerry's initiatives.

Jerry introduced the issue at hand: The unit was evaluating a psychiatric intern who had repeatedly missed his turns of duty at evaluation clinics. Jerry gave a brief history of the intern's problems and summarized his attempts to talk to the intern. In particular, Jerry asked the intern what a proper attendance rate should be. The intern ventured a ten percent absentee rate as an adequate figure. Jerry introduced this figure as a standard and then asked the others, "What do you think?" The psychologist and one social worker, Megan, asked what the intern's excuse is, and Jerry responded with a lengthy answer detailing the excuses and offering commentary on them.

Laura then spoke, arguing that an absence rate of one day every two months is more than enough. Megan, one of the two social workers, jumped in, and this exchange followed:

Megan: You shouldn't even give him that *(once every two months)* . . . I mean, if an emergency comes up that's one thing. If you say you're gonna get off . . .

Jerry: *(interrupting)* This is not . . . This is not time that we expect him to take. This is how often we expect emergencies to occur.

Megan: But he's going to interpret it as if we're gonna give him a day or two every two months if we say it.

Jerry: *(shaking his head as Megan speaks and speaking immediately on her last word)* It depends on how we want to say it, but what we had in mind was, if you look at how often he's here or not here—it's sort of a gross way to do an evaluation, but it's one possibility. And one could say, "If emergencies come up with more frequency, you need more time to attend to your emergencies, and we could make an exception." How you word it might vary, but I think what we need is some kind of sense for what's tolerable.

(continued)

CASE 8.1 Continued

Liu: *(the other social worker)* What about the things he has done when he shows up— expectations as far as staying or leaving early? Which is . . . I think, one of many things. After his last patients, five or ten minutes later he's gone. And yesterday that happened and five minutes later we had a walk-in who really needed medical help, and I was the only one there and I could have used (help) . . . that was, you know, it was like 11:15 and he didn't show up. Don't we expect the interns to check to see if there are any walk-ins before they leave?

Jerry: *(interrupting)* We can talk about that as another issue.

Liu: *(interrupting)* Well, it's another expectation that needs to be addressed.

At this point Laura clarified her position on the intern's attendance, and the issue raised by Frank was dropped. Laura and Jerry then pursued a long exchange in which they tried to define an acceptable level of participation for interns. Here is an excerpt from that exchange to give you an idea of its tone.

Laura: *(after a long speech)* . . . to vanish from sight (when patients need him), I just don't find that acceptable. *(pause)*

Jerry: On the other hand, if it's 11:15, and you don't have any patients . . .

Laura: *(interrupting)* That's a different issue.

Jerry: We don't have to provide any options. We can say that we recognize that over a year and a half your participation has been mitigated because of unusual circumstances, and that's the end. I mean, we don't have to make a deal at all.

As the discussion progressed, they tried to set an acceptable number of absences for the intern. After some discussion, the group determined that setting an ideal attendance rate was impossible. Rather, members decided to talk to the intern in order to make him aware of the problem and then to reevaluate the situation in two months. Throughout this process Jerry moderated the discussion. The following are excerpts from the discussion:

Laura: I guess I agree. I want to give him time off . . . but if he's gonna be there, then he has to be there.

Jerry: But we have to come up with some kind of sense that if he exceeds we have to say "thank you, but no thank you."

Laura: I'd say more than once in two months, or maybe twice in two months more than an hour late. Nobody else does that . . . that I know of . . . in terms of missing times.

Megan: *(talking over Laura's last sentences)* Rather than just specifically making a case for him, maybe we should decide what's appropriate—what the expectations are for all the residents.

Jerry: (interrupting) I think we are. I think you're right that the kind of sense we're generating is not necessarily specific. . . . It turns out that he's going to be the one for whom it's an issue . . . and we also have to acknowledge that there will be individual circumstances that . . . change. We may need to face that. But I need to have some type of sense of what we expect of him and at what point we should acknowledge that he should or should not participate. And one way—it's sort of simple and artificial—is to do attendance, to say "How many hours are you late? How many times are you late?" That avoids in part coming to grips with, you know, an overall kind of evaluation, and maybe we don't want to use a numerical scale. I'm open to lots of different suggestions. The one that I wasn't willing to accept was that if others in the subspecialties used their own internal sets I wasn't going to ask them to change (such as, other departments could evaluate the intern according to their own criteria).

Alberto: I think there's a double-barreled threat *(from the intern's absences)*. Dr. Jacobs

(continued)

CASE 8.1   Continued

(director of the hospital) is coming and in casual conversation says *(the intern)* is OK when he's here, but he's never here, then clearly that's another, that's a threat . . .

Jerry: *(summarizing the group's decision)* I'm comfortable if what the group wants to do, then, is take it back to (the intern) and say we have a set of expectations that include your participation—your full participation—in this program. That we will reassess our impression of that participation—and we hope you will assess it—on a monthly basis or something and that if we need to—because there's some question of whether or not your participation is complete—then we'll meet and we'll need to talk about it.

Discussion Questions:

- Did this group go through the two stages of the normative model, differentiation and integration?
- Did this group follow the principles for promoting collaboration discussed in this chapter?
- How might the group have done things differently if they had followed the conflict management procedure outlined above?
- Would Problem-Purpose Expansion be useful for this group? Why or why not?
- Compare this case to the Women's Hotline Case (Case I.1a and b, pages 2 and 3). Which case exhibited more effective conflict management?

8.5 Summary and Review

How does the normative model from Chapter 1 relate to conflict management?

The normative model posits that for effective conflict management the conflict process must go through stages of differentiation and integration. The normative model serves as the basic pattern for conflict management: parties must first differentiate without falling into spiraling escalation or rigid avoidance, then they must make a transition from differentiation into integration, and finally they must engage in collaborative problem-solving.

Is competing necessarily counterproductive in conflict management?

Handled properly and in moderation, competing can be quite useful. It can be used to signal priorities and issues and it can be used to demonstrate a party's strength and resolve, thus indicating that the conflict cannot be solved by force. This can, in turn, promote a move toward more positive approaches to conflict, such as collaborating.

What are some useful techniques for navigating differentiation?

During differentiation there is a danger that spiraling escalation or rigid avoidance will develop. One way to counteract these tendencies is to be careful to frame problems or issues in a positive, non-confrontational manner. We introduced a formula for doing so. Second, adopting a constructive attitude toward conflict will help. We outlined a number of beliefs that make up this attitude. Finally, experimental integration can be used to test the waters as to whether the other party is open to shifting to integration. Experimental integration involves offering someone safe concessions that are meaningful to him or her without putting the party in danger. The other party's response to this concession can then be observed for signs that the other is interested in moving in a productive direction. Experimental integration is premised on the assumption that parties often incorrectly assume that the other is competitive, when both want to collaborate. It is therefore one way of overcoming attribution problems in conflict situations. GRIT and reformed sinner are two specific processes for experimental integration.

How does the Conflict Management Procedure help in managing conflict?

The Conflict Management Procedure outlines five steps for managing conflict. It is designed to help parties avoid potential problems by structuring discussion so they do not consider solutions until they understand the problem. The procedure attempts to keep parties' minds open to the problem rather than focused on particular resolutions. Premature focus on solutions often blinds us to important aspects of the conflict and may lead to less effective resolutions. It also asks parties to develop a vision of a future without conflict to given them something positive to work toward. The procedure encourages parties to explore a range of options when considering resolutions to the conflict and to evaluate each option thoroughly. During this process of generating and evaluating options, parties often accidentally stumble onto integrative solutions they would not otherwise have considered. This process may also produce a different view of the conflict, leading parties to recycle to earlier steps to redefine or reanalyze their problem.

Why is it important to consider feelings when working with conflicts?

There is a tendency in the U.S. culture to assume that emotions get in the way of clear, rational thinking. In fact, acknowledging and coming to terms with feelings about the conflict is often essential in moving forward toward a workable resolution. This is why Filley suggests that the initial steps of conflict management must surface and help parties understand one anothers' emotional reactions to the conflict.

What is the Problem–Purpose Expansion Technique?

The Problem–Purpose Expansion Technique is designed to help parties find different ways to frame conflicts. It asks them to consider their goals and how a goal at one level relates to goals at higher or lower levels. Higher-level goals indicate *why* we are trying to do something, whereas lower-level goals indicate *what* we have to do to achieve our immediate goal. By moving up and down this goal ladder, we often see the conflict differently. These insights can help us reframe the conflict in a productive way.

How do superordinate goals contribute to integration?

One classic integrative tactic is to find a superordinate goal that both parties value. If managing the conflict can be connected to this goal, parties often work together to attain it and to achieve an integrative resolution.

8.6 Conclusion

In one sense, people involved in a conflict are always intervening in their own interactions. Each move or response directs interaction, at least for the moment. Not all moves contribute to conflict management, however. To work with the conflict, parties must diagnose the forces that are pushing the conflict in a destructive direction and develop the ability to act in a way that mitigates those forces. Conflict management is difficult because parties may not see the destructive turn interaction has taken until repetitive patterns are firmly in place. Moreover, when someone who is involved in a conflict attempts to alter interaction with the interests of all in mind, motives can be questioned and moves misinterpreted.

Despite formidable obstacles, there are a number of ways in which parties can diagnose their conflicts and act to redirect them. Previous chapters discussed how people can change a group's climate, assess power differentials and develop ways to deal with power imbalances, facilitate face-saving, and select styles that are appropriate for the situation and move the conflict in productive directions. This chapter focused on processes for collaborating.

We do not mean to present the procedures discussed in this chapter as pat, surefire solutions because conflicts simply have too many variables. It is a mistake to apply any formula strictly and without careful consideration; however, the techniques and procedures provided here do give general guidelines that can be useful in conflict management.

Although these and other procedures can be quite valuable, it is important to remember that they, too, can become trained incapacities. None of these procedures is appropriate under all conditions, and all must be tailored to fit specific situations. So be ready to improvise when you try to manage your conflicts.

9

Third-Party Intervention

Chapter 1 noted that conflict interaction tends to be self-perpetuating. This characteristic of conflict has important implications for understanding how patterns of interaction develop, how escalation cycles gain momentum, and how constructive or destructive climates are sustained. This property is also important in understanding why people who are not parties in a conflict intervene in ongoing disputes. The self-perpetuating nature of moves and countermoves, actions and reactions, can stifle parties' attempts at self-regulation of conflict, even when they try assiduously to track or alter these patterns. Moreover, trained incapacities can prevent parties from even recognizing the problems in their interaction patterns or detract from parties' efforts at finding acceptable solutions to real problems. An outsider has some distance from a conflict and can often see persistent cycles and ways of altering them. By necessity, the mere entry of a third party alters a conflict, if for no other reason than that the intervenor's moves become part of the unfolding interaction.

The term *third-party intervention* connotes a wide range of activities that span diverse conflict contexts, from the spontaneous attempts of parents to settle conflicts between siblings, to the carefully planned attempts to mediate the release of hostages across international borders. Third parties may be fact-finders, process consultants, go-betweens, ombudspersons, clergy, managers, conciliators, mediators, group facilitators, attorneys, friends of the court, arbitrators, or government diplomats. As this list suggests, third parties enact different roles and have different responsibilities in different conflict settings.

Over the past twenty years, there has been increasing interest in using a variety of third-party roles in diverse conflict settings (Donohue, 2006). For example, more than 300 community dispute–resolution programs have been established in the United States in recent years. These programs often use trained volunteers to intervene in neighborhood, small claims, or landlord–tenant disputes. In the past, if these cases were severe enough, they might end up in court. In many cases, conflicts simply festered because the parties had no recourse outside the courts to help resolve them (Merry, 1979; Marks, Johnson, & Szonton, 1984; Folger, 1991). In divorce cases, mediators are now used in many states to try to settle issues related to child custody or jointly owned property rather than having a judge impose a decision about such matters (Bush & Pope, 2004; Nichols, 2006).

In business environments, a market has developed for dispute-resolution services that can provide out-of-court settlements for a wide range of conflicts (Singer, 1990). In addition, changes in employer–employee relationships have brought changes in third-party roles within organizations. Businesses, medical facilities, and educational institutions have developed intervention roles, such as hearing officers, ombudspersons, and client representatives, to address conflicts "in-house." Middle managers have increasingly been viewed as dispute resolvers who intervene in conflicts among subordinates or between department members.

This chapter examines how third parties influence the course of conflict. No matter what intervention they perform, the moves third parties make can be examined in light of their impact on parties' conflict interaction. This chapter provides a framework for thinking about and analyzing conflict interaction as influenced by third-party intervenors.

This analysis of third-party intervention is organized around the four conflict interaction properties introduced in Chapter 1. Although conflict interaction is often quite different when a third party is involved, it is still shaped by such factors as moves and countermoves, exertion of power, self-perpetuating momentum, episodic structure, predictable themes, and relational influences. Each of the properties points to important and unique features of third-party intervention and its impact on the conflict. This chapter examines how these four properties help describe and explain the effects of third-party involvement in conflict.

9.1 Property 1: Conflict Interaction Is Constituted and Sustained by Moves and Countermoves During Interaction

When third parties intervene in conflicts, they become active participants in the parties' interaction. Third parties make moves—initiatives that spark reactions and launch sequences of interaction. They also respond with countermoves—reactions to disputants' moves. In this sense, the third party is as vulnerable to the moment-to-moment influences of action and reaction as the disputing parties themselves. Although the conflict issues may be of more (or different) consequence for the parties than the intervenor, the conflict interaction has consequences for both: The interaction emerges as the product of the third party's and disputants' actions, it has moment-to-moment effects on the third party's moves, it shapes the third party's interpretations of unfolding events, and it has relational consequences for the intervenor.

The moves a third party makes clearly influence the conflict interaction. What gives third parties the ability to shape conflict? What powers are available to any particular intervenor? Given a third party's available power, what influences the moves he or she actually makes? To understand how third-party influence occurs, it is important to understand that the potential for third-party influence stems from two primary sources: the third party's mandate—the ascribed source of power the intervenor holds—and the third party's responsiveness to the unfolding conflict interaction among the parties.

9.1.1 Third-Party Mandate

Any move a third party makes is rooted in the power he or she is able or willing to exert. In this sense, the basis of third-party moves is identical to that of the disputing parties. However, the sources of third-party power are often quite different from those held by the disputants. This is because the type of interdependence between third parties and disputants is very different from what defines the disputants, relationships. Disputants are dependent on intervenors for such functions as structuring the interaction, reducing hostilities, and providing expertise on specific substantive or legal issues. These sources of dependency stem from the authority or *mandate* given to the third party by the disputants (Auvine et al., 1977; Shubert & Folger, 1986; Kaufman & Duncan, 1989).

Like the forms of power discussed in Chapter 4, the third party's mandate is fundamentally relational: It is power endorsed by the disputing parties and thereby gives the intervenor certain resources that can be drawn from to control the interaction and substantive issues. If endorsement of the mandate is withdrawn or questioned, the ability of the third party to act is altered or curtailed (Merry & Silbey, 1984). Of course, some third-party mandates, such as those given to judges, stem from broadly based endorsements that societies or large groups of people provide. Disputing parties are sometimes under strong pressures to endorse third-party mandates when they are so widely accepted. This pressure often occurs, for example, when diplomats from a super-power intervene in international conflicts between less powerful countries or ethnic groups (Crocker, Hampson, & Aall, 2004).

A third party's mandate—as an endorsed basis of power—can stem from formal or informal sources (Kaufman & Duncan, 1989). Many third-party roles carry *formal endorsements,* which authorize certain types of interventions in specific conflict arenas. Such roles are typically established by law, societal traditions, or rules of an organization. The adjudicative role that judges play in legal contexts and the ombudsperson role employed to settle disputes within organizations are examples of formally defined third-party mandates (Kolb, 1987 & 1989; Rowe, 1987).

Other third-party mandates are granted *informally,* usually via the implicit expectations people have about who can appropriately intervene in conflicts. These informal mandates are often the result of resources the third party holds, such as specialized knowledge or skill in intervening, or of the third party's relationship to the disputants. Informal mandates are given to a wide range of individuals, including managers in organizations, parents or older siblings in families, group members who are skillful at framing problems, community leaders, and clergy. Informal mandates are also held by some interveners who work in ethno-political conflicts in international settings such as leaders of religious or social organizations who intervene in violent conflicts (Chigas, 2005). When third-party mandates are informal and hence less clearly specified, questions may arise about the appropriateness of or limits on intervention. In such cases, the nature of the third party's mandate may require explicit negotiation among the parties in order for the intervention to proceed.

Third-party mandates can carry with them a range of possible powers to conflict interaction. Specifically, three forms of third-party influence can be distinguished: process control, content control, and motivational control (Sheppard, 1984).

Process Control.   Process control refers to the third party's ability to organize or structure the procedures that disputants follow during interaction. *Process control* includes such diverse activities as arranging when and where the parties should meet, setting time limits on speaking turns or intervention sessions, establishing how decisions will be made, setting rules for decorum and specifying moves the third party will enact to support the conflict (Kraybill, 2004). Third parties whose mandates are formally established often impose clearly specified forms of process control, which can be stated explicitly to the parties at the outset. Process control is often less clearly specified when a third party's mandate emerges informally. Frequently, less forethought is given to the procedural rules, which are more likely to emerge during intervention than be stated initially. For example, a group member who is trying to intervene in a conflict among other members may ask that each person speak in turn rather than allowing a free-for-all to escalate.

Content Control.   Third parties also vary in the amount of content control they have in the dispute. *Content control* refers to the third party's influence over the arguments and substantive positions taken by the parties or over the terms parties accept as a final agreement. Third parties differ in their ability or willingness to refute or attack specific points made by the parties; interpret, frame, or add issues; present additional information relevant to the topics under discussion; or suggest or impose the terms that the parties adopt as an agreement or solution.

For some third-party mandates, the amount of control over outcomes is the most important defining feature of the intervention. Based on these we can distinguish three different forms of intervention, which differ in numerous ways but whose character stems primarily from the degree of control a third party has over the outcomes of a conflict:

- *Arbitrators* have clear control over the terms of a final agreement. An *arbitrator* is given authority to hear all sides of a case, discuss it with each party, and then make a final decision on how the dispute will be settled, much like the judge in a legal case. In most cases, the parties are compelled by law or prior agreement to enact the terms an arbitrator imposes. One less widely used form of arbitration is called *nonbinding arbitration*. In this form of arbitration, the third party follows the same general process, but the arbitrator's decision is not one the parties are bound by law or prior agreement to accept. Rather, the arbitrator's decision is a neutral opinion that the parties can consider and that might have an influence on the parties' continued negotiation.

    An arbitrator often has special background knowledge that enables him or her to grapple with the specific issues underlying the conflict. For example, arbitrators generally are used for highly technical disputes, such as labor contracts, which require knowledge of both economics and labor law. Arbitrators can also be used in "hopeless" cases for which a decision must be made but repeated attempts to settle have proved impossible or in difficult public conflicts that jeopardize community welfare (e.g., labor management conflicts in schools or hospitals).

- Less authority over settlement terms is given to *mediators*. Mediators are third parties who facilitate parties' interaction. The key characteristic of mediation is that final resolution rests with the parties themselves. Mediators intervene mostly by allowing the parties to clarify their choices, resources, and decision points and by recognizing each other's perspectives (Bush & Folger, 2005).

For example, mediators frequently intervene in environmental disputes (Mernitz, 1980; Riesel, 1985; Singer, 1990; Crowfoot & Wondolleck, 1990). In these types of disputes, a number of parties are involved, such as government representatives, citizens, and industry spokespeople. The objective is to help diverse parties negotiate an acceptable resolution to issues such as land use, watershed preservation, or highway construction.

Although mediators have traditionally been used in environmental and labor disputes, over the last three decades they have been employed in a wider array of contexts. Volunteer or professionally trained mediators now attempt to assist parties in reaching agreements in community and neighborhood disputes, student conflicts, landlord–tenant conflicts, small claims issues, consumer and business disputes, divorce and child custody cases, and international peacemaking efforts (Folberg & Taylor, 1984; Beer, 1986; Stulberg, 1987; Haynes & Haynes, 1989; Duffy, Grosch, & Olezak, 1991; Jones & Brinkman, 1994; Garcia, 2000; Bercovitch & Kadayifci, 2002; Lederach, 2005).

Although there are a range of mediator styles and differences in how willing mediators are to risk influencing outcomes, the important point to note here is that mediators have no explicit mandate to make or implement choices for the parties. They do, however, have a mandate to support the deliberation of choices the parties discuss during an intervention and sometimes point disputing parties toward specific outcomes. It is not uncommon, for example, for divorce mediators to offer suggestions or solutions that the parties have not thought of, based on solutions the mediator has seen work for other couples (Lemmon, 1985).

Some mediators go further and actually offer evaluations of parties' positions or choices in an effort to achieve what they consider a fair or just outcome or consciously or inadvertently promote certain substantive choices over others (Folger & Bernard, 1985; Shailor, 1994; Schwerin, 1995; Noll, 2003). For example, a divorce mediator may push for an agreement that gives one spouse greater financial autonomy once the marriage is dissolved. Such a move is often controversial because it may overstep the bounds of a mediator's mandate or be seen as a potential breach of neutrality (Bernard, Folger, Weingarten, & Zumeta, 1984). Pushing for financial autonomy for one spouse may cause the other spouse to view the mediator as biased. The mediator, on the other hand, may believe the spouse's autonomy will contribute to a more workable settlement. In a similar vein of mediator directiveness, ethno-political conflict mediators have been found to influence the direction of the conflict by offering external incentives for the parties or issuing ultimatums to them (Bercovitch, 2005).

- Even less involvement with settlement terms is enacted by third-party *facilitators* or *conciliators.* Facilitators and conciliators are process experts who have neither extensive expertise related to the issues under discussion nor the power to make a final decision (Schwarz, 2002; Lieberman, Baker, & Fraser, 2005). They are often brought in when the parties believe they can reach a resolution through direct negotiations, but need help managing the process.

Although the two roles are quite similar, the labels "facilitator" and "conciliator" are used to describe third parties who intervene in somewhat different settings. The *facilitator* label is used most often to describe a third party who intervenes in ongoing decision-making groups such as management teams, boards of directors, or department staff. The *conciliator* label is used to describe third parties who intervene in multiparty disputes among recognizable adversaries such as those involved in public policy disputes, environmental conflicts, or race-related issues.

Facilitators or conciliators offer process expertise but are not at the "center" of the interaction. They can, nonetheless, be an active force directing the conflict. However, all the impetus for substantive movement—proposals, compromises, changes in position—arises from the parties themselves. Facilitation and conciliation differ from arbitration or mediation not because they are more passive forms of intervention, but because they carry a narrower range of possible involvement with substantive issues. The third party called into the Riverdale Halfway House (Case 6.1, page 178) was a facilitator. He chaired several meetings at which members tried to talk out their problems and offered assistance in clarifying needs and proposals, but he did not try to direct the discussion in any forceful or intrusive way.

An important consideration in determining the degree of process and content control to exert is how fair parties perceive the intervention to be. Thibaut and Walker (1975) argue that perceived fairness of intervention styles varies according to the nature of the dispute. In disputes involving highly intense conflict, and high degrees of interdependence among parties, arbitration (high process and content control) is often perceived as the fairest approach (Sheppard, Saunders, & Minton, 1988). On the other hand, for conflicts that are less intense, mediation, with its lower degree of control, is perceived as more useful. Arbitration was also found to be preferred in disputes for which a settlement seemed very difficult to attain, whereas mediation was preferred for cases where a settlement seemed possible (Heuer & Penrod, 1986). Finally, other things being equal, participants who have some say in the selection of the third-party role generally seem to perceive the intervention to be fairer than those who do not (Sheppard et al., 1988).

Motivational Control. Besides process and content control, third-party mandates also differ in the motivational control they grant to the intervenor. *Motivational control* refers to the degree to which the third party can induce parties to perform desired actions. Some informal third-party intervenors, such as parents or managers, control incentives that can influence the parties and ultimately the outcomes of a dispute. Managers, for example, can indicate that they might reallocate or demote a recalcitrant employee if he or she does not address an ongoing dispute with a co-worker. In an attempt to encourage movement, a labor mediator may indicate that he or she is going to tell the press that one side in a dispute is making unreasonable demands (Sheppard, 1984). An international mediator might threaten to withdraw economic resources from the countries in conflict if they do not agree to stop violent attacks (Crocker, Hampson, & Aall, 2004). Many third parties, including parents, clergy, and teachers, have a significant motivational influence over disputants.

9.1.2 Responsiveness to Emerging Interaction

The third party's mandate provides the broad framework of endorsed powers, the possible bases third parties can draw on in making interventions. However, a third-party mandate only delimits the range of possible moves perceived to be appropriate or expected. It does not entirely account for the moves a third party actually makes in the interaction or the timing of those moves. Even though a third party is involved, the conflict interaction still unfolds turn-by-turn and is subject to all the momentary forces—such as defensiveness cycles, power tactics, immediate face threats—at play in any emergent interaction. Third-party moves can start from some formally or informally defined sense of what the nature of the intervention will be and what role the third party will adopt, but any given act is inevitably responsive: It is part of the stream of interaction and is, in a fundamental sense, a product of it.

In many discussions of third-party intervention and dispute processing there has been an increasing recognition of the emergent nature of conflict intervention processes (Felstiner, Abel, & Sarat, 1980–1981; Mather & Yngvesson, 1980–1981; Sarat, 1988). Theorists and critics have attempted to debunk what they see as a static image of disputes, dispute processing, and third-party intervention. This static image depicts disputes as fixed entities that are brought to third parties and are then acted on by intervenors to achieve some goal, such as reaching a settlement or handing down a decision. The conflict that the parties bring to the table is seen as relatively unchanged as the dispute moves through the intervention process. This image also implies that third parties and the intervention process remain unaffected by the dispute being addressed.

The critics of this image say that it is misleading and fails to capture all the dynamics—the elements of change and influence—in third-party interventions. They would replace this image with a less static conception—one that casts disputes and third-party processes as much more fluid and malleable activities. It has been argued, for example, that "disputes, even after they emerge and are articulated, are indeterminate. They do not exist in fixed form prior to the application of particular dispute processing techniques; they are instead constituted and transformed as they are processed" (Sarat, 1988, p. 708). In this view, the very act of presenting a dispute to a third party can reframe the conflict.

Several researchers have demonstrated how disputes are presented to intervenors in ways that "fit" the third parties' modes of intervention (Mather & Yngvesson, 1980–1981; Merry & Silbey, 1984; Conley & O'Barr, 1990). Courtroom disputants might, for instance, narrow the issues in a conflict, simplifying a complex history of events, injuries, and relationship struggles so that a judge can impose or suggest readily available settlement terms, such as monetary awards. In the organizational context, employees sometimes select issues and define disputes in ways that will increase the likelihood that they will be addressed by their managers (Kolb, 1986; Antes, Folger, & DellaNoce, 2001). Other research suggests that mediators in several conflict contexts influence the parties' views of the issues and may even take a strong hand in shaping attitudes toward possible settlement terms (Greatbatch & Dingwall, 1989; Lam, Rifkin, & Townley, 1989; Bush & Folger, 1994). In such cases, key dispute elements—how parties view the issues, what they think is reasonable or worth fighting for, what they are willing to agree to—are transformed as the intervention occurs.

Just as disputes are influenced by a third party and the intervention process, so too are third parties influenced by the disputes, the parties, and the context of intervention. In this more dynamic view of intervention, third parties are not unresponsive either. Because they are part and parcel of the interaction, they constantly adapt to contingencies that arise as interventions unfold.

To understand how third parties and intervention forums adapt to cases and disputing parties, third-party mandates must be seen as dynamic. For many third-party roles, even those for which the mandate is relatively clear, there is considerable leeway in the amount of process, content, or motivational control exerted in any given intervention. In practice, third parties acting as arbitrators, mediators, facilitators, or ombudsperson engage in a wide range of moves that often blur their mandates and can erode any hard-and-fast distinctions among the various forms of intervention. Parties who have clear arbitrative powers, such as judges or labor arbitrators, sometimes act as mediators (Wall & Rude, 1989; Phillips, 1990). Judges in divorce and custody cases, for example, often attempt to construct settlements rather than impose them. They may try to assess what terms are acceptable for both parties, encourage compromise, and involve parties in creating viable options.

There are also forms of arbitration that build in a certain degree of disputant control over the outcome. In "last-offer–best-offer" arbitration, the arbitrator decides a settlement for a dispute by having each party submit their last best offer and then chooses from among these options (Feuille, 1979). The decision of the arbitrator is limited to one of the settlement terms suggested by the parties. In this form of arbitration, the parties have somewhat more control over the substantive outcome of a final settlement than they would in "stricter" forms of arbitration because the options for settlement are determined by what they put forth.

In the same vein, mediators' actual behaviors during interventions have been found to vary considerably. Several different studies of mediators in diverse contexts paint a diverse picture of what mediators actually do in practice; at times, this picture blurs the line between mediators and arbitrators (Oberman, 2005; Davidheiser, 2006). Descriptive studies of labor mediation suggest that mediators adopt quite different styles of intervention (Kolb, 1983; Shapiro, Drieghe, & Brett, 1985). Some labor mediators have been characterized as *deal-makers* because they take an active role in shaping the substantive issues, put pressures on parties to move, and spend considerable time caucusing with each side in an active attempt to forge a deal (Kolb, 1983). *Orchestrators* take a different approach to mediation. This is a less impositional style in which mediators orchestrate the negotiations among the parties, setting up processes that allow them to keep talking and leaving substantive issues more directly under the disputants' control.

Differences have been found in intervention styles in other arenas of mediation as well (Noll, 2003; Donohue, 2006). Studies of those who intervene in community, neighborhood, and small claims disputes suggest that mediators adopt bargaining and therapeutic styles of intervention (Silbey & Merry, 1986). In the *bargaining* style, mediators place great emphasis on reaching settlements through control over the interaction and encouraging less direct discussion among the disputants. Caucuses—private discussions between the mediator and one of the parties—are more frequent in this style, as are explicit attempts to narrow issues, to push for compromise, and to synthesize arguments and positions. In the *therapeutic* style, mediators emphasize increasing understanding among the disputants and overcoming relationship problems. Face-to-face contact between the parties is maximized during the intervention, as are attempts to uncover underlying issues and veiled interests. The goal is not simply to reach agreements but to use the intervention as an opportunity to improve communication and to develop a foundation for addressing problems in general.

As might be expected in informally mandated third-party roles, there is as much or more leeway in how the third party intervenes. Studies of managers in organizations suggest, for example, that they also take on a range of roles (Kolb, 1986). In some instances, they adopt an *advisory* role, consulting with one or more of the parties in the dispute and suggesting moves parties might make to help direct a conflict. At other times, the same manager may become more of an *investigator,* collecting facts and assessing the source and nature of the problem. In other conflicts, the manager may become a *restructurer,* dealing with the conflict by moving personnel or reorganizing subunits or chains of command. In still other situations, the manager steps into a *mediative* role, guiding communication among the disputing parties and attempting creative problem-solving.

Given the range of third-party options in both formally and informally mandated third-party interventions, what influences the intervention style and thus the specific moves that third parties make? This is a difficult question to answer because of the range of factors that can influence the third party's moves—from habits individual third parties fall into to specific characteristics and demands of the case and disputing parties.

Third parties adapt to the conflict cases at hand in important ways. Consider Cases 9.1 and 9.2. These cases raise the type of questions about difficult intervention choices that third parties must face when they intervene in various types of conflicts.

These cases suggest that many different factors may influence the general approach and specific intervening moves third parties make. Although all possible contingencies have not been systematically studied, some attempts have been made to examine how third parties decide to intervene.

CASE 9.1 • *Organizational Co-Heads*

A large insurance firm decided to restructure one area of its business. Two separate businesses were being joined into one larger umbrella organization. Each of the separate businesses had been previously headed by fairly senior women, Sarah and Meghan. Both of these women had been with the firm for more than ten years, and they were both seen as highly competent leaders who had run successful businesses of their own. The two women knew each other but had never worked together. The firm felt that by joining the two groups and setting up one organization, the new, larger business unit could capitalize on the strengths of each leader and create strong, cross-client synergies. Sarah and Meghan accepted the co-leadership role with some skepticism but were willing to go along with the firm's vision for their future work. As Sarah put it, "when the firm asks you to do something like this, it is tough to say no without giving it a try."

The way the firm's management launched this reorganization created difficult obstacles from the outset. The firm combined the two business units and announced the co-head structure just before Meghan left for a three-month maternity leave. Meghan knew that this was extremely bad timing but felt she had no choice in the matter. She was adopting a child and although she had given the firm notice about the upcoming maternity leave, she was not able to provide a firm date until the adoption was approved. It was an unfortunate set of circumstances that challenged both women (as well as their employees) as the new business unit was formed.

(continued)

CASE 9.1   Continued

During the three-month period when Meghan was on leave, the two women tried to stay in contact with each other and to make joint decisions via phone and e-mail. At first this worked, but Meghan became increasingly frustrated as she realized that things were inevitably moving ahead—paths in the new business park were being worn—and she was simply not there day-to-day to contribute to the decisions and co-lead the organization. During this time, Meghan was also in contact with some of her former employees who told her that they felt Sarah was moving ahead with the planning without adequate input from their side of the business. Eventually Meghan simply stopped responding to Sarah's e-mails and calls. She felt that Sarah's activity was just skimming the surface and she did not want to appear to be going along with the decisions that were being made. Sarah realized that Meghan was becoming increasingly distant but wasn't exactly sure why. She felt she had no choice but to move forward leading the newly formed business. The result was that as the new business endeavor emerged, Sarah became the de facto day-to-day head of the organization for the first three months.

As Meghan's leave drew to a close, Sarah became increasingly frustrated and worried about what was going to unfold next. She went to the human resource department and told a senior representative that the newly formed business had gotten off to a bad start because the communication between Meghan and her was inadequate during Meghan's leave. She said she was afraid of how things were going to unfold when Meghan

returned to the division; some of Meghan's prior employees had become defensive and divisive and were withholding their support for the new business endeavor.

Human resources contacted an external consultant to come in to help address the conflict between Sarah and Meghan.

Discussion Questions:

Imagine you are the external intervenor in this conflict. How would you respond to the following questions?

- What would be your specific goals for conducting an intervention in this conflict?
- How would you first approach the two women—together or separately?
- What would be the risks of first meeting separately?
- Would you talk to upper management—those who had designed the reorganization—about how the business reorganization was implemented? And, if so, for what purpose?
- Under what conditions, if any, would you talk to the employees who work for Sarah and Meghan in the newly formed business unit?
- As the intervenor in this conflict, would you introduce your own ideas and suggestions about the possible ways to manage this conflict? What factors should you consider before suggesting how these two business leaders could best address the issues?

CASE 9.2 • *The Family Conflict*

Yolanda contacted a community mediation center in her city to obtain help with a difficult family conflict. During the standard intake interview at the mediation program, Yolanda gave the mediator an overview of the nature of the

conflict between herself, her brother Ted, and her sister Kate.

Yolanda said that she and her two siblings are in conflict over the arrangements for the care of their eighty-year old mother, Anna. Until recently,

(continued)

CASE 9.2   Continued

Anna was healthy enough to live on her own in a small condominium that she purchased after her husband died six years ago. Over the past five months, Anna began to have serious health problems. After a stay in the hospital, Anna could not return to her condominium because she could not live alone. Instead, she moved in with Yolanda and her family. This caused great stress for Yolanda because she has three children who are in middle and high school and she works full time. Although she has brought medical personnel into her home to assist with the care of her mother, the amount of attention and time that she needs to devote to her mother is overwhelming. She said she cannot continue to be the primary support person for her mother. She feels that her brother and sister need to step in to help with the care for their aging mother.

She feels her brother, Ted, should invite their mother to live with him. He lives alone and has a large guest bedroom on the first floor of his house, which would be comfortable as a living space for their mother. Ted disagrees and he believes that their mother needs to go to an assisted living residence because he does not feel he would be able to take care of her adequately, especially now that she is ill. He said he is willing to pay half of the costs of an assisted living site, if his two sisters cover the other half. Yolanda believes that her mother does not want to go to an assisted living home and that respecting her mother' wishes is critically important.

Yolanda and Ted's sister, Kate, said she would be willing to let her mother live with her. However, Yolanda also knows that her mother would not be comfortable living in Kate's home because Kate and her husband do not get along well and this will create a stressful living situation

for their mother. Kate said she does not have adequate resources to be able to contribute financially to support an assisted living situation for their mother.

Yolanda has asked for a mediator to attempt to resolve this difficult and emotional family conflict among the three siblings. She said she and her siblings have all agreed to try mediation. Yolanda says that they are all in agreement that they would like to try to resolve the situation without upsetting their mother so they do not want her present during their discussions about her future care and living arrangements.

Discussion Questions

If you were the mediator in this conflict, how would you respond to the following questions?

- Would you meet separately with Kate and Ted before gathering the three siblings together? Why or why not?
- Would you agree to the request to not involve Anna in the discussion among the three siblings? What factors would influence this decision?
- During the mediation with the family, would you bring up examples of how other families you have worked with have made similar decisions about parental care? Why or why not?
- If you felt that any of the siblings were being unreasonable about their positions would you meet with them separately to try to influence their point of view? How does such a decision influence the type of third-party role you would be enacting?

In one line of research, four general approaches to intervention have been studied (Carnevale & Pegnetter, 1985; Carnevale, 1986; Carnevale, Conlon, Honisch, & Harris, 1989; Carnevale, Putnam, Conlon, & O'Connor, 1991). In establishing a general orientation to intervention, third parties can (1) *integrate:* attempt to solve a conflict through encouraging negotiations and reaching a mutually acceptable agreement (a problem-solving approach); (2) *compensate:* persuade one or more of the parties to move or reach settlement by some reward or incentive offered by the third party (such as a manager acting as intervenor offering a "perk" in exchange for accepting some outcome in a conflict with a co-worker); (3) *be inactive:* allow the disputants to handle the conflict themselves; and (4) *press:* pressure disputants to change their goals or willingness to settle (for example, persuading a party to move from a currently held position, giving information that shapes perceptions of fairness). These four approaches were originally developed to apply to mediators, but they apply more broadly to any third party with some leeway in his or her general intervention mandate.

Research suggests that third-party selection of approaches depends on two primary factors (Carnevale et al., 1989). First, the choice seems to be contingent on how much value the third party attaches to the achievement of disputants' goals. The importance the intervenor places on this outcome may stem from a concern about the parties' welfare or it may come from some vested interest of the intervenor (such as a manager whose unit's performance is being influenced by the conflict). Second, the choice can also hinge on the third party's perception of whether there is sufficient common ground to reach a mutually acceptable solution. This factor suggests that third parties' approaches are influenced by an assessment of how likely it is that the disputants can reach an agreement.

Figure 9.1 summarizes the choices third parties are likely to make among the four approaches, given their concern for parties' aspirations and their perceptions of common ground. Third parties attempt integration when concern for the goals of the parties is great and the intervenor feels there is sufficient chance that the parties can reach an agreement. The third party is most likely to be inactive when there is a good chance of reaching agreement and he or she is concerned about a positive result. In this situation, he or she may believe that parties will reach an agreement on their own and thus third-party involvement is unnecessary.

Third parties are likely to compensate when they are highly concerned about the parties' reaching an agreement, but the chances for one appear slight. In this case, the third party has significant motivation to use available resources as incentives to promote agreements. Finally, the third party is most likely to press when the intervenor is not highly concerned about having the parties reach settlement and there appears to be little common ground on which to build the intervention. In this case the third party may feel there is nothing to lose in pressuring parties because the outcome is not seen as greatly significant. It has also been found that third parties may be more likely to use pressing tactics at later stages of the intervention because intervenors may become increasingly pessimistic about the amount of common ground as the intervention proceeds.

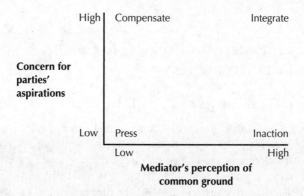

FIGURE 9.1   *Third-Party Intervention Approaches.*

Of the four intervention approaches in this model, the *press* stance has received the most attention in other studies of third party adaptation. Several other factors appear to influence whether third parties adopt a pressing strategy (Kressel, Pruitt, et al., 1989). There is a tendency for intervenors to become more directive when the intervenors' own values or interests clash with the parties'. One study of labor arbitrators found, for example, that arbitrators often settled labor grievances in ways consistent with the interests and rights of management rather than workers (Gross & Greenfield, 1986). Pressure tactics also appear to be more likely when the disputing parties are very hostile toward each other. For instance, mediators have been found to press for concessions, mention costs of failing to settle, and attempt to change bargaining expectations when parties are hostile (Kochan & Jick, 1978; Hiltrop, 1985 & 1989). Similarly, divorce and family mediators have been found to impose more procedural structure and control when parties became defensive (Donohue, 1991). Third parties may also be more directive under the pressures of a deadline, when they have well-defined formal mandates, or when they are biased toward one side (Kressel, Pruitt, et al., 1989; Zartman, 2005).

In addition to studies that bear on the general approaches to intervention, such as those discussed in the Carnevale and associates model, other more specific moves that third parties make are contingent on emerging factors as well. When bargainers bring too many issues to the table during negotiations, mediators often attempt to reduce the agenda, develop an overarching framework, or prioritize issues (Carnevale & Pegnetter, 1985). When bargainers lack experience, mediators also simplify agendas and try to educate parties in impasse processes. When issues have a potential impact on absent parties (such as children in a custody mediation) and absent parties' interests are not well represented by the disputants, third parties are more likely to reject suggestions and terms for settlement (Folger & Bernard, 1985).

Third-party intervenors are, in a real sense, part of the ongoing conflict. Their moves shape and define interaction in ways similar to the disputing parties' moves: Moves by third parties are possible because of endorsed power, they are adaptive to moment-to-moment influences in the unfolding conflict, and they are influential in shaping the overall conflict and its outcomes. When a third party is involved in conflict, conflict interaction is, in important ways, constituted by his or her moves and countermoves as well as those of the disputants. The next section examines the second property of conflict interaction and how it helps to describe and explain third-party involvement in conflict interaction.

9.2 Property 2: Patterns of Behavior in Conflict Tend to Perpetuate Themselves

9.2.1 Third Parties and Conflict Cycles

The self-perpetuating nature of conflict interaction is often a rationale for bringing a third party into a conflict. If interaction is self-perpetuating, if momentum becomes difficult for disputing parties to control or direct, or if cycles of interaction are difficult to recognize because parties contribute to them, then a third party may have the best chance to alter the repetitive tendencies. But the discussion of how the first property of conflict interaction applies to intervention shows that third parties do not stand apart from the conflict interaction—they are interactors themselves.

Does this mean that third parties' moves are vulnerable to the self-perpetuating tendencies of conflict interaction? Or that interaction involving third parties is itself self-perpetuating? In some instances, the answer is yes. While third parties can alter cycles and patterns of conflict interaction, interactions involving third parties are also susceptible to self-perpetuation.

Although there are a wide range of third-party mandates, most intervention roles put third parties in a position to alter repetitive patterns in conflict interaction. Many intervention moves are aimed specifically at the interaction itself and hence can counteract repetitive tendencies. Restructuring of conflict interaction occurs in diverse and often subtle ways. It occurs any time the third party sets time limits; organizes the agenda; controls when parties talk; focuses interaction on the problem before considering solutions; encourages parties to make statements in a clearer, less hostile, or more productive way; fosters an exchange of small concessions; or sets a climate that allows the parties to provide previously unstated information. These are just a few examples of the type of third-party moves that direct the process and thereby influence conflict interaction.

Parties immersed in the conflict often cannot easily monitor or control aspects of the interaction that third-party moves influence. As a result, disputing parties rarely address these issues themselves. In the midst of an unfolding conflict, people typically have their hands full tracking issues, dealing with emotions, and planning responses. It is difficult for parties to channel or control the interaction as a whole. Partly because disputants cannot easily make moves, these interventions are central to a third party's ability to alter well-grooved patterns and cycles of interaction.

There are some forms of intervention, such as arbitration or court hearings, in which the process is highly structured and the parties are prohibited from carrying on the interaction patterns that characterized the conflict before the intervention. The third party takes almost total control of the process and thereby ensures a radically different sequence of moves and countermoves, actions and reactions. Under some process rules, the parties may not even speak for themselves; for example, in a courtroom an attorney may speak for them. In these interventions, cycles of interaction are often broken. However, there are potential downsides to these interventions as well. Because existing patterns are altered by the strong hand of an intervenor, the process does little to foster new patterns that could be sustained by the parties themselves after the intervention ends. Moreover, these forms of intervention can, in some instances, exacerbate destructive cycles. Arbitration or other adjudicative procedures can encourage blaming or can dwell heavily on the history of the conflict, thereby reinforcing destructive tendencies.

Other forms of intervention attempt to strike a balance between controlling the process and allowing the parties to control their interaction. In these cases, third parties try to structure the interaction by setting ground rules and intervening in ways that redirect parties' moves. At the same time, the intervenor wants to encourage the parties to interact freely with each other so that they have a strong hand in shaping the outcome and new patterns of interaction are initiated. Most forms of mediation and facilitation are premised on this attempt to balance process control with free-form interaction. Particular mediators or facilitators may give more emphasis to either objective, but the intervention as a whole attempts to achieve a balance.

In interventions that attempt to balance control of the process and spontaneous interaction, there is variation in the success third parties have in altering the self-perpetuating cycles of interaction. If the intervenor leaves too much room for uncontrolled interaction, the parties' patterns of interaction can prevail. Surprisingly, third parties themselves can contribute to and become part of these patterns. The kinds of intervention that mediators rely on to achieve a balance include summarizing; pointing to common ground; redirecting the substantive focus of the interaction; and, in general, placing a high premium on controlling the process.

Becoming trapped in the disputants' destructive cycles is not the only problem the self-perpetuating nature of conflict interaction can cause in third-party interventions. The intervention itself is vulnerable to repetitive tendencies, much like other forms of conflict interaction. Two brief examples will show how self-perpetuating tendencies establish themselves in third-party interventions.

Studies of mediation in labor and business contexts suggest that third parties set up similar patterns of intervention across different cases (Shapiro et al., 1985; Kolb, 1986). Early in a case, mediators tend to assess and classify the dispute before them. In essence, they ask themselves: "What is possible in this case? How can this case develop? What outcomes are possible?" After answering these questions, they tend to draw from a small repertoire of favored approaches and choose one based on previous cases they have handled (Shapiro et al., 1985). The interaction following from this approach then becomes quite predictable and similar across cases. The third party may, for instance, pressure one of the parties to make concessions; or the intervenor may encourage negotiation; or the approach could be to separate the parties and shuttle back and forth between them in individual caucuses. The type of approach the mediator thinks will work for the dispute at hand shapes the mode of intervention and consequent interaction among the parties.

This work suggests that, just like disputing parties, intervenors find it useful to "know what to expect." Predictability is helpful in anticipating the way the parties may react and in planning future moves. In attempting to attain the security that comes with predictability, third-party approaches to intervention thus may become self-perpetuating. A limited number of solutions or intervention moves are applied across a wide range of cases. The danger is, of course, that the "canned" solutions favored by the intervenor may not work in new and different circumstances and that intervenors' well-defined scenarios may blind them to the need for different approaches (See Case 9.3).

Third-party interventions can become vulnerable to self-perpetuation in a second sense as well. The form of intervention applied in a case can shape future interventions. This tendency has been found in analyses of informal third-partyship, wherein the third party's mandate is an informal one such as those typically held by parents, managers, or even friends. In these settings, the same third party often becomes involved in a series of conflicts with the same parties over some length of time. Once a style of intervention is adopted with disputants, it may be reapplied in future conflicts. Although there is only anecdotal evidence to support this claim, several reasons to expect such repetition have been advanced (Sheppard, Blumenfeld-Jones, & Roth, 1989).

First, the type of resolution produced by an initial intervention is likely to shape the future direction of what may develop into an ongoing conflict. For example, a manager may

CASE 9.3 • *Neighbor Noise Problems*

This mediator's approach to addressing neighbor noise problems illustrates how third parties can easily fall into repetitive patterns as they intervene in conflicts.

A volunteer mediator in a court-annexed mediation center in New York proudly described how skillful he had become as a third-party intervenor in neighbor conflicts. He said that a lot of the cases referred to the mediation center where he works are neighbor conflicts that arise from noise disturbances. Most people in this neighborhood live in high-rise apartment buildings with people above and below them. As a result, there are a lot of conflicts that arise from an upstairs neighbor disturbing a neighbor living below because of the noise created when the residents walk around at various times of the day or night. This is particularly difficult when the upstairs neighbors have people entertain in the evenings or weekends. Sometimes these conflicts escalate over time and end up in court because they result in increasing tensions, retaliation, and even violence.

The mediator said that he now found these cases relatively easy to address. As soon as he hears that the conflict between the neighbors involves a noise problem, he knows right away what the likely solution is: the parties need to purchase a carpet or obtain a thicker carpet for the upstairs apartment. Of course, he said, you need to negotiate how the carpet is going to be paid for, who will purchase it, and where it needs to be placed in the apartment. The mediator said that relying on this obvious solution allows him to dispose of these neighbor cases in fifteen to twenty minutes. He says he is one of the courts' favorite mediators in the center because he can complete so many cases so quickly.

Discussion Questions

Consider the following questions about the mediator's intervention in this conflict:

- How is "knowing what to expect" shaping this mediator's approach to intervention?
- In what ways is this mediator's approach useful? Not useful?
- What is NOT being addressed in the intervention by relying on this approach to conflict intervention? What are the limits of taking this approach to mediation?

intervene in a dispute between two employees over how vacation time will be scheduled. The manager may decide to talk to each worker separately and then assign the vacation time in a way that he or she feels is fair. When the same issue comes up a year later, the workers may have learned little about how to interact with each other. Seeing that the employees are unable to deal with the second conflict, the manager may believe that he or she has no choice but to take the same approach—hand down a decision on how the issue should be settled.

Moreover, in interacting with an intervenor, the parties learn something about how the third party is likely to deal with the conflict. As a result, future conflicts with the same party may be shaped in ways that the intervenor is likely to address. For example, a parent might intervene in a sibling conflict by having each child state his or her case and then judging who was in the right. In future conflicts, the children are likely to get better at stating a defensible case because they know that is how the parent will decide things. So whereas they may have directly fought in the past, the children may instead turn to the parent with a prepared complaint.

Finally, the third party may be likely to approach future conflicts with the same parties similarly because the approach may be salient in memory or may be seen as "the" most effective way to respond to the parties. Interventions can be influenced by force of habit.

9.2.2 Third Parties and the Overall Shape of Conflict Behavior

Like other forms of conflict interaction, third-party interventions can be viewed as a series of episodes and phases unfolding over time that shape parties' understandings of what is going on at any point along the way. To the extent that third parties take a hand in establishing the unfolding interaction, they can significantly influence how people view their own conflict activity during the intervention. This principle of conflict interaction points to important ways in which third parties (1) steer broad stages of interaction by structuring the process and (2) shape specific conflict episodes by framing issues.

Considerable effort has been spent describing the way interaction develops over time during third-party interventions. This work suggests that third party interventions are characterized by broad, but recognizable, stages of interaction. Table 9.1 summarizes two different stage models of third-party interventions.

TABLE 9.1   *Two Stage Models for Third-Party Interventions*

Model 1 (Donohue, 1991)
Orientation
Parties gain an understanding of the process; set ground rules for the intervention

Background Information
Parties tell their stories, share information about the dispute, state objectives and desired outcomes

Issue Processing
Parties address points of difference, clarify preferences, and raise new underlying issues

Proposal Development
Parties attempt to reach agreements by negotiating, compromising, accommodating or dropping issues

Model 2 (Domenici & Littlejohn, 2001)
Introduction
Mediation process is explained, communication guidelines are established, mediator confidentiality is explained

Storytelling
Parties discuss their views about what happened and what might happen in the future to address the issues in the conflict

Problem-Solving
Mediators assist with the identification of interests that underlie parties' positions; an issue agenda is set and possible options for settlement are generated

Resolution
Summary of parties' commonalities; finding an agreement that is satisfactory to all parties; writing up the final agreement

It is important to note that not all mediations actually pass through these stages (Jones, 1988). At best these are likely to occur if the parties actually reach agreement. They are derived from recommendations about how mediations should unfold (Donohue, 1991; Domenici, 1996). In this sense, the four categories in the stages are based more on prescriptions about what interaction should look like than what actually does occur. Nonetheless, the stages capture a widely-held notion of how mediation develops, especially when the intervention is expected to move toward a mutually-acceptable agreement among the parties.

This last point suggests an important difference between stage development in third-party interventions, and other self-regulated forms of conflict. In interventions, third parties often make a conscious attempt to move interaction through a set of preconceived stages such as those described by either Donohue or Dominici and Littlejohn. Intervenors are often taught a prescribed series of stages as part of their training (Haynes, 1981; Folberg & Taylor, 1984; Moore, 1986; Stulberg, 1987); they use process rules that promote the emergence of the stages in sequence. Third parties also make specific moves, such as summaries, questions, or paraphrases, that help keep the interaction within a stage or move it from one stage to another (Kraybill, 2004). Moreover, intervenors may track the progress of the interaction through the stages as the intervention occurs and make the parties aware of the need to remain in, or move into, a particular stage. Without third-party involvement, there is rarely such a conscious attempt to envision and enact a sequence of stages by the parties themselves (See Exhibit 9.1).

EXHIBIT 9.1 • *Third Parties, Differentiation, and Integration*

Sharpening Conflicts

In many nonadjudicative contexts, an intervenor's most important and difficult task is to "sharpen" the conflict (Van de Vliert, 1985). A sharpened conflict results from a successful differentiation phase: When a conflict is sharpened, parties have an accurate, and often painful, understanding of the issues; see the consequences of not resolving the issues; and have some understanding of what a solution must do to reach the needs of all involved. The success or failure of an intervention ultimately rests on whether the third party can guide parties through differentiation without developing inflexible avoidance or spiraling escalation.

An effective third party will structure interaction in differentiation so that the concerns can emerge clearly without locking parties into solutions that stifle creative thinking, produce inflexibility, or promote escalation. Although the specific techniques that the third party must use to achieve this general goal depend on the specific conflict, the following three intervention functions can facilitate the sharpening of conflicts. Notice that these

parallel to some extent the process for managing conflicts outlined in Chapter 8.

Unearthing the Historical Roots of the Problem. By the time a third party is called in to help work through a conflict, the parties may have lost sight of important facts or events that played a significant role in shaping the problem. As they argue for preferred solutions and "fight things out" at this level, some dimensions of the problem itself may be lost. Having parties review the conflict chronologically may seem pointless at first, but it often provides important breakthroughs. It encourages parties to write a more careful definition of their own problems.

Encouraging a Statement of Needs Rather Than a Fight over Solutions. Successful differentiation can depend on a clarification of parties' needs. Any solution a party advocates meets some set of needs that he or she has. A problem exists not because people are pressing for different solutions or positions but because none of the

(continued)

EXHIBIT 9.1   Continued

solutions being considered or advocated meet all parties' needs (Fisher & Ury, 1981). Conflicts, in other words, stem from the apparent inability of the parties to meet diverse needs on some issue. The continual fight over solutions is a symptom that all parties' needs will not be met if any of the solutions being considered is adopted.

Third parties can take an active role in confronting parties with the incompatibility of needs. This often requires that the intervenor (1) make people clarify what their needs are, (2) discourage individuals from regarding each other as the cause of the problem, and (3) prevent people from suggesting solutions before all members' needs are clarified. The process of clarifying needs in a conflict can be straightforward and explicit. The third party can turn to each person and ask: "What needs of yours must any solution fulfill?" or "You have suggested that X be done. Why do you want to see this solution adopted? What needs of yours would it meet?" Third parties often find it beneficial to put people's need statements on paper or a board in front of the whole group. This method can allow for greater depersonalization of the conflict because specific needs become less associated with the parties who state them. People begin to see, almost in a literal sense, that the problem they need to address lies above the needs of any one individual and rests in the incompatibility of positions. There is a problem "out there" that the parties as a whole can attack.

Cutting Through Multiple Issues.   For the differentiation phase of conflict to be successful, issues must be clarified. Often parties are unable to work through their conflicts because the issues seem overwhelmingly complex. Multiple layers of problems may never be discussed separately. Issues may appear confused or ambiguous because parties' aggression is displaced and frustrations and anxiety from other unaddressed problems drive the interaction.

A third party is sometimes in a better position to see the multiple layers of problems than the parties themselves. An outsider can break the problem down into smaller, more manageable parts and separate areas on which parties already agree from

areas that still remain unsettled (Folberg & Taylor, 1984). To cut through multiple issues, the third party can watch for cues indicating that aggression or frustration is displaced. Heated discussions that seem to go nowhere or comments that imply a relational or face-saving problem (such as, "I'm sorry I can't answer that question because I feel like you're talking to me like a three-year-old") may be cues that aggression is displaced. The third party can talk to people individually to determine whether problems that have not surfaced are influencing the interaction. If the problems are critical to a successful resolution of the conflict, the third party can raise them and explain why the parties were hesitant to address them. Careful introduction of a problem enables discussion to start cautiously. The third party can place constraints on the interaction to help control issues that may be volatile or to enable people to vent frustrations and emotions in a safe climate.

Inducing Integration

When a conflict has been successfully sharpened, the parties move through a productive differentiation phase. People have a clear understanding of the differences among them, the needs of each person, and the likely consequences of not attaining a resolution. Helping the parties move from this phase to integration and acceptance of a solution is often a difficult task for a third party. The three approaches that some third parties employ to induce integration are: suggesting common goals, defining the integration process, and inducing cooperation.

Suggesting Common Goals.   In many conflict situations, there is often more agreement than parties realize because they become heavily focused on points of disagreement and lose sight of the commonalities. A third party can stay attuned to points of agreement and remind parties of these points at crucial times (Avery et al., 1981). People often share a common goal but differ over the means to achieve this goal. If the third party focuses attention on shared goals when conflicts escalate, the tension of the moment can be relieved and members may re-examine their commitments to specific solutions.

(continued)

EXHIBIT 9.1 Continued

Comments that point to shared goals allow parties to discover commonalities and may offer significant encouragement to those who feel discouraged, exhausted, or frustrated.

Defining the Integration Process. In suggesting common goals, the third party attempts to integrate the two sides around a shared issue. In essence, the third party sets up an agenda for the areas the parties will discuss and ground rules for discussion. By influencing the process, the third party tries to help the parties talk without letting the conflict escalate or de-escalate.

There are a number of procedures for integrative conflict management. Probably the best known is Filley's (1975) Integrative Decision-Making (IDM) Technique, which was the foundation of the procedure for conflict management outlined in Chapter 8. It is premised on several assumptions. First, it assumes people must untangle the substantive and emotional issues surrounding a conflict before they can develop a solution. Second, the technique assumes that people must have certain attitudes to successfully manage conflicts—including a belief in the possibility of a mutually acceptable solution, a belief that the other's position is legitimate (if not acceptable), trust in the other, and a commitment to work for an integrative outcome. Finally, in line with earlier discussions, the IDM model assumes that problem definition should be separated from solution generation.

Based on these assumptions, the third party can then guide the parties through management procedure outlined in Chapter 8.

Third parties impose ground rules, such as the procedure for managing conflict, to manage interaction. This is useful for several reasons. First, it makes parties discuss areas that must be clarified to attain an integrative solution. Often parties are simply unaware of the issues that have to be worked out to resolve a conflict; this agenda lets them know what they have to cover. Second, the agenda constrains parties to limited areas of discussion at any one time. This eliminates chaotic, "kitchen-sink" fights in which both sides toss in any comments or issues they think are to their advantage. Finally, ground rules offer tangible evidence of the third party's activity and willingness to intervene in the conflict. This can reassure the parties that they are not at each other's mercy and that there is an impartial person regulating the interaction.

Inducing Cooperation. In the third approach, the third party enlists one side as an ally in moves designed to get both sides to cooperate. A lack of trust and willingness to cooperate often prevents people from endorsing some solution that "on paper" seems to make good sense. Solutions may not be endorsed because parties do not trust that everyone will carry through on the commitments the solution requires. There is no assurance, in other words, that people are willing to cooperate even if they give their assent to a proposed solution or agreement.

Osgood's GRIT proposal (discussed in Chapter 8) can be used by a third party when disputants are locked in a bond of mutual distrust and "any innocent-seeming action is perceived as manipulative and threatening" (Lindskold, 1978, p. 777). The steps in the GRIT proposal may be most useful in cases where one of the conflicting parties wants to initiate concessions but is afraid to do so or is not being clear about his or her willingness to make concessions without a promise of reciprocity. In this instance, the third party can make sure that others recognize that a promise of concessions is being made, and that the concession is not linked to a demand for similar moves by others. The third party can also note when the promised concessions have been carried out and thereby point to the willingness of some parties to make a sincere effort to settle the conflict.

The third party's active involvement in clarifying the implicit steps in a GRIT-like offer can help establish a climate of mutual trust. He or she is a witness to the disputants' willingness to respond appropriately once a sincere conciliatory move has been made. If others fail to respond with reciprocal concessions or moves, it can be read by the third party as a sign of poor faith. There is some pressure on the responding parties to make reciprocal concessions or risk losing the third party's involvement in the process.

In using stages to steer interaction, intervenors frame interactions for the disputing parties. Through the explicit *labeling and control of stages* that third parties exert, disputants come to have a clear sense of what they are doing as the intervention process unfolds. Not only does this establish boundaries for what moves seem appropriate or inappropriate, but it also creates a redefining force much like that covered in the discussion of reframing interaction in Chapter 8. Part of the power of third-party intervention is its ability to transform disputants' goals. As parties enter various stages of intervention, their involvement in that interaction shapes their goals; it influences what they think can or should be done. The type of interaction the parties see themselves engaged in is influenced by the emerging interaction itself. Interaction is framed by what they see themselves doing rather than by what they planned to do. This effect reveals how the process itself holds the potential for creating significant change. The conscious use of stages in intervention—structuring interaction around sets of broad interactive goals that change over time—plays a key role in reframing the overall conflicts.

What propels movement through the stages in nonadjudicative forms of intervention? How is it that some interventions lead to settlement or proposal development and others do not? There is no single, easy answer to these questions. How interventions develop depends on a broad range of factors, including the issues in dispute, the extent of common ground among the parties, the third party's talent, the conditions under which the disputants enter the intervention, and the cultural influence of the intervenors (Davidheiser, 2006). What is clear is that all forms of nonadjudicative intervention attempt to move parties through the two broadest phases of conflict examined in detail in Chapter 1—differentiation and integration. Moving from storytelling to agenda setting and resolution in the Domenici and Littlejohn model is essentially a move from differentiation to integration.

Thus far, in examining the second property of conflict interaction, it has been shown that third party interventions can be viewed as developmental sequences and that intervenors play an active role in defining and controlling the unfolding conflict interaction. In addition to influencing broad stagewise development by conceiving of and enacting interventions in stages, third parties can also influence sequences of conflict interaction by the way in which they frame conflict issues. In discussing self-regulation, Chapter 8 noted that the way in which issues are framed by parties, influences perceptions of the conflict and in turn may direct or redirect the interaction. Third parties can have as great an influence on the framing of issues as the disputants themselves. As in self-regulation, the framing of issues directs the interaction.

When third parties first become involved with a conflict, their knowledge of the issues, events, and parties' relationships can be quite limited because the information is not always easily attainable. Conflicts are not isolated events that can be removed, unchanged, from the stream of interaction in which they have unfolded (Beer, 1986; Kolb, 1986). As we have seen in the discussion of third-party responsiveness to the conflict interaction, disputes are not fixed entities. The very act of presenting a case to a third party can alter the issues and mask or mute dimensions of the conflict that previously were pressing or important. How a third party comes to understand and represent the issues in a conflict may or may not reflect the way the conflict was understood or represented by the parties before the intervention process began.

How a third party eventually frames conflict issues depends on a number of factors, including how the parties present the issues to the intervenor, the third party's own interpretive assumptions about what the issues are or which issues need to be addressed, the third party's repertoire of intervention strategies (for example, which issues the intervenor feels capable of addressing), and the third party's willingness to cast issues in ways that promote agreements consistent with their values or interests. These factors suggest that, as a third party becomes involved, issues are likely to be reframed: The way the parties view the conflict can be changed dramatically or subtly (Lam et al., 1989). Moreover, the ensuing conflict interaction follows from the third party's casting of the issues. Unfolding episodes of interaction are, in direct ways, linked to the third party's framing of the issues (Putnam & Holmer, 1992).

As an illustration of the link between framing and interaction in third-party interventions, consider the options available in informal settings, such as when a parent intervenes in a dispute among siblings, or when a supervisor intervenes in a conflict among office workers. In these contexts, third parties try to get a sense of what the conflict is about; as they make sense of the situation, the problem is framed. Some research on framing suggests that third parties in informal settings draw from four broad framing strategies (Sheppard et al., 1989).

First, the third party can cast the conflict within a *right–wrong frame;* in this frame, the conflict issue is seen as one that stems from a violation of some rule or expectation. The problem requires identifying one party as right and the other as wrong.

Second, the conflict can be cast within a *negotiation frame;* here the problem is seen as one that requires compromise. It necessitates asking both parties to consider their interests and the interests of other parties simultaneously.

Third, the problem can be cast within an *underlying conflict frame;* in this case, the third party views the stated issue as a symptom of other issues not explicitly discussed. The conflict is complicated because issues are not all above board. Parties may be avoiding issues because they are riven with a history of painful or frightening experiences or because the status quo protects someone's interests. Once an issue is framed as an underlying conflict, the third party tends to believe that no satisfactory solution can be found until the buried concerns are unearthed.

Finally, a problem can be viewed as a *stop frame;* from this standpoint, the third party views the conflict as one that must be made to stop at almost any cost. When a conflict is cast in this frame, the issues themselves are downplayed. The third party has less concern for resolving issues than for making the conflict interaction cease. This occurs, for example, when a parent simply insists that two siblings stop fighting and makes no attempt to assess what problem instigated the ruckus.

Whatever framing a third party chooses, it is enacted through the sequence of moves as the intervention develops. The third party's framing of an issue is thus integrally tied to the way the conflict interaction is likely to unfold. For example, if a third party adopts a right–wrong frame, the interaction is likely to unfold as a series of question and response episodes regarding what the facts are, who actually did what, and what the understanding of the rule or expectation was. If the issue is perceived as one that requires negotiation, the third party is more likely to engage the parties in interaction sequences that seek possible compromises. Tit-for-tat exchanges and other forms of concession exchanges are likely. If the issue is cast within an underlying conflict frame, the third party is more likely to encourage a series of interaction episodes to foster diagnosis of deeper issues. The intervenor might, for example, prompt a series of self-disclosing exchanges followed by attempts at clarification and confirmation from the parties on what he or she thinks may be the real issues. In these interactions, intervenors often paraphrase a comment that a party has just made and, in the paraphrase, suggest an unspoken concern (Lemmon, 1985; Donohue, 1991).

In sum, understanding the framing of issues by third parties is important in understanding the influence they have on conflict interaction. Framing is sometimes done strategically by a third party to move interaction in a particular direction. In formal contexts, such as mediation, framing allows only certain forms of interaction to occur. Framing can also be inadvertent or unconscious, perhaps occurring with almost every substantive comment an intervenor makes. In these less strategic framings, third parties may exert influence over settlement terms by shaping values or preferences and by pursuing or dropping subissues.

9.3 Property 3: Conflict Interaction Is Influenced by and in Turn Affects Relationships

Throughout this book we have shown that the negotiation of relationships is an integral and inevitable part of conflict interaction. Relationships are defined and altered during any exchange of messages. In an attempt to be strategic, people often try to manage their own images, to define the image of the other party, and to establish particular types of relationships. Sometimes these attempts at controlling relational issues are in parties' self-interest and sometimes they are in the mutual interests of all sides. Regardless of strategic intent, the way in which relationships are defined and managed is as much a part of the "settlement" or "solution" as the substantive decisions. When people work through conflicts, they work through relationships as well.

When third parties intervene in a conflict, they establish relationships with the disputants. Third parties make conscious attempts to present certain images of themselves. These images differ depending on the third party's intervention role, but there are important commonalities as well. Foremost is the need for third parties to establish a credible image in the eyes of the disputants (Folberg & Taylor, 1984; Billikopf, 2004).

For adjudicators, credibility may rest on establishing that they have substantive expertise related to the issues; for example, labor arbitrators may try to show that they understand contract law, pension funds, fair labor practices, and so on. For mediators, facilitators, adjudicators, and many informal third-party intervenors, credibility rests on parties' perception that the intervenor is neutral (has no personal preference about the outcome of the dispute) and impartial (treats all parties in substantively and procedurally comparable ways) (Stulberg, 1987). For many third-party roles, credibility may rest on a sense that the third party is objective—that the intervenor has sufficient detachment to keep a clear head about the issues and unfolding interaction. Objectivity is linked to disputants' perceptions that third parties can maintain process control and establish safe climates while simultaneously tracking and fostering substantive movement on issues.

Like all images, the third parties' image is under continuous negotiation. Third parties make bids for an image. These bids can be accepted or rejected by the disputants.

If the expertise, neutrality, impartiality, or objectivity of the third party is challenged, there can be significant consequences for the intervention (Bernard et al., 1984). In such cases, the relationships between the third party and the disputants shift: Disputants may gain greater control over the interaction process and revert to patterns of interaction that existed prior to the intervention. Studies of mediation, for example, suggest that disputants are more likely to deadlock in sessions in which a mediator loses objectivity and becomes emotionally involved in the process (Donohue, 1989). Alternatively, if impartiality or neutrality is lost, one party may think the intervention is slanted against him or her and withdraw from the process.

Third parties do not just establish relationships with disputants, they alter relationships between the parties themselves. In particular, third parties influence face-saving between the parties. As discussed in Chapter 6, disputants are frequently concerned about appearing weak. They can suffer "image loss" if others in the dispute think they will make concessions or crumble easily under pressure (Pruitt, 1971). People may act tough and refuse to move from positions they are actually willing to concede, due to fear that giving an inch will mean conceding a mile. Third parties alter this dynamic in an interesting way; they allow movement without altering the relational image the disputants want to preserve.

When they move from an intransigent position, disputants can claim that it was the third party who suggested the idea or persuaded them to make the concession (Shapiro et al., 1985). As a result, parties can move without suffering damage to their images: They are not weak, they are simply acting under the guidance or pressure of the third party. Significant strides in breaking impasses can occur when third parties shoulder the responsibility for concessions or unpopular options (Carnevale, 1986; Hiltrop, 1989). Without the third party's presence, options that the parties are actually willing to accept may not even be explored.

Third parties alter relational dynamics in a second sense as well. Third parties alter the emotional tenor of the dispute and thereby change how parties see each other (Jones & Bodtker, 2001). We have noted that the presence of an intervenor may put parties, at least for a time, on their best behavior. This has important consequences. The presence of third parties has been found, for example, to dampen parties' desire for retribution (Peachey, 1989). It may be that simply having an outsider hear the issues makes parties feel as if they have already "gotten even" in some sense. Also, once parties know that someone else has heard about the mistreatment or grievance, it may be less important to take a tough stand on substantive issues. Similarly, third parties reduce defensiveness by encouraging disputants to talk about themselves, rather than defending the other party and by opening the possibility of apology (Jones, 1989; Schneider, 2000).

Third parties also alter the emotional tenor of a conflict by controlling how and when hostility is expressed. In the caucus—a separate and confidential meeting between each party and the intervenor—third parties have a powerful tool for channeling the expression of hostility. Disputants can release a great deal of hostility toward others in caucuses. Much of this hostility is often personalized attacks in the form of character assassination and venting (Pruitt, McGillicuddy, Welton, & Fry, 1989; McGillicuddy, Pruitt, Welton, Zubek, & Peirce, 1991); however, movement and creative solutions seem to come on the heels of releasing hostility. Third parties can use caucuses to facilitate private hostility release, fostering creative movement on issues without further damaging relationships (Beer, 1986).

Finally, intervenors can influence relationships by controlling or altering the distribution of power between disputants (Lemmon, 1985; Welton, 1991). In many intervention settings, third parties influence power by controlling process (Folger, 2001). Parties who have difficulty getting the floor or expressing their arguments, and thus are in a less powerful position vis-à-vis the interaction, may have a more level playing field during an intervention. The redistribution of power often comes as a result of interaction ground rules established by the intervenor.

Third parties also influence the balance of power in a conflict by controlling the exchange or provision of information. It is common in many types of disputes for some parties to have more information than others about the issues, legal options, or long-term consequences of possible settlement terms. In divorce, for example, one spouse may have more information about employment pensions, real estate laws, or financial investment programs. It has become general practice in private-sector divorce mediation for mediators to require each spouse to obtain legal and financial counseling before negotiating on these issues during the intervention. Mediators are reluctant to provide such information themselves because it may undermine their impartial stance. However, by encouraging parties to each have comparable information, the power distribution is altered during negotiations.

Third parties also equalize power by not allowing either party to lose ground when concessions are exchanged. As the rationale for the GRIT process described in Chapter 8 suggested, parties are often reluctant to make the first move because, if no concession is returned, the initiator may not be able to easily back away from the offer. The party "loses" because he or she moved first. When third parties act as go-betweens and caucus with each side, they often "test the waters," propose hypothetical concession exchanges, and arrange for simultaneous moves. This prevents either side from suffering what Pruitt (1971) calls "position loss"—the loss of bargaining ground during negotiations. Many third parties maintain equality of power by counterbalancing concessions and movement as negotiations unfold.

All of the preceding examples illustrate how third parties influence power during the intervention itself. There is good reason to believe that most third-party influence over power is limited to the time the intervenor is interacting with the parties. More long-term and fundamental influence over relationships is less likely to occur (Kressel, Pruitt, et al., 1989). There is a tendency for intervenors not to probe too deeply into underlying issues, or to have the parties rethink or change how they are dependent on each other (Kolb & Sheppard, 1985; Donohue, 1991). Given most intervenors' concerns of neutrality, impartiality, and objectivity, this restraint is not surprising.

9.4 Property 4: Conflict Interaction Is Influenced by the Context in Which It Occurs

This property of conflict interaction points to the way in which the prevailing ideologies and climate set expectations for behavior and, as a result, guide interaction and intervention.

9.4.1   Third Party Roles and Ideologies

Bush and Folger (2006) suggest that the third party's underlying ideological premises reveal important organizationally- and culturally-based assumptions that tend to guide the expectations for, and practices of, conflict interveners. There are several important characteristics of the ideological assumptions that underlie third party work.

First, the assumptions that third parties hold about human capability and the nature of conflict (described below) influence the types of conflict interventions they conduct. For example, one third party might believe that protracted competition brings out the worst in people. This third party might intervene by trying to break competitive interaction patterns. A different third party might believe that only after protracted competition will parties be motivated to work together. This third party might attempt to stimulate competition among parties, hoping to provoke a "crisis" that will bring the parties to their senses. Assumptions shape the discourse third parties create as they interact with parties during interventions.

Second, assumptions can be implicitly or explicitly held. In some instances, conflict interveners consciously adopt ideological commitments through self-reflection and careful analysis of their own predispositions and views about how they want to practice. In other instances, however, third parties may not be aware of their ideological assumptions. Third parties often learn their craft through experience, skill building, and training without examining their underlying assumptions.

Third, ideological assumptions are shaped by the third party's culture. Ideological premises are often part of an organization's, society's or community's world view and are thus linked to cultural identity in general. In many instances, these ideological assumptions are apparent in the organizational settings (e.g., courts, schools, businesses, faith-based communities) in which third parties practice. These organizational and institutional settings often set the ideological expectations for how conflict intervention work is conducted.

Table 9.2 summarizes the range of ideological beliefs that are directly relevant to conflict intervention work. These beliefs each have direct relevance to the choices third parties make and the strategies third parties adopt as they intervene in conflict. Third parties' overall approach to intervention as well as their specific moves and reactions will differ depending upon how conflict interveners respond to the questions associated with these beliefs.

Based on the range of ideological beliefs outlined in Table 9.2 on page 280, Bush and Folger see three primary ideological orientations that give rise to readily identifiable patterns of practice.

Individualist Ideology.   In this ideological orientation to practice, addressing the specific needs and interests of the individual parties in conflict is the paramount goal. Conflict is seen as a problem to be solved, and problems are shaped by the individual needs that clash with the needs of others. Constructive conflict intervention results in solutions, agreements or settlements that address the clash of needs. In this view, third parties often believe that conflict interaction between people is itself negative and destructive, because it is often emotional and irrational and gets in the way of finding useful solutions to problems the parties face. As a result, third parties often take an

TABLE 9.2   *Ideological Beliefs Relevant to Third-Party Work*

Views/Assumptions About Human Nature in Conflict
What are people capable of when they are in conflict?
What does the experience of conflict do to people?
What are the range of expected responses that people have to conflict?
How much capacity do people have to make "good" choices for themselves?

Views/Assumptions About the Nature of Conflict
What is conflict?
What gives rise to conflicts that are difficult for parties to manage on their own?

Views/Assumptions About What Productive/Destructive Changes in Conflict Are
When conflict moves in a productive direction, what happens?
When conflict moves in a destructive or negative direction, what happens?

Views/Assumptions About the Functions and Expectations for Social Institutions
What is the aim of institutions that serve and support people in conflict?
What should institutions try to accomplish?
What roles should social institutions promote to assist people who face difficult life challenges?

approach to practice that relies on minimizing the interaction among the parties and containing conflict through intervenor-led solutions and outcomes. Finding common ground, minimizing differences, and avoiding topics that are not readily solvable are hallmarks of this approach to conflict intervention.

Organic Ideology.   In this ideological orientation, communities and organizations are seen as having their own self-preserving order and structure that promote and sustain stability and social responsibility. This order is based on a set of values and beliefs that ties the members of a community together as a functioning unit. Conflict is seen as the disruption of the social order and a threat to the shared values and stability of relationships. Because of the emphasis on preserving relationships, conflict intervenors in this ideological framework work towards establishing interpersonal harmony. Successful conflict intervention restores social order while sustaining the commitment of the parties to the larger community. Conflict interaction is contained, not for the purposes of solving problems, but for the goal of maintaining the order that stable relationships provide. Avoidance of difficult issues and an emphasis on apology and forgiveness are hallmarks of this approach to conflict management. This approach is commonly invoked in non-Western cultures in some communities of faith, in victim–offender mediation programs, and in any communities where the preservation of relationships is a strong priority (Le Resche, 1992; Wall & Blum, 1991; Strang & Braithwaite, 2001; Zehr, 2002; Umbreit, Vos, Coates, & Brown, 2003).

Relational Ideology.   Relational ideology assumes that parties can address conflict through a simultaneous emphasis on both strength of self and connection to others. Conflict is not primarily meeting individual needs, nor is it necessarily about the preservation of an established relationship. Rather, it is about parties making clear, self-determined decisions that allow for consideration of others' points of view while staying true to themselves. This ideological orientation rests on the assumption that conflict is a crisis in human interaction. When parties are embroiled in conflict, their ability to interact productively over issues or differences is often undermined because conflict tends to throw them into states of weakness and self-absorption. In conflict, parties become unsettled, confused, fearful, disorganized and unsure of what to do. They also become self-protective, defensive, suspicious, and incapable of stepping outside of their own frameworks. When this happens, as it often does in the face of real differences and clashing viewpoints, the parties are unable to interact with each other in ways that allow them to productively address issues and make reasoned and useful decisions. If people in conflict receive assistance from third parties it helps to reduce their weakness and self-absorption; they gain greater capacity to deal with the conflict on their own.

Therefore, in the relational framework, the third party's goal is to support the transformation of the parties' interaction so that each person can move through the conflict with greater clarity for him or herself and with greater openness to the perspective of the other party—wherever this leads them on the issue at hand or however it ends up defining their relationship (See Exhibit 9.2).

EXHIBIT 9.2 • *Transformative Mediation: A Relational Approach to Conflict Intervention*

Bush and Folger and their colleagues (Bush & Folger, 2005; Folger & Bush, 2001; DellaNoce, Bush, & Folger, 2002) have developed an approach to conflict intervention that is rooted in relational ideology. Transformative mediation was designed as an alternative to the traditional individualistic approach to mediation that evolved in the United States and became the center of the alternative dispute resolution movement. In the transformative approach to mediation, mediators focus on supporting the transformation of the parties' interaction through fostering greater intra-party empowerment and inter-party recognition. In this approach, *empowerment* is achieved when parties experience a strengthened awareness of their own self-worth and their own ability to deal with whatever issues they encounter in conflict. Parties are empowered, for example, when they reach a clearer understanding of their goals, when they arrive at a better understanding of options open to them, when they realize that they have something of value to communicate to others, or

when they make choices based on a greater sense of clarity and focus than they had previously.

Recognition is achieved when parties experience an expanded willingness to acknowledge and be responsive to other parties' situations, perspectives, points of view, or common human qualities. Like empowerment, recognition can take a number of forms, including when a party realizes that it is valuable to reflect on and consider the other person's perspective; when a party can see that the other person's behavior may be caused by factors other than the ones they had previously assumed; when a party acknowledges that he or she could have done something differently in the eyes of the other; when a party acknowledges something he or she has done that hurt the other party and/or apologizes for it.

By supporting parties' shifts from weakness to greater empowerment and from self-absorption to greater recognition, the quality of the parties' interaction changes and, in this view, the conflict interaction becomes more productive regardless

(continued)

EXHIBIT 9.2 Continued

of whatever decisions are made. When common ground cannot be found, there are still important opportunities for parties to determine how they can live with difference. A transformative mediator attempts to ensure that parties develop their positions and arguments and understand each other so that, even if they do not come to an agreement or even if they decide to end a relationship, their views are clearer to themselves and their awareness of the other is enhanced. This provides for a more deliberate, focused, and reflective way of living with differences and making decisions about anything that arises between the parties.

Mediators reach the transformative goals of the process by focusing closely on the moment-to-moment interaction and intervening as facilitators who help parties elaborate their views and options. The mediator leaves control of the substantive issues clearly in the hands of the parties and does not interject his or her opinions or solutions in any way that directs the substantive outcomes or decision-making. Parties are encouraged to clarify their own perspectives and options and to make their own choices throughout the process. Empowerment is contingent on self-determined choice. Transformative mediators support perspective-taking by summarizing, reflecting, supporting, clarifying and checking-in on how the parties want the process and their interaction to unfold. Party control over the process is a hallmark of transformative intervention. This emphasis acknowledges the link between the content of a dispute and the process followed to address it, and it helps to ensure that during the intervention the parties interact in ways that they see as safe and productive for them (Folger, 2001).

9.4.2 Third-Party Roles and Climate

When third parties intervene in conflicts, shifts in climate are likely for several reasons. At the most basic level, third parties are "new" participants in the conflict. They contribute to establishing a climate that reflects different moves and responses (See Table 9.3).

In addition, intervenors are more than just additional interactors in the conflict; they are participants with mandates to control process or outcomes to a lesser or greater extent. The third party's mandate carries, in this sense, the power to enforce new expectations for behavior—to establish a new climate. Many of the process controls that third parties impose are aimed at managing parties' interaction. These controls may limit when and how long parties talk, stifle personal attacks, and/or arrange agenda items so that more explosive issues are surrounded by innocuous or mundane topics. As seen in the earlier discussions of climate, conflicts may not be well defined because parties feel it is not safe to state their positions or to express their emotions. The parties may believe that if they are honest, "things will get out of hand" or irreconcilable personal animosities will develop. Third party controls over interaction can establish a safe climate wherein conflicts can be sharpened without risk of spiraling escalation.

Third, because intervenors are initially "outsiders" to the dispute, the mere presence of a third party can change conditions considerably. When he or she first becomes involved, there is often a sense that parties need to "perform well"—to be on their best behavior—for the intervenor. Although this performance may seem inauthentic at first and can fade fast once the parties start interacting, it often encourages people to be more careful about word choices and style of presentation. Parties may be more descriptive than evaluative and less likely to blame others as they define the issues. Disputants begin to

TABLE 9.3 *How Third-Party Involvement Shifts Conflict Climates*

- Third parties enter the stream of parties' conflict interaction and influence it.
- Third parties direct process and set new expectations for communication.
- Disputants may want to look "good" for the third party and change their communication style accordingly.
- Third parties create a sense of optimism that alters expectations and party involvement in the conflict interaction.
- Parties listen to each other more attentively and achieve new understandings.
- Parties have a chance to think through what they really want to say to each other.
- Interventions are often conducted in places that are conducive to changes in climate.

recognize that more care is being taken in how others are stating their positions and making evaluations. This becomes a sign that people are trying to work on the issues without destructive escalation. Even though parties may suspect that others are on their best behavior because the third party is present, this period can allow for a greater clarification of issues than has ever been achieved previously. Moreover, climates change as interaction patterns change. Stepping through constructive exchanges, even under the guiding hand of a third party, creates the realization that such exchanges are possible.

Fourth, third parties acting in mediative or other nonadjudicative capacities often bring a sense of optimism that the parties may have lost in failed attempts to resolve the conflict on their own (Domenici & Littlejohn, 2001). When interventions start, there can often be a sense that something new is being tried and that the intervenor may have approaches, insights, or techniques that will ease tensions and settle issues. Third parties often begin an intervention by explicitly stating that they believe a constructive outcome is possible or that they have seen parties in more fractious disputes come to mutually satisfying agreements.

Finally, third-party interventions are often conducted in places conducive to changes in climate (Stulberg, 1987; Tueke, 2005). Facilitators and other intervenors often choose sites where threatening behavior is less likely because it seems inappropriate, such as a church or library. Any change in physical location may influence expectations about what behaviors are appropriate during the intervention.

Although all these factors contribute to third-party influence on climate, there is no guarantee that new climates will be sustained. As discussed earlier, the self-perpetuating tendencies in conflict interaction can overwhelm attempts at intervention. The parties' well-worn interaction patterns can recreate previous climates.

There is another way in which this fourth property of conflict interaction helps to clarify third-party interventions. Our discussion of third-party mandates suggests that there is usually considerable leeway within any mandate for third parties to select a variety of roles. In part, the approach a third party adopts may be explainable if the overarching climate is taken into account. The climate carries expectations for third-party behavior that influence his or her choice of style or approach.

For example, we have described how managers in organizations can adopt a range of roles in handling conflict among subordinates. These approaches vary from advisory, adjudicative, or restructurer roles, on the one hand, to less interventionist roles such as investigator, mediator, and problem-solver. Although quite a range of intervention roles is available, managers tend to prefer the more controlling advisory and adjudicative styles, which tend to impose outcomes rather than guide parties to construct their own solution (Sheppard et al., 1989). The explanation for this tendency is tied to established expectations for how managers act in their working environment—managers tend to feel responsibility for solving problems for people (Kolb & Sheppard, 1985; Kolb, 1986; Karambayya & Brett, 1989 & 1994).

Unlike third parties who intervene in legal settings, managers often have no pre-scribed guidelines for acting as an intervenor. As a result, managers tend to fall back on the authoritative stance they take in everyday supervisory activities such as planning, delegating work, conducting performance appraisals, and the like. Subordinates come to expect managers to take an authoritative stance when they act as third parties, and they sometimes misinterpret less authoritative intervention moves a manager may try to make. For instance, when managers offer mild suggestions in an attempt to encourage parties to settle their own dispute, subordinates may take these suggestions as binding directives (Kolb, 1986).

Besides the influence of their generally authoritative role, managers' adjudicative stance in intervention can be explained by a second reason. Managers are often "insiders" who hold vested interest in the outcomes of conflicts in which they intervene. The productivity or morale of their entire unit may ride on how an internal dispute turns out. Their concern for outcomes may predispose them to take a stronger adjudicative role when conflicts arise in managers' work units.

Intervenors in other settings may choose certain intervention roles because of established climates as well. In some divorce or community mediation programs, there are well-established climates that place a heavy emphasis on reaching high rates of agreement. At base, this emphasis on settlements may stem from financial concerns. Funding for mediation programs may be contingent on rates of reaching agreements in cases. But, like all climates, these expectations are established and embedded in interaction. Mediators in the programs talk to each other about their agreement rates, obstacles they have to overcome in attaining settlements, and/or intervention techniques that work for them to achieve settlements. Mediators who work in climates in which there is pressure to reach agreements may be more likely to adopt "strong arm" styles, shaping agreements in ways that other mediators might view as inconsistent with the goals of mediation (Pearson & Thoennes, 1989; Bush, 2002).

In other mediation programs, the climate may emphasize that mediators reserve judgment about substantive issues and not press for settlements (Harrington & Merry, 1988; DellaNoce, Folger, & Antes, 2002). In these programs, an expectation is set through interaction among mediators and program directors that the disputants should be allowed to construct their own solutions, even if it means that agreements are not reached. In this climate, intervenors are more likely to adopt a nonimpositional style of mediation, one in which mediators allow parties to exchange information and remain focused on the issues.

9.5 Summary and Review

What is a third-party intervention?

This refers to the case in which an outside party works with the principal parties to the conflict to help them manage and resolve it. There are a wide variety of third parties, from judges in formal judicial proceedings, to consultants serving in facilitator roles, to clergy, therapists, and even friends of the parties.

How do mandates influence third-party interventions?

A third party's mandate is the degree of authority he or she is given to manage the conflict. Sometimes mandates are formally granted; for example, in many mediations, participants discuss the "ground rules" and the role of the mediator at the outset and come to a formal agreement. In other cases, mandates are set informally. This is the case, for example, when there is an existing relationship between third and first parties—that is, a superior may try to mediate a conflict between two subordinates. Mandates differ in terms of the degree of process control, content control, and motivational control granted to the third party. Process control is the degree to which the third party is allowed to structure the procedures parties should follow. Content control is the degree to which the third party influences the content of the discussion. Motivational control is the degree to which the third party can influence the parties to come to a particular type of agreement.

Third-party roles differ in the degree of control they exercise, with facilitators being rather loose, mediators in an intermediate place (process control, but little content control), and arbitrators having the highest degree of control (high on process and content control).

How are third parties influenced as they work with conflicts?

Mandates define the power that the third party has and therefore depend on the relationship between parties and the third party. During the intervention, mandates may be redefined and renegotiated. We have emphasized throughout this book that conflicts are beyond the control of any party; so, too, they are greater than the third party and can attain a life of their own. Third parties attempt to channel interaction, but as they do so, their reputations and endorsement are influenced by the interaction, sometimes increased, sometimes maintained, and in some cases eroded. Mandates may change as the conflict interaction unfolds.

What are the different styles mediators can adopt?

Research has indicated a number of styles. Key distinctions to differentiate include: the dealmakers, who strongly shape the deal; the orchestrators, who help the parties work together; a bargaining style, which restricts contact among parties; a therapeutic style, which emphasizes increased understanding and direct contact among parties; and advisory, investigator, restructurer, and mediative roles.

What factors shape the styles third parties adopt?

Carnevale advanced one model that suggests that third-party styles depend on two factors: how much value the third party attaches to achievement of the disputants' goals, and the third party's perception of the degree of common ground. Depending on the values on these two factors, the third party will attempt to integrate, compensate, press, or be inactive.

Do third-party interventions affect relationships?

Third-party interventions shape relationships between the intervenor and the parties. Their credibility, impartiality, and expertise are continuously under negotiation as third parties work with the conflict. Third-party interventions also alter the relationships among the parties themselves, both during the intervention and through to the final resolution. During the intervention, third parties may influence participants to move from established positions, affect the emotional tenor of the interactors, and alter the balance of power between parties.

How does ideology influence third-party roles?

Ideological assumptions influence how third parties influence their practice. Differences among individualist, organic, and relational ideologies promote very different approaches to conflict intervention and different goals for third-party work.

How does transformative mediation differ from most approaches to third-party intervention?

Transformative mediation focuses on developing parties' ability for self-determination and insight into themselves and others. Whereas most third-party approaches regard achieving a satisfactory settlement as the primary goal, transformative mediation believes that achieving empowerment and recognition are prior conditions for a satisfactory settlement. When parties are empowered and recognize other parties' views, they have the best chance of creating outcomes that are truly their own.

How does a third party influence conflict cycles?

Evidence suggests that successful third parties are able to avoid being pulled into the cycles of behavior that emerge during conflicts. Instead, they help parties break these cycles. Ironically, though, third parties may themselves set up repetitive patterns in their own interventions that may become trained incapacities.

Are there recognizable phases in third-party interventions?

One pattern in interventions is composed of four phases: definition, discussion, alternative selection, and reconciliation. There may also be an orientation phase right after definition, in which the process for the intervention is clarified and defined. Interventions are more likely to follow this phase pattern when settlement-oriented styles are used.

What can third parties do to help participants move through differentiation and integration?

Effective third parties sharpen conflicts to help people move through differentiation. They can facilitate this by unearthing the roots of the problem; encouraging statements of needs rather than solutions; demonstrating the incompatibility of needs; and helping parties set high aspirations and sort out and define multiple issues. These actions help parties understand and appreciate the legitimacy of each other and motivate parties to seek a resolution.

Third parties may also induce integration by suggesting common points of agreement and common goals, defining the integrative process, inducing cooperation, and reframing issues. The Conflict Management Procedure was described as one means of defining the integrative process. Osgood's GRIT procedure is one means of inducing cooperation.

How do third parties influence climate?

Having a third party adds another interactor, which automatically affects climate. The third party's control over the process can shift the climate by, for example, increasing parties' feelings of safety. Third parties may also bring a sense of optimism to the situation, rejuvenating parties' hopes that a solution can be found. Third-party interventions can also be conducted in an unusual location, which may change the climate as well.

9.6 Conclusion

Any intervention in conflict is difficult and risky. Third parties always walk a slippery slope, and the principles of conflict interaction examined in this chapter suggest why. An intervention is never completely under the third party's control. Although intervenors may have mandates to control aspects of the process or influence the outcome, the spontaneous nature of conflict interaction can lead third parties down a variety of intervention paths. As participants themselves, third parties respond contingently to the issues on the table and the unfolding sequence of actions and reactions—they react and respond to events as they happen.

Although intervenors can break parties' destructive, repetitive cycles, they can just as easily contribute to existing cycles or become part of new ones. The momentum of parties' destructive patterns can overtake third parties' attempts to direct or redirect the interaction or to create collaborative, less hostile climates. If intervenors take unwarranted measures to control interactions or issues, they run the risk of losing credibility and, ultimately, their effectiveness.

Although the issues in a conflict may appear straightforward, they are often complex and malleable. They change as the parties present them to an intervenor and as the intervenor represents them to the parties during the intervention. The way third parties frame issues can influence the approach they take to intervention. If intervenors frame issues in ways that the parties themselves cannot understand or fully accept, any agreement will be difficult for the parties to enact. In this case, the third party runs the risk of addressing his or her own version of the dispute, rather than the parties'. Although third parties have useful techniques for altering the way parties relate to each other during an intervention, it is often more difficult to create long-term, stable changes in ongoing relationships. Intervention is difficult when it seeks more than short-term gains.

References

Abrams, D., Hogg, M. D., Hinkle, S., & Otten, S. (2005). The social identity perspective on small groups. In M. S. Poole & A. Hollingshead (Eds.) *Theories of small groups: Interdisciplinary perspectives* (pp. 99–138). Thousand Oaks, CA: Sage.

Adler, R. B. (1977). *Confidence in communication: A guide to assertive and social skills.* New York: Holt, Rinehart and Winston.

Alberts, J. (1990). The use of humor in managing couples' conflict interactions. In D. Kahn (Ed.) *Intimates in conflict: A communication perspective* (pp. 105–120). Hillsdale, NJ: Lawrence Erlbaum.

Allport, G. W. (1954). *The nature of prejudice.* New York: Anchor.

Alper, S., Tjosvold, D., & Law, K. S. (2000). Conflict management, efficacy, and performance in organizational teams. *Personnel Psychology, 53,* 625–642.

Antes, J., Folger, J. P., & DellaNoce, D. (2001). Transforming conflict interaction in the workplace: Documented effects of the USPS REDRESS program. *Hofstra Labor and Employment Law Journal 18,* 385–398.

Apfelbaum, E. (1974). On conflicts and bargaining. In L. Berkowitz (Ed.) *Advances in experimental social psychology* (vol. 7, pp. 103–156). New York: Academic Press.

Apfelbaum, E. (1979). Relations of dominance and movements for liberation: An analysis of power between groups. In W. G. Austin & S. Worchel (Eds.) *The social psychology of intergroup relations* (pp. 188–204). Monterey, CA: Brooks/Cole.

Applegate, J. L., & Delia, J. G. (1980). Person-centered speech, psychological development, and contexts of language use. In R. N. St. Clair & H. Giles (Eds.) *The social and psychological contexts of language* (pp. 245–282). Hillsdale, NJ: Lawrence Erlbaum.

Arendt, H. (1969). *On violence.* New York: Harcourt Brace Jovanovich.

Auvine, B., Densmore, B., Extrom, M., Poole, S., & Shanklin, M. (1977). *A manual for group facilitators.* Madison, WI: The Center for Conflict Resolution.

Avery, M., Auvine, B., Streibel, B., & Weiss L. (1981). *Building united judgment.* Madison, WI: The Center for Conflict Resolution.

Axelrod, R. (1984). *The evolution of cooperation.* New York: Basic Books.

Babcock, J. C., Waltz, J., Johnson, N. S., & Gottman, J. M. (1993). Power and violence: The relationship between communication patterns, power discrepancies, and domestic violence. *Journal of Consulting and Clinical Psychology, 61,* 40–50.

Bachman, G. F., & Guerrero, L. K. (2006). An expectancy violations analysis of factors affecting relational outcomes and communicative responses to hurtful events in dating relationships. *Journal of Social and Personal Relationships,* 943–963.

Bachrach, P., & Baratz. M. S. (1962). Two faces of power. *American Political Science Review, 56,* 947–952.

Bachrach, P., & Baratz, M. S. (1970). *Power and poverty.* New York: Oxford University Press.

Bandler, R., & Grinder, J. (1982). *Reframing.* Moab, UT: Real People Press.

Bartos, O. J. (1970). Determinants and consequences of toughness. In P. Swingle (Ed.) *The structure of conflict* (pp. 45–68). New York: Academic Press.

Bartunek, J. M., & Reid, R. D. (1992). The role of conflict in a second order change attempt. In D. M. Kolb & J. M. Bartunek (Ed.) *Hidden conflict in organizations* (pp. 116–143). Newbury Park, CA: Sage.

Bass, B. M. (1990). *Bass & Stogdill's handbook of leadership* (3rd ed.). New York: Free Press.

Baxter, L. A. (1982). Conflict management: An episodic approach. *Small Group Behavior, 13,* 23–42.

Baxter, L. A., Wilmot, W. W., Simmons, C. A., & Swartz, A. (1993). Ways of doing conflict: A folk taxonomy of conflict events in personal relationships. In P. J. Kalbfleisch (Ed.) *Interpersonal communication: Evolving interpersonal relationships* (pp. 89–107). Hillsdale, NJ: Lawrence Erlbaum.

Baxter, L., & Shepard, T. (1978). Sex-role identity, sex of other, and affective relationship as determinants of interpersonal conflict management styles. *Sex Roles, 4,* 813–824.

Bazerman, M. H. (1983). A critical look at the rationality of negotiator judgement. *American Behavioral Scientist, 27,* 211–228.

Bazerman, M. H., Magliozzi, T., & Neale, M. A. (1985). Integrative bargaining in a competitive market. *Organizational Behavior and Human Decision Processes, 35,* 294–313.

Bazerman, M. H., & Neale, M. A. (1983). Heuristics in negotiation: Limitations to dispute resolution effectiveness. In M. H. Bazerman & R. Lewicki (Eds.) *Negotiating in organizations* (pp. 51–67). Beverly Hills, CA: Sage.

Beckman, L. J. (1970). Effects of students' performance on teachers' and observers' attributions of causality. *Journal of Educational Psychology, 61,* 76–82.

Beier, E. G. (1951). The effect of induced anxiety on flexibility of intellectual functioning. *Psychological Monographs, 65,* 3–26.

Bercovitch, J., & Kadayifci, A. (2002). Exploring the relevance and contribution of mediation to peace-building. *Peace and Conflict Studies, 9,* 21–40.

Berger, C. R. (1994). Power, dominance, and social interaction. In M. L. Knapp & G. R. Miller (Eds.) *The handbook of interpersonal communication* (pp. 450–507). Newbury Park, CA: Sage.

Berk, M. S., & Anderson, S. M. (2000). The impact of past relationships on interpersonal behaviors: Behavioral confirmation in the socio-cognitive process of transference. *Journal of Personality and Social Psychology, 79,* 546–562.

Bernard, S., Folger, J. P., Weingarten H. R., & Zumeta, Z. (1984). The neutral mediator: Value dilemmas in divorce mediation. *Mediation Quarterly, 4,* 61–74.

Berryman-Fink, C., & Brunner, C. C. (1987). The effects of sex of source and target on interpersonal conflict management styles. *Southern Speech Communication Journal, 53,* 38–48.

Bies, R. J., Shapiro, D. L., & Cummings, L. L. (1988). Causal accounts and the management of organizational conflict. *Communication Research, 15,* 381–399.

Billig, M. (1976). *The social psychology of intergroup relations.* New York: Academic Press.

Bingham, L., & Nabatchi, T. (2001). Transformative mediation in the USPS REDRESS program: Observations of the ADR specialists. *Hofstra Labor and Employment Law Journal, 18,* 399–428.

Bippus, A. M., & Rollin, E. (2003). Attachment style differences in relational maintenance and conflict behaviors: Friends' perceptions. *Communication Reports, 16,* 113–123.

Blake, R. R., & Mouton, J. S. (1964). *The managerial grid.* Houston: Gulf Publishing.

Blake, R. R., Shepard H., & Mouton, J. S. (1964). *Managing intergroup conflict in industry.* Houston: Gulf Publishing.

Bolger, N., DeLongis, A., Kessler, R. C., & Schilling, E. A. (1989). Effects of daily stress on negative mood. *Journal of Personality and Social Psychology, 57,* 808–818.

Bono, J. E., Boles, T. L., Judge, T. A., & Lauver, K. J. (2002). The role of personality in task and relationship conflict. *Journal of Personality, 70,* 311–344.

Bormann, E. G. (1972). Fantasy and rhetorical vision: The rhetorical criticism of social reality. *Quarterly Journal of Speech, 58,* 396–407.

Boulding, K. (1990). *The three faces of power.* Newbury Park, CA: Sage.

Bourhis, R. Y., & Gagnon, A. (2003). Social orientations in the minimal group paradigm. In R. Brown & S. Gaertner (Eds.) *Blackwell handbook of social psychology: Intergroup processes* (pp. 89–111). Oxford: Blackwell.

Bower, B. (2007). Past impressions: Prior relationships cast a long shadow over our social lives. *Science News, 171,* 363–365.

Bowers, J. W. (1974). Beyond threats and promises. *Communication Monographs, 41,* ix–xi.

Bradley, G. W. (1978). Self-serving biases in the attribution process: A reexamination of the fact or fiction question. *Journal of Personality and Social Psychology, 36,* 56–71.

Brett, J. M., Shapiro, D. L., & Lytle, A. L. (1998). Breaking the bonds of reciprocity in negotiations. *Academy of Management Journal, 41,* 410–424.

Brewer, M. B., & Gaertner, S. (2003). Toward reduction of prejudice: Intergroup contact and social categorization. In R. Brown & S. Gaertner (Eds.) *Intergroup processes* (pp. 451–473). Malden, MA: Blackwell.

Brewer, N., Mitchell, P., & Weber, N. (2002). Gender role, organizational status, and conflict management styles. *International Journal of Conflict Management, 13,* 78–94.

Brown, B. R. (1977). Face-saving and face-restoration in negotiation. In D. Druckman (Ed.) *Negotiations* (pp. 275–300). Beverly Hills, CA: Sage.

Brown, L. D. (1983). *Managing conflict at organizational interfaces.* Reading, MA: Addison-Wesley.

Brown, P., & Levinson, S. (1987). *Universals in language usage: Politeness phenomena.* Cambridge: Cambridge University Press.

Burgoon, J. K. (2003). Spatial relationships in small groups. In R. Y. Hirokawa, R. S. Cathcart, L. A. Samovar, & L. D. Henman (Eds.) *Small group communication: Theory and practice* (pp. 85–96). Los Angeles: Roxbury.

Burgoon, J. K., Stern, L. A., & Dillman, A. (1995). *Interpersonal adaptation: Dyadic interaction patterns.* New York: Cambridge University Press.

Burgoon, J. K., & Hoobler, G. D. (2002). Nonverbal signals. In M. L. Knapp & J. A. Daly (Eds.) *Handbook of interpersonal communication* (3rd ed., pp. 240–299). Thousand Oaks, CA: Sage.

Burgoon, J. K., & Saine, T. J. (1978). *The unspoken dialogue: An introduction to nonverbal communication.* Boston: Houghton Mifflin.

Burke, K. (1935). *Permanence and change.* Berkeley: University of California Press.

Burke, R. J. (1970). Methods of resolving superior–subordinate conflict: The constructive use of subordinate difference and disagreements. *Organizational Behavior and Human Performance, 5,* 939–411.

Burrell, N. A., Buzzanell, P. M., & McMillan, J. J. (1992). Feminine tensions in conflict management as revealed by metaphoric analysis. *Management Communication Quarterly, 6,* 115–149.

Bush, R. B. (2002). Substituting mediation for arbitration: The growing market for evaluative mediation, and what it means for the ADR field. *Pepperdine Dispute Resolution Law Journal, 3,* 111–131.

Bush, R. B., & Folger, J. P. (1994). *The promise of mediation: Responding to conflict through empowerment and recognition.* San Francisco: Jossey-Bass.

Buzzanell, P. M., & Burrell, N. A. (1997). Family and workplace conflict: Examining metaphorical conflict schemas and expressions across conflict and sex. *Human Communication Research, 24,* 109–146.

Cahn, D. (1990a). *Intimates in conflict: A communication perspective.* Hillsdale, NJ: Lawrence Erlbaum Assoc.

Cahn, D. (1990b). Confrontation behaviors, perceived understanding and relationship growth. In D. Cahn (Ed.) *Intimates in conflict: A communication perspective* (pp. 153–166). NJ: Lawrence Erlbaum Assoc.

Cai, D. I., & Drake, L. E. (1998). The business of business negotiation: Intercultural perspectives. In M. Roloff (Ed.) *Communication yearbook 21* (pp. 153–189). Thousand Oaks, CA: Sage.

Cai, D. A., & Fink, E. L. (2002). Conflict style differences between individualists and collectivists. *Communication Monographs, 69,* 67–87.

Canary, D. J., Cupach, W. R., & Serpe, R. T. (2001). A competence-based approach to examining interpersonal conflict: Test of a longitudinal model. *Communication Research, 28,* 79–104.

Canary, D. J., & Lakey, S. G. (2006). Managing conflict in a competent manner: A mindful look at events that matter. In J. G.Oetzel & S. Ting-Toomey (Eds.) *The SAGE handbook of conflict communication* (pp. 185–210). Thousand Oaks, CA: Sage.

Canary, D. J., & Spitzberg, B. H. (1989). A model of the perceived competence of conflict strategies. *Human Communication Research, 15,* 630–649.

Canary, D. J., & Spitzberg, B. H. (1990). Attribution biases and associations between conflict strategies and competence outcomes. *Communication Monographs, 57,* 139–151.

Canary, D. J., Spitzberg, B. H., & Semic, B. A. (1998). The experience and expression of anger in interpersonal settings. In P. A. Andersen & Laura K. Guerrero (Eds.) *Handbook of communication and emotion: Research, theory, applications, and contexts* (pp. 189–213). San Diego, CA: Academic Press.

Carnevale, P. J. (1986). Strategic choice in mediation. *Negotiation Journal, 2,* 41–56.

Carnevale, P. J., Conlon, C. E., Hanisch, K. A., & Harris, K. L. (1989). Experimental research on the strategic-choice model of mediation. In K. Kressel, D. G. Pruitt, & Associates (Eds.) *Mediation research: The process and effectiveness of third party intervention* (pp. 344–367). San Francisco: Jossey-Bass.

Carnevale, P. J., & Pegnetter, R. (1985). The selection of mediation tactics in public sector disputes: A contingency analysis. *Journal of Social Issues, 41,* 65–81.

Carnevale, P., & Probst, T. (1997). Good news about competitive people. In C. DeDreu & E. Van DeViest (Eds.) *Using conflict in organizations* (pp. 129–146). London: Sage.

Carnevale, P. J., Putnam, L. L., Conlon, D. E., & O'Connor, K. M. (1991). Mediator behavior and effectiveness in community mediation. In K. Grover Duffy, J. W. Grosch, & P. V. Olczak (Eds.) *Community mediation: A handbook for practitioners and researchers* (pp. 119–136). New York: Guilford Press.

Caughlin, J. P., & Vangelisti, A. L. (2006). Conflict in dating and marital relationships. In J. G. Oetzel & S. Ting-Toomey (Eds.) *The SAGE handbook of conflict communication* (pp. 129–158). Thousand Oaks, CA: Sage.

Chertkoff, J. M., & Esser, J. K. (1976). A review of experiments in explicit bargaining. *Journal of Experimental Social Psychology, 12,* 464–486.

Christiansen, A., & Pasch, L. (1993). The sequence of marital conflict: An analysis of seven phases of marital conflict in distressed and nondistressed couples. *Clinical Psychology Review, 13,* 3–14.

Chusmir, L., & Mills, J. (1989). Gender differences in conflict resolution styles of managers: At work and at home. *Sex Roles, 20,* 149–163.

Clegg, S. (1989). *Frameworks of power.* Newbury Park, CA: Sage.

Cloven, D. H., & Roloff, M. E. (1991). Sense-making activities and interpersonal conflict: Communication cures for the mulling blues. *Western Journal of Speech Communication, 55,* 134–158.

Colquitt, J. A. (2001). On the dimensionality of organizational justice: A construct validation of a measure. *Journal of Applied Psychology, 8,* 386–400.

Conley, J. M., & O'Barr, W. M. (1990). Rules versus relationships in small claims disputes. In A. D. Grimshaw (Ed.) *Conflict talk* (pp. 178–196). Cambridge: Cambridge University Press.

Conrad, C. (1991). Communication in conflict: Style-strategy relationships. *Communication Monographs, 58,* 135–155.

Conrad, C., & Poole, M. S. (2004). *Strategic organizational communication,* 5th ed. Belmont, CA: Wadsworth.

Conrad, C., & Ryan, M. (1985). Power, praxis, and self in organizational communication theory. In P. K. Tompkins, & R. McPhee (Eds.) *Organizational communication: Traditional themes and new directions* (pp. 211–234). Newbury Park, CA: Sage.

Cooper, J., & Fazio, R. (1979). The formation and persistence of attitudes that support intergroup conflict. In W. G. Austin & S. Worchel (Eds.) *The social psychology of intergroup relations* (pp. 149–159). Monterey, CA: Brooks/Cole.

Coser, L. (1956). *The functions of social conflict.* New York: Free Press.

Cosier, R. A., & Ruble, T. L. (1981). Research on conflict handling behavior: An experimental approach. *Academy of Management Journal, 24,* 816–831.

Craig, R. T., Tracy, K., & Spisak, F. (1986). The discourse of requests: Assessment of a politeness approach. *Human Communication Research, 12,* 437–468.

Crenson, M. A. (1971). *The un-politics of air pollution: A study of nondecision making in the cities.* Baltimore: Johns Hopkins Press.

Crockett, L. J., & Randall, B. A. (2006). Linking adolescent family and peer relationships to the quality of young adult romantic relationships: The mediating role of conflict tactics. *Journal of Social and Personal Relationships, 23,* 761–780.

Crohan, S. E. (1992). Marital happiness and spousal consensus on beliefs about marital conflict: A longitudinal investigation. *Journal of Social and Personal Relationships, 9,* 89–102.

Cronen, V., Pearce, B., & Snavely, L. (1980). A theory of rule-structure and types of episodes and a study of perceived enmeshment in undesired repetitive patterns URPs. In D. Nimmo (Ed.) *Communication yearbook 3* (pp. 225–240). New Brunswick, NJ: Transaction Books.

Crowfoot, J., & Wondolleck, J. M. (1990). *Environmental disputes: Community involvement in conflict resolution.* Washington, DC: Island Press.

Cupach, W. R., & Metts, S. (1994). *Facework.* Newbury Park, CA: Sage.

Dalton, M. (1959). *Men who manage.* New York: Wiley.

DeDreu, C. W., Harnnick, W., & Van Vianen, A. M. (1999). Conflict and performance in groups and organizations. In C. L. Cooper & I. T. Roberston (Eds.) *International review of industrial and organizational psychology, Vol. 14.* (pp. 369–414). Chichester, UK: Wiley.

DeDreu, C. W., Weingart, L., & Kwon, S. (2000). Influence of social motives on integrative negotiations: A meta-analytic review and test of two theories. *Journal of Personality and Social Psychology, 78,* 889–905.

DeDreu, C. W., & Van Vianen, A. M. (2001). Managing relationship conflict and the effectiveness of organizational teams. *Journal of Organizational Behavior, 22,* 309–328.

DellaNoce, D. (2001). Recognition in theory, practice, and training. In J. Folger & R. B. Bush (Eds.) *Designing mediation: Approaches to training and practice in a transformative framework* (pp. 96–111). New York: Institute for the Study of Conflict Transformation.

DellaNoce, D., Bush, R. B., & Folger, J. (2002). Clarifying the theoretical underpinnings of mediation: Implications for practice and policy. *Pepperdine Dispute Resolution Law Journal, 3,* 39–66.

DellaNoce, D., Folger, J., & Antes, J. (2002). Assimilative, autonomous or synergistic visions: How mediation programs in Florida address the dilemma of court connection. *Pepperdine Dispute Resolution Law Journal, 3,* 11–38.

Deschamps, J. C., & Brown, R. (1983). Superordinate goals and intergroup conflict. *British Journal of Social Psychology, 22,* 189–195.

Deutsch, M. (1973). *The resolution of conflict.* New Haven: Yale University Press.

Deutsch, M., & Krauss, R. M. (1962). Studies of interpersonal bargaining. *Journal of Conflict Resolution, 6,* 52–76.

Dillard, J. P., Anderson, J. W., & Knoblach, L. K. (2002). Interpersonal influence. In M. L. Knapp & J. A. Daly (Eds.) *Handbook of interpersonal communication* (3rd ed., pp. 423–474). Thousand Oaks, CA: Sage.

Dirks, K. T., & Ferrin, D. L. (2002). Trust in leadership: Meta-analytic findings and implications for research and practice. *Journal of Applied Psychology, 87,* 611–628.

Distefano, J. J., & Maznevski, M. L. (2000). Creating value with diverse teams in global management. *Organizational Dynamics, 29,* 45–63.

Domenici, K. (1996). *Mediation: Empowerment in conflict management.* Prospect Heights, IL: Waveland Press.

Domenici, K., & Littlejohn, S. W. (2001). *Mediation: Empowerment in conflict management.* Prospect Heights, IL: Waveland Press.

Donnellon, A., Gray, B. & Bougon, M.G. (1986). Communication, meaning and organized action. *Administrative Science Quarterly, 31,* 43–55.

Donohue, W. A. (1981). Development of a model of rule use in negotiation interaction. *Communication Monographs, 48,* 106–120.

Donohue, W. A. (1989). Criteria for developing communication theory in mediation. In M. Rahim (Ed.) *Managing conflict: An interdisciplinary approach* (pp. 71–91). New York: Praeger.

Donohue, W. A. (1991). *Communication, marital dispute and divorce mediation.* Hillsdale, NJ: Lawrence Erlbaum.

Donohue, W. A. (2001). Resolving relational paradox: The language of conflict in relationships. In W. F. Eadie & P. E. Nelson (Eds.) *The language of conflict and resolution* (pp. 21–46). Thousand Oaks, CA: Sage.

Donohue, W. A. (2006). Managing interpersonal conflict: The mediation promise. In J. G. Oetzel & S. Ting-Toomey (Eds.) *The SAGE handbook of conflict communication* (pp. 211–233). Thousand Oaks, CA: Sage.

Donohue, W. A., Diez, M. E., & Hamilton, M. (1984). Coding naturalistic negotiation interaction. *Human Communication Research, 10,* 403–425.

Donohue, W. A., Diez, M. E., & Stahle, R. B. (1983). New directions in negotiation research. In R. W. Bostrom (Ed.) *Communication yearbook 7* (pp. 249–279). Beverly Hills, CA: Sage.

Donohue, W. A., & Kolt, R. (1992). *Managing interpersonal conflict.* Newbury Park, CA: Sage.

Douglas, A. (1962). *Industrial peacemaking.* New York: Columbia University Press.

Dovidio, J. F., Kawakami, K., & Beach, K. R. (2003). Implicit and explicit attitudes: Examination of the relationship between measures of intergroup bias. In R. Brown & S. Gaertner (Eds.) *Intergroup processes* (pp. 175–197). Malden, MA: Blackwell.

Downs, C. W., Smeyak, G. P., & Martin, E. (1980). *Professional interviewing.* New York: Harper and Row.

Duane, M. J. (1989). Sex differences in styles of conflict management. *Psychological Reports, 65,* 1033–1034.

Duffy, K., Grosch, J. W., & Olczak, P. V. (Eds.) (1991). *Community mediation: A handbook for practitioners and researchers.* New York: Guilford Press.

Ebert, R. J., & Wall, J. A. (1983). Voluntary adoption of negotiation processes. In M. Bazerman & R. Lewicki (Eds.) *Negotiating in organizations* (pp. 91–113). Beverly Hills, CA: Sage.

Edwards, R., Honeycutt, J. M., & Zagacki, K. S. (1988). Imagined interaction as an element of social cognition. *Western Journal of Speech Communication, 52,* 23–45.

Eidelson, R. J., & Eidelson, J. I. (2003). Dangerous ideas: Five beliefs that propel people toward conflict. *American Psychologist, 58,* 182–192.

Eisenberg, A. R., & Garvey, C. (1981). Children's use of verbal strategies in resolving conflicts. *Discourse Processes, 4,* 149–170.

Ellis, D., & Fisher, B. A. (1975). Phases of conflict in small group development. *Human Communication Research, 1,* 195–212.

Ellis, D., & Maoz, I. (2002). Cross-cultural argument interactions between Israeli-Jews and Palestinians. *Journal of Applied Communication Research, 30,* 181–194.

Elsayed-Ekhouly, S. M., & Buda, R. (1996). Organizational conflict: A comparative analysis of conflict across cultures. *The International Journal of Conflict Management, 7,* 71–81.

Emerson, R. M. (1962). Power-dependence relations. *American Sociological Review, 24,* 31–41.

Endler, N. S., & Magnusson, D. (1976). Toward an interactional psychology of personality. *Psychological Bulletin, 83,* 956–974.

Epstein, S. (1962). The measurement of drive and conflict in humans: Theory and experiment. In M. R. Jones (Ed.) *Nebraska Symposium on motivation.* Lincoln: University of Nebraska Press.

Etzioni, A. (1967). The Kennedy experiment. *Western Political Quarterly, 20,* 361–380.

Fehr, B., Baldwin, M., Collins, L., Patterson, S., & Benditt, R. (1999). Anger in close relationships: An interpersonal script analysis. *Personality and Social Psychology, 25,* 299–312.

Felstiner, W. L., Abel, R. L., & Sarat, A. (1980–1981). The emergence and transformation of disputes: Naming, blaming, claiming. *Law and Society Review, 15,* 631–654.

Feuille, P. (1979). Selected benefits and costs of compulsory arbitration. *Industrial and Labor Relations Review, 33,* 64–76.

Fiedler, K., & Schmid, J. (2003). How language contributes to persistence of stereotypes as well as other, more general, intergroup issues. In R. Brown &

S. Gaertner (Eds.) *Blackwell handbook of social psychology: Intergroup processes* (pp. 261–280). Oxford: Blackwell.

Filley, A. (1975). *Interpersonal conflict resolution.* Glenview, IL: Scott, Foresman.

Fink, E. L., & Chen, S. (1995). A Galileo analysis of organizational climate. *Human Communication Research, 21,* 494–522.

Finkelstein, S. (2003). *Why smart executives fail.* New York: Portfolio.

Fisher, R. (1964). Fractionating conflict. In C. Smith (Ed.) *Conflict resolution: Contributions of the behavioral sciences* (pp. 157–169). South Bend, IN: University of Notre Dame Press.

Fisher, R. (1969). *International conflict resolution for beginners.* New York: Harper and Row.

Fisher, R., & Ury, W. (1981). *Getting to yes: Negotiating agreement without giving in.* Boston: Houghton Mifflin.

Fitzpatrick, M. A., & Caughlin, J. P. (2002). Interpersonal communication in family relationships. In M. L. Knapp & J. A. Daly (Eds.) *Handbook of interpersonal communication* (3rd ed., pp. 726–778). Thousand Oaks, CA: Sage.

Fletcher, J. (1999). *Disappearing acts: Gender, power, and relational practice at work.* Cambridge, MA: MIT Press.

Folberg, J., & Taylor, A. (1984). *Mediation: A comprehensive guide to resolving conflicts without litigation.* San Francisco: Jossey-Bass.

Folger, J. P. (1991). Assessing community dispute resolution needs. In K. Grover Duffy, J. W. Grosch, & P. V. Olczak (Eds.) *Community mediation: A handbook for practitioners and researchers* (pp. 53–69). New York: Guilford Press.

Folger, J. P., & Bernard, S. E. (1985). Divorce mediation: When mediators challenge the divorcing parties. *Mediation Quarterly, 10,* 5–23.

Folger, J. P., & Bush, R. B. (2001). *Designing mediation: Approaches to training and practice within a transformative framework.* New York: Institute for the Study of Conflict Transformation.

Folger, R., & Cropanzano, R. (2001). Fairness theory: Justice as accountability. In J. Greenberg & R. Cropanzano (Eds.) *Advances in organizational justice* (pp. 1–55). Palo Alto, CA: Stanford University Press.

Fraser, B. (1981). On apologizing. In F. Coulmas (Ed.) *Conversational routine.* New York: Moulton Publishers.

French, R. P., & Raven, B. (1959). The bases of social power. In D. Cartwright (Ed.) *Studies in social power* (pp. 150–167). Ann Arbor: University of Michigan Press.

Freud, S. (1925). *The unconscious.* Translated by J. Riviere. London: Hogarth Press.

Freud, S. (1947). *The ego and the id.* Translated by J. Strackey. London: Hogarth Press. (Original work published in 1923.)

Freud, S. (1949). *An outline of psychoanalysis.* Translated by J. Strackey. New York: Norton.

Freud, S. (1953). *The interpretation of dreams.* Translated by J. Strackey. London: Hogarth Press. (Original work published in 1900.)

Frost, J. H., & Wilmot, W. (1978). *Interpersonal conflict.* Dubuque, IA: Wm. C. Brown.

Fry, D. P., & Fry, C. B. (1997). Culture and conflict-resolution models: Exploring alternatives to violence. In D. P. Fry & K. Bjorkqvist (Eds.) *Cultural variation in conflict resolution: Alternative to violence* (pp. 9–23). Mahwah, NJ: Lawrence Erlbaum Associates.

Gaelick, L., Bodenhausen, G. V., & Wyer, R. (1985). Emotional communication in close relationships. *Journal of Personality and Social Psychology, 49,* 1246–1265.

Garcia, A. (2000). Negotiating negotiation: The collaborative production of resolution in small claims mediation hearings. *Discourse and Society, 11,* 315–343.

Garcia-Prieto, P., Bellard, E., & Schneider, S. C. (2003). Experiencing diversity, conflict, and emotions in teams. *Applied Psychology: An International Review, 52,* 413–440.

Gayle, B. M., & Preiss, R. W. (1998). Assessing emotionality in organizational conflicts. *Management Communication Quarterly, 12,* 280–302.

Gaylin, W. (2003). *Hatred: The psychological descent into violence.* New York: Public Affairs.

Geist, P. (1995). Negotiating whose order? Communicating to negotiate identities and revise organizational structures. In A. M. Nicotera (Ed.) *Conflict and organizations* (pp. 45–64). Albany, NY: State University of New York Press.

Gelfand, M. J., Nishii, L. H., Holcombe, K., Dyer, N., Ohbuchi, K., & Fukomo, M. (2001). Cultural influences on cognitive representations of conflict: Interpretations of conflict episodes in the U.S. and Japan. *Journal of Applied Psychology, 86,* 1059–1074.

Gibb, J. (1961). Defensive communication. *Journal of Communication, 2,* 141–148.

Gibbons, P. A., Bradac, J. J., & Busch, J. D. (1992). The role of language in negotiations: Threats and promises. In L. Putnam & M. E. Roloff (Eds.) *Communication and negotiation* (pp. 156–175). Newbury Park, CA: Sage.

Giles, D., & Wiemann, J. (1987). *Language, social comparison and power.* In C. R. Berger and S. H. Chaffee

(Eds.) *The handbook of communication science* (pp. 350–384). Beverly Hills, CA: Sage.

Glen, E. S. (1981). *Man and mankind: Conflict and communication between cultures.* Norwich, NJ: Ablex.

Goffman, E. (1955). On facework: An analysis of ritual elements in social interaction. *Psychiatry, 18,* 213–231.

Goffman, E. (1967). *Interaction ritual: Essays on face-to-face behavior.* Garden City, NY: Doubleday.

Goodwin, M. H. (1982). Processes of dispute resolution among urban black children. *American Ethnologist, 9,* 76–96.

Gordon, T. (1970). *Parent effectiveness training.* New York: Wyden.

Gormly, J., Gormly, A., & Johnson, C. (1972). Consistency of sociobehavioral responses to interpersonal disagreement. *Journal of Personality and Social Psychology, 24,* 221–224.

Gottman, J. M. (1979). *Marital interaction: Experimental investigation.* New York: Academic Press.

Gottman, J. M. (1994). *What predicts divorce? The relationship between marital processes and marital outcomes.* Hillsdale, NJ: Lawrence Erlbaum.

Gottman, J. M., Driver, J., Yoshimoto, D., & Rushe, R. (2002). Approaches to the study of power in violent and nonviolent marriages, and in gay male and lesbian cohabiting relationships. In P. Noller & J. A. Feeney (Eds.) *Understanding marriage: Developments in the study of couple interaction* (pp. 323–347). New York: Cambridge University Press.

Gouldner, A. (1954). *Wildcat strike.* Yellow Springs, OH: Antioch Press.

Gouldner, A. W. (1960). The norm of reciprocity: A preliminary statement. *American Sociological Review, 25,* 161–178.

Gouran, D. S., & Hirkokawa, R. Y. (2003). Effective decision-making and problem solving in groups: A functional perspective. In R. Y. Hirokawa, R. S. Cathcart, L. A. Samovar, & L. D. Henman (Eds.) *Small group communication: Theory and practice* (pp. 27–38). Los Angeles: Roxbury.

Greatbatch, D., & Dingwall, R. (1989). Selective facilitation: Some preliminary observations on a strategy used by divorce mediators. *Law and Society Review, 23,* 613–641.

Grice, H. P. (1975). Logic and conversation. In P. Cole and J. L. Morgan (Eds.) *Syntax and semantics, Vol. 3* (pp. 41–58). New York: Academic Press.

Grimshaw, A. D. (Ed.) (1990). *Conflict talk: Sociolinguistic investigations of arguments in conversations.* Cambridge: Cambridge University Press.

Gross, J. A., & Greenfield, P. A. (1986). Arbitral value judgements in health and safety disputes: Management rights over worker's rights. *Buffalo Law Review, 34,* 645–691.

Gross, M. A., Guerrero, L. K., & Alberts, J. K. (2004). Perceptions of conflict strategies and communication competence in task-oriented dyads. *Journal of Applied Communication Research, 32,* 249–270.

Guerrero, L. K., & La Valley, A. G. (2006). Conflict, emotion, and communication. In J. G. Oetzel & S. Ting-Toomey (Eds.) *The SAGE handbook of conflict communication* (pp. 69–96). Thousand Oaks, CA: Sage.

Guetzkow, H., and Gyr, J. (1954). An analysis of conflict in decision-making groups. *Human Relations, 7,* 367–381.

Hall, J. (1969). *Conflict management survey: A survey on one's characteristic reaction to and handling of conflicts between himself and others.* Monroe, TX: Teleometrics International.

Hall, J., & Watson, W. H. (1970). The effects of a normative intervention on group decision-making performance. *Human Relations, 23,* 299–317.

Harre R., & van Langenhove, L. (1999). *Positioning theory.* Oxford, UK: Blackwell.

Harrington, C., & Merry, S. E. (1988). Ideological production: The making of community mediation. *Law and Society Review, 22,* 709–737.

Hatfield, E., Cacioppo, J. T., & Rapson, R. L. (1994). *Emotional contagion.* Cambridge: Cambridge University Press.

Haynes, J. M. (1981). *Divorce mediation: A practical guide for therapists and counselors.* New York: Springer.

Haynes, J. M., & Haynes, G. L. (1989). *Mediating divorce.* San Francisco: Jossey-Bass.

Heider, F. (1958). *The psychology of interpersonal relations.* New York: Wiley.

Heuer, L. B., & Penrod, S. (1986). Procedural preferences as a function of conflict intensity. *Journal of Personality and Social Psychology, 51,* 700–710.

Hewitt, J. P., & Stokes, R. (1975). Disclaimers. *American Sociological Review 40:* 1–11.

Hilgard, E., & Bower, G. (1966). *Theories of learning.* New York: Appleton-Century-Crofts.

Hiltrop, J. M. (1985). Mediator behavior and the settlement of collective bargaining disputes in Britain. *Journal of Social Issues, 41,* 83–99.

Hiltrop, J. M. (1989). Factors associated with successful labor mediation. In K. Kressel, D. G. Pruitt, & Associates (Eds.) *Mediation research: The process and effectiveness of third-party intervention* (pp. 241–262). San Francisco: Jossey-Bass.

Hofstede, G., & Bond, M. (1984). Hofstede's culture dimensions. *Journal of Cross-Cultural Psychology, 15,* 417–433.

Hogg, M. A. (2003). Social categorization, depersonalization, and group behavior. In M. A. Hogg & S. Tindale (Eds.) *Blackwell handbook of social psychology: Group processes* (pp. 56–85). Oxford: Blackwell.

Holmes, M. (1992). Phase structures in negotiation. In L. Putnam & M. Roloff (Eds.) *Communication and negotiation* (pp. 83–105). Beverly Hills, CA: Sage.

Holsti, O. R. (1971). Crisis, stress and decision-making. *International Social Science Journal, 23,* 53–67.

Hu, H. C. (1944). The Chinese concept of "face." *American Anthropologist, 46,* 45–64.

Hunger, J. D., & Stern, L. W. (1976). An assessment of the functionality of the superordinate goal in reducing conflict. *Academy of Management Journal, 19,* 591–605.

Infante, D. A., & Wigley, C. J. (1986). Verbal aggressiveness: An interpersonal model and measure. *Communication Monographs, 53,* 61–69.

Ivy, D. K., & Backlund, P. (1994). *Exploring genderspeak: Personal effectiveness in gender communication.* New York: McGraw-Hill.

Jameson, J. K. (2001). Employee perceptions of the availability and use of interest-based, rights-based, and power-based conflict management strategies. *Conflict Resolution Quarterly, 19,* 163–196.

Janeway, E. (1980). *Powers of the weak.* New York: Morrow-Quill.

Janis, I. (1972). *Victims of groupthink.* Boston: Houghton Mifflin.

Janis, I., and Mann, L. (1977). *Decision-making.* New York: Free Press.

Janssen, O., van de Vliert, E., & Veenstra, C. (1999). How task and person conflict shape the role of positive interdependence in management groups. *Journal of Management, 25,* 117–141.

Jehn, K. A. (1995). A multimethod examination of the benefits and detriments of intragroup conflict. *Administrative Science Quarterly, 40,* 256–282.

Jehn, K. A., & Chatman, J. A. (2000). The influence of proportional and perceptual conflict composition on team performance. *International Journal of Conflict Management, 11,* 56–73.

Jewell, L. N., & Reitz, H. J. (1981). *Group effectiveness in organizations.* Glenview, IL: Scott, Foresman.

Johnson, D. W., & Johnson, F. P. (1975). *Joining together.* Englewood Cliffs, NJ: Prentice-Hall.

Johnson, K. L., & Roloff, M. E. (1998). Serial arguing and relational quality: Determinants and consequences of perceived resolvability. *Communication Research, 25,* 327–343.

Jones, E. E., Gergen, K. J., & Jones, R. G. (1963). Tactics of ingratiation among leaders and subordinates in a status hierarchy. *Psychological Monographs, 77,* 120–144.

Jones, E. E., & Nisbett R. E. (1971). The actor and the observer: Divergent perceptions of the causes of behavior. In E. E. Jones, E. Kanouse, H. H. Kelley, R. E. Nisbett, S. Valins, & B. Weiner (Eds.) *Attribution: Perceiving the causes of behavior* (pp. 79–94). Morristown, NJ: General Learning Press.

Jones, R. E., & Melcher, B. H. (1982). Personality and preference for modes of conflict resolution. *Human Relations, 35,* 649–658.

Jones, R. E., & White, C. S. (1985). Relationships among personality, conflict resolution styles, and task effectiveness. *Group and Organization Studies, 10,* 152–167.

Jones, T. S. (1988). An analysis of phase structures in successful and unsuccessful divorce mediation. *Communication Research, 15,* 470–495.

Jones, T. S. (1989). Lag sequential analyses of mediator-spouse and husband-wife interaction in successful and unsuccessful divorce mediation. In M. Rahim (Ed.) *Managing conflict: An interdisciplinary approach* (pp. 93–107). New York: Praeger.

Jones, T. (2001). Emotional communication in conflict. In W. F. Eadie & P. E. Nelson (Eds.) *The language of conflict and resolution* (pp. 81–104). Thousand Oaks, CA: Sage.

Jones, T. S., & Bodtker, A. (2001). Mediating with heart in mind: Addressing emotion in mediation practice. *Negotiation Journal, 17,* 217–244.

Jones, T., & Brinkman, H. (1994). "Teach your children well": Recommendations for peer mediation programs. In J. P. Folger & T. Jones (Eds.) *New directions in mediation: Communication research and perspectives* (pp. 159–174). Newbury Park, CA: Sage.

Karambayya, R., & Brett, J. M. (1989). Managers handling disputes: Third-party roles and perceptions of fairness. *Academy of Management Journal, 32,* 687–704.

Karambayya, R., & Brett, J. M. (1994). Managerial third parties: Intervention strategies, process, and consequences. In J. P. Folger & T. Jones (Eds.) *New directions in mediation: Communication research and perspectives* (pp. 175–192). Newbury Park, CA: Sage.

Kaufman, S., & Duncan, G. T. (1989). Third-party intervention: A theoretical framework. In M. A. Rahim (Ed.) *Managing conflict: An interdisciplinary approach* (pp. 273–289). New York: Praeger.

Keck, K. L., & Samp, J. A. (2007). The dynamic nature of goals and message production as revealed in a sequential analysis of conflict interactions. *Human Communication Research, 33,* 27–47.

Kelley, H., Cunningham, J., Grishman, J., Lefebvre, L., Sink, C., & Yablon, G. (1978). Sex differences in comments made during conflict within close heterosexual pairs. *Sex Roles, 4,* 473–492.

Kelley, H. H. (1965). Experimental studies of threats in interpersonal negotiations. *Journal of Conflict Resolution, 9,* 79–105.

Kelley, H. H. (1979). *Personal relationships: Their structure and processes.* Hillsdale, NJ: Lawrence Erlbaum.

Kim, M. S., & Leung, T. (2000). A multicultural view of conflict management styles: Review and critical synthesis. In M. Roloff (Ed.) *Communication yearbook 23* (pp. 227–269). Thousand Oaks, CA: Sage.

Kipnis, D. (1990). *Technology and power.* New York: Springer-Verlag.

Kipnis, D., Schmidt, S., & Wilkerson, I. (1980). Intraorganizational influence tactics: Explorations in getting one's way. *Journal of Applied Psychology, 65,* 440–452.

Kluwer, E. S., C. deDreu, K. W., & Buunk, B. P. (1998). Conflict in intimate vs. nonintimate relationships: When gender role stereotyping overrides biased self-other judgment. *Journal of Social and Personal Relationships, 15,* 637–650.

Kochan, T. A., & Jick, T. A. (1978). The public sector mediation process: A theory and empirical examination. *Journal of Conflict Resolution, 22,* 209–241.

Kolb, D. (1983). *The mediators.* Cambridge, MA: MIT Press.

Kolb, D. (1986). Who are organizational third parties and what do they do? In R. J. Lewicki, B. H. Sheppard, & M. H. Bazerman (Eds.) *Research on negotiation in organizations* (pp. 207–278). Greenwich, CT: JAI Press.

Kolb, D. (1987). Corporate ombudsman and organizational conflict. *Journal of Conflict Resolution, 31,* 663–692.

Kolb, D. (1989). Labor mediators, managers and ombudsmen: Roles mediators play in different contexts. In K. Kressel, D. G. Pruitt, & Associates (Eds.) *Mediation research: The process and effectiveness of third-party intervention* (pp. 91–114). San Francisco: Jossey-Bass.

Kolb, D., & Bartunek, J. M., (Eds.) (1992). *Hidden conflict in organizations.* Newbury Park, CA: Sage.

Kolb, D., & Sheppard, B. H. (1985). Do managers mediate or even arbitrate? *Negotiation Journal, 1,* 379–388.

Komorita, S. S. (1977). Negotiating from strength and the concept of bargaining strength. *Journal of the Theory of Social Behavior, 7,* 65–79.

Korabik, K., Baril, G., & Watson, C. (1993). Managers' conflict management style and leadership effectiveness: The moderating effect of gender. *Sex Roles, 29,* 405–420.

Kozan, M. K. (1991). Interpersonal conflict management styles of Jordanian managers. In K. Avruch, P. W. Black, & J. A. Scimecia (Eds.) *Conflict resolution: Cross-cultural perspectives* (pp. 85–105). Westport, CT: Greenwood Press.

Kozan, M. K. (1997). Culture and conflict management: A theoretical framework. *The International Journal of Conflict Management, 8,* 338–360.

Kramer, R. M., & Carnevale, P. J. (2003). Trust and intergroup negotiation. In R. Brown & S. Gaertner (Eds.) *Blackwell handbook of social psychology: Intergroup processes* (pp. 431–450). Oxford: Blackwell.

Krauss, E. S., Rohlen, T. P., & Steinhoff, P. G. (Eds.) (1984). *Conflict in Japan.* Honolulu: University of Hawaii Press.

Kressel, K., Pruitt, D. G., & Associates (Eds.) (1989). *Mediation research: The process and effectiveness of third-party intervention.* San Francisco: Jossey-Bass.

Kritek, P. B. (1994). *Negotiating at an uneven table.* San Francisco: Jossey-Bass.

Kuhn, T., & Poole, M. S. (2000). Do conflict management styles affect group decision-making? Evidence from a longitudinal field study. *Human Communication Research, 26,* 558–590.

Kurdeck, L. A. (1994). Conflict resolution styles in gay, lesbian, heterosexual nonparent, and heterosexual parent couples. *Journal of Marriage and the Family, 56,* 705–722.

Lakey, S. G., & Canary D. J. (2002). Actor goal achievement and sensitivity to partner as critical factors in understanding interpersonal communication competence and conflict strategies. *Communication Monographs, 69,* 217–235.

Lam, J. A., Rifkin, J., & Townley, A. (1989). Reframing conflict: Implications for fairness in parent–adolescent mediation. *Mediation Quarterly, 7,* 15–31.

Larson, C. E., & LaFasto, F. M. (1989). *Teamwork.* Newbury Park, CA: Sage.

Lazarus, R. S. & Lazarus, B. N. (1994). *Passion and reason: Making sense of our emotions.* New York: Oxford University Press.

Leary, T. (1957). *Interpersonal diagnosis of personality.* New York: Ronald Press.

Lederach, J. P. (1991). Of nets, nails, and problems: The folk language of conflict resolution in a Central American setting. In K. Avruch, P. W. Black, & J. A. Scimecia (Eds).*Conflict resolution: Cross cultural perspectives* (pp. 165–188). Westport, CT: Greenwood Press.

Lemmon, J. A. (1985). *Family mediation practice.* New York: Free Press.

Leveque, C., & Poole, M. S. (1998). Systems thinking in organizational communication. In P. Salem

(Ed.) *Organizational communication and change* (pp. 79–98). Creskill, NJ: Hampton.

Levinger, G. (1976). A social psychological perspective on marital dissolution. *Journal of Social Issues, 32,* 21–47.

Lim, T., & Bowers, J. W. (1991). Face-work: Solidarity, approbation, and tact. *Human Communication Research, 17,* 415–450.

Lindskold, S. (1978). Trust development, the GRIT proposal, and the effects of conciliatory acts on conflict and cooperation. *Psychological Bulletin, 85,* 772–793.

Lindskold, S. (1979). Managing conflict through announced conciliatory initiative backed by retaliatory capacity. In W. G. Austin & S. Worchel (Ed.) *The social psychology of intergroup relations* (pp. 274–287). Belmont, CA: Wadsworth.

Lindskold, S., Betz, B., & Walters, P. S. (1986). Transforming competitive or cooperative climates. *Journal of Conflict Resolution, 30,* 99–114.

Long, W., & Brecke, P. (2003). *War and reconciliation: Reason and emotion in conflict resolution.* Cambridge, MA: MIT Press.

Lovelace, K., Shapiro, D. L., & Weingart, L. R. (2001). Maximizing cross-functional new product teams' innovativeness and constraint adherence: A conflict communications perspective. *Academy of Management Journal, 44,* 779–793.

Luchins, A., & Luchins, E. (1959). *Rigidity of behavior.* Eugene: University of Oregon Books.

Lukes, S. (1974). *Power: A radical view.* London: MacMillan.

Lyles, M. A., & Mitroff, I. I. (1980). Organizational problem formulation: An empirical study. *Administrative Science Quarterly, 25,* 102–119.

Mackey, R. A., & O'Brien, B. A. (1998). Marital conflict management: Gender and ethnic differences. *Social Work, 43,* 128–141.

Mansbridge, J. (1990). *Beyond self-interest.* Chicago: University of Chicago Press.

Markey, P. M., Funder, D. C., & Ozer, D. J. (2003). Complementarity of interpersonal behaviors in dyadic interactions. *Personality and Social Psychology Bulletin, 29,* 1082–1090.

Marks, J., Johnson, E., & Szanton, P. L. (1984). *Dispute resolution processes in America: Processes in evolution.* Washington, DC: National Institute for Dispute Resolution.

Mather, L., & Yngvesson, B. (1980–1981). Language, audience and the transformation of disputes. *Law and Society Review, 15,* 775–821.

Maurer, R. (1994). *Feedback toolkit.* Portland, OR: Productivity Press.

McGillicuddy, N. B., Pruitt, D. G., Welton, G. L., Zubek, J. M., & Peirce, R. S. (1991). Factors affecting the outcome of mediation: Third-party and disputant behavior. In K. Grover Duffy, J. W. Grosch, & P. V. Olczak (Eds.) *Community mediation: A handbook for practitioners and researchers* (pp. 137–149). New York: Guilford Press.

McLaughlin, M. L. (1984). *Conversation: How talk is organized.* Beverly Hills, CA: Sage.

McLaughlin, M. L., Cody, M. J., & Rosenstein, N. E. (1983). Account sequences in conversations between strangers. *Communication Monographs, 50,* 102–125.

McRae, B. (1998). *The art of creating and claiming value.* Thousand Oaks, CA: Sage.

Menkel-Meadow, C. (1985). The transformation of disputes by lawyers: What the dispute paradigm does and does not tell us. *Journal of Dispute Resolution, 2,* 25–44.

Mernitz, S. (1980). *Mediation of environmental disputes.* New York: Praeger.

Merry, S. E. (1979). Going to court: Strategies of dispute resolution in an American urban neighborhood. *Law and Society Review, 13,* 891–925.

Merry, S. E., & Silbey, S. S. (1984). What do plaintiffs want? Reexamining the concept of dispute. *Justice System Journal, 9,* 151–178.

Messman, S. J., & Canary, D. J. (1998). Patterns of conflict in personal relationships. In B. H. Spitzberg & W. R. Cupach (Eds.) *The dark side of interpersonal relationships* (pp. 121–152). Mahwah, NJ: Lawrence Erlbaum.

Metts, S. (1994). Relational transgression. In W. R. Cupach & B. H. Spitzberg (Eds.) *The dark side of interpersonal communication* (pp. 217–239). Hillsdale, NJ: Lawrence Erlbaum.

Meyer, H. H., Kay, E., & French, Jr., J. R. P. (1965). Split roles in performance appraisal. *Harvard Business Review, 43,* 123–129.

Mikolic, J. M., Parker, J. C., & Pruitt, D. G. (1997). Escalation in response to persistent annoyance: Groups versus individuals and gender effects. *Journal of Personality and Social Psychology, 72,* 151–163.

Miller, A. (1976). Constraint and target effects in the attribution of attitudes. *Journal of Experimental Social Psychology, 12,* 325–339.

Miller, G. R., Boster, F., Roloff, M., & Seibold, D. (1976). Compliance-gaining message strategies: A typology and some findings concerning effects of situational differences. *Communication Monographs 44:* 37–51.

Miller, J. B. (1991). Women's and men's scripts for interpersonal conflict. *Psychology of Women Quarterly, 15,* 15–29.

Moberg, P. J. (2001). Linking conflict strategy to the five-factor model: Theoretical and empirical foundations.

International Journal of Conflict Management, 12, 47–68.

Moore, C. W. (1986). *The mediation process.* San Francisco: Jossey-Bass.

Moore, J. C. (1968). Status and influence in small group interaction. *Sociometry, 31,* 47–63.

Morley, I. E., & Stephenson, G. M. (1977). *The social psychology of bargaining.* London: Allen and Unwin.

Morris, G. H., & Hopper, R. (1980). Remediation and legislation in everyday talk: How communicators achieve consensus. *Quarterly Journal of Speech, 66,* 266–274.

Moscovici, S. (1976). *Social influence and social change.* New York: Academic Press.

Mura, S. S. (1983). Licensing violations: Legitimate violations of Grice's conversation principle. In R. T. Craig & K. Tracy (Eds.) *Conversational coherence: Form, structure and strategy* (pp. 101–115). Beverly Hills, CA: Sage.

Musser, S. J. (1982). A model for predicting the choice of conflict management strategies by subordinates in high-stakes conflicts. *Organizational Behavior and Human Performance, 29,* 257–269.

Neale, M. A., & Northcraft, G. B. (1986). Experts, amateurs, and refrigerators: Comparing expert and amateur decision making on a novel task. *Organizational Behavior and Human Decision Processes, 38,* 305–317.

Newell, S. E., & Stutman, R. K. (1988). The social confrontation episode. *Communication Monographs, 55,* 266–285.

Newell, S. E., & Stutman, R. K. (1989/1990). Negotiating confrontation: The problematic nature of initiation and response. *Research on Language and Social Interaction, 23,* 139–151.

Newell, S. E., & Stutman, R. K. (1991). The episodic nature of social confrontation. In J. A. Andersen (Ed.) *Communication yearbook 14* (pp. 359–392). Beverly Hills, CA: Sage.

Nicotera, A. M. (1994). The use of multiple approaches to conflict: A study of sequences. *Human Communication Research, 20,* 592–621.

Nicotera, A. M., & Dorsey, L. K. (2006). Individual and interactive processes in organizational conflict. In *The Sage handbook of conflict communication* (pp. 293–326). Thousand Oaks, CA: Sage.

North, R. C., Brody, R. A., & Holsti, O. (1963). Some empirical data on the conflict spiral. *Peace Research Society Papers, I,* 1–14.

Northrup, T. (1989). The dynamic of identity in personal and social conflict. In L. Kreisberg, T. Northrup, & S. Thorson (Eds.) *Intractable conflicts and their transformation* (pp. 55–82). Syracuse, NY: Syracuse University Press.

Oakes, P. (2003). The root of all evil in intergroup relations? Unearthing the categorization process. In R. Brown & S. Gaertner (Eds.) *Blackwell handbook of social psychology: Intergroup processes* (pp. 3–21). Oxford: Blackwell.

Oetzel, J. (1998). The effects of ethnicity and self-construals on self-reported conflict styles. *Communication Reports, 11,* 133–144.

Oetzel, J., Meares, M., & Fukumoto, A. (2003). Cross-cultural and intercultural work group communication. In R. Y. Hirokawa, R. S. Cathcart, L. A. Samovar, & L. D. Henman (Eds.) *Small group communication: Theory and practice* (pp. 239–252). Los Angeles: Roxbury.

Oetzel, J. Ting-Toomey, S., Masumoto, T., Yokochi, Y., Pan, X., Takai, J., & Wilcox, R. (2001). Face and facework in conflict: A cross-cultural comparison of China, Germany, Japan, and the United States. *Communication Monographs, 68,* 235–258.

Olson, L. N., & Braithwaite, D. O. (2004). "If you hit me again, I'll hit you back:" Conflict management strategies of individuals experiencing aggression during conflicts. *Communication Studies, 55,* 271–285.

Operario, D., & Fiske, S. T. (2003). Stereotypes: Content, structures, processes, and context. In R. Brown & S. Gaertner (Eds.) *Blackwell handbook of social psychology: Intergroup processes* (pp. 22–44). Oxford: Blackwell.

Osgood, C. E. (1959). Suggestions for winning the real war with communism. *Journal of Conflict Resolution, 3,* 295–325.

Osgood, C. E. (1962). *An alternative to war or surrender.* Urbana: University of Illinois Press.

Papa, M. J., & Natalle, E. J. (1989). Gender, strategy selection, and satisfaction in interpersonal conflict. *Western Journal of Speech Communication, 53,* 260–272.

Peachey, D. E. (1989). What people want from mediation. In K. Kressel, D. G. Pruitt, & Associates (Eds.) *Mediation research: The process and effectiveness of third-party intervention* (pp. 300–321). San Francisco: Jossey-Bass.

Pearce, W. B. (1976). The coordinated management of meaning: A rules-based theory of interpersonal communication. In G. R. Miller (Ed.) *Explorations in interpersonal communication* (pp. 17–36). Beverly Hills, CA: Sage.

Pearce, W. B., & Cronen, V. E. (1980). *Communication, action and meaning.* New York: Praeger.

Pearce, W. B., & Littlejohn, S. W. (1997). *Moral conflict: When social worlds collide.* Thousand Oaks, CA: Sage.

Pearson, J., & Thoennes, N. (1989). Divorce mediation: Reflections on a decade of research. In K. Kressel,

D. G. Pruitt, & Associates (Eds.) *Mediation research: The process and effectiveness of third-party intervention* (pp. 9–30). San Francisco: Jossey-Bass.

Penman, R. (1991). Goals, games and moral orders: A paradoxical case in court? In K. Tracy (Ed.) *Understanding face-to-face interaction* (pp. 21–42). Hillsdale, NJ: Lawrence Erlbaum.

Pfeffer, J. (1978). *Organizational design.* Arlington Heights, IL: AHM Publishing.

Phillips, E., & Cheston, R. (1979). Conflict resolution: What works? *California Management Review, 21,* 76–83.

Phillips, S. U. (1990). The judge as third party in American trial-court conflict talk. In A. D. Grimshaw (Ed.) *Conflict talk* (pp. 197–209). Cambridge: Cambridge University Press.

Pinkley, R. L., & Northcraft, G. B. (1994). Conflict frames of reference: Implications for dispute processes and outcomes. *Academy of Management Journal, 37,* 193–205.

Planalp, S. (1999). *Communicating emotion: Social, moral, and cultural processes.* New York: Cambridge University Press.

Pondy, L. R. (1967). Organizational conflict: Concepts and models. *Administrative Science Quarterly, 12,* 296–320.

Poole, M. S. (1981). Decision development in small groups I: A comparison of two models. *Communication Monographs, 48,* 1–25.

Poole, M. S. (1983). Decision development in small groups III: A multiple sequence theory of decision development. *Communication Monographs, 50,* 321–341.

Poole, M. S. (1985). Communication and organizational climates. In R. D. McPhee & P. Tompkins (Eds.) *Organizational communication: Traditional themes and new directions* (pp. 79–108). Beverly Hills, CA: Sage.

Poole, M. S., & Garner, J. T. (2006). Perspectives on work-group conflict and communication. In J. G. Oetzel & S. Ting-Toomey (Eds.) *The SAGE handbook of conflict communication* (pp. 267–292). Thousand Oaks, CA: Sage.

Poole, M. S., & McPhee, R. D. (1983). Bringing intersubjectivity in: A structurational analysis of climate. In L. Putnam & M. Pacanowsky (Ed.) *Communication and organizations: An interpretive approach* (pp. 195–220). Beverly Hills, CA: Sage.

Poole, M. S., & Roth, J. (1989). Decision development in small groups IV: A typology of decision paths. *Human Communication Research, 15,* 323–356.

Pruitt, D. G. (1971). Indirect communication and the search for agreement in negotiation. *Journal of Applied Social Psychology, 1,* 205–239.

Pruitt, D. G. (1981). *Negotiating behavior.* New York: Academic Press.

Pruitt, D. G. (1983). Achieving integrative agreements. In M. Bazerman & R. Lewicki (Ed.) *Negotiating in organizations* (pp. 35–50). Beverly Hills, CA: Sage.

Pruitt, D. G., & Carnevale, P. J. (1993). *Negotiation in social conflict.* Pacific Grove, CA: Brooks/Cole.

Pruitt, D. G., & Johnson, D. F. (1970). Mediation as an aid to face saving in negotiation. *Journal of Applied Social Psychology, 14,* 239–246.

Pruitt, D. G., & Kimmel, M. J. (1977). Twenty years of experimental gaming: Critique, synthesis, and suggestions for the future. *Annual Review of Psychology, 28,* 363–392.

Pruitt, D. G., & Lewis, S. (1977). The psychology of integrative bargaining. In D. Druckman (Ed.) *Negotiations* (pp. 161–192). Beverly Hills, CA: Sage.

Pruitt, D. G., McGillicuddy, N. B., Welton, G. L., & Fry, W. R. (1989). Process of mediation in dispute settlement centers. In K. Kressel, D. G. Pruitt, & Associates (Eds.) *Mediation research: The process and effectiveness of third-party intervention* (pp. 368–393). San Francisco: Jossey-Bass.

Pruitt, D. G., Rubin, J., & Kim, S. (1994). *Social conflict: Escalation, stalemate, and settlement* (2nd ed). New York: McGraw-Hill.

Putnam, L. L. (1990). Reframing integrative and distributive bargaining: A process perspective. In R. J. Lewicki, B. H. Sheppard, & M. H. Bazerman *Research on negotiation in organizations, Vol. 2* (pp. 3–30). Greenwich, CT: JAI Press.

Putnam, L. L. (2006). Definitions and approaches to conflict and communication. In J. G. Oetzel & S. Ting-Toomey (Eds.) *The Sage handbook of conflict communication* (pp. 1–32). Thousand Oaks, CA: Sage.

Putnam, L., & Folger, J. P. (1988). Communication, conflict and dispute resolution: The study of interaction and the development of conflict theory. *Communication Research, 15,* 349–359.

Putnam, L., & Holmer, M. (1992). Framing, reframing and issue development. In L. L. Putnam & M. E. Roloff (Eds.) *Communication and negotiation* (pp. 128–155). Beverly Hills, CA: Sage.

Putnam, L., & Jones, T. (1982a). The role of communication in bargaining. *Human Communication Research, 8,* 262–280.

Putnam, L., & Jones, T. (1982b). Reciprocity in negotiations: An analysis of bargaining interaction. *Communication Monographs, 49,* 171–191.

Putnam, L., & Poole, M. S. (1987). Conflict and negotiation. In F. Jablin, L. Putnam, K. Roberts, & L. Porter

(Eds.) *Handbook of organizational communication* (pp. 549–599). Beverly Hills, CA: Sage.

Putnam, L., & Wilson, C. E. (1982). Communicative strategies in organizational conflicts: Reliability and validity of a measurement scale. In M. Burgoon (Ed.) *Communication yearbook 6* (pp. 629–652). Beverly Hills, CA: Sage.

Putnam, L., Wilson, S., Waltman, M. S., & Turner, D. (1986). The evolution of case arguments in teachers' bargaining. *Journal of the American Forensic Association, 23*, 63–81.

Quinn, R. W., & Dutton, J. E. (2005). Coordination as energy in conversation. *Academy of Management Review, 30*, 36–57.

Rahim, M. A. (1983). A measure of styles of handling interpersonal conflict. *Academy of Management Journal, 26*, 369–376.

Rapaport, A. (1960). *Fights, games and debates.* Ann Arbor: University of Michigan Press.

Raven, B., & Kruglanski, A. (1970). Conflict and power. In Paul Swingle (Ed.) *The structure of conflict* (pp. 69–109). New York: Academic Press.

Reich, N. M., & Wood, J. T. (2003). Sex, gender and communication in small groups. In R. Y. Hirokawa, R. S. Cathcart, L. A. Samovar, & L. D. Henman (Eds.) *Small group communication: Theory and practice* (pp. 218–229). Los Angeles: Roxbury.

Reicher, S. (2003). The psychology of crowd dynamics. In M. A. Hogg & S. Tindale (Eds.) *Blackwell handbook of social psychology: Group processes* (pp. 182–208). Oxford: Blackwell.

Riesel, D. (1985). Negotiation and mediation of environmental disputes. *Ohio State Journal on Dispute Resolution, 1*, 99–111.

Ridgeway, C. L. (2003). Social status and group structure. In M. A. Hogg & S. Tindale (Eds.) *Blackwell handbook of social psychology: Group processes* (pp. 352–375). Oxford: Blackwell.

Riggs, C. J. (1983). Communication dimensions of conflict tactics in organizational settings: A functional analysis. In R. W. Bostrom (Ed.) *Communication yearbook 7* (pp. 517–531). Beverly Hills, CA: Sage.

Roberts, L. J., & Krokoff, L. J. (1990). A time series analysis of withdrawal, hostility, and displeasure in satisfied and dissatisfied marriages. *Journal of Marriage and the Family, 52*, 95–105.

Rogan, R. G. (2006). Conflict framing categories revisited. *Communication Quarterly, 54*, 157–173.

Rogan, R. G., & LaFrance, B. H. (2003). An examination of the relationship between verbal aggressiveness, conflict management strategies, and conflict interaction goals. *Communication Quarterly, 51*, 458–469.

Roloff, M. E. (1976). Communication strategies, relationships, and relational changes. In G. R. Miller (Ed.) *Explorations in interpersonal communication* (pp. 173–196). Beverly Hills, CA: Sage.

Roloff, M. E. (1981). *Interpersonal communication: The social exchange approach.* Beverly Hills, CA: Sage.

Roloff, M. E. (1987a). Communication and conflict. In C. Berger & S. H. Chaffee (Eds.) *Handbook of communication science* (pp. 484–535). Beverly Hills, CA: Sage.

Roloff, M. E. (1987b). Communication and reciprocity within intimate relationships. In M. E. Roloff & G. R. Miller (Eds.) *Interpersonal processes: New directions in communication research* (pp. 11–38). Beverly Hills, CA: Sage.

Roloff, M. E., & Campion, D. E. (1985). Conversational profit-seeking: Interaction as social exchange. In R. L. Street, Jr. & J. N. Cappella (Eds.) *Sequence and pattern in communicative behavior* (pp. 161–189). London: Edward Arnold.

Roloff, M., & Cloven, D. (1990). The chilling effect in interpersonal relationships: The reluctance to speak one's mind. In D. D. Cahn (Ed.) *Intimates in conflict: A communication perspective* (pp. 49–76). Hillsdale, NJ: Lawrence Erlbaum.

Roloff, M. E., & Ifert, D. E. (1998). Antecedents and consequences of explicit agreements to declare a topic taboo in dating relationships. *Personal Relationships, 5*, 191–206.

Roloff, M. E., & Miller, C. W. (2006). Social cognition approaches to understanding interpersonal conflict and communication. In J. G. Oetzel & S. Ting-Toomey (Eds.) *The SAGE handbook of conflict communication* (pp. 97–128). Thousand Oaks, CA: Sage.

Roloff, M. E., & Soule, K. P. (2002). Interpersonal conflict: A review. In M. L. Knapp & J. A. Daly (Eds.) *Handbook of interpersonal communication* (3rd ed., pp. 475–428). Thousand Oaks, CA: Sage.

Roloff, M. E., Soule, K. P., & Carey, C. M. (2001). Reasons for remaining in a relationship and responses to relational transgressions. *Journal of Social and Personal Relationships, 18*, 362–385.

Ross, L. (1977). The intuitive psychologist and his shortcomings: Distortions in the attribution process. In L. Berkowitz (Eds.) *Advances in experimental social psychology* (vol. 10, pp. 174–220). New York: Academic Press.

Ross, M. H. (1993). *The culture of conflict: Interests, interpretations and disputing in comparative perspective.* New Haven: Yale University Press.

Ross, R. G., & DeWine, S. (1988). Communication messages in conflict: A message-focused instrument to assess conflict management styles. *Management Communication Quarterly, 1*, 389–413.

Roth, S. (1993). Speaking the unspoken: A work-group consultation to reopen dialogue. In E. Imber-Balck (Eds.) *Secrets in families and family therapy* (pp. 268–291). New York: Norton.

Rothbart, M. (2003). Category dynamics and the modification of outgroup stereotypes. In R. Brown & S. Gaertner (Eds.) *Blackwell handbook of social psychology: Intergroup processes* (pp. 45–64). Oxford: Blackwell.

Rousseau, D. M., Sitkin, S. B., Burt, R. S., & Camerer, C. (1998). Not so different after all: A cross-discipline view of trust. *Academy of Management Review, 23,* 393–404.

Rowe, M. (1987). The corporate ombudsman. *Negotiation Journal, 3,* 127–141.

Rubin, J. Z., & Brown, B. (1975). *The social psychology of bargaining and negotiation.* New York: Academic Press.

Rubin, L. (1983). *Intimate strangers.* New York: Harper and Row.

Ruble, T. L., & Thomas, K. W. (1976). Support for a two-dimensional model of conflict behavior. *Organizational Behavior and Human Performance, 16,* 143–155.

Rummel, R. J. (1976). *Understanding conflict and war, Vol. 2.* Beverly Hills, CA: Sage.

Rusbult, C. E., Drigotas, S. E., & Verette, J. (1994) The investment model: An interdependence analysis of commitment processes and relationship maintenance phenomena. In D. J. Canary & L. Stafford (Eds.) *Communication and relational maintenance* (pp. 115–139). San Diego, CA: Academic Press.

Sambamurthy, V., & Poole, M. S. (1992). The effects of variations in capabilities of GDSS designs on management of cognitive conflict in groups. *Information Systems Research, 3,* 224–251.

Sarat, A. (1988). The "new formalism" in disputing and dispute processing. *Law and Society Review, 21,* 695–715.

Savage, G. T., Blair, J. D., & Sorenson, R. L. (1989). Consider both relationships and substance when negotiating strategically. *The Academy of Management Executive, 3,* 37–48.

Scarf, M. (1987). *Intimate partners: Patterns in love and marriage.* New York: Ballantine Books.

Scheff, T. J. (1967). Toward a sociological model of consensus. *American Sociological Review, 32,* 32–46.

Scheidel, T., & Crowell, L. (1979). *Discussing and deciding.* New York: Macmillan.

Scherer, K. R. (1994). Affect bursts. In S. H. M. Van Goozen, N. E. Van Poll, & J. A. Sergeant (Eds.) *Emotions: Essays on emotion theory* (pp. 161–193). Hillsdale, NJ: Lawrence Erlbaum.

Schermerhorn, J. R., Jr., Hunt, J.G., & Osborn, R. N. (2005). *Organizational behavior* (9th ed.). New York: Wiley.

Schneider, C. D. (2000). What it means to be sorry: The power of apology in mediation. *Mediation Quarterly, 17,* 265–280.

Schwarz, R. M. (2002). *The skilled facilitator.* San Francisco: Jossey-Bass.

Schwerin, E. (1995). *Mediation, citizen empowerment and transformational politics.* Westport, CT: Praeger.

Selznick, P. H. (1969). *Law, society, and industrial justice.* New York: Russell Sage Foundation.

Shailor, J. G. (1994). *Empowerment in dispute mediation.* Westport, CT: Praeger.

Shapiro, D., Drieghe, R., & Brett, J. (1985). Mediator behavior and the outcome of mediation. *Journal of Social Issues, 41,* 101–114.

Sharkey, W. F. (1988, May). *Embarrassment: A review of literature.* Paper presented at the International Communication Association conference, New Orleans.

Shaw, J. C., Wild, E., & Colquitt, J. A. (2003). To justify or excuse: A metaanalytic review of the effects of explanations. *Journal of Applied Psychology, 88,* 444–458.

Shawn, W., & Gregory, A. (1981). *My dinner with André.* New York: Grove Press.

Shenkar, O., & Ronen, S. (1987). The cultural context of negotiations: The implication of Chinese interpersonal norms. *Journal of Applied Behavioral Science, 23,* 263–275.

Sheppard, B. H. (1984). Third-party conflict intervention: A procedural framework. In B. Staw & L. L. Cummings (Ed.) *Research in organizational behavior,* (vol. 6, pp. 141–190). Greenwich, CT: JAI Press.

Sheppard, B. H., Blumenfeld-Jones, K., & Roth, J. (1989). Informal third partyship: Studies of everyday conflict intervention. In K. Kressel, D. G. Pruitt, & Associates (Eds.) *Mediation research: The process and effectiveness of third-party intervention* (pp. 166–189). San Francisco: Jossey-Bass.

Sheppard, B. H., Lewicki, R. J., & Minton, J. W. (1992). *Organizational justice: The search for fairness in the workplace.* New York: Lexington Books.

Sheppard, B. H., Saunders, D. M., & Minton, J. W. (1988). Procedural justice from the third-party perspective. *Journal of Personality and Social Psychology, 54,* 629–637.

Sherif, M., Harvey, O. J., White, B. J., Hood, W. R., & Sherif, C. W. (1961). *Intergroup conflict and cooperation: The robber's cave experiment.* Norman, OK: University Book Exchange.

Shubert, J., & Folger, J. P. (1986). Learning from higher education. *Negotiation Journal, 2,* 395–406.

Silbey, S. S., & Merry, S. E. (1986). Mediator settlement strategies. *Law and Policy, 8,* 7–32.

Sillars, A. L. (1980a). Stranger and spouse as target persons for compliance gaining strategies. *Human Communication Research, 6,* 265–279.

Sillars, A. L. (1980b). Attributions and communication in roommate conflicts. *Communication Monographs, 47,* 180–200.

Sillars, A. L. (1980c). The sequential and distributional structure of conflict interactions as a function of attributions concerning the locus of responsibility and stability of conflicts. In D. Nimmo (Ed.) *Communication yearbook 4* (pp. 217–235). New Brunswick, NJ: Transaction Press.

Sillars, A. L., Canary, D. J., & Tafoya, M. (2004). Communication, conflict, and the quality of family relationships. In A. L. Vangelisti (Ed.) *Handbook of family interaction* (pp. 413–466). Mahwah, NJ: Lawrence Erlbaum.

Sillars, A. L., Coletti, S. F., Parry, D., & Rogers, M. A. (1982). Coding verbal conflict tactics: Nonverbal and perceptual correlates of the "avoidance-distributive-integrative" distinction. *Human Communication Research, 9,* 83–95.

Sillars, A. L., & Parry, D. (1982). Stress, cognition and communication in interpersonal conflicts. *Communication Research, 9,* 201–226.

Sillars, A. L., & Weisberg, J. (1987). Conflict as a social skill. In M. E. Roloff & G. R. Miller (Eds.) *Interpersonal processes: New directions in communication research* (pp. 140–171). Beverly Hills, CA: Sage.

Simmel, G. (1955). *Conflict.* New York: Free Press.

Simon, B., Aufderheide, B., & Kampmeier, C. (2003). The social psychology of minority-majority relations. In R. Brown & S. Gaertner (Eds.) *Blackwell handbook of social psychology: Intergroup processes* (pp. 303–323). Oxford: Blackwell.

Simons, T. L., & Peterson, R. S. (2000). Task conflict and relationship conflict in top management teams: The pivotal role of intragroup trust. *Journal of Applied Psychology, 85,* 102–111.

Singer, L. R. (1990). *Settling disputes.* Boulder, CO: Westview Press.

Smart, C., & Vertinsky, I. (1977). Designs for crisis decision units. *Administrative Science Quarterly, 22,* 640–657.

Smith, K. K. (1989). The movement of conflict in organizations: The joint dynamics of splitting and triangulation. *Administrative Science Quarterly, 34,* 1–20.

Smith, K. K., & Berg, D. (1987). *Paradoxes of group life.* San Francisco: Jossey-Bass.

Snead, K. C., & Ndede-Amadi, A. A. (2002). Attributional bias as a source of conflict between users and analysts in an information systems development context. *Systemic Practice and Action Research, 15,* 353–365.

Snyder, M., & Jones, E. E. (1974). Attitude attribution when behavior is constrained. *Journal of Experimental Social Psychology, 10,* 585–600.

Staw, B., Sandelands, L. E., & Dutton, J. E. (1981). Threat-rigidity effects in organizational behavior: A multilevel analysis. *Administrative Science Quarterly, 26,* 501–524.

Sternberg, R. J., & Soriano, L. J. (1984). Styles of conflict resolution. *Journal of Personality and Social Psychology, 47,* 115–126.

Stokes, R., & Hewitt, J. P. (1976). Aligning actions. *American Sociological Review, 41,* 838–849.

Straus, D. (2002). *How to make collaboration work.* San Francisco: Barrett-Koehler.

Street, R. L. Jr., & Cappella, J. N. (1985). Sequence and pattern in communication behavior: A model and commentary. In R. L. Street and J. N. Cappella (Eds.) *Sequence and pattern in communicative behavior* (pp. 243–276). London: Edward Arnold.

Stulberg, J. B. (1987). *Taking charge/managing conflict.* Lexington, MA: Lexington Books.

Stutman, R. K. (1988). *Denying persuasive intent: Transparently false disavowals of intention to influence.* Paper presented at the Western Speech Communication Association convention, San Diego.

Tajfel, H. (1978). *Differentiation between social groups: Studies in the social psychology of intergroup relations.* London: Academic Press.

Tajfel, H., & Turner, J. (1979). An integrative theory of intergroup conflict. In W. G. Austin & S. Worchel (Eds.) *The social psychology of intergroup relations* (pp. 33–48). Monterey, CA: Brooks/Cole.

Taylor, P. J. & Donald, I. (2003). Foundations and evidence for an interaction-based approach to conflict negotiation. *International Journal for Conflict Management, 14,* 213–232.

Tedeschi, J. T. (1970). Threats and promises. In P. Swingle (Ed.) *The structure of conflict* (pp. 155–191). New York: Academic Press.

Tedeschi, J. T., & Riess, M. (1981). Identities, the phenomenal self, and laboratory research. In J. T. Tedeschi (Ed.) *Impression management theory and social psychological research.* New York: Academic Press.

Thibaut, J., & Walker, L. (1975). *Procedural justice: A psychological analysis.* Hillsdale, NJ: Lawrence Erlbaum.

Thomas, K. W. (1975). Conflict and conflict management. In M. Dunnette (Ed.) *Handbook of industrial psychology* (pp. 889–935). Chicago: Rand McNally.

Thomas, K. W., & Kilmann, R. H. (1974). *Thomas-Kilmann conflict MODE instrument.* Tuxedo, NY: Xicom.

Thomas, K. W., & Pondy, L. R. (1977). Toward an "intent" model of conflict management among principle parties. *Human Relations, 30,* 1089–1102.

Thompson, L. (1998). *The mind and heart of the negotiator.* Englewood Cliffs, NJ: Prentice Hall.

Tingley, J. (2001). *The power of indirect influence.* New York: Amacon Books.

Ting-Toomey, S. (1983). An analysis of verbal communication patterns in high and low marital adjustment groups. *Human Communication Research, 9,* 306–319.

Ting-Toomey, S. (1999). *Communicating across cultures.* New York: Guilford.

Ting-Toomey, S., & Kurogi, A. (1998). Facework competence in intercultural conflict: An updated face-negotiation theory. *International Journal of Intercultural Relations 22,* 187–225.

Tjosvold, D. (1995). Cooperation theory, constructive controversy, and effectiveness: Learning from crisis. In R. A. Guzzo, E. Salas, & Associates (Eds.) *Team effectiveness and decision making in organizations* (pp. 79–112). San Francisco: Jossey-Bass.

Tjosvold, D., & Huston, T. L. (1978). Social face and resistance to compromise in bargaining. *Journal of Social Psychology, 104,* 57–68.

Tracy, K. (1991). The many faces of facework. In H. Giles & R. Robinson (Eds.) *The handbook of language and social psychology* (pp. 209–226). Chichester: Wiley.

Tucker, J. (1993). Everyday forms of employee resistance. *Sociological Forum, 8,* 25–45.

Turner, L., & Henzel, S. (1987). Influence attempts in organizational communication: The effects of biological sex, psychological gender and power position. *Management Communication Quarterly, 1,* 32–57.

Ury, W. L., Brett J. M., & Goldberg, S. B. (1988). *Getting disputes resolved: Designing systems to cut the costs of conflict.* San Francisco: Jossey-Bass.

Van de Vliert, E. (1985). Escalation intervention in small group conflicts. *Journal of Applied Behavioral Science, 21,* 19–36.

Vangelisti, A. L., Daly, J. A., & Rudnick, J. R. (1991). Making people feel guilty in conversations: Techniques and correlates. *Human Communication Research, 18,* 3–39.

Volkan, V. D. (1994). *The need to have enemies and allies.* Northvale, NJ: Jason Aronson.

Volkema, R. J. (1981). *An empirical investigation of problem formulation and problem-purpose expan-sion.* Unpublished Ph.D. Thesis, University of Wisconsin, Madison.

Volkema, R. J. (1983). Problem formulation in planning and design. *Management Science, 29,* 639–652.

Vuchinich, S. (1984). Sequencing and social structure in family conflict. *Social Psychology Quarterly, 47,* 217–234.

Vuchinich, S. (1986). On attenuation in verbal family conflict. *Social Psychology Quarterly, 49,* 281–293.

Vuchinich, S. (1990). The sequential organization of closing in verbal family conflict. In A. D. Grimshaw (Ed.) *Conflict talk* (pp. 118–138). Cambridge: Cambridge University Press.

Wall, J. A., & Blum, M. (1991). Community mediation in The People's Republic of China. *Journal of Conflict Resolution, 35,* 3–20.

Wall, J. A., & Rude, D. E. (1989). Judicial mediation of settlement negotiations. In K. Kressel, D. G. Pruitt, and Associates (Eds.) *Mediation research: The process and effectiveness of third-party intervention* (pp. 190–212). San Francisco: Jossey-Bass.

Wall, V. D., Galanes, G. J., & Love, S. B. (1987). Small, task-oriented groups, conflict, conflict management, satisfaction, and decision quality. *Small Group Behavior, 18,* 31–55.

Wall, V. D., & Nolan, L. L. (1987). Small group conflict: A look at equity, satisfaction, and styles of conflict management. *Small Group Behavior, 18,* 188–211.

Walton, R. (1969). *Interpersonal peacemaking: Confrontations and third-party consultation.* Reading, MA: Addison-Wesley.

Wanberg, C. R., Bruce, L. W., & Gavin, M. B. (1999). Perceived fairness of layoffs among individuals who have been laid off: A longitudinal study. *Personnel Psychology, 52,* 59–84.

Watson, C. (1994). Gender versus power as a predictor of negotiation behavior and outcomes. *Negotiation Journal, 10,* 117–127.

Watzlawick, P., Beavin, J., & Jackson, D. (1967). *The pragmatics of human communication.* New York: Norton.

Wehr, P. (1979). *Conflict regulation.* Boulder, CO: Westview Press.

Weingart, L. R., Hyder, E. B., & Prietula, M. J. (1996). Knowledge matters: The effect of tactical descriptions on negotiation behavior and outcome. *Journal of Personality and Social Psychology, 70,* 1205–1217.

Weisinger, J. Y., & Salipante, P. F. (1995). Toward a method of exposing hidden assumptions in multicultural conflict. *The International Journal of Conflict Management, 6,* 147–170.

Welton, G. L. (1991). Parties in conflict: Their characteristics and perceptions. In K. G. Duffy, J. W. Grosch, & P. V. Olczak (Eds.) *Community mediation: A handbook for practitioners and researchers* (pp. 105–118). New York: Guilford Press.

Wenzlaff, R. M., & Luxton, D. D. (2003). The role of thought suppression in depressive rumination. *Cognitive Therapy & Research, 27,* 293–308.

White, R., & Lippitt, R. (1968). Leader behavior and member reaction in three "social climates." In D. Cartwright & A. Zander (Eds.) *Group dynamics* (3rd ed. pp. 318–335). New York: Harper and Row.

Wilson, S. (1992). Face and facework in negotiation. In L. Putnam and M. E. Roloff (Eds.) *Communication and negotiation* (pp. 176–205). Newbury Park, CA: Sage.

Worchel, S., Anderoli, V. A., & Folger, R. (1977). Intergroup cooperation and intergroup attraction: The effect of previous interaction and outcome of combined effort. *Journal of Experimental Social Psychology, 13,* 131–140.

Yelsma, P., & Brown, C. (1985). Gender roles: Biological sex and predisposition to conflict management. *Sex Roles, 12,* 731–747.

Zand, D. E. (1972). Trust and managerial problem-solving. *Administrative Science Quarterly, 17,* 229–239.

Zuckerman, M. (1979). Attribution success and failure revisited, or: The motivational bias is alive and well in attribution theory. *Journal of Personality, 47,* 245–287.

Zupnik, Y. K. (2000). Conversational interruptions in Israeli–Palestinian "dialogue" events. *Discourse Studies, 2,* 85–110.

Index

Note: Page numbers followed by a "f" indicate figure, and page numbers followed by a "t" indicate table.